Women in the Cities of Asia

Westview Replica Editions

The concept of Westview Replica Editions is a response to the continuing crisis in academic and informational publishing. Library budgets for books have been severely curtailed. Ever larger portions of general library budgets are being diverted from the purchase of books and used for data banks, computers, micromedia, and other methods of information retrieval. Interlibrary loan structures further reduce the edition sizes required to satisfy the needs of the scholarly community. Economic pressures on the university presses and the few private scholarly publishing companies have severely limited the capacity of the industry to properly serve the academic and research communities. As a result, many manuscripts dealing with important subjects, often representing the highest level of scholarship, are no longer economically viable publishing projects—or, if accepted for publication, are typically subject to lead times ranging from one to three years.

Westview Replica Editions are our practical solution to the problem. We accept a manuscript in camera-ready form, typed according to our specifications, and move it immediately into the production process. As always, the selection criteria include the importance of the subject, the work's contribution to scholarship, and its insight, originality of thought, and excellence of exposition. The responsibility for editing and proofreading lies with the author or sponsoring institution. We prepare chapter headings and display pages, file for copyright, and obtain Library of Congress Cataloging in Publication Data. A detailed manual contains simple instructions for preparing the final typescript, and our editorial staff is always available to answer questions.

The end result is a book printed on acid-free paper and bound in sturdy library-quality soft covers. We manufacture these books ourselves using equipment that does not require a lengthy make-ready process and that allows us to publish first editions of 300 to 600 copies and to reprint even smaller quantities as needed. Thus, we can produce Replica Editions quickly and can keep even very specialized books in print as long as there is a demand for them.

Women in the Cities of Asia: Migration and Urban Adaptation

edited by James T. Fawcett, Siew-Ean Khoo, and Peter C. Smith

Women in Asia are on the move. The migration of women from village to city has increased dramatically in the past decade, and many of these new migrants are young single women seeking jobs. In several Asian countries, women migrants now outnumber men by a substantial margin. Along with the physical movement from rural to urban areas come new roles for women, new problems associated with living in cities, and the prospect of radical changes in status—upward or downward.

This book is the first comprehensive examination of female migration and the situation of urban women in Asia. Drawing upon the studies and insights of sociologists, anthropologists, economists, geographers, and demographers, it documents the striking changes that are in progress and looks in depth at the causes and consequences of emerging patterns of female mobility. Particular attention is given to the ways in which public policies can be more responsive to the needs of women who are urban, poor, and burdened with special responsibilities as working mothers or heads of household.

The Asian situation is placed in perspective through comparative and theoretical contributions. In addition, the editors provide integrative themes in the introductory and concluding chapters. Changes in the migration patterns of women are shown to be a major factor in economic development and social change, providing new insights about the modernization process and suggesting that an understanding of female mobility is essential in any picture of the Asian future.

JAMILAH ARIFFIN. Lecturer, Faculty of Economics and Administration, University of Malaya, Kuala Lumpur, Malaysia.

FRED ARNOLD. Research Associate, East-West Population Institute, East-West Center, Honolulu, Hawaii.

JANET BAUER. Postdoctoral Fellow, Carolina Population Center, University of North Carolina, Chapel Hill, North Carolina.

JUDITH BRUCE. Associate, International Programs, The Population Council, New York, New York.

RODOLFO A. BULATAO. Consultant, The World Bank, Washington, D.C.

ELIZABETH U. EVIOTA. Ph.D. Candidate, Department of Sociology, Rutgers University, New Brunswick, New Jersey.

JAMES T. FAWCETT. Research Associate, East-West Population Institute, East-West Center, Honolulu, Hawaii.

ROBERT W. GARDNER. Research Associate, East-West Population Institute, East-West Center, Honolulu, Hawaii.

STELLA P. GO. Research Associate, Research Center, and Assistant Professor, Behavioral Sciences Department, De La Salle University, Manila, Philippines.

NANCY B. GRAVES, Research Associate, Oakes College, University of California, Santa Cruz, California.

SAWON HONG. Research Associate, Association for Voluntary Sterilization, New York, New York.

NORA CHIANG HUANG. Associate Professor, Department of Geography, National Taiwan University, Taipei, Taiwan, China.

SIEW-EAN KHOO. Visiting Fellow, Department of Demography, Australian National University.

SUWANLEE PIAMPITI. Associate Professor, School of Applied Statistics, National Institute of Development Administration, Bangkok, Thailand.

PETER PIRIE. Research Associate, East-West Population Institute, East-West Center, and Professor, Department of Geography, University of Hawaii, Honolulu, Hawaii.

NASRA M. SHAH. Research Fellow, East-West Population Institute, East-West Center, Honolulu, Hawaii.

ANDREA MENEFEE SINGH. Project Officer, Rural Women's Employment Promotion, International Labour Office, New Delhi, India.

PETER C. SMITH. Research Associate, East-West Population Institute, East-West Center, Honolulu, Hawaii.

JUDITH STRAUCH. Associate Professor of Anthropology, Department of Sociology and Anthropology, Tufts University, Medford, Massachusetts.

VEENA N. THADANI. Staff Associate, Center for Policy Studies, The Population Council, New York, New York.

MICHAEL P. TODARO. Professor of Economics, New York University, and Senior Associate, Center for Policy Studies, The Population Council, New York, New York.

PAUL A. WRIGHT. Assistant Professor of Geography, University of California, Riverside, California.

Published in cooperation with the
East–West Population Institute, East–West Center, Honolulu

Women in the Cities of Asia

Migration and Urban Adaptation

edited by
James T. Fawcett
Siew-Ean Khoo
Peter C. Smith

Westview Press / Boulder, Colorado

A Westview Replica Edition

Copyright © 1984 by Westview Press, Inc.

Published in 1984 in the United States of America by
    Westview Press, Inc.
    5500 Central Avenue
    Boulder, Colorado 80301
    Frederick A. Praeger, President and Publisher

Library of Congress Cataloging in Publication Data
Main entry under title:
Women in the cities of Asia.
    (Westview replica edition)
    1. Women—Asia—Social conditions—Addresses, essays, lectures. 2. Rural-urban migration—Asia—Addresses, essays, lectures. 3. Urbanization—Asia—Addresses, essays, lectures. 4. Women—Asia—Case studies—Addresses, essays, lectures.
I. Fawcett, James T., 1935–   . II. Khoo, Siew-Ean, 1949–   . III. Smith, Peter Colin, 1943–   .
HQ1726.W66 1984   305.4'095   83-19835
ISBN 0-86531-814-X

Printed and bound in the United States of America

10 9 8 7 6 5 4 3 2 1

Contents

List of Tables

List of Figures

Preface

Like most books, this volume reflects cross-currents of ideas and issues at a particular time. And, like all edited collections, it owes its existence to the efforts of many.

In the 1970s, "women's studies" emerged as a distinctive subject of scholarly concern. This academic activity was often linked to the issues raised by women's social action groups, having to do with equity under the law and in the marketplace. At the international level, those concerned with Third World issues, notably some agencies of the United Nations, highlighted the role of women in less developed societies. Under the rubric of "women in development," they directed attention to the important economic contributions of women in many developing societies, while placing under increasing scrutiny the cultural constraints on women's activities and certain detrimental effects of economic change. Such concerns were highlighted during International Women's Year in 1975 and its follow-up activities.

These trends naturally had an impact on the population field, mainly owing to interest in how women's changing status and roles were affecting fertility. Only recently have gender-related issues in connection with migration emerged as an important area of research. This lag reflects in part the meager resources devoted to the general topic of migration, compared with fertility. It also indicates certain biases in theory, data collection, and data analysis, issues explored in the chapters that follow.

This book is the first attempt to assess comprehensively female migration and the role of urban women in Asia. It draws upon the contributions of scholars from many countries who represent a variety of academic disciplines. Not all countries in Asia are covered—China is a notable omission —but those that are represent the major cultural systems and subregions within this vast part of the world. The chapters vary in emphasis, ranging from theoretical analysis to policy prescriptions, from demographic profiles to case studies of women migrants. Together they constitute a state-of-the-art report on female migration in Asia that we hope will serve as both a stimulus and a building block for future work on this important topic.

The main impetus for this book can be traced to the presentations and discussions at a Working Group Meeting on Women in the Cities, held at the East-West Center in Honolulu in 1979. The three-week meeting, consisting of intensive discussions among 32 scholars from nine countries, precipitated a variety of follow-up activities, including research projects in several parts of Asia. We are grateful to the participants for the ideas and insights they contributed, many of which are reflected in the chapters of this volume. We also want to express deep appreciation to Dr. Lee-Jay Cho, director of the East-West Population Institute, for his support of the meeting and related activities, including preparation of this book. The Population Council co-sponsored the meeting, for which we are grateful, and Judith Bruce of the Population Council staff played a key role in the organization and conduct of the working group.

Books with an international roster of contributors require a great deal of editorial care. Don Yoder's thoughtful editing of the entire manuscript has greatly enhanced the quality and readability of the contributions. Sandra Ward's editorial management and Lynn Garrett's careful proofreading have further improved quality and brought the pieces together into a whole. Gail Yamanaka and the secretarial staff of the East-West Population Institute competently and helpfully produced more than one version of the manuscript, and Lois Bender of the East-West Center Publications Office produced all the tables, improving them greatly in the process. Our deepest thanks go to these and many other people who helped bring this book to fruition.

Honolulu, Hawaii, and Canberra, Australia
August 1983

James T. Fawcett
Siew-Ean Khoo
Peter C. Smith

INTRODUCTION

Chapter 1

Urbanization, Migration, and the Status of Women

James T. Fawcett
Siew-Ean Khoo
Peter C. Smith

This book examines research and policy issues at the intersection of two major social transformations: increasing urbanization and changes in the status of women. That the world's population is becoming more urban is well known, as is the related fact that migration from rural to urban areas contributes to urban growth. Less attention has been given, however, to recent changes in the composition of migrant populations—notably the higher proportions of women moving from rural to urban areas. In many of the countries where such female migration is increasing, this change is associated with new occupational roles for women in the urban economy. Entry into these roles implies not only a different status for women who come from rural backgrounds but also new policy issues that have economic, cultural, and demographic dimensions.

The geographic focus of this book is Asia, with some attention given to the Pacific. The Asian region is notable for its diversity. In this volume we include studies of countries as distant from one another, culturally and physically, as the Republic of Korea and Iran. Not all of Asia is included, but the eight countries chosen reflect a wide range of economic and social conditions. All have market economies, though, a fact of some significance in relation to the actual and potential impact of the international economic system on patterns of female migration. Such structural influences are currently of major concern to some countries in the region and are likely to become important in others soon, as the internationalization of economic activities crosses new political and sectoral boundaries.

But it is not only economics that has an important relationship to the cityward migration of women, and it is not the migration of women itself that is a matter for research interest and policy concern. Rather, the significance of female migration lies in the linkages among migration, which is a spatial process of adjustment, the societal changes that provoke it, and the ensuing consequences. The focus on migration, then, gives one a perspective on a variety of issues related to socioeconomic development. But is there a need for special research and policy attention to women migrants?

Does it make any difference, in understanding the processes of urbanization and development, whether migrants are women or men? There are at least five reasons why it does make a difference.

First, women represent a different human resource than men—a difference indicated by the explicit preference for women workers in certain industries and occupations. Such preferences may be regarded as inappropriate or unjustified, but they are a reality in the current labor market. Similarly, women in rural areas have distinctive economic roles; their out-migration may have consequences on rural development.

Second, the causes of female migration are different from the causes of male migration. There are sex-specific cultural constraints on female mobility, as in the Islamic practice of purdah, and such factors as wage discrimination imply differences in economic expectations for women migrants. And, more so than for men, there are important distinctions between married and single migrants regarding motivations for migration. A better understanding of the causes of migration, and more accurate projections of future trends, may be achieved by a separate focus on men and women.

Third, the consequences of female migration are different from those of male migration. Apart from the economic consequences mentioned above, there are significant social effects. With regard to single women migrants, there is a deep concern in some countries about the erosion of their moral values through exposure to modern urban life-styles. From a practical viewpoint, there are special problems for single women in finding suitable housing in the city. Married women migrants tend to play a different role in the urban labor market than single women, often supplementing the family income through part-time work in the informal sector. Most of these women also need maternal and child health services and child-care facilities in the city. Development planners should take these distinctive needs and contributions of women into account.

Fourth, changes in the family as an institution are a central component of modernization, and analysis of female migration can help to detect trends in family processes. The loosening of traditional family bonds may be reflected more sensitively by changes in female (as opposed to male) migration, for example. The prevalence of female-headed households depends partly on whether married women move with their husbands or remain behind, so that female migration is a component of this fundamental dimension of family structure. And, of course, there are important and complex relationships between migration and fertility. The analysis of these relationships depends on improved knowledge about the migration of both married and single women (the latter gaining relevance partly through potential effects on age of marriage).

And fifth, attention to female migrants is warranted for purposes of better social accounting in developing countries and to provide the basis for more informed judgments and policy decisions on a wide range of issues. Until recently, women were virtually invisible in migration processes, because of the assumption that most were merely passive movers who followed the household head. The striking increases in the proportion of young single women in certain migrant streams were slow to be detected, and even now the dimensions and implications of these changes are poorly understood. Yet, as we will see, patterns of female migration are both a reflection and a cause of some of the major social and economic transformations taking place in the Asia-Pacific region.

This volume is organized into four parts. Part I, consisting of three chapters, provides an empirical and conceptual overview of the topic of female migration. In Part II, the situation in six countries is reviewed. Each country's trends and patterns of female migration are analyzed and policies affecting women in urban areas are discussed. The chapters in Part III present results of four case studies, each based on interviews with selected groups of migrant and nonmigrant women. Part IV focuses generally on the adaptation of female migrants in urban settings, and specifically on their occupational roles. In a concluding chapter, generalizations are derived from the preceding chapters and issues of public policy are discussed.

The following paragraphs highlight various sections and chapters of the book. An overview of this kind is necessarily selective and requires simplified presentation of complex issues. Nevertheless, it can serve a useful purpose by providing a broad context within which more detailed analyses of particular issues may be viewed. We hope the preview given here will entice the reader to pursue various topics in the chapters where they are explored in greater detail.

Chapter 2, by Smith, Khoo, and Go, provides a historical perspective and a global context for the topic of female migration. Of particular interest are the analyses comparing different regions of the world. Women dominate migration streams in Latin America—it is no coincidence that most studies of female migrants have been conducted in this region—as well as in Western Europe and certain areas of European settlement. By contrast, male dominance characterizes most migration streams in Africa, the Middle East, and South Asia. A tendency toward balance of the two sexes in migration is evident in East and Southeast Asia, but there is substantial diversity among countries within this region.

As our focus sharpens, the picture naturally becomes more complex. When age of migrant is considered, for example, there is some evidence in Africa of a transition from male dominance to female dominance at more mature ages. Type of migration also makes a difference. In India, men dominate migration streams to large cities, but women dominate in short-distance moves within rural areas. The latter trend reflects mainly migration because of marriage, where custom requires that the bride move to the husband's village. Thus the purposes of migration may also be differentiated by sex.

Smith, Khoo, and Go discuss the cultural forces that influence female migration in Asian countries, and they point out the importance of labor markets in understanding migration trends. In their analysis of recent data from nine Asian countries, they reveal a pattern of male dominance for urbanward migration in Japan, Singapore, Malaysia, and Iran; in contrast, female dominance is characteristic of Thailand, the Philippines, and Korea. Differences in sex ratio of migrants by type of destination are especially evident in India and Indonesia. Also of interest is the finding that age selectivity—the concentration of migrants in younger age groups—is more pronounced for women than for men.

Chapter 3, by Thadani and Todaro, takes a more theoretical approach, aiming for a model of the structural forces that determine female migration patterns. After reviewing relevant literature, the authors discuss differences between men and women with respect to the purposes and outcomes of migration. A few differences are singled out as analytically powerful. Sex differentials in the labor market, for example, with respect to both type of job and level of pay, typically reflect discrimination against women. If the model is to reveal the true causes of migration, it must consider characteristics of both rural and urban labor markets. This analysis includes the distinctions between formal and informal sector employment and, ideally, should take into account preferences for different types of jobs (the relative attractiveness of factory work and domestic service, for example, given equal incomes).

Another factor stressed by Thadani and Todaro is marriage. In some cultures, marriage is a major avenue of upward social mobility for women, and this may imply moving to an urban area in search of a higher-status husband. Another kind of marriage-related migration involves the subordinate status of women in following their husbands or the custom of the bride moving to the husband's home. These types are distinguished in the Thadani-Todaro model, as is a factor to assess culturally enforced sex-role constraints on female migration. In combination, such structural factors are said to explain differences in the level of female migration over societies or across time within a society.

In Chapter 4, Strauch looks at female migration from the perspective of social relationships, especially family linkages both before and after marriage. She argues that the rural/urban dichotomy used by migration researchers is not very meaningful to individuals, who tend to think of movement in relation to their network of social relationships, including those in the past as well as future expectations. Recent changes in transportation, communications, and the job market have made it possible for a female to have value in places other than at home—that is, to produce income by moving to where the jobs are—without breaking traditional family ties. Because of her new access to resources, however, the female migrant has greater power and status. This change may cause strains and conflict within the family, but it also gives young women a greater sense of their own worth and a stronger basis for self-esteem. Strauch not only discusses these issues in conceptual terms but also illustrates them with material drawn from her studies of Chinese communities in Malaysia and Hong Kong.

Part II of the book consists of six country studies: India, Pakistan, Malaysia, Thailand, the Philippines, and Korea. Each chapter presents a substantial body of demographic data, as well as discussing aspects of female migration and policies for urban women. In the paragraphs that follow we select just a few highlights from each country report.

India is an enormous country with uneven development and a variety of cultural influences. As noted earlier, much of the female migration entails short moves within rural areas related to marriage. As pointed out in Chapter 5 by Singh, however, there are many other forms of female migration in India that have not received much attention. For example, women are included in the large mobile work force in rural areas, which moves partly in response to seasonal demands. In urban areas, many of the lowest-status jobs—such as working as coolies—go to migrant women. These and part-time domestic jobs are often missed in official statistics. A topic discussed at length in this chapter is the difference between northern and southern India. The stronger influence of Islam in the north constrains female migration and work participation through customs related to female seclusion. Singh also points out that many households in India are headed by women as sole providers; for the very poor migrant family, the wife's "supplementary" income may in fact be essential to survival. Since policy-makers in India tend to regard all women as dependents, they have not made provision for women in other statuses, including migrant women.

In Pakistan, a strongly Islamic society, most women are in fact protected, secluded, and dependent. Purdah continues to be widely practiced, females receive little education, and few women work. Most female migration is marriage migration, or movement as part of family migration. As pointed out by Shah in Chapter 6, however, there is little research on which to base conclusions about female migration in Pakistan. Her own analyses suggest greater female mobility in recent years and show that age, marital status, and education differentiate female migrants. Because of the weak research base, however, many of the conclusions must remain speculative.

Knowledge about female migration is substantially greater in Malaysia, as shown in Chapter 7 by Khoo and Pirie. Migration streams across state boundaries are dominated by males, whereas intrastate moves are mainly female—again reflecting the influence of marriage-related migration. But important differences in migration patterns are shown for Malaysia's main ethnic groups—Chinese, Malays, and Indians—with interactions involving age, sex, and destination of migrants. Particularly noteworthy in Malaysia is the recent establishment of certain industries that have purposely recruited young Malay village women as factory workers. This trend has led to various problems—including intergenerational conflict, ethnic tension, public concerns about morality, and mental stress for the workers themselves.

The situation in Thailand differs in a number of ways because of the country's cultural homogeneity and flexible social structure. There has been a massive increase in the migration of young single women to Bangkok in recent years, but this influx seems to have been absorbed with few problems. Among all migrants to Bangkok, women now outnumber men by a 3:2 ratio. About half the women come from the poor northeastern section of the country and many have virtually no schooling. Most find work easily in the service sector, where they have low status but usually consider themselves better off than before their move. Chapter 8, by Arnold and Piampiti, reviews the striking changes in female migration patterns in Thailand and discusses the need for certain public services, especially in Bangkok.

Compared with Thailand, the Philippines has a longer history of strong female migration and a more dispersed pattern of urbanward migration of women. As pointed out in Chapter 9 by Eviota and Smith, the Philippines pattern seems closer to the experience in Latin America than to that of other Asian countries. Domestic service is the main occupation of female migrants, whereas white-collar occupations are dominant for nonmigrant women in urban areas. Like men, many women too are drawn to cities for higher education. Eviota and Smith discuss occupational patterns and raise a fundamental question about the extent to which these patterns arise from demand or supply considerations. They also note the absence of programs directed toward improving the job skills of single women migrants.

Korea too shows a pattern of female domination of urbanward migration streams, apparently a recent development related to the country's rapid industrial growth. Unlike the Philippines and Thailand, in Korea a high proportion of female migrants is classified in the production sector (although the service sector continues to absorb many migrants as well). In the case of Korea one gets a sense of rapid change for which cultural adjustments are still in progress. As Hong points out in Chapter 10, the status of Korean women is strongly traditional, even by Asian standards.

Yet the evidence she presents on migration patterns for single women, on premarital sex, and on changing educational levels and occupational patterns points to a substantial change in recent years. Hong offers a particularly useful analysis of basic needs, differentiated by sex and marital status and discussed in the context of feasible government intervention.

Part III of the book contains case studies of female migrants in four countries. Jamilah Ariffin's Chapter 11, which focuses on Malay factory workers, shows that most of these young women come from poor rural families with many children. Their own educational level is relatively high, however, and most women migrants find factory jobs quickly, mainly in the electronics and textile industries. Economic motives are the main reason given for moving to urban areas, but, interestingly, secondary motives involve freedom and autonomy or escape from the constraints imposed on young women in traditional Malay-Muslim village settings. As Ariffin points out, this freedom implies adjustment to a new life-style. Some of the main adjustments involve working in close contact with men, earning money and using it independently, working regular hours and, conversely, having leisure time on a regular basis. From these and other experiences, contemporary young Malay women are being socialized in ways very different from their forebears, with potentially profound social consequences.

In Chapter 12, by Piampiti, findings are reported from a major study of female migration in Thailand. More than 2,000 women were interviewed —mainly migrants to Bangkok but also nonmigrants in rural provinces as well as nonmigrants in Bangkok. Most of the migrant women were young, single, and had four years or less of education. As in Malaysia, young women find jobs quickly in Bangkok, usually with assistance from a friend. This chain migration may cause a disproportionate out-migration from certain rural areas. Piampiti presents a useful discussion of the demographic effects of high out-migration on sending areas, such as a higher dependency ratio and a lower birth rate. These effects in rural areas are seldom studied. Piampiti also discusses the need for migration assistance programs, particularly the dissemination of job information to aid employment market efficiency and equity.

The case study from Taiwan, outlined in Chapter 13 by Huang, is also based on interviews conducted both in the city and in rural areas. Female migrants in Taipei are found in diverse occupations, no doubt largely because of Taiwan's high level of development. Many young women also come to Taipei for further education and training, presumably directed toward careers, although Huang's interviews suggest that most migrant women do not have a strong commitment to work. Rather, they prefer a homemaker's role and most leave their jobs after marriage when they can afford to. The migrants interviewed had mixed views of city life and tended to visit their home villages often. Remittances were also common, and frequently used to pay siblings' school tuition. This practice reflects the Confucian tradition of filial piety as well as a generally strong commitment to family.

The last case study, Chapter 14 by Bauer, focuses on women migrants to Tehran. Iran is dramatically different from the countries in East and Southeast Asia, mainly because of its conservative Islamic traditions. Bauer describes the seclusion of most Iranian women, the ways in which their lives are circumscribed, and the effects on traditional women of rural-to-urban migration. Although the urban setting may remain highly restrictive, especially for married women, change and exposure to new ideas affect both the migrants and the women remaining in the home village, with whom contact is maintained. The clash between old and new ways is particularly striking in Iran, because of the mixture of religious ideologies with political and administrative actions. Bauer's analysis of the situation illustrates these conflicts.

Part IV deals with the economic activity and adjustment of female migrants, drawing upon a variety of data sources including censuses and large-scale surveys. Chapter 15, by Shah and Smith, serves as a useful introduction to this section because it presents a general framework for the forces influencing female labor-force participation. The authors report results from a comparative analysis of data from Indonesia, Korea, Malaysia, Pakistan, and Thailand. The analysis is not designed to test the full framework, but it does examine the effects of some demographic variables. Although detailed results vary by country, some interesting generalizations emerge. Migrants tend to have lower unemployment rates than other groups, for example, and within the migrant group those who are young, single, and female have especially high rates of labor-force participation.

Chapter 16, by Gardner and Wright, is one of two in this volume dealing with international migration. Using data from Hawaii, the authors compare the experiences of different female immigrant groups—Chinese, Filipinos, Japanese, and Koreans—with each other, with comparable male immigrants, and with comparable nonimmigrants. The overall experience of immigrants in Hawaii is good. Although they start with jobs of low status and low pay, they move up the socioeconomic scale fairly rapidly to achieve status comparable to that of nonimmigrants. The analysis by Gardner and Wright reveals that female immigrants are relatively disadvantaged, however, especially in the income level they can achieve. And, among the immigrant groups studied, Filipinos tend to be worse off than others.

Bulatao's Chapter 17 focuses on the status of Filipino women in communities of varying size: barrios (villages), small cities, large cities, and Manila. His analysis is based on an extensive survey that collected objective and subjective data on the roles and status of women. The most consistent conclusion of this study, as shown by a variety of measures, is that women in small cities are better off. The author speculates why this should be so, but perhaps the main value of the chapter is in showing that community size and other characteristics of place should be incorporated into future studies of migrant satisfaction.

The adjustment of different ethnic groups in urban areas of New Zealand is the topic of Chapter 18 by Graves, who compares the Pakeha (Caucasians), the Maori, and Polynesian island immigrants. Using a conceptual framework with a social-psychological orientation, Graves describes different strategies of migrant adaptation: self-reliant, peer-reliant, and kin-reliant. She then illustrates how these strategies are implemented by various groups, including women migrants. This chapter provides a clear demonstration that cultural values can have a major effect on the style and success of migrant adaptation, quite apart from economic opportunities and other situational forces that are more commonly studied.

Chapter 19, the concluding chapter of this volume, extracts some integrative themes from the preceding chapters and offers recommendations for policy and research. The themes involve the role of female migrants in urban labor markets, the effects of industrialization programs and education on female migration, and the consequences of female migration—on the women themselves, on their families, and on rural areas. Another topic discussed at some length is the provision of adequate services for women, especially migrant women in urban areas. Toward that end, we suggest a typology of client groups and their needs that should be useful to planners. Finally, we discuss priorities for research that would shed light on important unresolved issues concerning female migration and women in cities.

PART 1

OVERVIEW AND THEORETICAL PERSPECTIVES

Chapter 2

The Migration of Women to Cities: A Comparative Perspective

Peter C. Smith
Siew-Ean Khoo
Stella P. Go

The large-scale migration of women to urban areas is not entirely a recent phenomenon, nor is it equally common in all parts of the world. Accounts of the growth of cities and the industrialization process in Europe and North America during the nineteenth century frequently refer to large numbers of female migrants in cities and industrial towns, where they were mostly engaged in domestic service or factory work. And comparative studies of urbanization and migration patterns in today's developing world often note the predominance of one sex over the other in the urbanward migration streams in the different world regions. In some countries males dominate the migration pattern; elsewhere females are more numerous.

We begin this chapter with a brief examination of female migration in the western countries before and during the Industrial Revolution and in the developing regions of the world today. With this perspective as background, we then present a comparative analysis of the geographic mobility of women in Asia, drawing mainly upon migration data from the 1970 round of censuses to examine the extent to which women are participating in the migration process and, specifically, in migration to cities in the various countries and subregions. We conclude by discussing some of the issues raised by this analysis.

FEMALE MIGRATION IN THE INDUSTRIALIZING WEST

The empirical country-level studies offered elsewhere in the volume and the comparative analysis presented later in the chapter indicate that a substantial volume and variety of female migration is an integral and apparently growing part of the process of economic change in Asia today. As we begin to explore these Asian migration patterns we would do well to study whatever guide maps are available. A glance backward to the European societies of the Industrial Revolution has often been useful, and we take this tack now. What we find is in some respects unique to the nineteenth-century European milieu, but much is germane to today's developing countries as well. In fact, the degree of similarity is notable, and the analytic models that have been applied to the past may well be of use in understanding the movement of women to Asian cities today.

Much of the literature on European development presumes that men dominate the processes of urbanization and economic change. Most models of these transformations link men, machines, and markets—through factor mobility and especially through male migration. Even as perceptive an observer as Simon Kuznets (1966:125) has incorrectly viewed the European migration entirely in male-dominant terms while others (Parish 1973, for example) see little sex differential.

More dynamic characterizations of the European migration system are offered by authors such as Bogue (1969:chap. 19) and Tilly (1978). In Bogue's view the earliest rural-to-urban migration was male-dominant, just as rural-to-rural frontier movement was generally dominated by men. Later, he argues, the migration streams matured, took on sexual balance, and finally became female-dominant as the character of the urban economy shifted from a predominance of manual to nonmanual occupations. There is some truth in this simple scheme, but the evidence also shows substantial female migration quite early in the European industrialization process.

Charles Tilly captures the process in richer detail when he proposes a typology of the kinds of migration that can occur as economic development proceeds. His typology is based on the distance and the definitiveness of moves. Within this scheme he is able to locate local, circular, chain, and career migrations, each with a characteristic pattern of sex composition and change over the course of economic development.

Another useful perspective is gained by studying specific cities with varying economic specializations. Lesthaeghe (1977), for example, describes extensive female migration to many of the provincial towns of Belgium where occupational opportunities existed in textile manufacturing and domestic services. This pattern contrasts, for example, with the coal-mining centers of Europe (Wrigley 1961; Haines 1979), where male migrants predominated. These differences across cities and towns were sharp enough to influence the social milieu and cause, for example, quite different marriage patterns to emerge.

It is the net result of all these local patterns that Weber (1899) describes in his analysis of nineteenth-century census materials. In his thorough empirical study he observes a "general surplus of women in cities which exceeds that of rural districts" (p. 276). Women, he notes, were primarily short-distance migrants moving within the same province or county, usually because of marriage or in response to the demand for domestic servants in the cities. Men, in contrast, traveled longer distances, usually in search of better labor markets. Ravenstein (1885) summarizes these patterns with one of his well-known laws of migration: "Females are more migratory than males."

Thus female migration was a significant component of the European migration system. It was linked closely to the pattern of economic transition, and it reflected important elements of the European sociocultural milieu. Before proceeding further, we want to outline certain aspects of social organization in Europe, especially northwestern Europe, that bear on the broad regional comparison we wish to make.

Much of rural life in Europe was organized around the principle that marriage must be based on certain material prerequisites—usually land (in the countryside) or a stable occupation (in the towns). Many believe that this feature of social organization sets European society apart from other regions and accounts for much of the pattern of migration experienced during the Industrial Revolution. The inheritance that prevailed, usually in its primogeniture form, had several results: late marriage for both sexes, substantial out-migration of male nonheirs, and the related out-migration of females—all integral features of the rural marriage market. It is apparent that these are important features of European rural society from the standpoint of freeing labor of both sexes for urban employment.

Another European institution is "life cycle servanthood" (Laslett 1977), often described as one of the central features of the European family system. For families, it operated as a mode of adjustment of rural labor supply to labor needs as the family pool of workers expanded and then contracted over the domestic cycle (Thadani 1980). For individuals, servanthood was a means of acquiring the material prerequisites for marriage. For the society and economy as a whole, the institution facilitated the systematic transfer of rural labor out of agriculture, either temporarily or permanently, and often the easy recruitment of rural labor into urban employment.

In this respect, Asian societies have been quite different. Since the joint family systems of South and East Asia permit the early sharing of parental resources, they allow and even encourage early marriage. These systems are characterized by low levels of rural out-migration from villages of birth on the part of male offspring, though frequently they are associated with extensive female migration for the purpose of marriage; this migration is almost always local and rural-to-rural in character (Libbee and Sopher 1972). But these systems of partible inheritance have not inhibited village out-migration very much in recent years, since the scarcity of rural land has forced more elaborate strategies of occupational choice for male offspring, often involving urbanward migration. Thus Asia's quite different rural land system may be producing a result much the same as in Europe: out-migration of male offspring and many of their sisters.

Another important set of contrasts, to which we now turn, centers on the nature of the economic and social revolutions characteristic of Europe and Asia. The rapidly changing economic and social milieu of nineteenth-century Europe was the dynamic element in the migration system that emerged there. Our description will stress contrasts with Asia.

The first contrast concerns a basic demographic difference. Expansion of industry and population in Asian cities is rapid in relation to nineteenth-century Europe, but so is the overall rate of population growth. As a result, we find two crucial differences between the regions. First, while the cities of Asia have grown very rapidly indeed, often at rates of 4 percent a year or greater, the structural transformation from a rural to an urban economy has been relatively slow; in particular, urban job creation relative to rural population growth has been quite slow. Second, the rural sector in Asia is continuing to grow rapidly in absolute terms. Whereas European urbanization absorbed all rural population growth during the Industrial Revolution, the Asian rural population continues to grow at an average rate of 2 percent a year (Davis 1975).

The structural significance of migration differs as a corollary of this demographic difference. Rural-to-urban migration was always the major source (and often the only source) of urban growth in Europe, but in Asia these transfers account for only about one-third of urban population growth. The net result in Europe was a rural-to-urban migration system that involved substantial rates of population transfer owing less to rural pressure than to the labor needs of the expanding factory system in cities and towns.

This demographic contrast brings us to a crucial difference in sectoral growth patterns that figures prominently in the comparative literature. Where European urbanization is said to have been led by the growth of manufacturing industry, followed later by growth in the services sector, Asian urbanization has had a much larger services component from the outset. Whether one views massive services employment as a permanent feature or as a passing phase, as a lifelong career for a large part of the urban labor force or as a temporary condition of lesser significance (Mazumdar 1979), the fact remains that in many Asian cities a remarkably high percentage of the youthful labor force, especially the young migrant population in cities, is engaged in service activities. Two further aspects make this point of great relevance here: First, this service employment is generally in the poorly capitalized and organized, ill-protected, "informal" sector; second, the service occupations are disproportionately the preserve of women.

Finally, the role of education in the Asian social transformation and the emerging rural-to-urban migration system cannot be overemphasized. The contrast with nineteenth-century Europe is again instructive. The fact that Europe prior to the Industrial Revolution was characterized by higher literacy and more sex equality in literacy than was found at a comparable time in Asia only highlights the significant transformation of Asia that has begun to occur. Whether the rise of educational attainment should be viewed as a reflection of a near-global ideology favoring concern for the human potential or as an incidental legacy of colonialism, the fact is that Asia in the twentieth century has been characterized by rapid improvement in literacy and rapid convergence of the sexes in educational attainment in all but a few countries.

This development, perhaps the most revolutionary change to occur in Asia in this century, has had major implications for rural-to-urban migration. There is much evidence that rural-to-urban migrants are positively selected on their schooling. This holds true for women as well as men. It is not unreasonable to suggest as a working hypothesis that the rise of female migration and the convergence of male and female patterns in many Asian countries reflect, at least in part, the rise of female relative to male education as the critical preparation for participation in urban labor markets.

A GLOBAL VIEW OF REGIONAL PATTERNS

In the absence of internationally comparable data directly assessing the volume of male and female migration, one can obtain indirect evidence of the sex composition of migrants from rural to urban areas by comparing urban and rural age and sex ratios. The various indexes that can be calculated from these data also provide a basis for comparing regions and countries regarding the degree of female participation in rural-to-urban migration. In analyzing these data researchers have used two indexes for making comparisons among countries: the urban residence ratio and the comparative urbanization level. The urban residence ratio (URR) measures the percentage urban for each age-sex group within each country: the comparative urbanization level (CUL), a logistic transformation of the URR, adjusts for the widely varying levels of urbanization across countries to make cross-national comparisons more interpretable and allow regional aggregation of the national data (United Nations 1970, 1971).

The United Nations analysis identifies four dimensions of international variation in urban and rural age-sex composition. Two of these are of interest to us here because they reflect the sex composition of migration. One reflects the degree to which one sex or the other dominates at the peak ages of migration (15 to 24). The other measures the extent to which the elderly are urbanized as well as the sex differential in the degree of urbanization among the older population. In order to draw out the points of greatest interest to us, we have plotted the UN's CUL indexes for these two dimensions (Figure 2.1),[1] with the sex ratio of youth migration on the vertical axis (female dominant toward the top) and the extent of old-age migration among women displayed along the horizontal axis. That these two aspects of rural-to-urban population transfer are positively associated is made clear in the plot of regional levels; the correlation of the two dimensions across the ten regions is 0.81, while the same correlation across 73 countries is 0.48. These data also indicate two distinct patterns of age-sex selective migration at the regional level. One pattern involves female-dominant migration at both young and older ages; the predominance of women in youth migration is usually accompanied by a high level of migration among older women. Such a pattern is observed in Latin America, Western Europe, and the areas of European settlement. The other regional pattern involves male-selective youth migration and low levels of old-age migration among women. This pattern is found in Africa, the Middle East, and South Asia; it is less evident in East and Southeast Asia and Eastern Europe, however, where more balanced sex ratios are observed among young migrants.

The foregoing results are based on data from the 1960 round of censuses. More recent data (1965–75) are examined briefly in another analysis of world urbanization (United Nations, 1980). Based mainly on direct comparisons of urban and rural age-specific sex ratios as indicators of the sex composition of rural-to-urban population transfers and limited to regional results, this analysis establishes that the main features noted in the 1960 census data persist in recent censuses—including both the regional sex patterns at the peak ages of youth migration and the pattern of female-dominant urbanization at older ages. Latin America is again singled out for its significant degree of older female urbanization, as well as for its female-dominant migration generally.

Another analysis of a similar body of recent data on age-sex composition uses indexes to adjust for sex differentials in survivorship; this analysis too yields results that correspond fairly closely to those based on CULs (Youssef et al. 1979).[2] As an indication of this correspondence we have obtained a zero-order correlation of 0.58 between the United Nations' CUL youth migration dimension and Youssef and colleagues' index of migrant sex composition.[3]

The regional patterns of female migration suggested by these indexes are corroborated by the findings of a growing body of studies using more direct data on female migrants for specific countries and areas. Now we discuss Asia and examine comparative data on the participation of women in migration to the cities in selected countries.

Figure 2.1 Regional patterns of youth and old-age migration of women: all countries

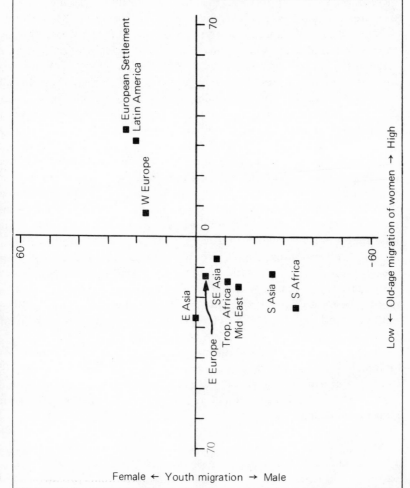

THE MIGRATION OF WOMEN IN ASIA

Although the literature on Asian migration in general is abundant (see Simmons et al. 1977; Pryor 1977), little attention has been given to the migration of *women* in Asian countries. In the past the typical migrant in Asia has been described as a young adult male, usually in the 15–24 age group, who is either pushed off the land in a rural area because of population pressure and forced to look for work in the cities or is attracted by the various social and economic amenities available in urban areas. Moreover, the migration of Asian women has traditionally been associated with marriage or the migration of their spouses and families. There has been, therefore, little interest in studying female migrants. Women migrants have not been thought to have much social or economic impact on their places of origin or destination—mainly because of the assumption that they are not economically active but only members of the households of their migrant spouses.

Recently, however, it has become common in both census and survey analysis and in the observations of urban sociologists and anthropologists to assert that more and more young women are joining the migrant flow to the cities. Many of them are said to be unmarried. Although some of them move to the cities with their families as a unit, others are said to have migrated autonomously to find work in the service, manufacturing, or informal sectors. Aside from these general observations, however, there are virtually no studies on the migration of women in Asian countries. Much of what we know today of female migration in Asia is drawn from reports based on census and survey data on the changing sex ratio of migrants and from passing references to migrant women in related studies.

In this section, we examine the migration literature as well as direct data on female and male migrants for several Asian countries. We focus specifically on four aspects: the sex composition of the migrants, the age composition of migrants, the direction of migration, and the prevalence of female migrants in the cities.

SEX COMPOSITION

The migration literature for Asia indicates that the degree to which women participate in rural-to-urban migration varies considerably among subregions and even among countries within each subregion. Systematic data on the sex composition of migrants are available mainly from the 1970 round of censuses for nine Asian countries: five in Southeast Asia, two in East Asia, and two in South Asia. In Table 2.1 we compare the sex ratios of migrants in the peak ages of migration with those of the total and nonmigrant populations. The general picture that emerges supports much of

Table 2.1 Sex ratios (males per 100 females) of the total population, nonmigrants and migrants 15—19 and 20—24 years old: selected Asian countries

Country and age group	Total population	Nonmigrants	Migrants Total	Migrants Rural	Migrants Urban	Migrants Metropolitan
Indonesia (1976)						
15—19	95.0	96.1	72.5	76.1	70.4	60.4
20—24	93.7	92.9	108.1	104.6	110.6	120.3
Malaysia (1970)						
15—19	98.0	96.3	106.8	97.8	129.0	108.6
20—24	96.0	95.4	97.8	86.0	125.5	93.4
Philippines (1970)						
15—19	89.4	97.0	55.4	73.9	43.6	41.5
20—24	88.4	91.7	71.0	77.8	65.1	68.9
Singapore (1970)						
15—19	105.2	105.7	101.0	na	na	101.0
20—24	102.6	104.0	97.1	na	na	97.1
Thailand (1970)						
15—19	97.2	97.5	95.0	96.9	91.2	81.0
20—24	97.1	90.1	132.7	97.1	135.8	123.8
Japan (1970)						
15—19	101.9	98.8	127.5	111.6	130.4	131.3
20—24	99.4	98.2	106.7	77.0	114.4	134.3
Korea (1970)						
15—19	103.8	108.4	77.6	80.0	77.3	74.8
20—24	86.0	115.8	66.8	71.5	65.5	69.0
India (1971)						
15—19	113.4	170.6	46.9	33.1	107.9	139.6
20—24	100.2	230.5	38.6	25.1	96.3	142.0
Iran (1966)						
15—19	99.2	98.7	102.0	99.0	102.6	na
20—24	89.2	76.8	141.5	120.0	146.3	na

Note: Lifetime migrants in India and Iran, five-year migrants in all other countries.

na—not applicable.

Sources: Indonesia: 1976 Indonesian Intercensal Population Survey; Malaysia: Malaysia, DOS (1973: table 4.4); Philippines: Philippines, NCSO (1974: vol. 2, table 4.11; vol. 1, table 4.14); Singapore: Singapore, DOS (1970: table 1); Thailand: Arnold and Boonpratuang (1976: tables 4 and 10); Japan: Japan, BOS (1973); Korea: Korea, NBS (1970); India: tabulations from the 1971 census; Iran: ISC (1969: tables 1 and 2).

the literature on the topic, though caution is needed in sorting out genuine sex-ratio patterns from distortions of various kinds.

Among Southeast Asian countries, the Philippines stands out as having a highly female-selective migration pattern comparable to that in Latin America. The migrant sex ratios at ages 15 to 19 in the urban and metropolitan streams in the Philippines are quite remarkable: Two out of three migrants to metropolitan areas are women. Previous studies of migration in the Philippines have indicated the predominance of women in rural-to-urban migration streams (Pryor 1975; Smith 1977), and Chapter 9 in this volume discusses how this pattern has come to replace a pattern of male-dominant rural-to-urban flows.

In Indonesia and Thailand, greater female selectivity in migration occurs in the younger (15–19) age group. Studies of migration in Indonesia by Pryor (1975) and Hugo (1975) found that there were more women than men among migrants to Jakarta in the 15–19 age group. A study by Mowat (1977) as well as a series of annual surveys of migration to Bangkok have reported a low sex ratio among young migrants, ranging from 84 in 1974 to 55 in 1977 (Thailand, NSO 1977, 1978, 1979). In Malaysia and Singapore, however, males appear to be in the majority among urban migrants.

In East Asia, Japan shows male-dominant migration streams, but Korea shows considerable female migration in both rural and urban streams, especially in the 20–24 age group. Data for Taiwan in 1967–68 indicate that men are more migratory than women in most age groups except the 15–19 age group, where the female migration rate (migrants per thousand women at the place of origin) exceeded the male migration rate by 50 percent (Speare 1971:13).

In both Iran and India, the majority of migrants to urban areas are male. In India, however, rural migration among the young adults is predominantly female. Several studies have suggested that this movement is related to marriage (Zachariah 1964; Libbee and Sopher 1972). A study by Premi (1979) using both 1961 and 1971 census data indicated the same pattern of sex composition among internal migrants in India. Behind these aggregate figures, however, are important variations among regions and social groups; these differences are described further in Chapter 5. Comparable data for Pakistan were not available for inclusion in Table 2.1; however, one study of migrants to urban areas in 1951–61 found the sex ratio to be 150 males per 100 females (Afzal 1967). A later study shows a decline in the sex ratio of the urban population in Pakistan between 1951–61 and 1961–72, but this trend was thought to reflect male-selective outmigration to other countries and more family migration from rural areas (Afzal and Abbasi 1979).

AGE COMPOSITION

In Table 2.2 we have assembled data for eight countries showing one important indicator of the age composition of recent migrants: the percentage in the 15–24 age group for the nonmigrant and total populations. A uniform pattern is observed across the six countries in East and Southeast Asia and can be summarized as follows: Disproportionate numbers of migrants are aged 15 to 24; the age concentration at age 15 to 24 is especially true of female migrants; and the age concentration at age 15 to 24 among both male and female migrants increases from rural to urban to metropolitan sectors.

Although the opposite pattern is observed for India and Iran, this is probably because the data refer to lifetime migrants instead of recent (five-year) migrants. (In these instances the age at census is not an indication of the age at migration, so that the concentration of migrants in specific age groups cannot be seen.)

The strength of the urbanward and metropolitan age selectivities in East and Southeast Asia is remarkable. In Japan, Korea, Malaysia, and Thailand, about half of all recent female migrants were aged 15 to 24 at the time of the survey or census (compared with no more than about one-third in the age group among nonmigrants). In Indonesia and the Philippines, well over half of all urbanward migrants were in the same age group, as were more than 60 percent of all migrants in the metropolitan sector.

URBAN VERSUS RURAL DESTINATIONS

Even in countries where men predominate in migration, the sex ratio of migration streams can vary according to distance and the size and degree of urbanization of the destination. Singh (1978) notes that data for the 1955–58 period in India show more women than men migrating to urban areas (the migrant sex ratio was 89), particularly to towns with a population of less than 300,000 (with a migrant sex ratio of 80), but there were more men migrating to the four largest cities (their migrant sex ratio was 120). Hugo (1975) finds that the proportion of female migrants varies with migration stream in Indonesia, although on average men form the majority of migrants. The migrant stream from West Java to Jakarta is predominantly female; the sex ratio is 93 according to 1971 census data and 80 according to a 1967 survey.

A comparison of the destinations of female and male migrants aged 15 to 24 (data not shown) indicates some important differences among countries. In Japan, Korea, Indonesia, and Iran, the net flow was toward urban and metropolitan areas; in Malaysia, the Philippines, Thailand, and India, one-third to one-half of all migrants moved to urban destina-

Table 2.2 Percentage of population 15–24 years old, by migrant status and place of residence: selected Asian countries

Country and sex	Migrant population[a]				Nonmigrant population			
	Total	Rural	Urban	Metropolitan[b]	Total	Rural	Urban	Metropolitan
Indonesia (1976)								
Female	52.6	45.0	59.1	60.9	31.4	30.5	35.7	37.2
Male	45.1	36.5	53.6	56.2	31.8	30.8	36.3	35.7
Malaysia (1970)								
Female	48.0	47.4	49.8	51.3	32.0	32.5	35.5	35.8
Male	42.2	38.8	51.0	52.7	33.4	32.8	34.8	34.9
Philippines (1970)[c]								
Female	48.7	42.8	54.3	63.2	33.1	32.4	34.3	36.5
Male	36.1	33.8	38.8	50.8	32.4	32.2	32.6	33.4
Thailand (1970)								
Female	43.6	40.8	51.6	52.3	32.6	32.5	33.5	34.4
Male	40.3	37.2	49.9	52.8	33.1	33.1	33.0	34.5
Japan (1970)								
Female	46.4	42.7	47.4	54.7	22.7	20.7	23.5	24.9
Male	44.8	34.0	47.3	57.4	22.3	21.9	25.0	28.5
Korea (1970)								
Female	45.8	37.3	48.1	50.6	37.9	36.0	38.6	31.0
Male	35.8	27.4	38.4	41.8	36.8	29.4	39.2	28.7
India (1971)								
Female	25.6	25.4	30.4	25.5	25.6	32.0	41.5	47.8
Male	25.5	25.5	25.6	23.9	29.3	27.7	38.3	41.4

Iran (1966)

Female	28.3	26.9	28.6	na	30.2	28.7	33.4	na
Male	27.9	23.7	28.8	na	26.3	23.5	32.7	na

Note: Denominator refers to population 15 years old and above.

a. Five-year migrants only except for India and Iran, where the data refer to lifetime migrants.

b. Refers to the capital cities in Indonesia, Japan, Korea, Philippines, and Thailand; to cities with over 75,000 population in Malaysia; and to cities with over 1 million population in India.

c. Excludes those whose age or place of residence in 1965 is not stated.

na—not applicable.

Sources: Same as for Table 2.1.

tions. With the exception of Indonesia, the proportions of female and male migrants moving to urban areas are different in all the countries although the differentials are usually slight. A greater proportion of male migrants in Japan, Malaysia, India, and Iran are urbanward migrants. The male/female differential is greatest in India, where more than 40 percent of male migrants but only 19 percent of female migrants moved to urban areas. As indicated by the migration literature, female migration in India is largely related to marriage and mainly rural. In Korea, the Philippines, and Thailand, a larger proportion of female migrants than males moved to urban destinations, particularly among migrants in the 15–19 age group. The female/male differential is largest among migrants aged 15 to 19 in the Philippines, where 61 percent of female migrants but only 50 percent of male migrants are found in urbanward migration streams.

There are also important variations in the metropolitan concentration of all migrants and urbanward migrants. In the Philippines, where more than half of all migrants moved to urban areas, no more than 6 to 9 percent moved to the metropolis. Of the urbanward migrants, about one in seven moved to Manila. In Thailand, where about 30 percent of the migrants moved to urban areas, well over half of these (and about one in five among all migrants) moved to Bangkok. The result of this metropolitan concentration of migration in Thailand is a very high metropolitan prevalence. The more dispersed urbanward migration of Filipinos seems to be a feature unique to that country and is discussed further in Chapter 9.

There is a similar contrast in East Asia between Japan and Korea. In both countries, the majority of migrants went to urban areas, but in Korea more than half went to Seoul while in Japan the urbanward streams were more dispersed. One in five Japanese urbanward migrants moved to Tokyo compared to about two of three Korean urbanward migrants moving to Seoul.

In summary, both the literature and the data we have examined suggest several situations. First, in a few countries female migration is mainly rural-to-rural and is likely to be marriage migration. Northern India is typical of this pattern. In certain other countries, female as well as male migration is disproportionately toward urban and metropolitan areas. And in a few of these countries, especially in the Philippines, women dominate numerically in these urbanward flows.

THE PREVALENCE OF FEMALE MIGRANTS

It is important to realize that the volume of female and male migration varies from country to country and that the significance of the patterns we are describing may vary as well. To illustrate this point we have calculated a rough measure of the prevalence of migrants in rural, urban, and metropolitan areas (Table 2.3). Again we focus on the key age groups: 15 to 19 and 20 to 24.

Table 2.3 shows, for each sector, ratios of recent migrants to the sector's total population, specific by age. This ratio reflects only part of the effect of migration in each sector since it ignores the prevalence of out-migration from another sector as well as the impact of cross-canceling moves within the reference period. The urban ratios are treated as proxies for the prevalence of rural-to-urban migrants in urban populations. It should be remembered, though, that the numerators include some urban-to-urban migrants as well.

The prevalence of migrants in the 15–24 age group is generally highest in the metropolitan areas and lowest in the rural areas, reflecting the net rural-to-urban flow of population and especially the movement to large centers. In five of the eight countries shown in Table 2.3, migrant prevalence in the rural areas is around 10 percent or less, increasing to between 10 and 29 percent in the urban areas and to over 30 percent in the metropolitan centers of Korea. The prevalence of migrants is also high among males aged 20 to 24 in metropolitan areas in Malaysia and Thailand and among the female metropolitan population aged 15 to 19 in the Philippines. The main exceptions are Malaysia, where the migrant prevalence in rural areas is relatively high and probably due to organized rural relocation, and India, where the exceptionally high migrant prevalence among the female population is perhaps the clearest indication of village exogamy among rural women.

A higher prevalence of migrants among women is observed in Korea and the Philippines in both the 15–19 and 20–24 age groups and in the 15–19 age group in Indonesia and Thailand. The differential is greatest among the urban and metropolitan population in the Philippines, where 25 to 30 percent of the female population aged 15 to 19 are migrants (compared with 14 to 17 percent of the male population). The prevalence of migrants is higher among males than females in Japan and Malaysia, indicating male dominance in migration in both countries. The prevalence of migrants in India shown in Table 2.3 agrees with the finding of Singh (1978) mentioned earlier: Although more women than men migrate to smaller towns and cities, more men than women migrate to metropolitan centers.

PATTERNS AND PERSPECTIVES

The preceding discussion has compared the patterns of female and male migration in eight countries in Southeast Asia, East Asia, and South Asia. The diversity in the patterns is striking. There is no consistent predominance of one sex over the other in the migration process, even within the same subregion, except perhaps in South Asia, confirming the observations in the regional comparisons in the preceding section based on indirect data. Instead the sex ratios of urbanward migration streams vary from country to country, resulting in sex differentials in migrant destination and

Table 2.3 The prevalence of migrants in the 15—24 age group: selected Asian countries

Country and age group	Ratio of migrants to:					
	Rural population		Urban population		Metropolitan population	
	Male	Female	Male	Female	Male	Female
Indonesia (1976)						
15—19	.018	.022	.102	.136	.145	.210
20—24	.032	.028	.148	.136	.245	.223
Malaysia (1970)						
15—19	.170	.169	.189	.147	.177	.165
20—24	.234	.259	.280	.218	.325	.220
Philippines (1970)						
15—19	.071	.093	.140	.242	.171	.306
20—24	.106	.120	.185	.228	.189	.224
Thailand (1970)						
15—19	.102	.102	.255	.265	.218	.256
20—24	.189	.136	.392	.295	.346	.268
Japan (1970)						
15—19	.067	.059	.159	.125	.219	.186
20—24	.109	.125	.156	.140	.157	.144
Korea (1970)						
15—19	.028	.038	.191	.247	.315	.390
20—24	.057	.096	.199	.283	.287	.374
India (1971)						
15—19	.144	.486	.344	.381	.367	.328
20—24	.188	.705	.465	.585	.543	.522
Iran (1966)						
15—19	.050	.047	.261	.377	na	na
20—24	.095	.059	.502	.399	na	na

Note: Five-year migrants except for India and Iran, where the data refer to lifetime migrants.
na—not applicable.
Sources: Same as for Table 2.1.

migrant prevalence. One common pattern is that in all countries where the data indicate age at migration, 50 to 60 percent of both female and male migrants are in the 15–24 age group. Overall the data indicate that where migration to urban and metropolitan areas is female selective, the women who migrate tend to be more concentrated in the younger age groups, resulting in higher migrant prevalences among the urban and metropolitan female populations. These patterns are shown most clearly for the Philippines and Korea and, to a lesser extent, for Thailand and Indonesia, where sex differentials in migration patterns are smaller and shift with the age group. The reverse pattern is observed in Japan, Malaysia, India, and Iran, where migration to urban and metropolitan areas appears to be male-selective, the prevalence of migrants is higher among the urban and metropolitan male population, and female migrants are not disproportionately younger than male migrants.

The comparative perspective we have adopted thus far is cross-sectional, focusing on patterns across various countries and regions at a similar point in time. An issue of current interest, however, is whether the sex composition of migrants is changing in Asia and, specifically, whether female migration to cities is increasing. Recent research suggests such a trend in a few countries. In a study of migration patterns in Thailand, Arnold and Boonpratuang (1976) found that male interprovincial *(interchangwat)* migrants exceeded female migrants by 31 percent during the 1955–60 period, but for 1965–70 male migrants exceeded female migrants by only 15 percent. Successive rounds of the Survey of Migration to Bangkok have documented a decrease between 1974 and 1978 in the sex ratio of migrants (Thailand, NSO, 1975–79). Data for India show that the sex ratio of the rural population held steady at about 104 in the rural areas between 1961 and 1971, but the urban sex ratio decreased from 118 to 109 during the same period, perhaps indicating increasing numbers of rural women migrating to urban areas (Singh 1978). In a study of population mobility in Java, Hugo (1975) suggests an increased importance of female migration, especially to Jakarta. He notes that the sex ratio in Jakarta declined from 104 in 1961 to 100 in 1971 and that there were more women than men whose duration of residence in Jakarta was less than two years.

These data are not unambiguous, however, and could reflect, in the case of Java, generally shorter durations of stay in Jakarta for female migrants. Even the reported reductions in the sex ratios of urban migrants in Thailand do not necessarily mean an increase in the number of female migrants, since the trend could imply an increase in the duration of urban stay among female migrants relative to male migrants. The decline in urban sex ratios over time in India and the Philippines could mean either an increase in female in-migration to cities or increasing out-migration of males from cities.

Aside from these observations of changes in the sex ratio of various population groups, more direct data on changes in migrant composition are,
unfortunately, not available. Although the evidence from the literature is
persuasive, it is certainly not conclusive. There are indications that increasing numbers of women relative to men are migrating to the cities in
some Asian countries, but not enough is known about trends in other
countries to conclude that female migration is increasing significantly
everywhere in Asia.

NOTES

1. We have plotted differences between female and male CULs, taking simple averages of the UN's five-year CUL values. The youth dimension describes ages 15 to 24;
the old-age dimension covers ages 60 and above. The CULs make global comparisons
more valid by rescaling. Because of the complex rescaling method used, no meaning
should be attached to the absolute CUL levels.

2. In the study by Youssef et al., the sex ratio is defined as the ratio of females to
males; we have inverted all the results to make them comparable with the other material reviewed and with our own analysis.

3. The correlation relates the CUL for ages 15 to 24 with Youssef and colleagues'
female migration index (FMI).

BIBLIOGRAPHY

Afzal, Mohammad
    1967   Migration to urban areas in Pakistan. *Proceedings of the International Union for
            the Scientific Study of Population Conference.* Sydney, Australia.

Afzal, Mohammad, and Nasreen Abbasi
    1979   *Urbanization and Internal Migration in Pakistan: 1951–1973.* Islamabad: Paki-
            stan Institute of Development Economics.

Arnold, Fred, and S. Boonpratuang
    1976   *1970 Population and Housing Census: Migration.* Subject Report No. 2. Bang-
            kok: National Statistical Office.

Bogue, Donald J.
    1969   *Principles of Demography.* New York: Wiley.

Boserup, Ester
    1970   *Woman's Role in Economic Development.* New York: St. Martin's Press.

Chapman, Murray
    1978   Circulation in cross-cultural perspective: the Melanesian case. Paper pre-
            sented at the Symposium on Population Distribution in Africa, University
            of Ahmadu, Zaire, Nigeria.

Davis, Kingsley
  1975   Asia's cities: problems and options. *Population and Development Review* 1(1): 71–86.
Durand, John D.
  1975   *The Labor Force in Economic Development.* Princeton: Princeton University Press.
Goldstein, Sidney
  1978   *Circulation in the Context of Total Mobility in Southeast Asia.* Papers of the East-West Population Institute, No. 53. Honolulu: East West Center.
Goldstein, Sidney, Visid Prachuabmoh, and Alice Goldstein
  1974   *Urban-Rural Migration Differentials in Thailand.* Research Report No. 12. Bangkok: Institute of Population Studies, Chulalongkorn University.
Haines, Michael
  1979   *Fertility and Occupation: Population Patterns in Industralization.* New York: Academic Press.
Herrick, Bruce H.
  1965   *Urban Migration and Economic Development in Chile.* Cambridge, Mass.: M.I.T. Press.
Hugo, Graeme
  1975   *Population Mobility in West Java.* Jogjakarta, Indonesia: Gadjah Mada University Press.
Ibarra, Teresita E.
  1979   Women migrants: focus on domestic helpers. *Philippine Sociological Review* 27(2):77–92.
Iranian Statistical Center (ISC)
  1969   *National Census of Population and Housing, 1966.* Tehran.
Japan, Bureau of Statistics (BOS)
  1973   *1970 Population Census of Japan.* Vol. 7, pt. 2. Tokyo.
Korea, National Bureau of Statistics (NBS)
  1970   *1970 Population and Housing Census Report.* Vol. 2. Seoul.
Kuznets, Simon
  1966   *Modern Economic Growth: Rate, Structure and Spread.* New Haven: Yale University Press.
Laslett, Peter
  1977   Characteristics of the western family considered over time. *Journal of Family History* 2(2):89–116.
Lesthaeghe, Ron
  1977   *The Decline of Belgian Fertility, 1800–1970.* Princeton: Princeton University Press.
Libbee, M. J., and D. E. Sopher
  1972   Marriage migration in rural India. Paper submitted to the IGU Commission on Population Geography for its Symposium on Internal Migration, Edmonton.

Malaysia, Department of Statistics (DOS)
1973   *1970 General Report: Population Census of Malaysia.* Vol. 2. Kuala Lumpur.

Mazumdar, Dipak
1979   *Paradigms in the Study of Urban Labor Markets in LDC's: A Reassessment in the Light of an Empirical Survey in Bombay City.* World Bank Staff Working Paper No. 366. Washington, D.C.: International Bank for Reconstruction and Development.

Mowat, Susanne
1977   *Education and the Urban Migrant: Comparative Analysis of Case Studies in Bangkok, Manila and Jakarta.* Bangkok: UNESCO Regional Office for Education in Asia.

Parish, William L.
1973   Internal migration and modernization: the European case. *Economic Development and Cultural Change* 21:591–609.

Philippines, National Census and Statistics Office (NCSO)
1974   *1970 Census of Population and Housing.* Vol. 2. Manila.

Premi, Mahendra K.
1979   *Patterns of Internal Migration of Females in India.* Occasional Paper, Center for the Study of Regional Development, School of Social Sciences. New Delhi: Jawaharlal Nehru University.

Pryor, Robin J.
1975   The migrant to the city in South-East Asia—can and should we generalize? Paper presented at a specialist symposium on the migrant and the city, Institute of Australian Geographers, 13th annual conference, Wollongong University.
1977   Bibliography of internal migration in South-East Asia. Working paper in demography, Department of Demography, Australian National University.

Ravenstein, E. G.
1885   The laws of migration. *Journal of the Statistical Society* 48(pt. 2):167–235.

Simmons, Alan, Sergio Diaz-Briquets, and Aprodicio A. Laquain
1977   *Social Change and Internal Migration: A Review of Research Findings from Africa, Asia and Latin America.* Ottawa: International Development Research Center.

Singapore, Department of Statistics (DOS)
1970   *Report on the Population Census 1970.* Vol. 2. Singapore.

Singh, Andrea Menefee
1978   Rural-urban migration of women among the urban poor in India: causes and consequences. *Social Action* 28:326–56.

Smith, Peter C.
1977   The evolving pattern of interregional migration in the Philippines. *Philippine Economic Journal* 16(182):121–59.

Speare, Alden
1971   *Urbanization and Migration in Taiwan.* Taiwan Population Studies, Working Paper No. 11. Ann Arbor: Population Studies Center.

Thadani, Veena N.
   1980   *Property and Progeny: An Exploration of Intergenerational Relations.* Center for Policy Studies, Working Paper No. 62. New York: The Population Council.

Thailand, National Statistical Office (NSO)
   1975   *The Survey of Migration in Bangkok Metropolis 1974.* Bangkok.
   1976   *The Survey of Migration in Bangkok Metropolis 1975.* Bangkok.
   1977   *The Survey of Migration in Bangkok Metropolis 1976.* Bangkok.
   1978   *The Survey of Migration in Bangkok Metropolis 1977.* Bangkok.
   1979   *The Survey of Migration in Bangkok Metropolis 1978.* Bangkok.

Tilly, Charles
   1978   Migration in modern European history. In William H. McNeill and Ruth S. Adams (eds.), *Human Migration: Patterns and Policies.* Bloomington: Indiana University Press.

United Nations
   1970   *Sex and Age Patterns of the Urban Population.* New York: United Nations, Population Division.
   1971   *Comparative Regional Typology of Urbanization Patterns by Sex and Age.* New York: United Nations, Population Division.
   1972   *Sex-Age Composition of the Urban and Rural Population of the World, Major Areas, Regions, and Individual Countries in 1960.* New York: United Nations, Population Division.
   1980   *Patterns of Urban and Rural Population Growth.* New York: United Nations.

Weber, Adna
   1899   *The Growth of Cities in the Nineteenth Century.* New York: Macmillan.

Wrigley, E. A.
   1961   *Industrial Growth and Population Change: A Regional Study of the Coalfield Areas of North-West Europe in the Later Nineteenth Century.* Cambridge: Cambridge University Press.

Yap, Loreen
   1975   *Internal Migration in Less Developed Countries: A Survey of the Literature.* World Bank Staff Working Paper No. 215. Washington, D.C.: International Bank for Reconstruction and Development.

Youssef, Nadia H., Mayra Buvinic, and Ayse Kudat
   1979   *Women in Migration: A Third World Focus.* (Mimeographed.) Washington, D.C.: International Center for Research on Women.

Zablan, A.
   1977   *Causes and Effects of Rural-Urban Migration: A Study of 1972 Cebu City Immigrants.* SEAPRAP Research Report No. 16. Singapore: SEAPRAP.

Zachariah, K. C.
   1964   *A Historical Study of Internal Migration in the Indian Subcontinent, 1901–1931.* New York: Asia Publishing House.

Chapter 3

Female Migration: A Conceptual Framework

Veena N. Thadani
Michael P. Todaro

From the volume and diversity of recent research on rural-to-urban migration in developing countries emerge certain common issues and unifying elements. One element common to almost all of the varied approaches is the striking absence of analysis of female migration. Implicit in these approaches is the assumption that the patterns of female migration are likely to mirror those of male migration. Consequently, gender-related variations in the causes, consequences, and patterns of migration have not been considered significant enough to warrant specific analysis (see, for example, Standing 1978).

Speculation, however, about possible gender-related differences in the migratory process summons to mind a variety of forces that may indeed affect male and female migrants differently. In the general model of migration put forth by Lee (1966) emphasizing the causes of migration—area of origin, area of destination, intervening obstacles, and personal factors— the potential differences between male and female migrants are fairly obvious. The possibility of social constraints against the autonomous migration of women, or even the associational migration of wives in some cases, is merely one clear area of difference between males and females. Cultural norms may well promote the migration of males while impeding the migration of females. The places of origin and destination are also likely to involve gender-related differences in the push or pull variables involved in migration. Thus the subordinate position of women in the traditional social hierarchy of the village of origin may be a powerful push factor unique to women.

Although the significance of these gender-related differences is a matter for empirical verification, male/female differences in migration are clearly evident. If, for example, the goal of migration is, as is generally assumed, the improvement of one's economic and social status via education and employment, then the divergence between male and female attainment strategies is immediately apparent. Whereas education and employment are usually the sole avenue of economic betterment and status mobility for men, marriage to an upwardly mobile man may be an alternative approach for women.

These gender-related differences in the migratory process suggest the need for a specific analysis of female migration. Recent research provides preliminary evidence of the steadily expanding stream of female migration, both the associational migration of wives accompanying migrant spouses and the autonomous migration of unattached women. It is particularly this latter category of new migrants—unattached women—that reveals the inadequacy of present approaches to the study of migration. These studies have taken female migration into account but focus on household or family migration or, occasionally, on marriage migration. Bogue, for example, has attemped to explain the early male dominance and subsequent female dominance in the migration streams in terms of the household; because the first migratory moves were always attended by uncertainty, both economic and noneconomic, males usually migrated first. As migration became a routine manner, wives and families followed and gradually the migration of females began to equal or even exceed that of males (Bogue 1969:764).

Along the same lines, accounts of marriage migration represent a variation on the theme of household migration. These explanations have focused on marriage customs and the demographic imbalances in sex ratios that result in the migration of women, and sometimes men, in the pursuit of desirable alliances. In the Cameroons, for example, Podlewski finds female mobility more important than male mobility. He suggests that exogamy accounts for the sex variation in migratory flows: "[Since] the members of a same clan are usually united in the same villages, and as the wife usually goes to live in the husband's clan, a great volume of female migration is recorded" (Podlewski 1975:559). In India, too, where village exogamy and group endogamy prevail, female migration has been attributed entirely to marriage migration. Bose, for example, states (1973:142): "The predominant female migration in India is what may be called 'marriage migration' (on account of village exogamy in several parts of India) and 'associational migration' (accompanying their migrant husbands). Economic causes are relatively unimportant in India."

It is perhaps these a priori assumptions—as well as the lack of information about the migration of women and the invisibility of women who merely accompany or join migrant males—that account for the paucity of analysis of migrant women. It has been almost axiomatic in the literature that patterns of female migration reflect patterns of family or household migration. It has been suggested, moreover, that this assumption can be traced to prevailing patrilineal patterns and the subordinate position of women that deters their autonomous migration in many societies (Connell et al. 1976).

The attempt to focus on female migration is not without its problems, however. It may be problematic in some cases to identify female migration that is independent of household or family migration. Even where female migration is responsive to wage and opportunity differentials in urban areas, it is difficult in cases of family migration to ascertain whether the decision to migrate was based on the incentives for the household head (assuming male head of household) or for the women in the household. The responsiveness of female migration to income and opportunity differentials in urban relative to rural areas may also be considerably affected by cultural constraints relating to the migration of women.

These difficulties in disentangling the diverse causes of female migration may account for the prevalence of two assumptions: (1) that it is mainly family or marriage migration and thus reflects male migration or (2) that if it is a response to perceived urban/rural differentials in opportunities, it is unlikely to differ significantly from male migration.

Given these assumptions regarding female migration and the preponderance of males in the migration streams until recently (excluding those in Latin America and the Philippines), analyses of migration have been based almost entirely on information gathered from male migrants. These analyses, assumed to apply to both male and female migration, are, in fact, sex-specific theories—specific to male migration. For in the absence of a gender-differentiated analysis or with the neglect of subsample variation between males and females, the results of empirical inquiry cannot be tacitly assumed to apply to both sexes. Responses to various aspects of social change, including migration, are inevitably differentiated by gender, and theories of migration that have not taken women into account—or have overlooked gender variations—must be regarded as special theories rather than general ones. In the absence of research on female migration, these male-specific theories of migration have been perpetuated and reinforced.

The framework proposed here is gender-specific also—focused specifically on the migration of women—in an effort to redress the male bias in approaches to migration and to analyze the specific causes of female migration with a view to assessing the significance of gender in migration.

EVIDENCE AND INTERPRETATION

Recent studies provide evidence of the gradually expanding stream of female migration and particularly the autonomous migration of unattached women.[1] However, most explanations of this increased pace and volume of female migration are related to family migration—the associational migration of wives or daughters accompanying the primary male migrant—or, in the case of unattached female migration, to the existence of economic and employment opportunities in the urban areas. Therefore, their motivations for migrating are no different from those of men.[2] The nature of urban wage and employment activities for female migrants has in turn been related to their economic roles in the rural areas, suggesting a continuity in their urban and rural economic roles.[3] Thus it has been argued that the "activity pattern of immigrant women in the town is determined primarily by the customary pattern of female employment in the village, and especially by the extent to which women participate in non-agricultural activities in the village" (Boserup 1970:175).

The generalization that urban activity patterns are "determined primarily" by rural activity patterns does not, however, appear to be the case in Latin America, Africa, or India, as is suggested in this simplified table (Boserup 1970:186):

Country group	Female activity Rates in village	Female activity Rates in town
Arab countries	Low	Low
Latin America	Low	High
Southeast Asia	High	High
Africa and India	High	Low

In the rural areas of Latin America, as the table indicates, women's participation in agriculture and other economic activities is low. Rural women are primarily engaged in domestic activities, whereas women in urban areas have a high level of participation in both modern and traditional sectors (Boserup 1970:186–87).

The migration of women from places with no employment opportunities to places where employment may be found is evident in the capital cities of Chile, Argentina, Mexico, Colombia, and Costa Rica. It is in these Latin American countries that the predominance of female migration has been most marked.[4] Boserup (p. 187) explains why sex patterns of migration in Latin America are radically different from those in developing countries in other continents.

In Latin America, young rural women are attracted to the towns because they offer them better employment opportunities than the rural areas. Poor farmers send their daughters to town to become domestic servants, because they are not needed at home if the mother does little more than domestic duties. Moreover, there is little agricultural work for them to do, except in regions where female labor is needed for plucking the principal crop. In town, on the other hand, women find many employment opportunities ranging from domestic service for the daughters of poor farmers to clerical jobs for the educated daughters from better-off families. As a result the flow of women from the countryside to the towns is larger than that of men.

Owing to this high rate of rural-urban migration of young girls, Latin American towns, in sharp contrast to other towns in developing countries, have a higher proportion of women than the rural areas.

The predominance of females in the migration streams in the Philippines has been regarded as resembling the Latin American pattern. These predominantly female streams are attributed in both the Philippines and Latin America to the structure of urban employment opportunities (Connell et al. 1976:204). However, a closer look at the sex composition of migration streams in other Southeast Asian countries reveals that female migration is not confined to the Philippines alone. Remarking on the widely held notion that migrants tend to be males rather than females, Pryor (1977:7) has commented that "the notion of male dominance is either incorrect or there has been a marked change in the late 1960s." He has observed further (p. 7) that "overall there is a significant predominance of females among migrants to Manila (sex ratio 64 males to 100 females), Surabaja (Indonesia), and Bangkok." The significant shift in the sex composition of migration streams has also been observed recently in Malaysia, where there has been a dramatic increase in the volume of female migrants from the rural areas to urban industrial centers (Chapters 7 and 11 of this volume).

In the simplified table presented earlier, the Southeast Asian pattern is characterized by high levels of female activity in both village and town. Not only are women active in agriculture and other productive endeavors in the rural areas but the wide range of economic opportunities offered by the cities in both the informal sector and the modern sector is reflected in high levels of female employment (Boserup 1970:189).[5]

The Southeast Asian pattern of considerable female participation in economic activities in both urban and rural areas is found also in West Africa, where women are active in agricultural as well as market and trading activities. The existence of urban economic opportunities, given other predisposing conditions, has led to a considerable increase in the volume of female migration, resulting in shifting sex ratios in the cities and new migration patterns during the 1960s and 1970s (Carynnyk-Sinclair 1974). The presence of a substantial number of female migrants in most West African towns and cities and the growing proportions of migrant women led Caldwell to suggest that "the female propensity for rural-urban migration is rising faster than the male" (1968:368). As Sudarkasa has noted (1977:178): "This 'propensity' is, of course, a predictable response to actual and perceived opportunities for employment, education, and/or marriage in the cities."

The typical female migrant in West Africa is described by Sudarkasa (p. 183) as a commercial migrant:

> The vast majority of women move from the rural areas to the cities. This is the direction of most internal migration. Because they do not have the formal educational qualifications required for the types of wage employment open to women, many female rural-urban migrants have had to enter market trade or similar occupations. In the past two decades, however, more and more young women with some degree of formal education have been moving to the cities in the hope of obtaining jobs in the "modern sector." As often as not, these young women do not find the clerical, industrial or technical jobs they seek, and they, too, have to turn to trading on their own account or with female relatives in order to eke out a living.

In contrast to the West African situation of considerable female participation in both agriculture and nonagricultural economic activities, rural women in East Africa are engaged primarily in agricultural work (Mair 1969:63). In fact their productivity, along with the limited employment opportunities open to them in the cities, even in the informal sector, inhibits their migration to the urban areas (Thadani 1978). As Boserup's generalization suggests, the low level of participation in nonagricultural activities appears to limit the options for urban economic participation.

Although most African migrants are males, there has been a shift in the sex composition of migration in recent years: Female migration has been steadily increasing. Ominde (1968:189) has noted the marked increase, in both absolute and relative terms, of the movement of women to the urban areas of Kenya during the 1960s. Moreover, Heisler (1974:63) has reported that during the 1960s in Zambia the migration of women to the cities exceeded that of men.

In India, female migration has been characterized as exclusively family or marriage migration induced by the movement of either the parental or the marital household (Joshi and Joshi 1976:138). Other reasons for migration, such as employment or education, are not believed to be of importance. There is, however, one interesting exception reported in the literature—that of Moti Ghadal in Gujarat, where female migration, which comprises 32 percent of total migration, is unexpectedly high because many young women migrate for education (Connell et al. 1976:181). If there are other exceptions, they have yet to be detected.

THE FIELD

The striking feature about the study of migration is its diversity. This diversity can be traced, in large part, to the wide range of disciplinary perspectives in the field and to the different levels of analysis that can be applied. Different disciplines—each with its special vocabulary and conceptual framework—have focused on different elements of the migration process. Economists study migration at the macrolevel and focus on labor transfer and adjustments in the labor market; sociologists concentrate on the study of motivation, social mobility, and the assimilation and adaptation of migrants; geographers examine spatial patterns of mobility and relate them to broad social, economic, and environmental changes.[6]

Moreover, each discipline must deal with the issue of which level of analysis to apply: micro or macro, structural or individualist. From the perspective of economics, for example, it is possible to view the migratory process at the macrolevel as an inevitable consequence of the unequal distribution of factors of production; thus migration is determined by the strategy of overall development and the allocation of scarce resources. At the microlevel, the inducement to migrate can be traced to severe imbalances in employment opportunities and income levels in the city versus the countryside. The issue, as Parkin sees it (1975:9), is this: "How much analytical emphasis should be placed on the individual migrant as being free to decide between alternative courses of action, and how much on the wider political, economic, and ecological factors directing and constraining migratory flows of particular groups?"

It is specifically in relation to the place of women in the migratory process that the issue of analytic emphasis has been raised. In a short but strident piece, Anthony Leeds has vigorously decried the study of women in the migratory process. He contends that the analysis of "men" and "women" involves an "individualistic, reductionist, and motivational" emphasis that reduces all "structural elements to epiphenomena" (1976:73). Migration ought to be analyzed, according to Leeds, in terms of the structural flows of resources, including human labor capacity and money, and shifts in these flows entailed by migration. He argues further (p. 73) that the focus on migrants and the reductionism that this involves "has a strong ideological element . . . emphasis on which serves to divert people, including social scientists, from closer examination of dominating forms of economy and polity and their major institutions, e.g., capitalist exploitation, as these shape migration."

Along similar ideological lines, Samir Amin (1974:88–89) argues that "the decision of the migrant to leave his region of origin is . . . completely predetermined by the overall strategy determining the 'allocation of factors' "—that is, the overall strategy of development. It is here, he says, that the ultimate cause of migration lies. Amin dismisses the possibility of rational choice on the part of the migrant as mere rationalization: "a platitude which leads nowhere."

Amin's argument suggests that the emphasis on macrostructure precludes the need for analysis at other levels. Others, however, have pointed to the necessity for analysis at both levels (Parkin 1975; Taylor 1969). In this case, the two levels are viewed as alternative approaches rather than incompatible ones—simply different perspectives posing different questions. Parkin, for example, suggests that the macrocontext can be regarded as a given in a microstudy of migrants. He continues: "Since a macrocontext *does* change over time (e.g., government and political systems are altered, economic expansion alternates with recession, etc.), then the relationship between its changing nature and alterations in the choices open to individuals requires analyses at both levels" (1975:13). Although few analyses have explicitly attempted to incorporate both the macrocontext and the microlevel of migration, Parkin (1975:12–16) cites two attempts; for another, see Jackson (1969).

The specific link between macrostructural forces and the problems of individual migration from rural to urban areas, while undoubtedly plausible, requires considerable clarification. Morever, although macrostructural factors may create the internal imbalance conducive to migration, a wide variety of social, cultural, and individual forces determines *who* actually migrates. The expectations of prospective migrants regarding opportunities, the financial resources needed to migrate, and the sociocultural norms favoring (or at last sanctioning) migration affect their propensity to migrate no less than the macrocontext. Thus Mitchell makes an apt distinction between the "underlying determinants" predisposing toward migration and the specific motives that cause an individual to migrate (Mitchell 1959).

It is at the microlevel that research has been concentrated overwhelmingly on the causes of migration (Brown and Newberger 1977:446). There are three basic questions at this level: Who migrates? Why? And what are the consequences for the individual, the family, and the sending and receiving communities? The question "Who migrates?" may be answered in terms of age, sex, marital status, education, and level of occupation, employment, and income. The causes of migration are generally traced to economic, sociocultural, and environmental determinants. Economic explanations center on the search for better opportunities of income and employment; sociocultural explanations center on the desire of migrants to break away from traditional constraints and inequities; environmental explanations center on the lure of the cities and migration induced by disaster, displacement, and demographic pressures or imbalances.

Because migration often involves elements of all these forces, narrow studies of migration have been found to be inherently unsatisfactory (Shaw 1975). Although economic models of the migration in terms of urban/rural wage differentials and expectations of employment are the principal explanations in the field, and although there is considerable evidence for the expected-income model (Todaro 1976; Fields 1979; House and Rempel

1979), the emphasis on economics alone has often been regarded as too simplistic. Where migration has become an intrinsic part of the life cycle, for example, it has acquired the significance of a rite of passage into adulthood or social status. Among youths in Talara, Peru, migration is considered crucial to social maturation (McIrvin 1970). In northern Thailand, Keyes (1966:329) found that "every young man considers it a part of his maturation to spend a few months or even years working in an urban center before returning to the village to settle down, marry, and follow the traditional village way." Similarly, in parts of Africa the early patterns of periodic or circular migration have gradually become integrated into the life cycle of young males (Gugler 1968). These sociocultural functions of migration may in some cases counteract its economic utility. Thus an argument is often made against relying totally on any unidimensional system of explaining migration, given the complex webs of conflicting pressures and interests (Connell et al. 1976; Du Toit and Safa 1975; Shaw 1975).

Diverse models have been developed to organize the interacting causes of migration: various forms of push-pull theories emphasizing the negative push factors at the place of origin and the positive pull factors at the place of destination; cost-benefit models that include both push and pull factors; and gravity models that center on the characteristics of the origin and destination and the distance between them. There is also the general model of migration articulated by Lee (1966), which emphasizes the characteristics of origin and destination as well as intervening obstacles and personal factors. The framework proposed here is an effort to identify the forces uniquely involved in the migration of a specific group: women.

THE FRAMEWORK

Speculation about the causes of migration of women has tended to focus on unattached women who migrate independently. Women migrating with their families—either parents or spouse—are assumed to be merely accompanying the primary migrant. This type of migration has been characterized as "associational" migration. But even the associational migration of women may be induced, in part, by the expectation of urban employment and the dislocation of their traditional economic activities. Certainly the expectation of urban employment is likely to influence associational migration. Given the often substantial contribution of rural women to the support of their families, the lack of urban opportunities may conceivably deter associational migration. Conversely, the possibility of urban employment may promote it.

The associational migration of women may be impelled also by the dislocation of their rural economic activities. The introduction of modern methods of agriculture and mechanized farming has, in some cases, driven women out of agricultural labor and thus out of economic activity (Boser-up 1970). Development programs for agricultural training, cooperatives, and credit and market improvement, by neglecting women, have some-times undermined their economic activities (Tinker 1973). Thus where women have played important roles in agriculture and other economic activities such as rural crafts or trading in the bazaar, the declining impor-tance of their traditional activities may induce greater associational migra-tion. Such changes also tend to exacerbate urban/rural differences in income and employment opportunities.

Explanations of the autonomous migration of unattached women, in contrast to associational migration, have ranged over a variety of issues. It has been suggested that, in Africa, migration from village to city offers women an escape—an escape from their traditional ascribed status, per-haps an escape from obedience to male kinsmen, and an escape from a life of exceedingly hard work: "It is hardly surprising that there should be a widespread desire among African women to exchange a village life of hard toil for an urban life of leisure" (Boserup 1970:191). It has also been sug-gested that women move to towns in search of husbands. Some seek to escape customary sanctions (which vary from tribe to tribe) against un-married mothers. Then there are the women who are divorced or have deserted their husbands. They may be runaways from unhappy, broken, or barren marriages (Little 1973:19–22). Or they may come as ayahs—young girls, usually from poor families, who come to the city as live-in maids or babysitters. Their situation is not dissimilar to that which obtains in Latin America, where employment opportunities for unschooled and low-income women in domestic service have led to a preponderance of females in the migration flows from rural to urban areas (Schultz 1971: 175–63).

Regardless of whether female migrants are single or married at the time of migration, and especially given the fluidity of marital status, it has been suggested that women, like men, tend to move out of areas where eco-nomic opportunities are limited to areas where employment is available. Thus the economic motive is seen as the principal force in female as well as male migration (Standing 1978:212; Fields 1979).

The migration of women, like that of men, is indeed likely to be job-oriented; employment opportunities and wage differentials, actual or per-ceived, between rural and urban areas are of central significance. A distin-guishing feature of female compared to male migration, however, is the importance of marriage as a reason for migration. Marriage could be, as Pryor (1977) has phrased it, an "unavoidable correlate" of migration—as in India, where marriage involves the bride's move to the parental house-hold of her spouse, dictated by the practice of village exogamy and group endogamy: *marriage migration*. Moreover, marriage itself could also be the goal of migration, as in West Africa, where the dissatisfaction of young women with marriage prospects in their rural villages has been suggested as a reason for migration: *marital migration* (Gugler 1969). Marriage could also be an alternative route to socioeconomic status and social mobility: *mobility marriage*. As Pryor (1977:8) has noted, female migrants tend to return to their rural village if they neither marry nor obtain jobs in the city.

Accordingly, the central variables involve income and employment opportunities, marriage as a means to financial betterment and status mobility (mobility marriage), plus the two other aspects of marriage suggested above (marriage migration and marital migration). Marriage migration refers to the movement involved *in* marriage—such as the bride's move to her spouse's place of residence. Marital migration refers to migration *for* marriage—that is, marriage for the sake of marriage rather than for economic betterment, although such betterment may well be a secondary effect. Mediating the effect of these causes of female migration are intervening factors such as sex-role constraints, which may impede the migration of women, and the usual factors of cost, transport, amenities, and the like, which are common to both male and female migration. The ensuing discussion elaborates on these variables: employment and income differentials (in the formal sector and informal sector), mobility marriage, marital migration/marriage migration, and sex-role constraints.

EMPLOYMENT AND INCOME DIFFERENTIALS

The relevance of urban/rural differentials in employment and income for female migrants, including wives accompanying migrant husbands, has been suggested earlier. Apart from the largely spatial migration involved in marriage migration, and aside from situations where, traditionally, the strict seclusion of women prevails, female migrants to cities, irrespective of their marital status, are likely to be influenced by the perceptions of urban/rural differentials.

The mainstream economic theory of rural-to-urban migration, the Todaro model, identifies the expected difference between urban and rural real wages as the key determinant. The expected differential is determined by the interaction of two variables: the actual urban/rural wage differential and the probability of obtaining employment in the city (Todaro 1969: 138–48). The model makes no distinction between men and women, however.

Differentials in the Formal Sector. In the case of women, data on urban/rural wage differentials in the formal sector require modification to account for the sex discrimination frequently encountered by women seeking employment in the modern sector—a situation found not only in developing societies but also in developed ones. This discrimination is manifested in the significant differences in employment opportunities and considerable differences in pay for equal work.[7]

In many developing societies, women are often underrepresented in the modern sector—industrial, professional, and white-collar jobs—even after allowances have been made for educational disparities between women and men. In Kenya, for example, women constitute only 15 percent of the modern employment sector, whereas they constitute more than 30 percent of the educated, urban labor force (ILO 1972:53, 59).

Sexual inequality in the labor market has been abundantly documented. (For studies of discrimination in the U.S. labor market, see Epstein [1970] and Kreps [1971]. See Boserup [1970:chap. 8] for discrimination in the developing countries.) But it is the degree to which sex discrimination affects the probability of obtaining employment as well as the rural/urban wage differential that needs to be incorporated in models of female migration. The framework presented in the next section attempts to do this.

Differentials in the Informal Sector. Corresponding to the sex discrimination that affects the urban/rural differential in the formal sector, the traditional roles of women and their control over the distribution of agricultural products and other activities in the rural areas directly influence the extent of the rural/urban differential in the informal sector. As Friedl (1975) has pointed out, control over distribution is a critical economic aspect of the status and power differentials between men and women. Because women are often in a subordinate position in the traditional social hierarchy and lack the autonomy derived from control over resources, urban migration may represent the promise of freedom and economic independence. To the degree that women do lack power in the rural areas, the promise of income from informal-sector work in the cities will result in a greater positive differential for women compared to men.

MOBILITY MARRIAGE

The importance of marriage as a means of upward social mobility for women, in both developed and developing societies, has been generally acknowledged. (For several references to the marital mobility of women in the west, see Glenn et al. [1969]; see Little [1972:276] for the situation in Africa.) It has been suggested that whereas males rely largely on occupational achievement for social mobility, women can acquire social status through marriage. Implicit in this idea is an "exchange theory" of marriage that posits a marriage market (see Becker 1974)—not dissimilar to the market in which economic goods and services are exchanged—females offer the characteristics sought after by males in exchange for the characteristics and status they desire from males. Implicit also is the idea that rational, status-seeking considerations are important in the marital choices of females, although this assumption has not gone unchallenged. (See Taylor and Glenn 1976.)

Marital mobility thus applies only to women and may be of special benefit to low-status women, who are at a competitive advantage over low-status men in the marriage market. Whereas high-status males may not be reluctant to marry lower-status females, the reverse—high-status females marrying lower-status males—is less probable.

As Little perceptively points out, the acquisition of an upwardly mobile, professional, and urbane husband has become part of the West African woman's dream.[8] He cites a ditty about a young girl's fondest fantasies (1972:276):

> What shall I do to get a man of that type?
> One who is a been-to,[9]
> Car full and fridge full,
> What shall I do to obtain a man like that?

MARITAL MIGRATION AND MARRIAGE MIGRATION

The migration of married women and the migration of women in the pursuit of improved marital prospects are two different aspects of marital migration. The requirements of customary marriage practices, as in village exogamy, often necessitate the migration of women. It has been suggested that this type of marriage migration is generally rural-to-urban and involves only short distances (Connell et al. 1976:42). But in addition to this sort of migration dictated by customary practices is the type of marital migration induced by a simple imbalance in sex ratios, or an imbalance in the sex ratios within certain status groups, that may result in the migration of females.[10] Little (1972) suggests that this may be the case for West African women who find few eligible husbands left in rural areas after previous periods of male migration.

Does this aspect of marital migration and mobility marriage limit the relevance of our explanation to young and marriageable women? To some degree it does. But, as used here, the term "marriage" includes a wide variety of arrangements and forms of cohabitation and is not confined to a formal, legal, or western definition of marriage. In Kenya, for example, the range of possibilities includes Christian marriage, recognized by the law courts; tribal marriage, based on African customary practices; and free marriage, which involves cohabitation with varying degrees of permanence. Sometimes these forms of marriage overlap—as when a couple living on terms of free marriage undertakes to have a Christian or tribal marriage later. The complex array of types of marriage—"multiple" marriage, "serial" marriage—has been identified in several contexts. (See, for example, Rodman 1977, and Brown 1975.) Because of the diversity of domestic arrangements and the diversity of forms of consensual union that fall outside the purview of marriage strictly defined, the initial impression that the marriage factors included here pertain only to eligible young women is perhaps unwarranted. The dependence of poor and unschooled women on men in urban areas, given the absence of alternative economic options (Van Allen 1974), reinforces the idea of marriage, loosely construed, as an economic as well as social explanation of migration.

Taking into account the marital status of rural women at the time of migration and their employment status in the city, four variants of female migration can be identified:

1. Married women in search of urban employment and induced to migrate by perceived urban/rural differentials
2. Unmarried women in search of urban employment and induced to migrate for economic or marital reasons
3. Unmarried women induced to migrate solely for marriage reasons
4. Married women engaged in associational migration with no thought of employment.

SEX-ROLE CONSTRAINTS

Sex role in this context refers to the sociocultural valuation of migration and the differences in attitudes toward male and female migration. For men, migration may be regarded as necessary and routine—necessary to the attainment of status in the community and routine as an accepted stage in the life cycle. For women, however, the stigma attached to their position in some cities, which until recently were largely "male-towns" (reflecting in many countries the colonial policy of recruiting men for indigenous labor in the mining sites, for example), may well deter the migration of unattached women (Boserup 1970:85–86).

Attitudes toward female migration are diverse. Positive valuations are evident in West Africa among the Nupe of northern Nigeria, for example, where the itinerant aspects of women's market and trading activities require a mobility that is socially sanctioned (Levine 1966). Similarly, Caldwell (1968, 1969) in his study of rural-to-urban migration in Ghana found that rural parents admitted no societal constraint on the migration of women to urban areas. Ross (1975) reports considerable opposition in Kenya to the migration of women to the cities, however, and Little notes strict regulation of the migration of women in Zambia in order to preserve tribal stability and induce the return of migrating males (Little 1972: 18–20).

Sociocultural evaluations may be an effective constraint on the migration of women, particularly unattached women. The autonomous migration of women may indeed be found only where values supporting, or at least sanctioning, their mobility prevail. It is not inconceivable, however, that even where female migration is currently restricted by cultural mores, the growing disparities between urban and rural areas and increasing rural impoverishment may in fact influence social deterrents to female migration. Sheer economic stress may impel the migration of women from rural areas in search of a means of support for themselves and their families. It is the interaction between these forces—between urban/rural differentials in income and employment opportunities and the strength of culturally prescribed economic and social roles of women—that must be considered in the analysis of female migration. Sex differentials in urban employment and the sociocultural norms associated with marriage and motherhood are likely to have specific effects in either encouraging or discouraging the migration of women.

AN EMPIRICAL APPROACH

The measures proposed here for the analysis of female migration estimation call for a judicious combination of quantitative as well as qualitative information. Thus results of survey research need to be amplified by anthropological and sociological analysis of family structures, customs, and legal and social sanctions in different communities. Our focus here, however, is primarily on survey research methods as we spell out the determinants of female migration.

Having set forth in previous sections the rationale for a migration model for women, we can now specify the components of our theory. The migration of women (both unattached and associational), whatever the level of their education, is assumed to be determined jointly by economic and social forces while being constrained by cultural sex-role prescriptions. There are five key variables in our model:

1. The differential between expected urban income (both in the modern and informal sectors) and average rural income. This differential takes into account the degree of sex discrimination in both job hiring (thus affecting the probability of successful job search) and salary scales (affecting actual wages paid).
2. The mobility-marriage factor expressed in terms of marriage probabilities to males either engaged in or actively searching for work in the modern sector.
3. The customary-marriage differential reflecting the relative probability of marriage to *any* eligible male in urban as opposed to rural areas.

4. The strength of sex-role constraints on any kind of spatial mobility for women from particular areas of origin.
5. All other residual factors, including distance, amenities, extended-family contacts, and size of origin and destination areas, that might modify the pace and direction of female migration.

Clearly some of these variables also have sex biases (amenities, extended-family contacts, and so forth). But here we want to focus on the first five variables as the major determinants of female migration in general and unattached female migration in particular. Associational migration may also be influenced to some degree by variables 1, 2, and 5, but economic opportunities for the husband may well be the principal reason for the household's decision to migrate.

Our specific migration equation is then formulated as follows:

$$\frac{M_{ij}}{P_i} = f(Y_{ij}, m^Y_{ij}, m^P_{ij}, \mathcal{Q}_i, Z)$$

where:

$\dfrac{M_{ij}}{P_i}$ is the dependent variable representing the gross flow of female migrants between, say, the ages of 15 and 45 over a given period of time from one area i to another area j (M_{ij}) divided by the same age-specific population in the origin area at the beginning of the period (Pi). For our purposes, i and j represent rural and urban areas respectively. One would also want to adjust M_{ij}/P_i for education and to distinguish between associational and unattached female migration.

Y_{ij} is the expected modern sector urban (j)/rural (i) income differential where, as shown below, expected income is expressed both in terms of actual urban/rural female wage differentials and employment probabilities for women in the modern and informal urban sectors.

m^Y_{ij} is the mobility-marriage income differential reflecting an unattached female migrant's chances of achieving a certain expected income through marriage to a male in the modern sector who is either gainfully employed or searching for a job.

m^P_{ij} is the customary-marriage differential reflecting the relative probability that an unattached female can find any spouse in urban as distinct from rural areas. Whereas m^Y_{ij} is an income concept reflecting potential socioeconomic mobility through marriage, m^P_{ij} is a cultural concept reflecting social pressures on women to marry *independently* of the financial status of their potential spouse.

φ_i is a sex-role constraint variable designed to measure the sociocultural obstacles to geographic mobility faced primarily by women qua women. It is one of Lee's intervening obstacles that affects female migrants in particular (Lee 1966). This variable can range from zero (total constraint mobility) to 1 (no constraint). It may vary according to the nature of origin and destination areas as well as the ethnic, caste, or religious groups that dominate those areas.

Z is a residual variable reflecting all other influences on female migration—distance, personal contacts, range of amenities, and so forth—that for the present are assumed not to exert any differential affect on female as distinct from male migrants.

Regarding the anticipated relationship between the four major independent variables and the rate of female rural-to-urban migration, we hypothesize that:

1. $F'(Y_{ij}) > 0$. The higher the expected urban/rural income differential, the greater the female migration rate.
2. $F'(m_{ij}^Y) > 0$. The higher the probability or urban mobility marriage, the greater the female migration rate.
3. $F'(m_{ij}^P) > 0$. The higher the unattached male/female ratio in urban compared with rural areas, the greater the propensity for female out-migration.
4. $F'(\varphi_i) < 0$. The stronger the sex-role constraint on mobility, the lower the rate of female rural out-migration.

For additional details of the model presented here and a discussion of methodological issues of measurement and estimation, see Thadani and Todaro (1979).

CONCLUSION

Females now predominate in the migration streams throughout Latin America and parts of Asia. They also represent a growing proportion of internal migrants in Africa. Given the greater access to primary and secondary education, the gradual relaxation of discrimination in hiring, and the inexorable labor displacement and mechanization of traditional agriculture, all indications point to an even greater influx of young and increasingly independent women into the cities of developing nations.

Most governments in the developing world have expressed great concern with their growing problems of rapid urbanization and rising unemployment. Numerous policy alternatives designed either to modify the pace of internal migration or to accommodate expected increases in urban migrants have been proposed. Some countries—South Korea, Indonesia, the Philippines, Tanzania, Cuba, and Venezuela, for example—have adopted specific measures to slow the growth of their major cities resulting from natural increase and especially rural-to-urban migration.

Yet when the discussion turns to policy options to deal with migration, whether in the scholarly literature or in government legislative bodies, the causes and consequences of female as opposed to male migration are never considered. One reason for this oversight is the failure of researchers and government statistical offices to recognize the growing numbers of women in internal migration. Lacking either a theory to explain this female migration or a sense of its empirical significance in a male-oriented society, developing nations are unlikely to devise judicious urbanization policies if they do not begin to recognize the unique role of women in the development process.

In this essay we have provided a framework for analyzing the special characteristics and circumstances of female migration in developing countries. By focusing on income and employment opportunities in the urban labor market (in the context of wage and job discrimination) as well as the role of the urban marriage market and the special institutional, cultural, and political constraints on women's migration, we believe this framework can serve as the basis for organizing empirical research on female migration in developing nations.

NOTES

The authors wish to thank the Compton Foundation for financial support of their research.

1. The literature surveys listed in Note 5 include some references to studies of female migration. But because the shifts in the sex composition of migration streams are of quite recent origin, documentation of the trends in female migration lags considerably behind the initial evidence.

2. As Standing (1978:209–10) puts it: "The migration of men, other than of men moving to retire or for education, can be expected to be related to relative employment opportunities, but the widespread tendency for women to migrate independently of their families is an indication that migration plays a similar function of many women in those economies, since it is usually for the purpose of seeking employment."

3. The extent to which migration to urban areas involves women in significant changes in both economic and social roles and life options is highly variable, in cultural, subcultural, and class terms, and not amenable to ready generalizations.

4. For the predominance of female migration by country, see Herrick (1965) and

Elizaga (1966) for Chile; Findley (1977) for Argentina; Jelin (1977) for Mexico; Schultz (1971) for Colombia; and Carvajal and Geithman (1974) for Costa Rica.

5. Although migration in Southeast Asia is believed to be largely family migration (Standing 1978:209), there is evidence of substantial independent female migration. For the Philippines, see Hart (1971) and Anderson (1975); for Indonesia, see Heeren (1955) and Suharso (1975); for Thailand, see Pryor (1977) and Piampiti (1977).

6. Among the many literature surveys of migration, the following are perhaps the most comprehensive: Findley (1977), Shaw (1975), Todaro (1976), Simmons et al. (1977), Stark (1976) and Yap (1977).

7. In the case of Colombia, for example, Fields provides data indicating that women can expect to earn approximately 63 percent as much as men with similar educational backgrounds and in similar jobs (Fields 1979:24–25).

8. Barbara Lewis describes the situation among Ivoirian urban women (Schlegel 1977:172):

> As young women, they hope to attract boyfriends who will both pay them the customary flexible allowance, and better still, find them jobs. Some have boyfriends who, while employed, are unlikely to have such connections. Others have been befriended by more successful men. . . . At the optimistic extreme is the hope that the liaison will lead to marriage. . . . Some hope for help in finding a job or funds to attend one of the many professional training courses available in Abidjan. Others settle for more immediate gains such as gifts of cash. . . . Because they are young and more desirable than uneducated women, they gamble for the long shot—a good job they find themselves, a good marriage, or a job opportunity through some male connection —rather than accepting the hard competitive business of petty trade.

9. A "been-to" is a person who has lived in the United Kingdom. Meillassoux (1968:130–42) reports that in Bamako, Mali, young people of the literate class have the same respectful attitude toward fellow Africans who have lived in France, especially Paris.

10. Although marriage migration is usually believed to be chiefly female, male marriage migration has been reported in a rural region in the Philippines where considerable female migration resulted in the paucity of eligible wives for the young men left behind (Anderson 1975).

REFERENCES

Abu-Lughod, Janet, and Richard Hay, Jr. (eds.)
    1977   Third-World Urbanization. Chicago: Maaroufa Press.

Acker, Joan
    1972   Women and social stratification: a case of intellectual sexism. American Journal of Sociology 78(4):936–45.

Amin, Samir (ed.)
    1974   Modern Migrations in Western Africa. London: Oxford University Press.

Anderson, James N.
    1975   Social strategies in population change: village data from Central Luzon. In

John F. Kantner and Lee McCaffrey (eds.), *Population and Development in Southeast Asia.* Toronto: Heath.

Anthropological Quarterly
1976   Special Issue: Women in Migration. 49(1).

Barnum, H. N., and R. H. Sabot
1975   Education, employment probabilities and rural-urban migration in Tanzania. Paper presented at the 1975 World Congress of the Econometric Society, Toronto.

Becker, Gary S.
1974   A theory of marriage. In T. P. Schultz (ed.), *The Economics of the Family: Marriage, Children, and Human Capital.* Chicago: University of Chicago Press.

Bogue, D. J.
1969   Migration: internal and international. In D. J. Bogue (ed.), *Principles of Demography.* New York: Wiley.

Bose, A.
1973   *Studies in India's Urbanisation.* New Delhi: Institute of Economic Growth.

Bose, S.
1967   Migration streams in India. *Proceedings of the 1967 (Sydney) Conference.* Liege: International Union for the Scientific Study of Population.

Boserup, Ester
1970   *Woman's Role in Economic Development.* New York: St. Martin's Press.

Brown, Alan A., and Egon Newberger (eds.)
1977   *International Migration: A Comparative Perspective.* London: Academic Press.

Brown, Susan E.
1975   Love unites them and hunger separates them: poor women in the Dominican Republic. In Rayna E. Reiter (ed.), *Toward an Anthropology of Women.* New York: Monthly Review Press.

Caldwell, J. C.
1969   Determinants of rural-urban migration in Ghana. *Population Studies* 22(3): 361-77.
1970   *African Rural-Urban Migration: The Movement to Ghana's Towns.* New York: Columbia University Press.

Carvajal, Manual J., and David T. Geithman
1974   An economic analysis of migration in Costa Rica. *Economic Development and Cultural Change* 23(1):105-22.

Carynnyk-Sinclair, Natala
1974   *Rural to Urban Migration in Developing Countries, 1950-1970: A Survey of the Literature.* Working paper for the World Employment Programme. Geneva: International Labour Office.

Connell, John, et al.
1976   *Migration from Rural Areas.* Delhi: Oxford University Press.

Du Toit, B., and H. Safa (eds.)
1975   *Migration and Urbanization*. The Hague: Mouton.

Ekwensi, Cyprian
1961   *Jagua Nana*. London: Hutchinson.

Elizaga, J. C.
1966   A study of migration in Greater Santiago (Chile). *Demography* 3(2):352–77.

Epstein, Cynthia Fuchs
1970   *Woman's Place: Options and Limits in Professional Careers*. Berkeley: University of California Press.

Fields, Gary S.
1975   Rural-urban migration, urban unemployment and under-employment, and job-search activity in LDCs. *Journal of Development Economics* 2:165–87.
1979   Lifetime migration in Colombia: tests of the expected income hypothesis. *Population and Development Review* 5(2):247–65.

Findley, Sally
1977   *Planning for Internal Migration: A Review of Issues and Policies in Developing Countries*. Washington, D.C.: U.S. Bureau of the Census.

Friedl, Ernestine
1975   *Women and Men: An Anthropologist's View*. New York: Holt, Rinehart & Winston.

Glenn, Norval D., Adreain A. Ross, and Judy Corder Tully
1969   Patterns of intergenerational mobility of females through marriage. *American Sociological Review* 39:683–99.

Gugler, J.
1968   The impact of labour migration on society and economy in Sub-Saharan Africa: empirical findings and theoretical considerations. *African Social Research* December:463–86.
1969   On the theory of rural-urban migration: the case of Sub-Saharan Africa. In J. A. Jackson (ed.), *Migration*. Cambridge: Cambridge University Press.
1974   Migrating to urban centers of unemployment in tropical Africa. Paper presented at the Eighth World Congress of Sociology, Toronto.

Hart, D. V.
1971   Philippine rural-urban migration: a view from Caticugan, a Bisayan village. *Behavior Science Notes* 6(2):103–37.

Heeren, J. H.
1955   *The Urbanisation of Djakarta*. Djakarta: University of Indonesia.

Heisler, H.
1974   *Urbanisation and the Government of Migration: The Interrelation of Urban and Rural Life in Zambia*. London: Hurst.

Herrick, Bruce
1965   *Urban Migration and Economic Development in Chile*. Cambridge, Mass.: M.I.T. Press.

House, William J., and Henry Rempel
1979   *The Determinants of Interregional Migration in Kenya.* (Mimeographed) Nairobi: Department of Economics, University of Nairobi.

International Labour Office (ILO)
1972   *Employment, Incomes and Equality: A Strategy for Increasing Productive Employment in Kenya.* Geneva.

Jackson, J. A. (ed.)
1969   *Migration.* Cambridge: Cambridge University Press.

Jelin, Elizabeth
1977   Migration and labor force participation of Latin American women: the domestic servants in the cities. *Signs: Journal of Women in Culture and Society* 3(1):129–41.

Joshi, Heather, and Vijay Joshi
1976   *Surplus Labour and the City: A Study of Bombay.* Delhi: Oxford University Press.

Kantner, John F., and Lee McCaffrey (eds.)
1975   *Population and Development in Southeast Asia.* Toronto: Heath.

Keyes, C. F.
1966   Peasant and nation: a Thai-Lao village in a Thai state. Unpublished doctoral dissertation, Cornell University.

Knowles, J. C., and R. Anker
1977   The determinants of internal migration in Kenya: a district level analysis. Population and Employment Working Paper No. 56. Geneva: International Labour Office.

Kreps, Juanita
1971   *Sex in the Marketplace: American Women at Work.* Baltimore: Johns Hopkins Press.

Lee, E. S.
1966   A theory of migration. *Demography* 31:47–57.

Leeds, Anthony
1976   Women in the migratory process: a reductionist outlook. *Anthropological Quarterly* 49:69–76.

Lenski, Gerhard E.
1966   *Power and Privilege.* New York: McGraw-Hill.

Levine, Robert A.
1966   Sex roles and economic change in Africa. *Ethnology* 5:186–93.

Little, Kenneth
1972   Voluntary associations and social mobility among West African women. *Canadian Journal of African Studies* 6(2):275–88.
1973   *African Women in Towns.* London: Cambridge University Press.

McIrvin, R. R.
1970   Adaptation to sociocultural change: a study of young Talaernos. Unpublished doctoral dissertation, University of Kansas.

Mair, Lucy
    1969   *African Marriage and Social Change.* London: Cass.

Margulis, M.
    1968   *Migracion y Marginalidad en la Sociedad Argentina.* Buenos Aires: Paidas.

Meillassoux, Claude
    1968   *Urbanization of an African Community.* Seattle and London: University of Washington Press.

Mitchell, Clyde J.
    1959   The causes of labour migration. *Bulletin of the Inter-African Labour Institute* 6:12–47.

Ominde, S.
    1968   *Land and Population Movements in Kenya.* Evanston: Northwestern University Press.

Parkin, David (ed.)
    1975   *Town and Country in Central and Eastern Africa.* London: Oxford University Press.

Piampiti, Suwanlee
    1977   Female migrants in Bangkok Metropolis. Paper prepared for the Seminar on Women and Development, Bangladesh Institute of Law and International Affairs, Dacca, March 28–April 1.

Podlewski, A.
    1975   Cameroon. In John C. Caldwell (ed.), *Population and Socioeconomic Change in West Africa.* New York: Columbia University Press.

Pryor, Robin J.
    1977   The migrant to the city in South East Asia—can and should we generalise? Paper delivered at IUSSP General Conference, Mexico City.

Rodman, Hyman
    1977   Affluence, poverty, and the family's future: the case of Trinidad. *Studies in Comparative International Development* 12(1):115–22.

Ross, Marc H.
    1975   *Grass Roots in an African City: Political Behavior in Nairobi.* Cambridge, Mass.: M.I.T. Press.

Safa, Helen I., and Brian M. Du Toit (eds.)
    1975   Migration and development. In *World Anthropology.* The Hague: Mouton.

Sapir, André
    1977   The Todaro hypothesis for internal migration: a case study for Yugoslavia 1954–1972. Belgian National Foundation for Scientific Research and The Johns Hopkins University.

Schlegel, Alice (ed.)
    1977   *Sexual Stratification.* New York: Columbia University Press.

Schultz, T. P.
    1971   Rural-urban migration in Colombia. *Review of Economics and Statistics* 53(2): 157–63.

Shaw, R. Paul
  1975   *Migration Theory and Fact: A Review and Bibliography of Current Literature.* Phila-
          delphia: Regional Science Research Institute.

Simmons, A., S. Diaz-Briquets, and A. Laquian
  1977   *Social Change and Internal Migration.* Ottawa: Migration Review Task Force,
          International Development Research Centre.

Standing, Guy
  1978   *Labour Force Participation and Development.* Geneva: International Labour
          Office.

Stark, Oded
  1976   *Rural-to-Urban Migration and Some Economic Issues: A Review Utilizing Findings
          of Surveys and Empirical Studies Covering the 1965–1975 Period.* Working Paper
          No. 38 for the World Employment Programme. Geneva: International
          Labour Office.

Sudarkasa, Niara
  1977   Women and migration in contemporary West Africa. *Signs: Journal of Women
          in Culture and Society* 3(1):178–79.

Suharso et al.
  1975   *Migration and Education in Jakarta.* Leknas, Lipi: Indonesian Institute of Sci-
          ences.

Taylor, Patricia Ann, and Norval D. Glenn
  1976   The utility of education and attractiveness for females' status attainment
          through marriage. *American Sociological Review* 41:484–98.

Taylor, R. C.
  1969   Migration and motivation: a study of determinants and types. In J. A.
          Jackson (ed.), *Migration.* Cambridge: Cambridge University Press.

Thadani, V.
  1978   Women in Nairobi: the "paradox" of urban progress. *African Urban Studies*
          (Winter).

Thadani, V., and Michael P. Todaro
  1979   *Female Migration in Developing Countries: A Framework for Analysis.* Center for
          Policy Studies Working Paper No. 47. New York: Population Council.

Tinker, Irene
  1973   Women in Development. *International Development Review* 2:39–43.

Todaro, Michael P.
  1969   A model of labor migration and urban unemployment in less developed
          countries. *American Economic Review* 59(1)(March):138–48.
  1976   *Internal Migration in Developing Countries.* Geneva: International Labour Of-
          fice.

Van Allen, Judith
  1974   Modernization means more dependency. *The Center Magazine* 7(3):60–67.

Yap, Lorene
  1977   The attraction of cities. *Journal of Development Economics* 4:239–64.

Chapter 4

Women in Rural-Urban Circulation Networks: Implications for Social Structural Change

Judith Strauch

Rural-urban migration and its effects have been the focus of considerable attention in anthropological and sociological literature for some time. Nonetheless, gaps remain in our understanding of the phenomenon and its ramifications. A significant advance of recent years is the wide recognition that migration is not necessarily a single, permanent, one-way move for an individual or a family, whether the distance covered is long or short. The relative ease of modern communications—specifically transport, postal, and telephone links—makes it possible for many Third World migrants to actively maintain close ties to the home community and facilitates frequent, perhaps eventually permanent, return. The applicability of the notion of a rural-urban dichotomy as such to traditional agrarian society is of course now sharply questioned. Any comparable conceptualization of the contemporary Third World is clearly even more suspect, for modern technology and labor markets have not merely linked the two spheres but have created a single social field in which mobile people live their lives with one foot in each domain. As Ross and Weisner put it, "rural and urban social systems, while spatially separated, are often socially, economically, and politically interdependent. . . . People seek to maximize relations in both places by using resources derived from one setting to strengthen social ties and make life more secure in the other" (1977:360–61).

The effects of circular mobility and related strategies and choices on social structures and kinship forms need to be explored more fully, both empirically and theoretically. As labor demand patterns are transformed in industrializing societies, so too are labor allocation patterns within the social groupings that traditionally constituted units of production and consumption—the family and household. The relationships of blood and marriage that found support in the mutually reinforcing web of affective bonding, ritual legitimation, and economic utility appear in a new light when one thread of the web takes on new and more complex forms and variations. In the present paper I will examine the implications of circular mobility for a particular set of kinship relations, those that shape the place of women within patrilineal systems. My analysis emerges from consideration of my field data drawn from rural Chinese communities in Malaysia and in Hong Kong, and from examination of other cases found in the literature on patrilineal societies, including India and Japan. I will argue that as patrilineal peasant societies incorporate wage labor into their economic structures alongside or in place of household-based agriculture, women's economic potential expands both directly and, less frequently noticed, indirectly, in such a way that severe pressure is placed on the exclusively patrifocal kinship system. In the context of economic systems based in part on circular labor migration, the seemingly dichotomous and exclusive roles of daughter and daughter-in-law may not be as sharply separable as they were in peasant societies based firmly on household agricultural production. A women who is at once a daughter and a daughter-in-law may have a wider range of choices open to her than either role alone once provided. The existence of such choices, as the data will demonstrate, moves social behavior in the direction of an effective bilateral orientation, regardless of continued intransigency of ritual forms, which may serve to ameliorate some of the harsher conditions of women's lives in changing patrilineal societies.

In the process of moving between villages and cities, people create new social relationships; but the old are seldom dissolved, merely altered. Village relationships, among friends or among kin, now often provide the basis for and links to urban connections, thereby adding a new dimension. A relationship that traditionally meant assistance offered at harvest time or the sharing of both the labors and the joys or sorrows of family transitions such as weddings, births, and deaths, might gain an added layer of value when one party moves to the city and thus becomes a potential link to new opportunities for others still in the village. Such a potential can radically re-value relationships that in traditional contexts were of only limited importance in either affective or instrumental terms, reactivating them with a strength that may eventually put pressure on accepted forms of social structure. Female mobility today results in just such re-valuation of kin connections that traditionally lay relatively dormant. In the material that follows I will first discuss traditional definitions of female roles and obligations in patrilineal societies, and then present findings from Malaysia and Hong Kong that suggest that despite the continuing strength of patrilineal ideology, a radical revision of actual kinship behavior is under way.

TRADITIONAL SOCIAL STRUCTURE AND FEMALE MOBILITY IN ASIAN PATRILINEAL SYSTEMS

The impact of increased female mobility opportunities on patrilineal systems is of particular interest because it is in such systems that female autonomy has traditionally been most severely circumscribed. In the classic patrilineal form a newly married couple resides with the groom's family; the children take their father's family name; ultimate authority rests with the males of the family; and only males inherit valued real property (land), passed down through the male line. This is of course a statement of a traditional ideal, and exceptions and variations were numerous in the past and are probably multiplying further under contemporary conditions. Nonetheless, people are far from immune to the dictates of cultural ideals. Even where legal modifications may today stipulate a more balanced relationship governing authority and inheritance, in practice the old ways are transformed only slowly.

Important elements of tradition that have direct bearing on the issue of female mobility are the strong preferences for village exogamy (drawing marriage partners from outside one's natal village) and patrilocal postmarital residence common among patrilineal societies. In southeastern China, for example, where villages have been organized for centuries by kinship rules, families headed by men of the same lineage—related by descent through the male line and sharing a single surname—lived together in groups that, if small, made up a neighborhood but in many cases were large enough to constitute an entire village or a group of several villages (see, e.g., Baker 1979). Since lineage and even surname exogamy was the rule, the daughters of the lineage were expected to leave the village on marriage. If the village included several surnames, a fictive kin link of sworn brotherhood often provided the rationale for the desired village exogamy (see, e.g., Strauch 1983). The same pattern of village exogamy, justified by a somewhat different kinship rationale, was and is prevalent in most of rural India as well (see, e.g., Vatuk 1972).

Thus from early childhood a girl was constantly made aware that the village of her birth was not to remain her home throughout her adult life. She knew that at some point she would face the difficult adjustment required by the move away from family and friends into a new social world peopled by total strangers, for she would not meet her husband or his family before the day of the wedding. Her family too knew that when she was grown and left the village to go to her husband's home, now to be hers, whatever investment they had made in her—material and emotional—would be lost to them. There are numerous stories, poems, laments, and proverbs in Chinese folk tradition to depict the trials of the new bride, and the loss incurred by her parents (see, e.g., Freedman 1970:183). Daughters were proverbially characterized as "bamboo growing on the other side of the fence" or "goods on which one loses." Daughters belong to somebody else, not to the house into which they are born; daughters have no value, they are worthless; rice given to feed daughters is rice thrown away.

Sons, by contrast, were valued among traditional Chinese, as in other patrilineal societies, as a source of security for parents' declining years. In most of these societies a boy grew up with the knowledge that his world was safely predictable. He would work with his father and brothers on land that would one day be his (divided equally among brothers),[1] and the important social beings in his world—the men—would remain the same, his uncles and lineage cousins, all referred to as "elder and younger brothers" *(xiongdi)*. It was perhaps a source of sadness to him that his sisters would one day leave the village and he would see them only rarely thereafter, when they made occasional visits, not as returning family members but as guests. It was probably with some excitement, possibly mixed with trepidation, that he contemplated the arrival of a strange young woman who would be brought in to be his bride. But his lot was "naturally" different from that of a girl. He lived his life in the bosom of his family and lineage; she went out at a young age to make her way in a world of strangers, a world to which she would have to adapt if she hoped to find contentment.

Female mobility at marriage was thus virtually a requirement of the patrilineal social structure. The specifically unilineal (patrilineal) nature of social organization was reinforced by mobility (female mobility).[2] At marriage a young woman severed ties with her natal family, and the door that was ritually slammed behind the Chinese bride as her brother spat or threw water on her departing sedan chair (Wolf 1972:136) powerfully symbolized the sharp change in relationship that had occurred. Closed doors prevent the family's good fortune from leaving with the departing daughter; spilled water can no more return to the container that once held it than a bride to her natal home. A daughter at marriage became a member of someone else's family, a stranger, no longer of social importance to her natal family once she was physically removed from them. (Emotional importance may be, of course, another matter.) In the single-lineage village of southeastern China, bound together economically and ritually by the corporate ties of a kinship group defined by male lines, as in the patrilineal extended kin groups of, for example, Indian and Japanese villages, the female born into a family was far from indispensable. Women contributed to production as surely as they did to reproduction, but only newly incorporated women, namely brides, could do both, so the loss of sisters and daughters was not grave. As one female married out, she was replaced by another female who married in.

The biological importance of the exchange of women to the male-centered kinship structure was of course undeniable, but analysts seemed for some time to have difficulty pinpointing an equivalent social importance. As Fried (1953:95) put it with reference to the Chinese: "Kin relations which are beyond the [lineage] . . . are quite difficult to describe, since they lack institutionalization and present few sweeping regularities on which generalizations may be based." This is not to say that affinal ties were valueless; they were simply difficult to bring coherent meaning to. As Freedman notes (1958:104): "Marriage opened up for any family possibilities of social contact with people in other communities . . . men were brought in touch with matrilateral kinsmen and affines, and the relations set up on these bases could clearly serve an important foundation for political and economic activity." In one of the few studies focusing specifically on the structural role of marriage alliances, Gallin (1960) argued that matrilateral and affinal ties in Taiwan can be seen to play important roles, in part because they are free from some of the rigorous demands and expectations that adhered to intralineage relationships. Nonetheless, even where the importance of affinal ties is acknowledged, it is the relationship between male affines that is critical. The woman is no more than a link; she has no further importance in and of herself.

In sum, the basic pattern of a woman's life in a traditional patrilineal society meant serial membership in three distinct primary groups: first, the family into which she was born; then the family into which she married; and, finally, the family that she and her husband headed when his parents were no longer present—that is, when the "big" family had divided or his parents had died. Her responsibilities were ideally unambiguous and her loyalties undivided. In fact, of course, she no doubt retained emotional ties to her own parents. Moreover, her selfish interests in the well-being of her nuclear family—or as Wolf (1972) terms it, her "uterine" family plus husband—were often instrumental in bringing about family division before the deaths of her parents-in-law. But the strains that any contending loyalties she might feel could put on the system were limited by well-established patterns. The major "move" of her life placed distance between her and her parents, thereby sapping the strength and salience of a potentially divisive affective tie. Thereafter she was unequivocally under the authority of her husband's parents, particularly her mother-in-law, until the natural progression of the domestic cycle removed that source of authority and her husband took on the role of family head. (In fact, as they grew older a couple might share roughly equal power, though ideally the husband, as long as he lived, held paramount status.) To each of these three families, exclusively and in succession, a woman contributed her labor, in household or agricultural work or both, and her emotional commitment. From each in turn she derived her sole source of material support as well as her sole sense of identity, meaning, and belonging.

URBAN LABOR MIGRATION: FEMALE MOBILITY WITH A DIFFERENCE

The implications of female mobility today appear far more complex than they did in the context of traditional systems. There is now a wider range of options open to a woman, as well as a wider range of demands and expectations placed on her by family units that may no longer compartmentalize their claims on her in a neat temporal sequence. Contemporary female mobility is of a sort quite different from that embedded in traditional social forms. It is now open to single as well as married women and offers involvement in new economic roles that produce new income as well as other less tangible but equally real benefits in the form of access to information and introduction networks. Although a woman still moves at marriage in most cases, today many women move even before marriage, to enter the urban labor market. Because of these new factors, female mobility no longer simply provides reinforcement for certain aspects of the social system; instead, it joins with other novel social and economic factors to exert pressure toward change of that system.

The sources of change are multiple, as several critical elements interact. Both the macrolevel economic structures that demand new supplies of mobile labor and the microlevel rise in "felt needs" as more goods become available induce families and individuals to enter the labor market. These factors are of course crucial to the total social formation, but their analysis lies beyond the scope of the present paper. Here I am concerned only with the interrelationships between social structure and labor mobility, especially as they pertain to women.

Of particular interest, I would suggest, is the relationship between female mobility and the unilineal focus of a patrilineal kinship system. In the context of traditional agrarian life in which a woman's families of both birth and marriage were likely to be peasant families, the natal family had no particular reason to be concerned about their daughter once she was safely married and the course of the remainder of her life thereby clearly charted. She had nothing more to offer her parents beyond continuing respect and affection, which in any case could be expressed but seldom, as distance and lack of leisure time, as well as the strictures of social form, precluded frequent visiting. In many cases, especially if the marriage was a satisfactory one, ties tended to weaken as the years went by and the young wife, soon a young mother, became involved in her new family and its welfare. At her former home, a new daughter-in-law was very likely taking over her old responsibilities and more, as the domestic cycle pursued its well-worn path.

Today, however, the urban wage labor market introduces new factors that underlie changes in family attitudes toward daughters, single or married, and provide new rationale for maintaining ties based on practical interest as well as affection, even after a daughter marries out. And for the parents-in-law of an in-marrying daughter-in-law, conflicts of interest emerge regarding the new opportunities she may have for mobility, which could bring both benefits and problems to them. Where marriage once meant the unambiguous transfer of a female from one family to another, it is today more likely to link together two families who may develop contending interests regarding the future employment and mobility choices of the woman who has formed the link. These two sets of interest may further conflict with those that the woman, along with her husband and children, perceive as most important to their own family unit as well as to their own personal wishes.

Thus, in the smooth operation of the kinship system that once provided for an orderly sequence of incorporation and allegiance, one family unit replacing another over time, there is now a snag, as all three families pile one upon another, sharing concurrent rather than consecutive interest in the woman who has membership in all three. The social adjustments that are required threaten to disrupt the basic unilineal principle of the traditional kinship organization.

The impact of urbanization as both form and process on kinship structures has not of course gone unnoticed. As early as 1958, Dore called attention to the increasing importance of matrilateral ties among urban Japanese families. Vatuk's important study of urban neighborhoods in a north Indian city (1972) reports a trend toward lesser incorporation of a married woman into her husband's kin network and a greater assertion of her ties to her natal kin than was typical in traditional rural India. Sweetser (1966) suggests that strongly patrilateral societies, under the impact of urbanization, evidence a trend toward bilateralism, and Vatuk acknowledges the validity of such a generalization for northern India, though noting that the asymmetrical affinal relationship in which bride-takers are conceived of as superior to bride-givers complicates and slows the process (Vatuk 1972:148). But these studies and others have focused attention on the urban situation itself. There is little explicit reference to continuing mobility between rural and urban settings, nor do they explain how changing female roles affect these trends.

As peasant women, single or married, move into cities, they cease to be peasant women bound to household or agricultural occupations that can bring instrumental benefit to only one family unit at a time, the family of current residence. Instead, as they take up wage labor or establish an urban household for a husband, their change of role opens up new potential for instrumental value that can be distributed among several families simultaneously.

In the rural setting, the ritual solidarity of the male-centered kinship group and the instrumental interdependence of the residentially concentrated family group as a unit of production and consumption were mutually supporting, and the countervailing force of affective bonds between females and their natal kin was weak. But as some family members move and others stay behind, the loss of residential concentration undermines the strength of instrumental exclusivity. The ideological component under-lying ritual solidarity may remain unchanged, but it now stands in isolation. Affective bonds assert their power and act to take control of a share of the newly generalizable instrumental value that the female migrant holds for both of the two families of orientation that remain behind in separate rural villages.

In an urban-oriented labor market, women—daughters and sisters as well as daughters-in-law or wives—may provide important benefits to their rural families (of birth or of marriage) in at least three forms: (1) monetary remittances; (2) introductions for younger relatives to coveted jobs through their own or their husbands' connections or in their husbands' businesses; and (3) secure and reliable homes for younger relatives moving to the city for the first time, whether for education or employment, affording village parents peace of mind, knowing their children are well cared for and well supervised. Any relationship offering such tangible benefits, one may safely assume, will not be neglected.

THEME AND VARIATIONS: TWO CHINESE CASES

The examination of change in the direction of bilateral balance requires detailed microlevel research and the collection of data that illustrate contemporary conditions in a wide range of situations. My research in Chinese communities in Malaysia and Hong Kong provides a start in this direction.[3] The patterns in these two cases, I would argue, suggest changes that are likely to be occurring in other patrilineal societies as well.

Sanchun (a pseudonym), located in southern Perak, is one of some 500 "new villages" that were formed in Malaysia in the early 1950s when the British military administration, waging war against communist guerrillas, forcibly relocated half a million rural people. From scattered hamlets, these people were brought together into fenced and curfewed settlements both to protect them and to prevent them from supplying aid to the guerrillas. Both guerrillas and resettled new villagers were predominantly ethnic Chinese. This community is discussed more fully in Strauch (1981).

Sanchun today is a rural Chinese market town of about 3,000. About a third of the community is primarily involved in commerce; the remainder includes rubber smallholders, vegetable farmers, and a large number of families dependent almost entirely on income from wage labor, much of it in the form of remittances from sons and daughters working and living elsewhere. In Sanchun, as in ethnic Chinese communities throughout Southeast Asia, the time-honored Chinese kinship fundamentals of patrilineality and patrilocality have been somewhat weakened by the more flexible modes of economic and social organization required in immigrant and frontier conditions. The land base prerequisite to the founding of a localized lineage community has been denied the overseas Chinese by various legal restrictions, and the necessary generational depth is also lacking. Though the elderly people of Sanchun, and the parents or grandparents of the others, came originally from the areas of southeastern China where single-lineage villages were numerous, Sanchun today is a heterogeneous mixture including not only a variety of surnames but a number of language and dialect groups as well. Although the extended kin groups of the homeland are lacking in Sanchun, patrifocal principles provide the template for self-identification (surname and "native place"), inheritance patterns, and numerous forms of family organization and marriage.

Patrilocal postmarital residence—in the same house sharing, in a manner of speaking, production and consumption—is still widely practiced and acknowledged by all to be the preferred form, though it is by no means universal. Neolocal residence is common, necessitated in part by housing structures packed so closely together that living space cannot always be expanded to embrace a new nuclear unit. Because of the community's heterogeneity, village exogamy, though still common, is no longer required. Many young people marry within the village, often setting up neolocal households that in village terms are both patrilocal and matrilocal. Moreover, a number of the women who live neolocally in Sanchun have chosen, and have been able to realize, matrilocal village residence even when marrying men from other communities. In most of these cases the men work in such jobs as construction or logging that keep them far from their home community much of the time, in transitory living quarters where wives cannot conveniently join them. Thus, rather than moving to a new community to live as a stranger in her mother-in-law's house while her husband works far away and returns only briefly every few months, the woman has established her home in her own parents' neighborhood, sometimes even in their house. But such de facto household matrilocality is conceptually denied, for a married-out daughter sharing her parents' home invariably pays rent, as would an outsider. She is not a family member as she would be in her parents-in-law's home.

A few daughters, mostly from shopkeepers' families, leave Sanchun to go to Ipoh or Kuala Lumpur for secondary education. Many daughters, from families of all socioeconomic groups, go to Ipoh, Kuala Lumpur, and even Singapore to work, and many find marriage partners in the cities. Others go to the cities or to other medium-sized towns or villages only after a match has been arranged, usually with the help of interested friends or relatives; in effect they marry according to the modern variant of the traditional pattern. And, finally, some who marry locally may find themselves eventually moving to another town or to the city to join husbands who have preceded them there; these women generally find work there themselves.

During my 18 months of residence in Sanchun over a period of seven years, I gathered considerable information on family relationships and attitudes, some of it through extensive household surveys done in 1972 and again in 1978 and some of it in the course of conversations with friends and neighbors and in observation of daily life. An attempt to quantify the data that support my thesis would be methodologically spurious and beside the point as well, for I am suggesting an emerging trend rather than describing a completed transformation.[4] Nonetheless, the direction of the trend is apparent in the ethnographic evidence.

In household interviews I often found family boundaries to be less sharply defined than the literature on Chinese society had led me to expect. I attribute this lack of sharp definition to the high mobility of some members and to the nascent shift from unilateral to bilateral emphasis. Though most absent sons were unequivocally regarded as family members and most sent remittances from their earnings (particularly if they were single or their wives lived in their parents' households), some parents refused to discuss sons whom they considered unfilial—those who sent little or no money home. Sons, of course, were expected to send money; not to do so was aberrant behavior subject to disapprobation. Daughters, however, if married, had no such obligation. But many parents chatted at length about married daughters, some of whom visited frequently or lived nearby or sent money home as "gifts" (*liwu*, a word seldom used in connection with remittances from sons, single or married, or from single daughters). Affective ties could remain warm even without gifts, and they could grow warmer with them. Unmarried daughters who had gone out to work in the towns and cities were, like their brothers, expected to contribute to the family coffers. In fact they were sometimes able to send more money home than brothers of the same age, for daughters were likely to go directly to jobs as seamstresses or household amahs—using skills they had already learned in Sanchun—while young sons often began as poorly paid apprentices in some trade that would prove more lucrative only in the future. Though remittances are difficult to quantify precisely, it is clear that money transfers link distant daughters, married and single, as well as sons, to the natal families in the home village.

The value of daughters and sisters in providing links to urban jobs or homes for new arrivals in the city was brought out repeatedly during the course of the interviews. The links most frequently cited were between generations: father's sister, mother's brother, and mother's sister or her husband were repeatedly credited with having introduced a young man or woman to a job or offering a place for a young relative to stay while studying in the city. Links between siblings were by no means uncommon, however, particularly in facilitating the moves of young single women to the city. Young men often left the village with friends, or to join friends, and sometimes made the move before the job was found, planning to look for work upon arrival. But young women rarely left Sanchun unless work was virtually guaranteed, often in the workplace of an elder married sister or an elder brother, and they almost always went to live with close kin, often with siblings. As employment opportunities in urban centers increase for young single women, in fact, it is in this provision of a home and a job introduction for a younger sister who will faithfully send remittances back to the village that the married-out daughter may prove to be particularly helpful to her natal family.

Male mobility too is undermining the strict construction of patrilocality, for it is women whose husbands are circular migrants in logging and construction who occasionally arrange to live in their own natal villages rather than their husbands'. In most cases of this sort, both in Sanchun and in the Hong Kong village where I conducted more limited research, the woman's matrilocality is particularly important to her parents because her brothers, like her husband, are circular migrants or out-migrants. Some of these absent sons were as yet unmarried, and some had taken their wives with them. The married daughter's proximity clearly helped to compensate for the lack of a resident daughter-in-law, both in household assistance and in companionship.[5]

Fung Yuen, the field site in the Hong Kong New Territories, is both more traditional and more modern than Sanchun, and comprises a social complexity of a different sort. (See Strauch 1983 for a general description of this community.) It is a small agricultural community just a few miles from Taipo, a major market town that is only half an hour from central Kowloon by train. The core of Fung Yuen's population of about 500 consists of a multilineage community whose ancestors settled the valley some 200 to 300 years ago. They maintain all the forms of the patrilineal village, including ancestral halls supported by income from ancestral land, inheritance of land by males only, and village exogamy. Two-thirds of the residents in the valley, however, are recent immigrants from the rural areas of Guangdong province to the north, now settled as tenant farmers growing vegetables for the urban market on land owned by the lineages and their members. The "outsiders" are lacking in extended kin groups, but the ideology they absorb in the lineage villages of Guangdong stays with them. Village exogamy remains the preferred form of marriage and is practiced virtually universally, despite the village's heterogeneity. For the young women who marry other outsiders or newcomers to the colony, who as first- or second-generation immigrants lack the rootedness that is axiomatic to the old system, the result is more likely to be neolocality than patrilocality.

The tendency toward operational bilaterality is slightly less pronounced among the lineage people of Fung Yuen than among the outsiders, owing as much to a differential impact of rapid change as to a stronger kinship ideology. Gifts or remittances from married-out daughters appear to be less common among this group in part because the need is markedly less. Lineage sons, many of them in lucrative restaurant jobs in England, have less trouble meeting their obligations than do sons of the recent immigrants and sons in Malaysia. Moreover, given the labor scarcity that characterizes Hong Kong today, personal introductions to jobs are far less crucial than in Malaysia. Proximity to the city and the efficiency of the urban system make information widely available to all, and unskilled or semi-skilled jobs are filled from applicant pools that depend only marginally on personal introductions.[6] Finally, the provision of a home in the city for a younger sibling is less important to families who in any case live within commuting distance, and many workers and students from Fung Yuen commute on a daily basis. These last two factors of course apply to outsiders and lineage people alike, but they do more to slow change among the settled population than among a group that is subject not only to rapid urbanization but also to the massive dislocation of recent flight from the homeland.

Marriages between local lineage youth of Hong Kong and more recent arrivals from China have had interesting implications for some lineage daughters in Fung Yuen and elsewhere. Four young lineage women who have in recent years married outsiders who came to the colony alone as single men have settled with their husbands in the valley. These families are defined as outsider households by the status of their male heads. Like other outsiders, they must occupy lineage land as tenants and build houses on rented land outside the lineage hamlets. But like the matrilocally resident daughters in Malaysia, these women provide both companionship and significant assistance to their natal families, substituting for daughters-in-law who have gone to Europe with their husbands. The labor exodus has not affected all lineage families alike, for some lineage sons take their wives only as far as urban Hong Kong, establishing neolocal homes close to their workplaces and returning regularly for ritual occasions.

Male mobility has wrought changes in the lineage ritual that are almost shocking to those who value the old ways. The sharp distinction of male and female ritual roles reported by Freedman (1958, 1966), which consigns worship in the ancestral hall exclusively to males and in the home to females, has broken down completely in Fung Yuen, where few men remain to perform the ritual observances that were their province in the past. The effects of this change might produce a mild countervailing force serving to slow the trend toward bilateral orientation, for a young wife who performs important ritual functions that define lineage membership may feel herself more completely incorporated into the kinship group than she would have felt in the past. But the shift in which wives may play the ritual roles of their husbands shows no immediate sign of being complemented by a parallel shift permitting daughters to take on their brothers' roles as coparceners in the family estate. Although current legal codes stipulate equal inheritance for sons and daughters alike, such a division of property remains unheard of in the valley.

A nascent shift toward a functional bilaterality in kinship relations is discernable in Fung Yuen, as in Sanchun, though structural contrasts in the two situations have thus far resulted in a somewhat stronger expression of bilateral orientation in the latter case. In neither community, however, does the gradual modification of kinship patterns receive formal recognition in the cultural models of the people among whom it is occurring, despite its impact on actual social relationships.

STRAINS IN THE SYSTEM

As the above material demonstrates, Chinese daughters are no longer goods on which one loses, even though they may still be seen as bamboo growing in someone else's yard. Today it is quite possible for them to provide benefits from either side of the fence. This implies a new potential value in maintaining ties with married-out daughters not only among Chinese but in other societies as well. But what of the family that lives on the other side of the fence? How do the new variables of mobility and urban job opportunities affect *their* relationship with their daughter-in-law?

Parents-in-law may of course benefit in the same ways that parents do, particularly as connections a daughter-in-law might make through her job are passed on to younger relatives. With regard to remittances, however, they may fare less well. A distant daughter-in-law faced with the problem of allocating limited resources to equally needy recipients is probably more likely to look after her own parents (if affective ties dating from childhood are strong) and her own children (anticipating old age herself and thus preparing for it by cementing bonds of loyalty and duty in the next generation), rather than her husband's parents. It is her duty to care for his parents too, but part of the husband's income is set aside for that purpose. If a woman's contribution to household income produces a surplus after the needs of the neolocal nuclear family have been met, she is likely to make presents to her own parents, particularly if she feels that they are not being adequately taken care of by her brothers. The village-based mother-in-law, despite her formal authority, has no means of influencing her urban daugher-in-law's decisions on such matters. Thus for parents-in-law the economic benefit derived from a working daughter-in-law may be little more than from a daughter-in-law who stays home, keeping them company and providing household labor in the village.

Another issue may be more important to parents-in-law than either monetary or practical benefits on the one hand or companionship and household labor on the other: A daughter-in-law can act either as an ally binding their son to them or as an enemy dragging him away. The agrarian base that held traditional Chinese society together has little relevance in either Fung Yuen or Sanchun today, as parents there and elsewhere know too well, and they must accept that sons as well as daughters often leave home. But it is the fond hope of parents that their sons will return. In the best of all possible worlds the son should visit frequently during his early working years while his parents are able to care for themselves; later, when they retire, he should return permanently to take over the few acres of family land or perhaps to live at home and commute to an urban job. If the absent son's wife and children remain in the village throughout his working life, he is likely to maintain closer filial ties to the parental home than if she has joined him in the city.

In Fung Yuen, conjugal units of husband and wife are seldom broken up residentially. If a son is married, either he lives in Fung Yuen with his wife and parents and commutes daily to work in the urban center,[7] or both he and his wife reside elsewhere and return occasionally for visits. In Sanchun, by contrast, the middle case highlights the issue at hand: Many daughters-in-law dutifully reside in the village with their children and parents-in-law while their husbands work elsewhere, either in a city or in logging tracts in the jungles, and return home for visits with wife and parents together. In 1972, a quarter of the households interviewed included a resident (usually female) whose spouse worked elsewhere and returned to Sanchun only occasionally.

The patrilocal home may be the logical residence for a wife whose husband lives in loggers' quarters or moves about every few weeks on construction jobs that range over most of the southern and central portions of Perak state. But if he holds a steady job in a town or city, as many husbands do, she might wish to join him, regardless of filial duty. She might point out to him and to his parents the financial contribution she could make if she too took an urban job. Moreover, if his parents are contemplating sending a younger child to the city as well, they might decide that a home with an elder brother and his wife would be a more suitable arrangement for the younger sibling than the "bachelor" establishment it would be without the wife. But the man's parents are no doubt well aware that potential advantages of the move are balanced by potential risks. If the daughter-in-law remains in the village, the son is more likely to come back eventually to settle down as well, in a pattern that has been followed by several Sanchun men now in their thirties and forties. Once the daughter-in-law settled with her husband in the city, however, parents might "lose" their son permanently to city life. A woman's parents-in-law thus find themselves caught between conflicting interests, in a dilemma that for them has no optimal solution in a time of changing life-styles and changing economic opportunities and demands.

The three families of orientation that can simultaneously claim a woman's loyalties today may have conflicting interests in her mobility choices. Her husband's parents are likely to feel ambivalence in the matter. They might prefer to forgo the advantages that could accrue from her move to the city in favor of maintaining the incentive for their son to return to the village to settle down with them in their old age. The woman's own parents (and perhaps her siblings as well), by contrast, have no expectations of her companionship in their later years and recognize the benefits they may receive if she moves to the city. Hence they might support her strongly should she wish to join her absent husband and "abandon" his parents. Theoretically, her natal family has no legitimate right to an opinion of any sort once a woman is married. But it seems clear to me from discussions and observations that parents do in fact hold opinions and make them known. Thus if those who are most directly involved—the wife and her husband, comprising her third family of orientation—decide that a common home in the city is in their best interests, even though contrary to the wishes of the husband's parents, who want to retain their traditional rights of authority over both daughter-in-law and son, the young couple might receive moral support from the wife's parents. Her first family of orientation, her natal family, in refusing to abrogate interest in their daughter's life choices, is flaunting traditional kinship rules. Strains toward the bilateral expression of kinship ties are apparent, as changing interest structures undermine the strength of the traditional unilineal system.

CONCLUSION

Links through women—daughters, sisters, wives—today prove to be as important as agnatic links in supplying access to coveted urban jobs and residences. The salience of these new links implies important changes in patterns of family relationships among Chinese in Malaysia and Hong Kong, and probably among other patrilineally oriented societies now participating in urban wage labor economies elsewhere as well. Women's lives, both in cities and in the countryside, will be powerfully affected by these changes, as women come to play significant roles throughout their lives vis-à-vis a wider range of kin, including their natal families. The added value women have for the several social groups to which they belong may lead their natal families to increase their investment in them, in childhood as well as in maturity. Females should realize concrete benefits such as improved nutrition and medical care as children and increased educational and training opportunities as they grow older. More importantly, perhaps, they will experience a more coherent lifelong identity unbroken by the psychological reorientation at marriage that was traditionally required of women in patrifocal societies.

A new sense of connectedness to one's natal family does not necessarily imply an abandonment of the husband's parents and the proper forms of times past. But it does provide a wider range of choices enabling women more actively to seek contentment and meaning in their lives, in accordance sometimes with old norms, sometimes with new. The elderly widow of a Fung Yuen man, who had moved with him to the city before their children were born, insists on bringing her grandsons back to the village their father has himself only visited, for proper ceremonial induction into the lineage through traditional lantern-raising ceremonies (Strauch 1983). But in Sanchun, a schoolteacher's wife, herself an educated young Cantonese who in 1972 suffered in obedient silence the trials and indignities of the role of daughter-in-law in a Hakka peasant home, had by 1978, to the great dismay of the parents-in-law, succeeded in moving husband and children back to the town of her own childhood, where her parents still reside. Change and continuity are processes that may exist side by side, offering women options that challenge oppressive patriarchy. As the transforming social forces of new economic formation act on traditional kinship systems, women, as social beings of considerable value to various social actors and groups simultaneously, may find themselves increasingly well situated in the ongoing effort of all people to shape satisfying, meaningful lives.

NOTES

1. Later-born sons in Japan, however, where primogeniture was and is the rule, lack this secure predictability.

2. The parenthetical insertions here could be replaced by their logical opposites: matrilineality reinforced by male mobility. This is in fact approximated in several ethnographic cases.

3. I first carried out research in a Chinese new village in Perak, a state on Malaysia's west coast, for 14 months in 1971–72, and I returned for two months in 1976 and again for a similar period in 1978. I conducted research in Fung Yuen, in the eastern part of Hong Kong's New Territories, for seven months in 1978 and two months in 1981. In my 1978 research in both sites I focused on labor circulation—its forms, its variations, and its effects on those involved in labor networks that take them away from home, and on their families and communities.

4. The 1972 surveys covered all family members of about half of Sanchun's Chinese households randomly selected; the 1978 survey covered half the original sample, again randomly selected. The data concern age, sex, education, marital status, occupation, and, for absent workers, frequency of return, frequency and amount of remittances, and information on each job held during each individual's complete working life—

duration, reason for change, connecting link to the new job, and so forth. I also encouraged informants (often mothers or fathers of absent workers) to describe their attitudes toward their children's mobility. While the surveys have produced a considerable body of data, the retrospective nature of some of it limits my confidence in its quantitative validity.

5. One of these women whom I knew quite well acknowledged that it was unusual for her to live with her own mother rather than with her absent husband's family in a village some 20 miles distant, but she maintained that her mother's home had more space and was "more convenient" (*fangbian*)—a euphemism that tactfully avoided mention of the familiar problems all too often inherent in relations with in-laws.

6. In one or two instances, however, a sister married out to another New Territories emigrant village has eventually provided a Fung Yuen man with a job in her husband's restaurant in England.

7. Since the handful of daughters-in-law resident in Fung Yuen all have small children, none work outside the valley. Some of them do vegetable gardening or piecework for Taipo factories (assembling parts of toys, for example, or doing finishing work on garments) in addition to household work.

REFERENCES

Baker, Hugh D. R.
    1979   *Chinese Family and Kinship*. New York: Columbia University Press.

Dore, Ronald P.
    1958   *City Life in Japan*. Berkeley: University of California Press.

Freedman, Maurice
    1958   *Lineage Organization in Southeastern China*. London: Athlone Press.
    1966   *Chinese Lineage and Society: Fukien and Kwangtung*. London: Athlone Press.
    1970   Ritual aspects of Chinese kinship and marriage. In Maurice Freedman (ed.), *Family and Kinship in Chinese Society*. Stanford: Stanford University Press.

Gallin, Bernard
    1960   Matrilateral and affinal relationships in a Taiwanese village. *American Anthropologist*. 62(4):632–42.

Geertz, Hildred
    1961   *The Javanese Family: A Study of Kinship and Social Organization*. New York: Free Press.

Potter, Sulamith Heins
    1977   *Family Life in a Northern Thai Village: A Study in the Structural Significance of Women*. Berkeley: University of California Press.

Ross, Marc H., and Thomas S. Weisner
    1977   The rural-urban migrant network in Kenya: some general implications. *American Ethnologist*. 4(2):359–76.

Strauch, Judith
1981   *Chinese Village Politics in the Malaysian State.* Cambridge, Mass.: Harvard University Press.
1983   Community and kinship in southeastern China: the view from the multilineage villages of Hong Kong. *Journal of Asian Studies* (forthcoming).

Sweetser, D. A.
1966   The effect of industrialization on intergenerational solidarity. *Rural Sociology.* 31:156–70.

Vatuk, Sylvia
1972   *Kinship and Urbanization: White Collar Migrants in North India.* Berkeley: University of California Press.

Wolf, Margery
1972   *Women and the Family in Rural Taiwan.* Stanford: Stanford University Press.

PART 2

TRENDS, POLICIES, AND PROGRAMS: NATIONAL PERSPECTIVES

Chapter 5

Rural-to-Urban Migration of Women in India: Patterns and Implications

Andrea Menefee Singh

The study of female migration in India is complicated by the enormous size of the country and its population, the incredible heterogeneity and diversity of the people, and the uneven patterns of economic development and urbanization within the country. In 1971 the population stood at 546 million. Although only 19.9 percent of the population lived in urban areas, the size of the urban population alone (109 million) was larger than the population of most countries in the world. About 50 percent of the urban population in 1971 lived in 143 cities that each had a population of 100,000 or more; the rest lived in 2,968 smaller cities and towns. While the urban population grew by 37.9 percent (compared to 24.8 percent for the country as a whole) between 1961 and 1971, the growth of the eight largest cities was an astounding 49.4 percent. Much of this urban growth was due to rural-to-urban migration, but the larger cities also attracted migrants from smaller towns and cities. Provisional figures from the 1981 census indicate that India's population today is nearly 684 million and that there are now 12 cities with a population of a million or more. Approximately 150 million people now live in urban settlements.

In view of these staggering figures, it is clearly impossible to give a comprehensive description of female rural-to-urban migration in the country as a whole. My purpose, therefore, is to identify the important patterns and characteristics of female rural-to-urban migration and, where possible, to illuminate these findings with information available from micro-level studies. Special emphasis is given to variations due to social and cultural forces in the different regions of the country. The final section discusses the policy implications of the findings with special reference to the urban poor.

DEMOGRAPHIC CHARACTERISTICS

Although women are outnumbered by men in India's population as a whole (108 men per 100 women in 1971),[1] they vastly outnumber men in rural-to-rural migration streams (29 men per 100 women) when estimated by place of birth (GOI 1974:34). In rural-to-urban migration streams, however, males outnumber females slightly, resulting in a sex ratio of 104. Urban-to-urban migration streams contain about equal numbers of men and women (sex ratio of 101).

The predominance of females in rural-to-rural migration streams has traditionally been attributed to the practice of village exogamy and patrilocal residence. It is important to remember, however, that village exogamy has not always been followed among the lowest castes or landless laborers (Cohn 1955; Gough 1962), among whom the changing demand for agricultural labor plays an important role in choice of residence. Among some groups, matrilineality accompanied by natolocal or matrilocal residence has predominated,[2] although historical evidence indicates that these practices are undergoing transition. Moreover, the growing commercialization of agriculture has, especially during the last decade, resulted in a rapidly growing rural migrant labor force, and women play an essential part in many agricultural operations such as sugarcane harvesting (Bremen 1979), tobacco harvesting and processing (Rao 1978; Mitra et al. 1980), cotton picking, and woodcutting (Ali 1981). Women also play an important role in rural construction, road works, dam building, and digging irrigation canals. It is estimated that women comprise about 10 percent of the labor force in construction. However, a recent study of the rural Employment Guarantee Scheme in Maharashtra indicates that around half of those employed off-seasonally in rural works are women (Jain 1979). Hence it is no longer possible to dismiss female rural migration as being due entirely to marriage or association.

While documentation of women's participation in rural migrant labor streams is as yet very unsatisfactory, it appears that it is not unrelated to patterns of female rural-to-urban migration. Rural-based work opportunities for women (as well as for men) are apparently increasing in some areas, particularly those involving seasonal rather than permanent migration. This trend may help to account for India's low rate of urbanization compared to other countries at a similar stage of development. The Punjab, for example, which gave birth to India's Green Revolution in the 1960s, experienced an extremely low rate of urbanization between 1961 and 1971 (D'Souza 1975). Moreover, it appears that some states that evince unusually high sex ratios in their migration streams to urban areas have large-scale participation of women in seasonal intrastate as well as interstate rural migrant labor. These states include West Bengal, Orissa, Bihar, and Uttar Pradesh.[3] This suggests that the rural-to-urban migration of women is not an isolated phenomenon and needs to be explored with reference to counterbalancing trends and opportunities in rural areas.

Female rural-to-urban migration in India, as indicated by aggregate data, is affected by distance and by city size. Table 5.1, though not disaggregated for rural and urban destination, shows that the majority of both men and women who migrate move only short distances. Although three times as many women as men migrate short distances, their numbers are nearly equal in long-distance migration.

Data collected in 1955–58 (NSS, n.d.) indicate that the larger the city, the higher the sex ratio in migration streams. The migrant sex ratio was lowest in towns with population below 300,000 (80 males per 100 females), nearly equal in towns of 300,000 and above (99:100), and highest in the four largest cities (120:100). Among the four largest cities, however, sex ratios of migrants ranged from 126:100 in Bombay to 107:100 in Madras. There are also regional differences to consider. While sex ratios tend to be much higher in big cities than in smaller urban areas in the north, they are much more even in cities of all sizes in the south (Joshi 1976:1308).

In a study of towns with greater out-migration than in-migration, Premi (1980:17–18) found that such towns generally have a population of less than 20,000, exhibit a depression in the age pyramid in the age group 20–49, and have a comparatively lower sex ratio, lower literacy rate, and higher participation rate of females in economic activities than other urban areas. In a microstudy of four such towns in Punjab and Haryana in 1972–73 he found that much of this female employment was in higher age groups —about 41 percent in professional and supervisory posts and 43 percent as unskilled workers (1980:76–78). Hence it is not unlikely that greater female migration to smaller urban areas and their tendency to stay behind when men migrate out of small towns may be linked to better employment opportunities for female migrants in smaller urban areas. The 1971 census showed that even in the largest cities, female migrants have considerably higher work-force participation rates than the female population as a

Table 5.1 Distance and migration: India, 1971

Migration type	Total (%)	Males (%)[a]	Females (%)	Males per 100 females
Short distance	67.4	52.7	72.8	33
Medium distance	21.5	26.6	19.4	59
Long distance	11.1	18.5	7.8	102
Total	100.0	100.0	100.0	43

a. Column does not sum to 100 because of rounding.
Source: GOI (1974:34).

whole. In some cases the rate for migrant women was twice as high—for example, in Hyderabad a participation rate of 16.8 for migrant women and 8.2 for all women.

The sex ratio of the country as a whole has been increasing since 1900, from 103 in 1901 to an estimated 107 in 1981. Among the urban population, however, it has been steadily decreasing, from 118 to 109 between 1961 and 1971 alone. This decline is due in part to increasing numbers of women migrating to urban areas and a decreasing tendency to marry city-raised daughters back into villages; it may also reflect what Joshi (1976: 1303) calls the "snowballing demographic effect of more women bearing children" in the city as well as better access of women to health services. Provisional census returns for 1981 for the 12 largest cities, compared to sex ratios since 1951, show that this is a consistent trend over the past 30 years. The 1951 census report noted that there were important differences between rural and urban sex ratios according to region; the difference was largest in eastern India, western India, and northern India and smallest in southern India and central India. Likewise the urban sex ratio was highest for eastern India (156), western India (140), and northern India (125) and lowest for southern India (106) and central India (107) according to Natarajan (1971:96). One could expect to find a similar pattern today, although the gap between highest and lowest sex ratios has been gradually decreasing.

The distribution of migrants in urban areas according to age and sex differs somewhat from the characteristics of the urban population as a whole. National Sample Survey (NSS) data for 1963–64 revealed little difference in the age distribution of the male and female urban population as a whole. For migrants, however, a much larger proportion of females than males fall into the 0–17 age group, whereas the proportion of males in the 18–44 age group far exceeds that of females. The proportion of migrants, both males and females, in the economically productive years (18 to 44) nonetheless exceeds that of the urban population as a whole. The distribution clearly reflects the younger age distribution of migrants compared to nonmigrants. The smaller proportion of migrants in the highest age group suggests that extended families are comparatively rare and that migrant women thus lack this traditional source of support with child care and domestic chores.

Data on the educational levels of migrants are limited. Youssef et al. (1979:64) note that 56 percent of the women compared to 35 percent of the men among lifetime migrants in India are illiterate; among those who are educated, men have significantly more education than women. The distinction between migrant workers and nonworkers yields further insight. Literacy rates in 1971 were the same for males regardless of worker status

(72 percent), for example, but were considerably lower for female workers (47 percent) than nonworkers (65 percent). Males also had a higher rate of literacy gained without education among both groups (25 percent among workers and 35 percent for nonworkers) than did females (8 percent and 28 percent respectively), according to Mehrotra (1974:56–61).

Hence there is little evidence of a link between education and employment among male migrants, but among female migrants the relationship appears to be negative—that is, those with the least education are the most likely to take up work. Youssef et al. (1979:64) point out that "the explanation for this pattern is probably not that these women are more likely to find work, but rather that they are willing to take up work that is available." It may be unreasonable to expect educated women to be willing to work in the low-paid and low-status occupations in which the majority of migrant women apparently find themselves: unskilled laborers, domestic servants, self-employed pieceworkers, sidewalk vendors, and the like (see Singh and de Souza 1980:88–103). Men with some education are also reluctant to take up demeaning work (see Karlekar 1979). Studies have also shown that women in Indian cities are seriously underrepresented in the organized sector, although their position has improved somewhat in recent years, especially in the public sector (Joshi 1976; GOI 1974). Hence, compared with men, their opportunities for urban employment are far more limited.

Earlier studies of reasons for migration reported that only a small minority of women migrate to urban areas for employment. An NSS survey conducted in 1955–58 (NSS, n.s.:table 2.6), for example, found that 46 percent of the women migrated for marriage compared to only 0.6 percent of the men, but 40 percent of the men migrated for employment compared to only 2.7 percent of the women. Women citing association or dependence as reasons for migration accounted for 28.4 percent compared to 18.5 percent of the males.

One problem with these studies is that respondents were required to give only one reason for migration. In India, as in many other cultural settings, it is considered inappropriate for women to emphasize their economic independence, especially if the interviewer is a stranger or a male. Similarly, if it is the male household head who provides information about female household members (or if a male family member is present when a female is interviewed), employment-related reasons for female migration are likely to be played down. While it is undoubtedly true that a large percentage of women migrate to urban areas for marriage or as dependents, this explanation does not account for the wide variations in sex ratios that are evident when data are disaggregated for caste, region of origin and place of destination. The sex-ratio differences, which are explored further in the next section, appear to be related to the work-force participation rates of women, which in turn are related to social and cultural forces. As noted earlier, migrant women have far higher work-force participation rates than nonmigrant women.

It is now generally accepted that the 1971 census significantly underenumerated the employment of women due to a shorter reference period and a change in the definition of work, emphasizing primary activity and full-time work (see Mitra et al. 1980:23–24). Because of these changes in definition, it is also likely that women in the organized sector and modern occupations were more accurately enumerated than those in the informal sector. The census data show that migrant women who were reported as workers tend to cluster at the top and at the bottom of the occupational hierarchy. Using Delhi as an example, the distribution of migrant female workers according to major occupational divisions and literacy is given in Table 5.2. The table shows that although a majority (54 percent) of migrant female workers in Delhi are literate and employed in modern occu-

Table 5.2 **Distribution of migrant female workers in Delhi by occupation and literacy: 1971**

Occupational category	Migrant female workers		% female of all migrant workers	% of migrant female workers who are literate
	Number	%		
Cultivators	68	0.1	6.2	27.6
Agricultural laborers	214	0.3	12.5	5.1
Professional, technical, and related workers	23,355	37.4	27.3	96.7
Administrative, executive, and managerial workers	1,097	2.1	1.8	96.4
Clerical and related workers	9,137	14.6	5.6	97.3
Sales workers	2,608	4.2	2.0	77.5
Service workers	11,838	18.9	11.2	15.6
Farmers, fishermen, hunters, loggers	158	0.3	1.9	15.8
Production workers, transport equipment operators and laborers	13,016	20.8	4.2	14.3
Workers not classified by occupation	1,020	1.6	4.6	61.3

Source: Census of India (1971).

pations, a high percentage (40 percent) are illiterate and are found in occupations that are generally low in status.

Although I have no information to question the accuracy of the census
figures related to female migrants in modern occupations, data collected
by the Town and Country Planning Organization (TCPO) in 1973 and
our own data (Singh and de Souza 1976) collected in 1975 for a "Madrasi
thatched-roof settlement" of about 300 households can be compared to
census figures in the primary census abstract. This comparison indicates
the accuracy of the migration tables with reference to the urban poor.
According to the census, 54 percent of all males and 19 percent of all
females in this settlement were employed; 97 percent of the female workers
were in the occupational category of "other services." According to the
TCPO study, however, 47 percent of all males and 42 percent of all females
were workers; 98 percent of the female workers were classified as unskilled
manual workers (including domestic service). Our study yielded almost
identical figures to those of the TCPO study. Most of the women referred
to themselves as "part-time utensil cleaners." Because they usually worked
in at least two or three households and went without a weekly holiday,
however, they worked about 40 hours per week, which is nearly equal to
the norm for full-time employment in any modern occupation. Hence
there is good reason to question the reliability of the census figures for
female workers of migrant status among the urban poor.

The comprehensive TCPO survey (1975) found that 18 percent of Delhi's population resided in squatter settlements whereas the housing tables
of the 1971 census reported that only 10 percent of the houses in Delhi
were *kachcha* (temporary or substandard). The TCPO study covered only
unauthorized squatter settlements whereas the census included these settlements as well as recognized slum areas in the old city and authorized
resettlement colonies. Hence it appears that the city's urban poor as a
whole were also greatly underenumerated in the census. The TCPO study
found that 93 percent of the household heads in squatter settlements were
migrants from rural areas. (The total squatter population was equivalent
to 60 percent of Delhi's total migrant population as reported in the census.) Hence it is worthwhile comparing the employment patterns of this
important segment of the migrant population with those reported in Table
5.2 for the city as a whole. The TCPO findings are summarized in Table
5.3. The study found that 38 percent of the adult females and 94 percent of
the adult males were employed, though it also cautioned that the employment of women, especially as part-time domestic workers, may have been
underreported for reasons of prestige and the assumption that their
meager earnings were marginal to the family's economy (TCPO 1975:
105–17).

As can be seen from Table 5.3, migrant women workers among the

Table 5.3 Occupational distribution of men and women in Delhi squatter settlements: 1973

Occupational category	% of working men	% of working women	Total
Hawkers and vendors, petty business, retail	5.2	5.7	8.2
Construction workers	34.7	65.1	42.5
Miscellaneous unskilled workers (porters, loaders, office help, cooks, waiters, domestic help, transport, repair shops)	30.6	23.4	28.6
Traditional trades and skills (launderers, tailors, barbers, sweepers)	10.3	4.0	8.8
White-collar and semiprofessional workers	1.4	—	1.1
Industrial workers	13.8	—	10.8

Source: TCPO (1975:116–17).

urban poor in Delhi are confined almost entirely to traditional occupations, blue-collar work, and small-scale self-employment. Their heavy representation in construction work is particularly disturbing because in this industry they are hired only as coolies and assigned the most arduous chores such as carrying earth, bricks, and cement, breaking stones, and loading and unloading (Bellwinkel 1973). Men in the construction industry also work as coolies, but they have opportunities for advancement and monopolize all the better-paid skilled and semiskilled jobs as carpenters, masons, painters, machine operators and supervisors. It should also be noted that the vast majority of women in the category of "miscellaneous unskilled workers" in Table 5.6 are employed as domestic workers. More remunerative work is the reserve of men. According to the 1971 census, in the 15–59 age group 44.3 percent of migrant women and 24.0 percent of migrant men were illiterate; in the areas covered by the TCPO study, 90 percent of the adult women and 46 percent of the adult men were illiterate. For Delhi's urban population as a whole, 34.6 percent of all males and 48.8 percent of all females were recorded as illiterate in the 1971 census, and 51.7 percent of the total urban population were classified as migrants.

The Delhi example shows how important it is to disaggregate data on migrant women by class and to seek out alternative sources of data to the census. Patterns vary somewhat from city to city, but the trends are similar with regard to high work-force participation of migrant women among the urban poor (see Singh and de Souza 1980). As a group, migrants are less literate and less educated than the nonmigrant population. Migrant women are not only more likely to be employed than nonmigrant women; they find work largely in the informal sector in the lowest-status, most arduous, and lowest-paid jobs available.

SOCIAL AND CULTURAL FACTORS

It has now been established that migration, at least to the large urban metropolises in India, is more likely to involve a single direct move rather than step migration from smaller towns to progressively larger cities (Majumdar 1977; Saxena 1977; Premi 1980). While the well-educated and those employed in the modern sector tend to rely on impersonal channels in seeking housing and employment, the urban poor rely heavily on their own personal networks based on kinship, caste, village, and region of origin. Hence the groups that share a common identity tend to cluster together in residence as well as in occupational categories (see also Majumdar 1977; Singh 1976, 1977, 1978; Singh and de Souza 1980). As Tables 5.2 and 5.3 show, migrant women tend to be clustered in fewer occupational categories than men, though among the well educated their participation in the modern sector appears to be growing (see also Mitra et al. 1980). The proportion of females in the high-status occupations was greater in the lower age group (15 to 29 years) than for males. As mentioned earlier, the urban sex ratios were the highest and the difference between the rural and urban sex ratios the greatest in the eastern, western, and northern regions of India, while the reverse was true of the southern and central regions. If we look at migration from the perspective of a single large city, a similar pattern emerges with regard to place of origin, regardless of distance implied in the migration. Using Delhi again as the example, a city located in the north, Table 5.4 gives the sex ratio of migrant streams in 1971 and the percentage of rural-born literate and employed women in each.

As can be seen from Table 5.4, there is a general negative association between sex ratios and female work-force participation. Exceptions are two northern states (Haryana and Punjab) that have sex ratios below the average but a very low percentage of females as workers, and Karnataka in the south, with a high sex ratio but an extremely high percentage of females recorded as workers. Note also that in Jammu, Kashmir, and West Bengal, female migrants have an unusually low percentage of rural-born among them and unusually high literacy rates. Hence it could be expected that migrants from these states are largely in the modern sector. The high percentage of rural-born and the low percentage of literates among female migrants from Rajasthan, though, would lead one to the opposite conclusion. This relationship between literacy and type of employment generally holds true for migrant workers from all states if one examines differences

Table 5.4 Sex ratio, rural birth, literacy, and work-force participation of female migrants in Delhi: 1971

Place of origin	Sex ratio[a]	% of females rural-born[a]	% of females literate[b]	% of females as workers[b]
Northern Zone				
Haryana	111	67.1	47.5	5.0
Himachal Pradesh	177	48.2	65.8	7.0
Jammu and Kashmir	142	14.6	75.6	7.9
Punjab	116	37.1	68.4	5.1
Uttar Pradesh	156	56.0	39.2	4.8
Eastern Zone				
Bihar	186	46.1	61.5	7.8
Orissa	159	36.3	72.4	5.8
West Bengal	129	8.0	80.7	7.9
Central Zone				
Gujarat	111	27.4	69.9	8.4
Madhya Pradesh	119	32.3	59.4	11.5
Maharashtra	118	12.7	77.8	10.8
Rajasthan	129	64.6	25.3	17.3
Southern Zone				
Andhra Pradesh	125	24.4	75.8	9.7
Kerala	126	36.1	85.8	24.7
Karnataka	147	13.8	81.2	14.3
Tamil Nadu	114	24.1	63.1	17.2
All migrants	132	24.2	53.2	7.7

a. Classified by place of birth.
b. Classified by last residence.
Source: Census of India (1971).

in occupational distribution by state. Some 65 percent of the migrant female workers from Jammu and Kashmir and 53 percent from Kerala are "professional, technical, and related workers," for example, whereas 77 percent from Rajasthan are "production and related workers, transport equipment operators, and laborers." The majority of migrant female workers from Tamil Nadu (56 percent) are "service workers." Although concentrations in certain occupational divisions vary among the different states of origin, the correspondence between sex ratio, work-force participation, and zone is generally consistent. In Delhi the relatively low sex ratios and high work-force participation rates among migrant streams from the Southern Zone are of special significance since this migration involves the greatest distance.

THE NORTH-SOUTH DISTINCTION

The striking difference between female rural-to-urban migration patterns in the north and in the south deserves further consideration since this is the most consistent variation to emerge from both macrolevel and microlevel data. By disaggregating data from north and south, we may gain a clearer picture of the causes and consequences of migration and the implications of these differences for policy-makers.

Premi (1979) examined 1971 census data on female migration in three northern states (Haryana, Himachal Pradesh, and Punjab) and three southern states (Andhra Pradesh, Kerala, and Tamil Nadu). He found (pp. 29–32) that the rate of female migration in northern India (51 percent) was considerably higher than in southern India (38 percent). The lowest rates were found in Kerala and parts of Tamil Nadu. Although the data were not disaggregated by rural or urban destination, Premi nonetheless attributes the low rates of migration in Kerala to two factors: (1) large village size, which may reduce the pressure for village exogamy, and (2) the tradition of natolocal residence among matrilineal groups in some parts of Kerala.

This explanation must be accepted with caution, however. First, there is evidence that among lower-caste and landless groups, even in the north, the practice of village exogamy and patrilocal residence has never been strictly adhered to; changes in residence among the rural poor may be greatly affected by the local demand for labor (Cohn 1955). In the south, the landed classes apply the rule of village exogamy fairly rigorously but the landless do not (Gough 1962). The second reason is that the traditional matrilineal system in the south has been gradually modified by both the colonial and modern legal systems, and natolocal residence now appears to be the exception rather than the rule (Saradamoni 1979). Even in Kerala, matrilineality was never practiced by a majority of the population. Further examination of the comparative data suggests the possibility of other reasons for differences in migration rates.

Table 5.5 presents data on the rural and urban destination of female migrants according to marital status, duration of residence, state, and region. This table shows that there are important differences between female migrants to urban areas in the north and in the south. Of particular interest is the percentage of female migrants who are widowed or divorced among recent migrants in the south: This number is almost double that of the north. Among migrants of all durations in both north and south (with

Table 5.5 Percentage distribution of female migrants to rural and urban areas by marital status and duration of residence, North and South Zones: 1971

State and duration of residence	Migrants to rural areas				Migrants to urban areas			
	Un-married	Married	Widowed and divorced	Total	Un-married	Married	Widowed and divorced	Total
All durations								
Haryana	9	81	10	100	19	71	10	100
Himachal Pradesh	11	75	14	100	32	60	8	100
Punjab	19	72	9	100	22	69	9	100
North Zone	14	75	11	100	24	67	7	100
Andhra Pradesh	13	71	15	99	24	63	13	100
Kerala	21	67	12	100	28	59	13	100
Tamil Nadu	15	71	14	100	26	61	13	100
South Zone	16	80	14	100	25	61	13	99
Overall	15	72	13	100	25	64	12	101
Duration less than 1 year								
Haryana	38	60	2	100	39	57	3	99
Himachal Pradesh	25	65	9	99	43	53	4	100
Punjab	48	49	3	100	42	54	4	100
North Zone	38	57	5	100	42	54	4	100
Andhra Pradesh	37	55	8	100	42	50	8	100
Kerala	44	50	6	100	50	42	8	100
Tamil Nadu	45	47	8	100	41	47	7	100
South Zone	41	51	7	100	45	47	8	100
Overall	40	54	6	100	44	50	6	100

Note: Totals do not add up to 100 in all cases because of rounding and because information on marital status of some migrants was not available. The averages at the state level or for the zones are unweighted averages of the district-level figures.

Source: Premi (1979:33).

the exception of Kerala), the percentage of widowed or divorced is some-what higher among migrants with rural destinations than among those with urban destinations. Among recent migrants, there is no consistent pattern at the state level, but at the aggregate level it is higher in rural than urban areas in the north. The reverse is true of the south—mainly because of the large difference exhibited by Kerala, where the percentage is much higher in urban than rural destinations. Premi (1979:34) suggests that the higher proportion of widows and divorcees among migrants in the south reflects "the relationship between destitution and migration," implying that the low proportion in the prosperous states of Punjab and Haryana means that fewer widows are forced to migrate for economic reasons. The high rates of migration of widows and divorcees in Kerala, however, seems to contradict his hypothesis that natolocal residence patterns affect the overall rates of migration in the south. Matrilocal and natolocal systems, after all, should provide more security for widowed or divorced women than patrilocal or even neonatal systems, provided that land and property holdings are sufficient.

At the aggregate level, the percentage of unmarried female migrants to both rural and urban destinations is also larger in the south than in the north, though this regional difference is less marked than that of widowed and divorced women. Of interest is the fact that the proportion of unmarried women among recent migrants far surpasses that of unmarried women among migrants of all durations, particularly among rural migrants. In the Punjab, Kerala, and Tamil Nadu, they are nearly equal to married female migrants in recent migration to rural destinations, and in Kerala they surpass married women among those moving to urban areas. Premi reports that district-level variations are even more marked than those observed at the state level in Punjab and Himachal Pradesh. Assuming that a large proportion of migrants moved upon marriage, especially those with residence of less than a year's duration, it cannot be assumed that all unmarried female migrants moved with their families. Surely a significant proportion of unmarried women are migrating on their own. Premi (1979:19–20) assumed that all married women who have moved within the past year have migrated for marriage; that half the unmarried women aged 20 to 24 and all unmarried women aged 25 and above have migrated for economic reasons; that all widowed and divorced women aged 25 to 49 have migrated for economic reasons; and that all other unmarried or widowed or divorced women reflect associational migration. Hence he concludes that only 2.6 percent of female migrants in the north and 4.4 percent in the south have migrated for economic reasons. Haryana had the lowest percentage (1.1) and Kerala the highest (6.3); the rest are assumed to have migrated for marriage or associational reasons.

While I would agree that female migration in the south in general, and Kerala in particular, is probably influenced more by economic forces than in the north, I believe the economic causes are seriously underestimated for two reasons. First, the assumptions mentioned above ignore the fact that large numbers of children migrate for economic reasons.[4] Second, the work-force participation rate of migrant females is generally higher than for the population as a whole. Premi (1979:39) assumes that associational migration (migration with parent or male relation) excludes economic motivations. As I have argued earlier, many women and children accompany other family members because they expect to work or have been assured employment; where migrant women have low rates of economic activity, high sex ratios in migration streams have prevailed. Economic motivations should be considered as important as associational reasons among those who have high rates of economic activity. Karlekar (1979) and Kasturi (n.d.) have both found, for example, that migrant women often work to sustain their families while male family members are gaining experience or education, or waiting for the right job to come along. Low-caste Tamil migrant women in the slums of Delhi frequently said they believed it was just as much the woman's responsibility as the man's to work and support the family (Singh and de Souza 1976).

Economic activity rates are not disaggregated by rural or urban place of destination in Premi's (1979) study, but the distribution of female migrant workers by industry of employment is given in Table 5.6. This table reveals that migrant women have a more diversified occupational structure in the south than in the north. Premi (1979:46–48) notes that migrant women in urban areas in the south are much more likely to engage in construction, manufacturing, and petty trade than in the north. Except for

Table 5.6 Percentage distribution of female urban migrant workers in broad industrial categories: 1971

State and region	Industrial category of workers			
	Primary	Secondary	Transport	Services
Northern Zone	10.14	12.55	5.27	72.04
Haryana	14.47	13.47	5.60	66.47
Himachal Pradesh	17.04	12.32	5.29	65.35
Punjab	2.36	12.15	5.05	80.45
Southern Zone	27.67	21.98	10.42	39.90
Andhra Pradesh	39.42	24.47	11.41	24.71
Kerala	17.92	15.27	6.05	60.76
Tamil Nadu	17.86	23.24	12.11	46.49
Overall	21.16	18.48	12.11	46.49

Source: Premi (1979:44)

Kerala, the proportion of female workers engaged in "trade and transport" in the southern states is more than double the proportion in the north; the reverse is true of "other services." In Andhra Pradesh there is an unusually large proportion of female workers in the primary sector. This finding is probably due to the large-scale participation of women in the tobacco industry in that state, particularly in *bidi* (an indigenous cigarette) rolling. (Raju (1981:55) notes that in 1961 some 77 percent of the *bidi* workers in Andhra Pradesh were women, compared to 61 percent in Maharashtra and 47 percent in Rajasthan.) The heavy concentration of female workers in "other services" in all the northern states and Kerala is more difficult to interpret because the category includes educated white-collar workers as well as domestic servants. A rough distinction could be made on the basis of literacy as in Table 5.4 for Delhi since nearly all white-collar workers are literate whereas domestic workers are more likely to be illiterate. Considering that Kerala has the highest female literacy rate in the country, however, it would probably be difficult to interpret the findings on the basis of literacy. Premi (1979:56) speculates that in the Punjab and Kerala the large proportion of migrant women in "service" represents an increasing number of educated women entering the work force in white-collar jobs in rural areas whereas in urban areas they are probably in domestic service. This hypothesis needs further substantiation. Mitra et al. (1980:88–91) find an unusually large increase in the participation of women in the service category of "nurses, pharmacists, etc." in both Kerala and Punjab between 1961 and 1971.

PURDAH, EMPLOYMENT, AND MIGRATION

The contrasting patterns and characteristics of female rural-to-urban migration in northern and southern India emerge consistently in both macrolevel and microlevel studies. South Indian rural-to-urban migration streams, compared to those of the north, have lower sex ratios but a greater representation of single women, widows, and divorcees, a higher rate of economic activity among women, and a greater occupational diversity among women—particularly with reference to "outside work" such as petty trading, which requires a public role. These differences are observed even among migrants to cities outside their own region, as illustrated above for Delhi and also elsewhere (Singh 1978) for other major cities. Raju's study (1981) finds a correlation between the propensity to work and the degree of occupational diversity among elite and depressed-class urban women at the regional and local level—providing further evidence that these patterns are related to specific sociocultural and historical influences.

The evidence strongly suggests that female employment and rural-to-urban migration are intimately related. Although the overall rate of migration is higher among women in the north, their proportions in rural-to-urban migration streams are considerably lower, as are their rates of economic activity in urban areas. Although it is impossible to prove a causal relationship between these factors on the basis of macrolevel data, a number of microlevel studies provide important insights into the process of migration, decision-making, coping strategies, and the consequences of rural-to-urban migration for women and the family. It will be argued here that a woman's propensity to work plays a critical role in her decision to migrate and, moreover, that this propensity is influenced differently in north and south by diverse customs, norms, and attitudes related to the seclusion of women and limitations on their public role.

As Boserup has noted (1970:71–72) in her remarkable worldwide review of the role of women in economic development, the pattern of female work-force participation in northern India resembles that of women in West Asian and North African Arab countries, whereas in central and southern India, where West Asian culture never penetrated to the same degree as in the north, the patterns resemble those of Southeast Asia. Raju (1981) has documented these differences down to the district level and finds the differences most marked in cities with a strong presence of Muslim elite culture. To see how this cultural norm might affect female migration and employment, it is necessary to understand the complex concept of purdah—a term that literally means "veil" or "curtain" but broadly refers to the many practices related to the seclusion of women.

Sharma (1980:213–14) studied the relationship between purdah and the use of public space by women in two northern Indian villages located in Punjab and Himachal Pradesh. She describes purdah as a complex of norms having three main dimensions. The first relates to rules governing the behavior of married women toward male affines and neighbors, including the practice of *ghungat* (the avoidance of certain males of the husband's family and village). These customs, Sharma claims, effectively cut women off from communication with decision-makers and those holding power both inside and outside the family. The second dimension comprises norms governing sex segregation. It is considered the responsibility of women (rather than men) to avoid situations that might lead to contact with the opposite sex and, moreover, to withdraw from contact when it does occur. Hence if a woman appears without male protection in a public place where contact is likely to occur, such as a bus or a bazaar, she is perceived as openly inviting contact or verbal abuse. The third dimension relates to a variety of norms that limit a woman's mobility and visibility outside the home. These norms reinforce all the other norms that define women's role as essentially domestic. According to Sharma, Hindus tend to emphasize the first dimension whereas Muslims emphasize the third, though variations occur within both groups according to local conditions, social class, caste practices, and so on. Sharma specifically notes the problem that purdah creates for women who engage in economic activities such as petty trade involving contact with unrelated men.

In a study of the structure of women's work in rural Bangladesh—a country located at the easternmost end of the Purdah Belt extending across the northern Indian subcontinent—Cain et al. (1979) describe an even more constraining pattern arising out of the norms of purdah. Women were found to be almost totally alienated from control over family resources; men control family property, income, and women's labor. This was true regardless of a family's class or ownership of property. Purdah restrictions on the movement of women outside the home excluded them from access to such economic opportunities as paid agricultural work and petty trading. Since women who are engaged in home production depend on men to do the marketing, men therefore control their income. This study appears to confirm Sharma's analysis regarding the Muslim emphasis on the woman's domestic role and limited mobility and visibility outside the home. By way of contrast, Bhatty (1980:208–09) and Jacobson (1974) have found important class differences at the village level regarding Muslim women's participation in agricultural activities in Uttar Pradesh and Madhya Pradesh, respectively. Nevertheless, although many of the Muslim women from lower classes worked as cultivators or wage laborers, they noted their desire to achieve a degree of economic security that would allow them to withdraw to the domestic sphere.

In southern India, as Lessinger (1980:4) notes, Hindu women are not required to maintain purdah but are nonetheless limited in their range of social contacts because of norms stemming from concepts of male and female nature, patterns of family relations, and class relations within a strongly hierarchical society. While they may not be required "to crouch, to cover their heads, or avoid all eye contact with strange men, they are required to speak softly, modestly, and respectfully, to use honorific forms of address, and to repress any tendency to argue and domineer. In relations between high-status men and low-status women, there is the implied threat of sexual exploitation." Hence although southern Indian Hindu women are certainly not without gender-based constraints on their economic activities, they certainly do not operate within the restrictive context of the north, which precludes active participation in petty business, or, as in Bangladesh, prevents them even from entering into financial transactions outside the household.

Although there are broad regional differences between northern and southern India that surface in macrolevel data and can be confirmed through microlevel studies, it is also important to note that there is considerable variation at the state, district, and city level within the major regions. These differences are in most cases related to caste differences in gender roles and often reflect the adaptation of traditional occupations in the urban setting. In Delhi's squatter settlements, for example, although female migrants from the northern state of Uttar Pradesh had on the whole much lower economic activity rates than those from the southern state of Tamil Nadu, among certain caste groups from Uttar Pradesh, namely Dhobis (launderers) and Balmikis (sweepers), women's labor-force participation rates nearly equaled those of men (Singh 1978:338). Raju (1981:32) found that the work-force participation rate of scheduled caste women was often high in cities of Uttar Pradesh where there is a large Muslim population and elite (ashraf) culture is strong. She postulates that women of the depressed classes may be filling jobs that are available because privileged women are not able or willing to work in these positions.

While the process of "immurement"—the withdrawal of women from the paid work force when the family's economic situation improves (Srinivas 1977:226)—is no doubt a process that occurs in both southern and northern India, there is reason to doubt the extent to which this process may be generalized. Migrant women from Tamil Nadu in Delhi's squatter settlements, for example, many of whom claimed that it is as much the woman's responsibility to support the family as it is the man's, also claimed that they would not give up working should their husband's income improve (Singh 1978). Similarly, Karlekar (1979) has found that continuation of female employment in traditional occupations (scavenging or sweeping) among migrant Balmikis in Delhi constituted a family strategy to assure a regular income, however meager, while the men looked for avenues of occupational mobility. These women continued to work even after the men were employed in higher-status positions. Ironically, while the women continued to occupy extremely low-status positions within the work force and the family, the gap between female and male economic and social status was rapidly widening (see also Alexander and Jayaraman 1977). Furthermore, recent evidence indicates that as privileged-class women gain access to higher education, they are increasingly entering the work force in modern occupations in certain states, including the northern state of Punjab where female work-force participation rates have always been low (Mitra et al. 1980).

In contrast to situations where large numbers of women accompany their husbands to the city or migrate on their own (as household heads, for example, or single women), there are regional and caste groups in which only the males migrate. This pattern is evident in the high sex ratios of migrant streams to the larger cities from certain northern and eastern states—namely Jammu and Kashmir, Himachal Pradesh, Punjab, Uttar Pradesh, Bihar, West Bengal, and Orissa (Singh 1978:335). Although these states have apparently seen recent increases in the participation of women agricultural workers in rural migrant labor, their movement to cities has increased only gradually over the last few decades. These changing patterns need to be explored further, as they have important implications for the integrated regional planning that constitutes a recent thrust in social development policy. In areas such as Himachal Pradesh and northern and eastern Uttar Pradesh, the high concentrations of women, children, and the aged in rural areas have crucial significance for agricultural development as well as social services. The following section deals explicitly with the policy and planning implications of the patterns and variations in female rural-to-urban migration.

POLICY, PLANNING, AND PROGRAM ISSUES

The migration of women to cities in India has long been dismissed as irrelevant to urban planning because of the assumption that women come as dependents of men. Their earnings, when they do work, are thus regarded as marginal and only supplementary to those of male earners in the household. This assumption finds support from a variety of sources mentioned above, including the census (which seriously underestimated the work-force participation rates of women, especially those in the informal sector) and the 1955–58 NSS report on reasons for migration in which only a minority of women mentioned employment as their primary motive. I have presented evidence from both macrolevel data as well as microlevel studies that casts doubt on these assumptions. In urban areas throughout the country, migrant women have significantly higher work-force participation rates than nonmigrant women. At the microlevel, several studies indicate that there may be an element of caste selectivity among migrants from states with low female work-force participation—a bias that favors female rural-to-urban migration among those groups in which women have traditionally worked and can adapt their skills to the urban situation. Hence a woman's employability may determine whether or not she will accompany her spouse to the city and, once the family reaches the city, influence its patterns of adaptation. This is clearly the case among a large portion of the urban poor and may also count among other classes as well.

Hence there is an urgent need for policy-makers to recognize that women who migrate to the towns and cities come not only as dependents but also as earners who play an integral role in the family economy. While most migrant women earn less than males, their contribution is often crucial to the family's survival. Furthermore, perhaps as many as 19 percent head their own households or provide the sole support for their families (Buvinic and Youssef 1978). The high rate of economic activity among migrant women in low-income groups is of special significance, as is their almost total dependence on informal employment.

At the national level, this recognition could lead to a number of useful policy initiatives that could shape urban development at the state and municipal level. Promoting a viable work-residence relationship, for example, especially for the poor, is a fundamental principle embodied in the master plans of most cities. In practice, however, it is usually based solely on the work-residence patterns of the male household head. Since proximity to place of work is undoubtedly more important for women (who carry the double burden of earning as well as child care and domestic responsibilities) than for men, priority should logically be given to female employment patterns when planning for a viable relationship. Not only do men have more time and money to spend on public or private transport; they also face fewer physical and social constraints in using them. Transport, credit, and child-care services could also respond more appropriately to the needs of migrant women (see Singh 1979).

It will be recognized by now, however, that the diverse patterns of female migration, work-force participation, and adaptation to urban life make it necessary to go beyond broad policy directives at a national level and consider the implications for planning programs at the regional, state, and local level. Some of these implications are discussed in the pages that follow. It will be seen that more sensitive planning for migrant women can lead to rapid and low-cost improvements not only in their lives but in the city as a whole.

The inverse association between sex ratios in rural-to-urban migration streams and the rates of female work-force participation among migrant groups present a number of practical implications for policy planning. The high sex ratios in urban migration streams originating from specific areas of the north should alert planners involved in rural development of special service needs of women, children, and the aged, as well as the need to bring women into training and extension activities related to agricultural development. In urban areas, the low sex ratios and high female work-force participation rates that prevail in migrant groups should signal the need to investigate the economic roles of these women and the need to design child care, health, transport, and credit services that are consistent with their needs. Since patterns and needs are bound to vary from city to city, this work must be carried out at the local level.

In some circumstances, predominantly male migration has important implications for female migrants. In Bombay, for example, thousands of low-income migrant women are self-employed as meal providers out of their one-room slum tenements for the textile mill laborers who have come individually to work in the industrial heart of the city. These women are normally invisible to the public and the planner's eye. Prema Purav, an imaginative and spirited social worker, has since 1975 organized nearly 5,000 meal providers into an association, the Annapurana Mahila Mandal, which has given women meal providers access to low-interest credit from a national bank (see Singh 1979; Krishna Raj 1980). As a result these women have been freed from the grip of local moneylenders, who often charge more than 100 percent interest a year. (The banks are happy since neighborhood committees collect loan repayments and the organization has a recovery rate of more than 95 percent.) In Ahmedabad and Madras, similar efforts by nongovernmental organizations provide low-income women (mainly women involved in petty trade) access to credit. In Delhi, where few women are engaged in petty trade, leaders have organized women who do embroidery work, carve metal and ivory, and make glass bangles at home. A thousand women have benefited from the program within a year. Since credit was not considered the most pressing need in Delhi, efforts focused first on stabilizing rates for various types of work and promoting savings accounts in a local bank. Most of these organizations have been able to expand benefits and services gradually into other areas such as insurance, health, child care, and family planning.

Another issue with important policy implications is child labor among female migrants. Nearly half the female child workers are concentrated in the four southern states, though less than a quarter of the country's population resides in the south. In Kerala the data clearly show that this labor is limited almost entirely to domestic services; in the other three states an equal or larger proportion work as "craftsmen and laborers." Other sources of information suggest that in the latter category there are significant concentrations of female child workers in the cottage match-making industry in Tamil Nadu and Karnataka, while the tobacco and bidi-rolling industry engage large numbers in Andhra Pradesh and Karnataka (Rao 1978; Raju 1981; *Times of India* 1979). Although legislation has banned child labor in the organized sector, it seems that little that can be done to limit their informal employment. There is also the troubling question of whether it is *right* to do so, since it is recognized that most children work because of compelling economic reasons. Hence a search is under way for policies that can improve their working conditions, earnings, skills, and access to supportive services.

Another vulnerable category of women migrants is the household heads. Studies indicate that between 20 and 35 percent of working women among low-income urban groups are the sole providers for their families—either because they are alone (widowed, divorced, deserted, or single) or because their husbands or other male adults in the household are unemployed, ill, handicapped, or simply irresponsible with their income. In Delhi there is evidence that around 9 percent of low-income migrant households are headed by women (Singh and de Souza 1976:44). Many of these women came to the city because they were unable to support a family alone in the village; others assumed the leading economic role in their families at some point after migration. Although these findings require more extensive documentation, they suggest that female workers among low-income migrants, because of the key role they play in the family economy and the statistically strong possibility that they are sole providers, are especially in need of programs and services, including health, nutrition, shelter, skill development, and child care—in addition to those that can enhance their earning capacity and job security.

Of major importance are variations in extent of migrant women's employment and type of occupation, especially differences between the north and south. While specific programs and policies need to be formulated at the city or state level after careful investigation of local patterns, differences at the state and regional level could be used to shape broad policy guidelines. The much higher participation of women in petty trade in southern and central India indicates that policies oriented toward supporting women in this important sector will have more widespread implications in these regions than in northern and eastern India. Because of the women's limited resources and need for a regular cash flow, extending low-interest credit to them has proved to be a remarkably successful strategy in Madras, Bombay, and Ahmedabad. In Andhra Pradesh, a government-sponsored women's finance corporation has also been successful in extending institutionalized credit to low-income women in both rural and urban areas on a statewide basis. A recent evaluation of the program indicates that self-employed, urban-based vendors have perhaps benefited the most (Rao 1979). Recovery rates are less than satisfactory (about 52 percent), however. Unlike the nongovernmental organizations that designate responsibility to local groups of women to recover loans, the government agency and banks so far lack a means of promoting community responsibility.

Other problems amenable to policy and planning include improving the access of women vendors to centralized wholesale markets, reducing their harassment by police or rich traders in profitable markets and providing them with protection from the elements. Child care, health, and functional literacy programs are other areas of need, though they are rarely accorded priority by the women themselves until their economic situation improves. In the north and east it appears that such strategies directed at women in trade would benefit only a small number of female migrants and hence may not be viable at all.

Others, however, such as the many migrant women working as coolies in urban construction, may be in need of special supportive services in the north. In Delhi the Mobile Creches, a nongovernmental organization, provides child care, health services, and informal education to thousands of such women, largely migrants from Rajasthan, at the construction site (see Singh 1979). Efforts to develop similar services for women construction workers in Bombay have proved more difficult, however, due to different patterns of organizing construction. In Bombay workers often have to commute long distances because there is no room at the site for temporary housing.

Finally, there is a need to investigate the relationship between city size, employment opportunities for female migrants, and the low sex ratios in small towns and cities. It seems clear that women migrating to the largest cities take on the most menial jobs or, at the other end of the occupational hierarchy, are increasingly entering the modern sector. Yet data indicate that employment opportunities for migrant women are greater in small towns and cities in the north. This finding suggests that short-distance migration to smaller towns would be more attractive for women not accompanying spouses or joining other relatives in the larger cities, and hence the incidence of women-headed households would be much higher in small urban areas. This topic is in need of further exploration if we are to understand the broad implications of urbanization and female rural-to-urban migration in India.

NOTES

This article was written prior to the author's appointment to the ILO. The views expressed herein are those of the author and not necessarily those of the ILO.

1. There is a marked difference between rural and urban areas; the sex ratio is 105 in the former and 117 in the latter. (The sex ratio is defined in this chapter, and throughout the book, as the number of males per 100 females. In Indian documents, it is usually defined as the number of females per 1,000 males.)

2. In natolocal residence, after marriage male and female children remain in the home of their mother, mother's brother, mother's mother, mother's mother's brother, and so forth. (Men have visiting rights with respect to their wives but do not stay with them.) In matrilocal residence, the husband moves to his wife's parents' home, which may include in the extended household wife's sisters, wife's sisters' spouses and children, and wife's unmarried brothers, in addition to his own wife and children. Natolocal residence is unusual, but it was once commonly practiced among the Nayars of Kerala.

3. The widespread participation of women in rural migrant labor originating in these states was brought out by several participants at a national seminar on migrant labor in India hosted by the National Labour Institute, New Delhi, 16–18 February 1981.

4. It is interesting to note that data on migrant children in the cities of India in 1971 (Sebastian 1979) show that young female workers constitute a larger percentage of all young workers than do young male migrant workers in all four of the southern states. The reverse is true of all other states except Madhya Pradesh, Rajasthan, Uttar Pradesh, and West Bengal. Among child migrants (0–14 years), the economic activity rates are consistently higher for females in the south than in the north. In Kerala there are even more migrant female child workers in the cities than males, 97 percent of

whom are in "services." In fact, 45 percent of all migrant female child workers in the cities of India are found in the four southern states where only 24 percent of the country's total population resides.

REFERENCES

Alexander, Sue C., and Raja Jayaraman
1977   The changing status of women in India. In Allen G. Noble and Ashok K. Dutt (eds.), *Indian Urbanization and Planning: Vehicles of Modernization.* New Delhi: Tata McGraw-Hill.

Ali, Nisar
1981   Some aspects of migratory labor in Jammu and Kashmir. Paper presented at the National Seminar on Migrant Labour in India, 16–18 February. New Delhi: National Labour Institute.

Bellwinkel, Maren
1973   Rajasthani contract labor in Delhi: a case study of the relationship between company, middleman and worker. *Sociological Bulletin* 22(1):78–97.

Bhatty, Zarina
1980   Muslim women in Uttar Pradesh: social mobility and directions of change. In Alfred de Souza (ed.), *Women in Contemporary India and South Asia.* New Delhi: Manohar Press.

Boserup, E.
1970   *Women in Economic Development.* New York: St. Martin's Press.

Breman, Jan
1979   Seasonal migration and cooperative capitalism: crushing of cane and of labor by sugar factories of Bardoli. Paper presented at the ADC-ICRISAT Conference on Adjustment Mechanisms of Rural Labor Markets in Developing Areas, 22–24 August, Hyderabad.

Buvinic, Mayra, and Nadia H. Youssef
1978   *Women-Headed Households: The Ignored Factor in Development Planning.* Washington, D.C.: International Center for Research on Women.

Cain, Mead, Syeda Rokeya Khanam, and Shamsum Nahar
1979   Class, patriarchy and the structure of women's work in rural Bangladesh. Paper presented at the ADC-ICRISAT Conference on Adjustment Mechanisms of Rural Labor Markets in Developing Areas, 22–24 August, Hyderabad.

Census of India
1971   *Migration Tables: Delhi.* Series 27, Part II-D. Delhi.
1981   *Provisional Population Totals.* Paper-1 of 1981. New Delhi.
n.d.   *Town and Village Directory: Delhi.* Village and Townwise Primary Census Abstract. Series 27. Delhi.

Cohn, Bernard S.
1955   The changing status of a depressed class. In McKim Marriott (ed.), *Village India.* Chicago: University of Chicago Press.

D'Souza, Victor S.
1975   Scheduled castes and urbanization in Punjab: an explanation. *Sociological Bulletin* 24(1):1–12.

Gough, Kathleene
1962   Caste in a Tanjore village. In B. R. Leach (ed.), *Aspects of Caste in South India, Ceylon and North-West Pakistan*. Cambridge: Cambridge University Press.

Government of India (GOI)
1974   *Towards Equality: Report of the Committee on the Status of Women in India*. New Delhi: Ministry of Education and Social Welfare.

Hindustan Times
1981   Provisional census figures show high population growth. 19 March.

Jacobson, Doranne
1974   The women of North and Central India: goddesses and wives. In Carolyn J. Mattiasson (ed.), *Many Sisters: Women in Cross-Cultural Perspective*. New York: Free Press.

Jain, Devaki
1979   *Impact on Women Workers—Maharashtra Employment Guarantee Scheme: A Case Study*. Paper prepared for the ILO. New Delhi: Institute of Social Studies.

Joshi, Heather
1976   Prospects and case for employment of women in Indian cities. *Economic and Political Weekly* 11:1303–08.

Karlekar, Malavika
1979   Balmiki Women in India. Paper prepared for the Indian Council of Social Science Research. New Delhi.

Kasturi, Leela
n.d.   South Indian domestic workers in New Delhi. Paper prepared for the Indian Council of Social Science Research. New Delhi.

Krishna Raj, Maithreyi
1980   *Approaches to Self-Reliance for Women: Some Urban Models*. Research Unit on Women's Studies, SNDT. Bombay: Women's University.

Lessinger, Johanna
1980   Women traders in Madras City. Paper prepared for the annual meeting of the Society for South India Studies, 17–19 March, Philadelphia.

Majumdar, Tapan K.
1977   The urban poor and social change: a study of squatter settlements in Delhi. *Social Action* 27(3):216–40.

Mehrotra, G. K.
1974   *Birthplace Migration in India*. Special Monograph. New Delhi: Census of India, 1971, Series 1, India: Special Monograph, No. 1. Office of the Registrar General, India.

Mitra, Asok, Lalit P. Pathak, and Shekhar Mukherji
1980   *The Status of Women: Shifts in Occupational Participation 1961–71*. New Delhi: Abhinav Publications.

Natarajan, D.
    1972   *The Changes in the Sex Ratio*. Census of India, 1971. Census Centenary Monograph No. 6. New Delhi: Office of the Registrar General, India.

National Sample Survey (NSS)
    n.d.   Report No. 53 on Migration, Report No. 182.

Premi, Mahendra K.
    1979   *Patterns of Internal Migration of Females in India*. Center for the Study of Regional Development, Occasional Paper No. 15. New Delhi: Jawaharlal Nehru University.
    1980   *Urban Outmigration: A Study of Its Nature, Causes and Consequences*. New Delhi: Sterling Publishers.

Raju, Saraswati
    1981   Sita in the city: a sociogeographical analysis of female employment in urban India. Discussion paper. Syracuse, New York: Department of Geography, Syracuse University.

Rao, M.S.A.
    1978   Tobacco development and labor migration: planning for labor welfare and development. *Economic and Political Weekly* 13(29).

Rao, Seshagiri
    1979   *A Case Study of the Functioning of A.P. Women's Cooperative Finance Corporation Limited and Impact of Assistance Extended by It* (Mimeographed). New Delhi: Indian Council of Social Science Research.

Saradamoni, K.
    1979   *Changing Land Relations and Women—A Case Study of Palghat District in Kerala* (Mimeographed). New Delhi: Indian Council of Social Science Research.

Saxena, D. P.
    1977   *Rural-Urban Migration in India: Causes and Consequences*. Bombay: Popular Prakashan.

Sebastian, A.
    1979   *State-Wise Child Migrants and Child Migrant Labor in the Cities of India* (Mimeographed). Deonar, Bombay: International Institute of Population Studies.

Sharma, Ursula M.
    1980   Purdah and public space. In Alfred de Souza (ed.), *Women in Contemporary India and South Asia*. New Delhi: Manohar Press.

Singh, Andrea Menefee
    1976   *Neighborhood and Social Networks in Urban India: Voluntary Associations of South Indian Migrants in Delhi*. New Delhi: Marwah Press.
    1977   Women and the family: coping with poverty in the bastis of Delhi. *Social Action* 27(3):241–65.
    1978   Rural-urban migration of women among the urban poor in India: causes and consequences. *Social Action* 28(4):326–56.
    1979   *Women in Cities: An Invisible Factor in Urban Planning in India*. Unpublished report prepared for the Population Council, New York.

Singh, Andrea Menefee, and Alfred de Souza
  1976   *The Position of Women in Migrant Bastis in Delhi*. Report prepared for the Ministry of Social Welfare. New Delhi: Indian Social Institute.
  1980   *The Urban Poor: Slum and Pavement Dwellers in the Major Cities of India*. New Delhi: Manohar Press.

Srinivas, M. N.
  1977   The changing position of Indian women. *Man* (n.s.) 12.

Times of India
  1979   Article on working children in the cottage match industry in Sivakasi, 11 September. Tamil Nadu.

Town and Country Planning Organization (TCPO)
  1975   *Jhuggi Jhonpri Settlements in Delhi: A Sociological Study of Low-Income Migrant Communities, Part II*. New Delhi: Ministry of Works and Housing, Government of India.

Youssef, Nadia, Mayra Buvinic, and Ayse Kudat
  1979   *Women in Migration: A Third World Focus*. Washington, D.C.: International Center for Research on Women.

Chapter 6

The Female Migrant in Pakistan

Nasra M. Shah

The urban population in Pakistan has grown from about 18 percent in 1951 to about 26 percent in 1972. There is general agreement among demographers that a substantial proportion of this increase can be attributed to internal migration from rural to urban areas. One estimate shows that 40 percent of the increase in urban population between 1959–60 and 1969–70 was a result of rural-to-urban migration (Mujahid 1975). Only a few studies in Pakistan have examined the levels of internal migration or looked at the characteristics of migrants. Even among studies that have raised the issue, estimates are often not available separately for males and females (Burki 1973b; Afzal 1967; and Mujahid 1975).

Afzal (1967) estimated migration rates between 1951 and 1961 using the census survival ratio technique. He calculated overall migration rates per hundred for the 1951 population of urban areas to be 18.7 percent for males and 18.2 percent for females. He interprets this close correspondence in rates to imply a tendency toward family migration in Pakistan. The finding that many people move as family units also finds support when sex ratios are examined. The sex ratio in towns was calculated to be 126 compared to 116 males per 100 females for the country as a whole in 1961 (Krotki 1963). This finding probably implies that although more males than females might be moving into urban areas, most of the moves are family moves. It might be noted that these sex ratios are for all ages, and migration might well be highly male-selective at certain ages, especially younger ages.

The apparent predominance of family movement in the migration streams was also found in a study of a small town in the Punjab (Naeem and Mahbub 1969). The sex ratios for the in-migrants to and out-migrants from Lulliani were 106 and 110, implying a trend toward family migration. Analysis of migrant registration records supports this finding. (Lulliani was an experimental project in which vital events—births, deaths, migration—were registered continuously for several decades in the 1960s.)

In a more recent study, Afzal and Abbasi (1979) have shown that female migration has increased during recent years relative to male migration. When they compared the two intercensal periods, 1951–61 and 1961–72, the authors found that the pace of female urbanization was higher than that of male urbanization during the latter period. This change represents a reversal of the trend during the earlier intercensal period. The authors interpret this finding as indicating a growing tendency toward family migration, increased marriage migration for females, or even greater female migration associated with the pursuit of education. Sex ratios in urban areas declined from 126 in 1969 to 119 in 1972, suggesting both a better coverage of females and a probable decline in male-only migration (Afzal and Abbasi 1979:table 6).

With regard to the age structure of male and female migrants, not many estimates are available for the country as a whole. One exception is a study by Krotki (1963). By plotting the age distributions of males and females in large and small towns and comparing them with the total population, he showed an excess of females in the 10–24 age group and an excess of males aged 10–44 in urban areas. Krotki argued that the excess of females might not necessarily result from in-migration but might simply indicate a substantial underenumeration of this age group (10–24) in the country as a whole. The largest proportion of male migrants are in the 20–24 age group, which is "perhaps the most venturesome and energetic age group not yet encumbered with family responsibilities" (Krotki 1963:122). If Krotki's assumption about the marital status of these younger males is correct, this is an indication of a high propensity among young single males to migrate.

The high mobility of young people and young families was also shown by the migration patterns in Lulliani. In this town, there were more women than men in the age group 20–34 among the migrants than among the nonmigrants. The higher mobility among women of these ages is probably related to their movement because of marriage—both into and out of Lulliani. On the basis of data for one town alone, however, not much can be concluded about the patterns and the reasons for migration in Pakistan.

In discussing the probable reasons for rural-to-urban migration in Pakistan, Burki argues that push factors combined with expectations about finding a job play a significant role. Analysis of the socioeconomic characteristics of migrants to the city of Karachi suggests that in-migrants were "considerably more impoverished, less skilled and educated, and less 'urbanized' than the rest of Pakistan's population" (Burki 1973b:167). Similarly, it has been suggested that the proportion of the urban labor force in low-paid occupations increased between 1963–64 and 1969–70, implying that the urban labor force has continued to absorb rural migrants in its low productivity and unskilled sectors (Mujahid 1975). Mujahid (p. 591) argues that the rapid in-migration from rural areas has created an employment and income structure that "does not offer better living conditions to prospective migrants."

If the average rural migrant is indeed an impoverished landless laborer, is unskilled and uneducated, and is moving with his family, such a move can have significant implications for the wife's subsequent role and her status in the family. Given the higher cost of living in the city, for example, larger numbers of wives (and daughters) might be forced to enter the labor force in order to supplement the family income than would have been necessary in the rural areas. General observation of Pakistani cities shows that there are numerous opportunities for women to find at least part-time jobs carrying out domestic chores like dishwashing, laundering, babysitting, and cooking. Yet few of these women might actually be able to enter the labor force because of lack of skills, lack of contacts, or general ignorance.

This brief review of the literature shows that we do not know very much about the female migrant in Pakistan. We know that the female rate of migration was slightly lower than the male rate during the decade 1951–61 but seems to have increased between 1961 and 1972. The declining sex ratio in urban areas could have been caused by increased family migration, or increased marriage migration for females, or simply better reporting of females in urban areas. It is difficult to determine what proportion of the decline can be attributed to each of these causes without a careful study of the dynamics of migration and the characteristics of migrants. In this essay I wish to examine the nature of female migration in Pakistan. I also want to compare the characteristics of the female migrant with her male counterpart in order to explore the dynamics of the migration process.

While this study cannot determine whether most migration in Pakistan is actually family migration, cultural conditions lead us to make certain educated guesses. Social norms in Pakistan generally dictate a highly sheltered (secluded) status for women, particularly younger women. Women are not expected to move from one place of residence to another without proper escort, particularly if they are young and unmarried. A substantial number of women do move on account of marriage itself, although the custom is for daughters to be married to men who reside in nearby areas. Young unmarried girls usually live with their parents or siblings; married women live in their husbands' home, visiting their own parental home occasionally; divorced women usually return to their parental home and live with parents or brothers; widowed women may continue to live in their husband's home or may return to their parental home, depending on duration of marriage, parity, and the relative economic status of the two families. Thus a woman is always attached to some form of family structure that affords her protection. In a situation like this, it is reasonable to assume that mobility of unattached females would be minimal except under exceptional circumstances such as utter destitution and lack of family support. It is because of these cultural conditions that women, when they move, must move with other members of the family. In Pakistan, young unmarried girls simply do not move to the city to find jobs in domestic service or industry. The few female migrants who work as domestic servants are usually older women who are widowed or divorced, although a substantial number of young unmarried migrant males do work as domestic servants.

THE DATA

This study is based on data collected as part of the 1973 Housing, Economic and Demographic (HED) Survey. The HED Survey, based on a nationwide sample of 255,000 households, was designed to supplement the 1972 census by providing information on education, fertility, mortality, labor force, migration, and housing conditions in the country. In the subsequent analysis, the data are weighted to represent the actual numbers for the country.

Three questions on migration were asked of each individual in the household:

1. In which district/country was_____born?
                              (name of person)
2. How long (years) has_____been living continuously in the
                   (name of person)
   current place of residence (district)?
3. What was the usual place of residence (district) of_____
                                           (name of person)
   when India attacked Pakistan in 1965?_____
                                         (Specify urban or rural place.)

In order to divide migrants into three groups for analysis, residence at three points in time was considered: (1) district of birth, (2) district of residence in 1965, and (3) district of present residence. If (1) and (2) were different but (2) and (3) were the same, the move was classified as having taken place *before 1965;* if all three were different, the person was classified as having moved both *before and after 1965.* Only when (1), (2), and (3) were all the same was the person classified as a *nonmigrant.* Although this classification scheme is somewhat more complex than a duration of residence measure, it has two distinct advantages over the latter. First, we are able to measure, even if crudely, the frequency of movement and its relationship to socioeconomic forces. Second, we can categorize the move as urban or rural for migrants who moved after the 1965 war.

It should be noted that the migration data were collected at the district level.[1] Only when an individual was living in a district other than the district of birth (or district in 1965) was he or she classified as a migrant. Estimates based on interdistrict migration might therefore be an underestimate of internal migration, particularly if there is much migration within the district. Some support for a high rate of within-district migration is found in the case studies of Peshawar city and Gujranwala city—40 percent of the migrants to Peshawar and 28 percent of the migrants to Gujranwala came from within the same district (BEE 1977; SSRC 1977).

Given these limitations, it is my objective here to present a comprehensive profile of migrant women in Pakistan. I have therefore analyzed data on the migrants' age, marital status, education, and employment and have compared male and female migrants for each characteristic, as well as female migrants versus female nonmigrants. My analysis has been restricted to migrants (and nonmigrants) ten years old or more mainly because the characteristics under study are age-selective: Data on labor-force participation and marital status are available only for persons aged ten and over; data on education are available only for persons aged five and over. Since it is reasonable to expect that migration decisions are made by adults, the group aged ten and over is a meaningful unit to consider in a study such as this one.[2]

THE RESULTS

A total of 5.4 million males and 4.5 million females were classified as migrants in the 1973 HED Survey, resulting in a sex ratio of 121, the same as the sex ratio for nonmigrants (Table 6.1). Among the males and females aged ten and over, however, exactly the same proportions (23.4 percent) of both sexes were reported as migrants. Almost 80 percent of all migrants had moved sometime before 1965 (that is, eight years before the survey), while the rest had moved only after 1965 or had made more than one move.

Information on the urban or rural nature of the move is available only for those who moved after 1965. In this subgroup, the majority of males and females migrated from urban to urban or rural to rural areas. The percentage of those who moved from rural to urban areas was only 18 percent for males and 16 percent for females, which indicates that rural-to-urban migration is only a small component of overall migration in the country. Of all the rural-to-urban migrants, however, 26 percent had moved to the largest city, Karachi, while 10 percent had moved to Lahore (data not shown).

The sex ratio among recent migrants (those who moved since 1965) was particularly low—107 compared to 143 among those who had moved more

Table 6.1 Numbers (in thousands) and percentages of male and female migrants ten years old and above, by migration status: Pakistan, 1973

Migration status and nature of move	Males		Females		Sex ratio (M/F X 100)
	No.	%	No.	%	
Migrant status					
Never moved	17,787.4	76.6	14,686.9	76.6	121
Moved before 1965	4,285.2	18.4	3,565.4	18.6	120
Moved after 1965	513.3	2.2	481.8	2.5	107
Moved before and after 1965	623.9	2.8	435.3	2.3	143
Total	23,209.8	100.0	19,169.4	100.0	121
Nature of move after 1965[a]					
Rural to urban	204.7	18.0	149.9	16.3	137
Urban to urban	444.0	39.1	352.2	38.4	126
Urban to rural	144.9	12.7	89.3	9.7	162
Rural to rural	343.7	30.2	325.7	35.5	105
Total	1,137.3	100.0	917.1	99.9	124

a. Includes all those who moved only after 1965 and those who moved before and after 1965.

Source: Data in this and subsequent tables are based on the author's tabulation from the HED Survey.

than once. The low sex ratio among recent migrants lends support to the suggestion of Afzal and Abbasi (1979) that female migration has increased in recent years. The markedly higher sex ratio among the twice-movers presents a more complex situation. This exceptionally mobile group perhaps represents a subgroup of achievement-oriented unattached males who have a greater tendency to migrate. This tentative idea is explored in some detail later.

In analyzing the characteristics of migrants by duration since migration (or date of migration), a researcher must deal with the obvious demographic changes that are likely to take place in a person's lifetime. Those who migrated a long time ago, for example, are obviously older at the time of the survey than those who migrated only recently. Similarly, earlier migrants are more likely to be widowed and divorced because they are older. Thus most of the demographic characteristics are confounded with the timing of migration, and the causal connections (for example, between marital status and migration) are impossible to disentangle, particularly for the earlier migrants. In the absence of adequate migration histories, one can only make tentative conclusions about the process.

MALE AND FEMALE MIGRANTS: SOME COMPARISONS

Recent migrants, particularly females who moved after 1965, were an exceptionally youthful group. Some 60 percent of the female migrants were below age 25 compared to 48 percent of the nonmigrant female population. A substantial proportion of the recent female migration seems to be related to marriage—68 percent of the female migrants were married compared to 57 percent of the nonmigrant females. The markedly low sex ratio of 63 among the recent married migrants further highlights the importance of marriage migration as an aspect of overall female migration in Pakistan.

Age has an intrinsic positive effect on widowhood, and earlier migration streams can be expected to have higher proportions of widowed men and women than recent streams. Divorce, however, cannot be expected to be intrinsically related with age (although older people have had a longer time in which to make a decision about divorce). Notably larger proportions of multiple movers (those with more than one move) were divorced compared with those who moved before 1965. The proportion of widowed men also seems to be exceptionally high among multiple movers, who have a sex ratio of 118 compared to 72 for nonmigrants and around 90 for other migrant groups. Whether divorce and widowhood themselves lead to higher mobility is an interesting question but one that cannot be answered with these data.

All groups of migrants had higher literacy rates than nonmigrants. The proportion of literate persons was only slightly higher for earlier migrants but was strikingly higher for recent migrants and particularly so for multiple movers. Only 37 percent of the male multiple movers were illiterate compared with 65 percent of nonmigrant males; the corresponding percentages for females were 62 percent and 89 percent. Similarly, the proportion of those with higher education (ten or more grades) was more than four times as high among multiple movers, both male and female, compared with their nonmigrant counterparts. One other point about male/female differences in education is worth noting: the lower discrepancy among all the migrant groups compared with nonmigrants, particularly among recent migrants. Sex differentials in education were smaller among recent migrants than nonmigrants as suggested by the sex ratios of 264 and 418 for the former and latter groups. Recent migrants (particularly females) are younger than nonmigrants, and their higher literacy rate may largely be a function of their youthfulness. Migration itself might have improved the chances for females to get an education, but this effect cannot be clearly demonstrated with cross-sectional data available for the present study.

While the rate of female labor-force participation was uniformly low for all groups, women who had moved more than once had a slightly higher rate than other groups—5 percent were currently employed compared with 4 percent of the nonmigrants. It should be noted that female employment rates reported in the HED Survey are much smaller than rates reported in the census or other studies in Pakistan.[3] A comparison of the sex ratios for different groups shows that while ratios for all groups were extremely high, the ratio among the multiple movers was relatively lower. The more mobile women were also more likely to be economically active, but a smaller proportion of the more mobile men were in the labor force compared to males in other groups. The unusual educational and employment patterns of the female multiple mover are examined in greater detail in the following sections.

EDUCATION AND ITS RELATION TO MIGRATION STATUS

The general pattern of higher literacy rates among migrants persisted after the age and marital status of women were controlled (data not shown). Within each of the marital status categories, migrants had a higher literacy rate than nonmigrants; the differences are particularly marked for those who moved both before and after 1965. Some 57 percent of urban single women who had moved at least twice were literate, compared with only 24 percent of single urban nonmigrants; the corresponding figures for married women were 29 percent and 4 percent.

Notably larger proportions of younger women were literate compared with older women in all categories except the single recent migrants and the single and divorced multiple movers. Higher literacy rates among younger women are consistent with expectations; while the exceptions present an interesting contrast to the general picture. Literacy rates of 60 percent among single and 83 percent among divorced multiple movers aged 45 and above are extremely high compared to 11 percent among single and 5 percent among divorced nonmigrants in this age group. The unusually high literacy rates among the migrant single and divorced older women are probably indicative of the exceptional circumstances that face these women. The older single and divorced women (45 and above) who do not have adequate economic support are likely to be under pressure to find employment. In some cases the search for work might involve migration, and here their literacy may prove of value. It should also be mentioned that restrictions on the movement of older women and their work participation are far less severe than in the case of young women.

Although the overall higher literacy rate of migrants was true for women of all marital categories, there were notable differences in magnitude between various groups. Single nonmigrant women had notably higher literacy rates than their married, widowed, and divorced counterparts. Among each of the migrant groups, however, a larger proportion of single women was literate compared with married and widowed women but not when compared with divorced women. The latter group of migrant women had an unusually high literacy rate. The phenomenon of higher literacy among single migrant women is interesting, since the majority of these women are very young. Given the Pakistani values regarding the physical protection of young daughters, most of the young single women are expected to have moved with their families. Thus the high mobility of the young, well-educated woman is highly likely to be related to her family's general socioeconomic level. The family must have been affluent and educated to be able (and *willing*) to educate the daughter. In some cases, the high mobility of such families might be related to the father's job, which might involve a transfer.

The pattern of higher literacy among migrant groups remained unchanged when the sample was divided by the rural or urban nature of current place of residence. Furthermore, the rural/urban differentials in literacy and education also varied by marital status. The differences were generally greater among nonmigrant compared to migrant groups. There were more than seven times as many literate married nonmigrant women in urban as compared to rural areas, for example; among the recent migrants, there were three times as many literate women in urban as compared to rural areas. Among widowed and divorced recent migrants, a notably larger proportion of rural women were literate compared to urban women, contrary to the general pattern. Some 21 percent of the rural widowed recent migrants were literate compared with 11 percent of their rural counterparts. Since the number of women in these categories is fairly small, however, the findings should be interpreted with caution. It is possible that some educated widowed and divorced women from urban areas or other rural areas migrated to rural areas, perhaps for employment.

Differences in educational level between migrants and nonmigrants were striking in the group of divorced women. Divorced migrant women had unusually high literacy rates in both rural and urban areas compared with nonmigrants. Furthermore, this was true of all groups of migrants, including the older migrants who moved before 1965; the literacy rate for earlier migrants was 48 percent compared to 58 percent for those who moved after 1965, 77 percent for the multiple movers and only 7 percent for nonmigrants. Within rural and urban areas, multiple movers again had notably higher literacy rates compared to other migrants and nonmigrants among the divorced women. Some 78 percent of urban and 77 percent of rural divorced multiple movers were literate compared to only 16 percent of urban and 5 percent of rural divorced nonmigrants. These findings strongly suggest that there is a positive relationship between migration and education for divorced women. It is not possible to assess the dynamics of this relationship from the available data, however. We do not know whether divorced women migrated in order to obtain further education, whether education itself was a factor in divorce, or whether educated divorced women migrated for some other reason such as employment. One must keep in mind while discussing this process that at least part of the movement of divorced women results from migration back to the parental home. Employment too, as we will see, could be a reason why women with certain educational levels migrated.

EMPLOYMENT AND MIGRATION

Table 6.2 presents data on percentages employed among women migrants and nonmigrants. Several subgroups of women were found to have distinctly higher employment rates than the average 4 or 5 percent. Literate women usually had higher participation rates than illiterate women for migrants and nonmigrants in all age and marital status categories, although the participation rates varied by educational level. Single women aged 25 to 44 and with ten or more grades of education had much higher participation rates than uneducated women. The employment rates among this subgroup were similar for migrants and nonmigrants except for the multiple movers. Unmarried multiple movers who were educated up to matriculation or more had a much higher participation rate (48 percent) compared with illiterate unmarried multiple movers (17 percent). Thus both migration and higher education seem to influence the employment of this subgroup. The employment patterns of the oldest single women (45 and above) were somewhat different—those with less than ten grades of education had consistently higher participation rates than the illiterate women, while the participation rate of those with ten or more grades was lower than that of the less educated group. Note that the participation rates of single women aged 25 and over are much higher than the participation rates for married women in the same age groups for both migrants and nonmigrants. Married women also had consistently lower employment rates compared with widowed and divorced women, although slightly more of the educated married women were in the labor force compared with the uneducated.

The widowed and divorced women constitute two groups who would theoretically be in greatest need of employment—particularly if the family structure that is expected to provide shelter and sustenance for these women is weak or absent. The last two panels of Table 6.2 show that participation rates were unusually high among widowed and divorced women who had less than ten grades of education and who were migrants, considering all ages together.[4] The higher participation rates for widowed and divorced migrants who had less than ten grades of education persist after age is controlled. Both the long-term migrants and those with multiple moves generally had significantly higher participation rates than the nonmigrants. Moreover, migrant women at the middle level of education had notably

Table 6.2 Percentages employed among migrant and nonmigrant women by age, marital status, and education: Pakistan, 1973

Age and migration status	Single			Married			Widowed			Divorced		
	Illit-erate	< Ma-tric	Ma-tric +	Illit-erate	< Ma-tric	Ma-tric +	Illit-erate	< Ma-tric	Ma-tric +	Illit-erate	< Ma-tric	Ma-tric +
Age 10–24												
Migrants												
Moved before 1965	4	3	10	3	6	5	5	44	8	2	37[a]	0
Moved after 1965	3	2	8	1	1	3	5	0[a]	7	0	0[a]	0
Moved before and after 1965	3	3	9	3	4	6	6	49	5	32[a]	47	4
Nonmigrants	3	1	8	4	3	8	3	17	9	8	14	61
Age 25–44												
Migrants												
Moved before 1965	7	24	37	2	4	12	14	27	21	10	37	11
Moved after 1965	8	47	39	3	6	9	19	13[a]	9	14	50[a]	0[a]
Moved before and after 1965	17	27	48	3	8	7	7	39	6	11	52	2
Nonmigrants	8	17	38	5	5	14	12	15	18	6	7	31
Age 45+												
Migrants												
Moved before 1965	20	38	17	3	8	8	5	20	6	8	52	2
Moved after 1965	31	68	40[a]	4	2	10	4	9	0[a]	24	0[a]	0[a]
Moved before and after 1965	16	30	18	2	13	6	3	35	6	0	55	0
Nonmigrants	8	37	29	5	9	10	4	20	8	6	39[a]	7[a]

All ages

Migrants

Moved before 1965	7	7	18	3	5	10	6	22	9	8	45	4
Moved after 1965	3	6	10	2	3	6	6	9	7	12	17[a]	0
Moved before and after 1965	5	7	13	3	8	7	3	37	6	11	52	2
Nonmigrants	4	2	10	5	5	11	5	18	11	7	13	25

a. Fewer than 10 unweighted cases in the cell.

higher participation rates than illiterate migrant women or those with higher levels of education. Among the divorced women who had moved more than once, for example, 52 percent of those with less than ten grades of education were employed compared with 11 percent of the illiterate and 2 percent of the women with ten or more grades.

In an earlier section I showed that unusually large proportions of divorced multiple movers were literate and had education up to ten or more grades. I also suggested that the higher mobility of this group is likely to be related to a need for employment. While this connection seems to be supported for divorced migrant women with medium education (less than ten grades), it does not hold true for the higher-educated divorced women. Assuming there were no reporting biases that influenced the results for the less and more educated women, it is possible that divorced women with medium levels of education belong to families that cannot support them financially and therefore endorse (or tolerate) their employment. The more educated women, on the contrary, might belong to more affluent families and thus do not need to work. These findings must be considered tentative, however, keeping in view the small numbers of educated widowed and divorced women.

Note that mobility was very high among all divorced women, particularly among migrants to urban areas (Table 6.3). Some 69 percent of all divorced women in urban areas and 49 percent of those in rural areas were migrants. The predominance of migrants among divorced women with ten or more grades of education is striking indeed in both urban and rural areas. Of all divorced women who had 10 or more grades of education, 95 percent in urban and 97 percent in rural areas were migrants. While the proportion of migrants was exceptionally high among the highly educated women, their mobility does not seem to be necessarily related to the search for employment. The greatest proportions employed among divorced women in both urban and rural areas were those with medium education (less than ten grades). There is also a clear connection between educational level and employment rate for migrant as well as nonmigrant single women aged 25 to 44 in urban areas (data not shown).

The positive association between education and migration was again supported by data on proportion of migrants in the educational and marital status categories shown in Table 6.3. The proportion of migrants was about twice as high among those with less than ten grades of education compared with the illiterate population within each of the marital status categories; it was even higher among those with ten or more grades of education. Among rural women with ten or more grades of education, 58 percent were migrants compared with only 15 percent of migrants among the illiterate group. It should be recalled here that 78 percent of migrants after 1965 to rural areas came from other rural areas, while 22 percent came from urban areas. It seems that a greater proportion of families with highly

Table 6.3 Percentages of migrants among females ten years old and above by marital status, education, and place of residence: Pakistan, 1973

Marital status and place of residence	Educational level			
	Illiterate	Less than 10 grades	10 or more grades	Total
Single	7	15	31	10
Urban	13	17	30	17
Rural	5	10	36	6
Married	27	55	65	29
Urban	53	62	68	55
Rural	19	37	58	20
Widowed	34	68	88	36
Urban	60	72	83	61
Rural	24	57	90	26
Divorced	38	73	97	55
Urban	54	79	95	69
Rural	34	66	97	49
Total	22	27	51	23
Urban	44	32	48	41
Rural	16	18	58	16

educated females (ten or more grades) were mobile compared with families with illiterate women or women with lower education. In the Pakistani context, the educational level of the women in the family can be treated as a good proxy for the family's socioeconomic status. These findings thus imply that migration to rural areas is exceptionally high among families of higher socioeconomic status. Among the divorced and widowed women, however, many of whom are employed in rural areas, migration might not involve the whole family. Some women might have moved on their own, although we do not expect their numbers to be large given the Pakistani sociocultural context.

SUMMARY AND CONCLUSION

The same proportion (23 percent) of males and females in Pakistan had migrated at least once during their lifetime. Most migration had taken place before 1965, and only 5 percent of the men and women had changed their district of residence during the eight-year period before the 1973 HED Survey. The overall sex ratio for migrants as well as nonmigrants was 121. Among recent migrants, however, the sex ratio was only 107— suggesting either that recent migrant women were being reported more accurately than before or that female migration had increased in recent years.

Three patterns of migration seem to typify the interdistrict movement of adult Pakistani women aged ten and above. Numerically, the predominant pattern is that of a married woman moving to another district with her family. Some 29 percent of all married women in the country had migrated at least once during their lifetime. Considerable migration took place on account of marriage itself, as shown by a high proportion of married women among migrants compared to nonmigrants—75 percent and 57 percent respectively.

The second pattern is that of a higher propensity to move among older single women, particularly those aged 45 and above. Some 64 percent of single women aged 45 and above were migrants compared to only 10 percent of single women in all age groups. Among single women aged 25 or more, the labor-force participation rate was several times higher than among married women. This proportion was true for migrants and nonmigrants. The disproportionately large labor-force participation rate among older single women perhaps points to certain changes in social structure that necessitate their employment and induce many of them to migrate in search of work.

The third pattern of migration relates to divorced women, particularly the ones who have achieved a high level of education. The proportion of migrants was noticeably higher among the divorced women compared to married as well as widowed women—55 percent of divorced women were migrants compared to 29 percent of married and 36 percent of widowed women. While the mobility of divorced women might be related to the incidence of divorce itself, education seemed to exert an exceptionally strong influence on their migration. Among the divorced women with ten or more grades of education, 97 percent were migrants; the corresponding figure for illiterate women was 38 percent. Thus both marital status and education seem to be important causes of migration of Pakistani women.

The positive relationship between literacy and migration was observed for all marital status categories and for all ages. This relationship was particularly strong for single and divorced women in all migrant groups and particularly the multiple movers. Literacy and level of education seem to have a strong relationship with multiple movers. Women who had moved both before and after 1965 had a literacy rate over three times as high as that of nonmigrant women in the country—38 percent and 11 percent respectively. The positive relationship persisted after age and marital status were controlled. Moreover, the subgroup of twice-movers to urban areas had a higher literacy rate (50 percent) than the nonmigrant urban population (34 percent). The greater mobility of the educated women might be associated with job-related transfers of fathers or husbands. In addition, there might be other factors related to educational attainment such as intention to look for a job. The Pakistani female migrant's level of education in many cases can serve as a proxy for the socioeconomic status of her family. I believe that most female migration is taking place in the form of family migration, and, further, that women are accompanying the family as daughters, wives, sisters, or mothers of the household head (who is often a male). Some exceptions to this pattern are probably represented by the migration of older single women and educated divorced women.

Migrants as a whole were not more likely to be in the labor force than nonmigrants. Specific subgroups of migrant women, however, were employed in much larger proportions than nonmigrants: single women aged 25 to 44 in all migrant groups who had some education; single women aged 45 and over; divorced women in general and divorced women with medium levels of education (less than ten grades); and widowed women with medium levels of education in the rural areas. The positive relationship between education and employment among both migrant and nonmigrant women probably indicates both the greater likelihood of women with some education finding jobs and the greater likelihood of their employment being reported more accurately.

In summary, then, the average migrant woman in Pakistan does not seem to represent the poorest and most illiterate section of the population. Most migration seems to be a response to opportunities for which the better educated are searching. Certain subgroups of widowed, divorced, and single migrant women might be faced with more difficult circumstances than women who move with their families. Although the women in these subgroups constitute a small proportion of all migrant women, they need special attention and further study.

NOTES

1. The district is an administrative unit. There were a total of 50 districts in Pakistan according to the census of 1972.

2. If one's objective is to assess the total magnitude of migration in a population, then those under age ten should also be included. An attempt to do this has been made by Afzal and Abbasi (1979).

3. The 1961 census, for example, using a reference period of one week similar to the HED Survey, reported a participation rate of 10 percent. The National Impact Survey (1968) and the Pakistan Fertility Survey (1975) reported participation rates of 19 percent and 17 percent respectively for currently married women who were working at the time of the survey. Thus the rate provided by the HED Survey seems to reflect underreporting of female labor-force participation.

4. The patterns discussed in this paragraph do not generally hold true for recent migrants (those who moved after 1965). Since this group contained only a few women (unweighted $N = 33$ for widows and $N = 6$ for divorced women), their patterns cannot be discussed in detail.

BIBLIOGRAPHY

Afzal, Mohammad
  1967   Migration to urban areas in Pakistan. In *Proceedings of the Conference of the International Union for the Scientific Study of Population,* Sydney. Liege: International Union for the Scientific Study of Population.

Afzal, Mohammad, and Nasreen Abbasi
  1979   *Urbanization and Internal Migration in Pakistan 1951–1973.* Islamabad: Pakistan Institute of Development Economics.

Belokvenitsky, Vyacheslav
  1974   The urbanization process and the social structure of the urban population in Pakistan. *Asian Survey* 14(3):244–57.

Board of Economic Enquiry, NWFP (BEE)
  1977   *Factors Influencing Migration to Urban Areas in Pakistan: A Case Study of Peshawar City.* Research Report No. 102. Islamabad: Pakistan Institute of Development Economics.

Burki, Shahid Javed
  1973a   Rapid population growth and urbanization: the case of Pakistan. *Pakistan Economic and Social Review* 11(3):239–75.
  1973b   Migration, urbanization and politics in Pakistan. In W. Howard Wriggins and James F. Guyot (eds.), *Population, Politics and the Future of Southern Asia.* New York: Columbia University Press.
  1974   Development of towns: the Pakistan experience. *Asian Survey* 14(8):751.

Koo, Hagen
  1978   Rural-urban migration and social mobility in Third World metropolises: a cross-national study. *Sociological Quarterly* 19:292–303.

Krotki, Karol J.
  1963   Temporariness of urban migration estimated from age distributions in large and small towns of East and West Pakistan. In *Proceedings of the Pakistan Statistical Association,* Vol. 2. Lahore: Institute of Statistics, Punjab University.

Mujahid, G. B. S.
  1975   Rural-urban migration, urban underemployment and earning differentials in Pakistan. *Weltwirtschaftliches Archiv* 3(3):585–98.

Naeem, Jamila, and Nasra Mahbub
  1969   A study of the characteristics of migration in Lulliani. *Pakistan Journal of Family Planning* 3(2):17–26.

Social Sciences Research Center (SSRC).
  1977   *Factors Influencing Migration to Urban Areas in Pakistan: A Case Study of Gujranwala City.* Research Report No. 101. Islamabad: Pakistan Institute of Development Economics.

Chapter 7

Female Rural-to-Urban Migration in Peninsular Malaysia

Siew-Ean Khoo
Peter Pirie

The migration of women in Peninsular Malaysia has not been the focus of much attention. Until recently, the proportion of women in migration streams in the peninsula has been slight and of little economic significance for both historical and cultural reasons. Peninsular Malaysia historically had an unbalanced, heavily male sex ratio because of the influx of male immigrants from China and India in the last century and the earlier part of this century. Moreover, women have traditionally been more restricted to the home than men and their migrations normally occurred at marriage or with their husbands and families. Consequently, migration research has focused on either male migrants and heads of household or the migration process itself and its relationship with urbanization and other aspects of socioeconomic development considered to be more useful in planning and policy-making. More recently, however, because of government policies and the effects of development, the migration of women to towns and cities seems to be increasing and may become an important issue in the process of social change in Malaysia.

This chapter examines the female component of migration patterns in Peninsular Malaysia both past and present. In an effort to define the causes of female migration, we examine the demographic and socioeconomic characteristics of a recent cohort of female rural-to-urban migrants —those who migrated during 1965–70, for whom detailed data are available from the 1970 census—and review several studies of migration in Malaysia and the implications of recent economic policies. Finally, we discuss the urgent priorities for research action in this area.

THE NATIONAL MIGRATION SYSTEM

The demographic history of Peninsular Malaysia can be broadly divided into two periods separated by World War II. Before the war, population growth and distribution in the peninsula were largely determined by the

Table 7.1 Sex ratios (males per 100 females) by community group and state: Peninsular Malaysia, 1911–70

Group and state	1911	1921	1931	1947	1957	1970
Community group						
Malays	112.5	104.2	102.8	99.0	98.7	98.7
Chinese	533.3	281.9	205.9	122.7	108.0	102.1
Indians	324.8	235.8	193.6	145.4	134.0	113.4
Others	114.0	118.4	131.0	112.2	164.1	124.0
Total	232.4	154.3	142.3	112.2	106.5	101.0
State						
Johore	na	193.9	177.8	120.7	110.6	100.5
Kedah	na	135.5	124.0	109.2	105.3	101.0
Kelantan	na	103.7	103.9	100.2	98.6	98.0
Malacca	na	144.6	128.7	101.6	98.3	95.4
Negri Sembilan	206.0	202.0	173.7	116.8	108.7	100.6
Pahang	155.4	151.0	141.4	117.6	111.0	107.4
Penang	na	150.4	137.5	109.5	106.0	99.5
Perak	229.8	172.4	154.3	114.0	106.7	100.0
Perlis	na	112.7	111.9	106.8	101.6	100.0
Selangor	302.3	199.6	159.1	118.6	110.4	105.1
Trengganu	na	100.6	105.6	99.4	99.0	98.3

na—not available.

Source: Chander (1977: vol. 1, tables 2.25 and 2.26).

immigration of large numbers of Chinese, Indians, and others from the surrounding countries who arrived in Malaya, as it was then known, in search of economic opportunities in the expanding tin and rubber industries. The indigenous Malay population was mainly engaged in agriculture and resided in rural villages while the growth of towns was due primarily to the influx of Chinese and Indian immigrants who were engaged in the commercial and mining sectors. Most of the immigrants were male, as reflected in the sex ratios according to the prewar censuses (Table 7.1). The 1921 and 1931 censuses recorded balanced sex ratios in only two states on the east coast, Kelantan and Trengganu, which were least affected by the immigration of Chinese and Indians, most of whom settled on the west coast near the tin mines and rubber estates. Among the Chinese and Indians in the prewar years males heavily outnumbered females. After World War II and the end of the immigration era in 1947, the imbalance between the sexes was progressively reduced. By 1970, balanced sex ratios had been attained for all states and community groups. During the period from 1947 to 1970, natural increase became the major cause of population growth, and the spatial distribution of the population was determined mainly by internal migration.

Data on internal migration before 1960 were very limited and quite incomplete. The only information relevant to the internal movement of the population recorded in the censuses up to 1957 pertained to place of birth and place of enumeration. Thus only lifetime migrants could be estimated —and multiple moves and migrants who returned to their places of origin would not be included. The figures in Table 7.2 on lifetime net migrants should be observed with these limitations in mind. They are presented primarily to show the basic trends and direction of interstate migration flows. Questions on the respondent's length of stay at the present locality and on previous place of residence were added to the 1970 census. It then became possible to estimate the magnitude and direction of migration flows during specific periods, in addition to estimating lifetime net migration.

The estimates of lifetime net interstate migrants in Table 7.2 indicate that the states of Selangor and Pahang have been destinations of a large proportion of migrants. Historically they have also been the focus of Malay migrants, but between 1957 and 1970 the volume of in-migration has increased tremendously in response to the government's efforts in rural development and the expansion of industries that have been concentrated in these two states. According to the 1970 population census report, the high sex ratios found in 1970 in these two states (Table 7.1) reflect the large number of males in the predominantly Malay migrant stream.

Estimates of male and female interstate lifetime migrants for each community group according to the 1957 and 1970 censuses are presented in Table 7.3. The number of lifetime migrants increased for all community groups between 1957 and 1970; the increase was noticeably greater for females than for males, however, as indicated by the decrease in the sex ratios of about 3 points for Malay and Chinese migrants and 2.4 points for all migrants. Among the Chinese and Indian migrants, the sex ratios have dropped below 100, indicating a majority of female migrants. Because of the higher proportion of Malays in the population and in the migrant streams and the higher geographic mobility of Malay men, however, males still formed the majority of lifetime interstate migrants up to 1970.

By contrast, there were more female than male intrastate migrants. According to the 1970 census, 828,093 males and 838,613 females moved within the state, giving a migrant sex ratio of 98.7. It appears that Ravenstein's law—that females are more migratory than males in short-distance moves whereas males tend to outnumber females in long-distance moves —holds true for Malaysia (Chander 1977:372). Only 21.6 percent of the intrastate migrants moved to urban destinations, however, compared with 38.0 percent of interstate migrants. This finding indicates that before 1970

Table 7.2 Lifetime net migrants, by community group and state: 1931–70 (in thousands)

State	Malays				Chinese				Indians	
	1931	1947	1957	1970	1931	1947	1957	1970	1957	1970
Johore	14.2	5.5	8.0	-5.4	4.6	12.0	4.4	-0.8	2.7	1.0
Kedah	10.7	10.1	1.9	-15.0	3.1	5.0	1.8	-7.6	2.2	-2.6
Kelantan	-8.4	-4.5	-17.0	-48.3	0.2	0.5	0	1.0	0	-0.5
Malacca	-12.7	-17.6	-20.0	-32.2	-1.5	-3.1	-3.7	-6.7	-1.0	-0.8
Negri Sembilan	-1.6	-4.9	-5.2	-17.2	1.7	4.5	6.4	-5.9	1.6	1.5
Pahang	2.5	4.6	12.1	46.1	0.9	4.1	4.1	13.7	1.8	5.9
Penang	-19.7	-15.0	-18.8	-12.4	-8.4	-11.0	-8.2	-6.7	-3.5	-0.5
Perak	4.1	-2.1	-5.2	-40.4	2.4	-5.5	-17.3	-53.7	-8.0	-19.8
Perlis	1.0	2.0	2.8	2.2	0.4	1.4	1.6	0.6	-0.2	0.2
Selangor	11.7	9.9	40.1	119.2	1.7	-5.1	9.8	64.1	4.2	15.0
Trengganu	na	-0.4	1.2	3.2	0.4	0.7	1.1	2.1	0.3	0.6

na—not available.

Sources: 1931, 1947: Report 14, 1957 Population Census, table 4.8; 1957: 1957 Population Census State Reports, No. 2-12, table 9; 1970: Chander (1977: vol. 1, table 5.11).

Table 7.3 Lifetime interstate migrants by community group and sex: 1957 and 1970 (in thousands)

Community group	1957			1970		
	Male	Female	Sex ratio	Male	Female	Sex ratio
Malays	136.4	115.9	117.7	270.4	237.1	114.0
Chinese	91.4	91.1	100.3	155.0	159.3	97.3
Indians	34.3	34.3	100.2	62.1	63.1	98.4
Others	6.1	6.1	99.8	3.2	3.4	95.7
Total	268.1	247.3	108.4	490.8	462.9	106.0

Source: Chander (1977: vol. 1, table 5.13).

the female intrastate migration occurred mainly in rural areas and could be related to marriage and, moreover, that the magnitude of female migration to urban areas for economic reasons might be relatively small.

URBANIZATION AND RURAL-TO-URBAN MIGRATION

The pace of urbanization by state and community group is shown in Table 7.4. Urbanization proceeded slowly before 1947. Between 1911 and 1947, the percentage of the population residing in towns of 10,000 persons and over increased from 10.7 to 15.9. That percentage rose to 26.5 in 1957, but by 1970 it had only increased to 28.8. The total urban population thus grew at 3.2 percent per year for the 1957–70 intercensal period. This rate of growth is not much higher than expected natural increase so that rural-urban migration played a lesser role in urban growth.

The slow rate of urbanization has been discussed by Hirschman (1976) in an analysis of population redistribution in Peninsular Malaysia between 1957 and 1970. He noted that the average growth rate of the largest towns (75,000 population and over) was below the national average, although the growth rate of towns of 10,000 to 74,999 was slightly above the average. Hirschman concluded that opportunities in urban areas have not been so great or rural conditions so poor as to push significant numbers of people to the cities. An examination of migrant flows between 1965 and 1970 shows that only 9 percent of all migrants aged ten and above moved from a rural to an urban area (Table 7.5). Some twenty percent were urban-to-urban migrants while 32 percent moved from urban to rural areas and 39 percent moved within rural areas.

Similar observations were made by Young (1977), who also used the 1970 census data to estimate migration flows during the 1965–70 period. Her examination of data on migrants of all ages showed that only 3.7 percent of migrants were rural-to-urban and that the largest flows were from

Table 7.4 Percentage of population residing in towns of 10,000 persons and over, by state and community group: 1911–70

State and group	1911	1921	1931	1947	1957	1970
State						
Johore	na	10.1	10.9	15.4	21.8	26.2
Kedah	na	3.4	4.3	8.2	13.3	12.5
Kelantan	4.4	3.5	4.1	5.1	9.8	15.1
Malacca	17.0	20.0	20.4	22.8	24.0	25.0
Negri Sembilan	na	9.7	9.2	13.2	17.8	21.5
Pahang	na	na	na	na	22.2	18.9
Penang	37.3	41.8	47.7	52.9	56.7	50.9
Perak	11.0	13.3	14.4	17.1	25.0	27.6
Perlis	na	na	na	na	na	na
Selangor	15.9	23.0	24.8	32.7	43.0	45.4
Trengganu	9.1	8.1	7.8	11.9	19.0	26.9
Total	10.7	14.0	15.1	15.9	26.5	28.8
Community group						
Malays	na	na	na	7.3	11.2	14.9
Chinese	na	na	na	31.1	44.7	47.4
Indians	na	na	na	25.8	30.6	34.7
Others	na	na	na	46.2	49.3	40.8
Total	na	na	na	15.9	26.5	28.7

na—not available.
Source: Chander (1977: vol. 1, table 2.9); Community Groups, p. 33.

urban to rural areas and between rural areas. Young suggested that the government's land settlement schemes in rural areas were the main reason for the high rates of urban-to-rural and rural-to-rural migration. These programs appear to be rather successful in retaining and redistributing people in rural areas as well as in attracting considerable numbers of people from urban areas to business and employment opportunities in the villages.

Because rural-to-urban migrants made up only a small proportion of the total number of migrants in the 1960s, one cannot expect the number of female rural-to-urban migrants in Peninsular Malaysia, at least until 1970, to be very large. It is estimated that only 36,500 women moved from rural to urban areas between 1965 and 1970. According to Table 7.5, fewer than 50 percent of the migrants in all streams during the period 1965–70 were women (except among Chinese rural-to-urban migrants, of whom 51 percent were women). More than half of the Malay female rural-

Table 7.5 Five-year migrants (1965–70), by community group and strata

Community group	Rural-urban	Urban-urban	Urban-rural	Rural-rural	Total
No. of migrants aged 10 and above (in thousands)					
Malays	42.0	76.2	142.9	244.8	505.9
Chinese	28.3	78.5	104.6	65.9	277.2
Indians	8.8	23.8	44.0	39.1	115.6
Total[a]	79.4	180.8	292.9	351.3	904.3
% distribution by strata					
Malays	8	15	28	49	100
Chinese	10	28	38	24	100
Indians	8	21	38	34	100
Total[a]	9	20	32	39	100
% female among migrants					
Malays	43	42	47	48	46
Chinese	51	49	47	45	48
Indians	46	44	49	49	48
Total[a]	46	45	47	47	47

Note: Migrants whose previous residence was abroad, unknown, or in Sabah or Sarawak were excluded. Settlements having 10,000 or more population are considered to be urban.

a. Includes other community groups not shown here.

Source: Tabulations from 1970 Census Sample Tape.

to-urban migrants moved to urban areas in the states of Selangor, Johore, and Perak. There were more Malay males than females migrating to cities in these states, however, as shown by the high sex ratios (between 116 and 145). Urban destinations favored by Chinese female migrants are in the three most urbanized states of Selangor, Penang, and Perak. In contrast to the sex distribution of Malay migrants to the cities in Selangor and Perak, Chinese migrants to urban areas in these two states are predominantly female (sex ratios of 94 and 56 respectively). In his study of migration and labor absorption in metropolitan urban Selangor, Narayanan (1977) reported that there were numerous Chinese women migrants, many of whom were active in the labor force, although he also found that migrants to Selangor were predominantly male.

Most of the Chinese female migrants were between 15 and 30 years old at the time of migration. Among Malays, however, male migrants outnumbered female migrants in this age group, particularly those between 15 and 19 years old. Although the data indicate that Malay women above age 60 are highly mobile, their sample size is too small to affect the overall sex ratio. Because the rural-to-urban migration stream is 53 percent Malay and 36 percent Chinese, males still make up more than 50 percent of all rural-to-urban migrants.

Notwithstanding the small rural-to-urban migration flow and its male majority, the steady decline in the urban sex ratios between 1957 and 1970 is an indication that the proportion of female migrants has increased. Part of the decline may be traced also to the rectification, through natural increase, of the previous imbalance of the sexes due to the predominantly male immigration before 1947. The comparatively low sex ratio of the Chinese in the urban areas is consistent, however, with the female majority in the Chinese rural-to-urban migrant stream and the predominantly male urban-to-rural migration stream.

Since 1970, industrial development has been concentrated in a few designated zones in the country, particularly around the capital city of Kuala Lumpur in Selangor state and parts of Penang and Johore. Although proximity to a pool of low-cost, high-quality labor influenced the location of these zones, the rapid growth of light manufacturing industries there and the increased demand for labor have stimulated migration from adjacent states. Because these industries have a need particularly for female labor they may have stimulated female rural-to-urban migration in recent years (see Chapter 11). Although national data on the magnitude and patterns of female migration after 1970 are not yet available, studies have shown that female employment in industry has increased rapidly (Blake 1975; Chew 1977) and that many of the women may be rural-to-urban migrants. Because the government's New Economic Policy requires 30 percent of employees in large businesses to be Malay, factory agents have been known to go to the villages to recruit young Malay women in order to meet the quota, thereby encouraging their migration to the cities.

The changes brought about by recent social and economic policies may mean a change in patterns of migration. With increasing female education in the 1960s and the expansion of employment opportunities for women in industry in the 1970s, male dominance of migration may now be a pattern of the past as women begin to migrate to the cities by themselves in search of better social and economic prospects.

CHARACTERISTICS OF FEMALE RURAL-TO-URBAN MIGRANTS

There are few references to rural-to-urban migrant women in Peninsular Malaysia. Although data on the age distribution of female migrants to Kuala Lumpur and four other cities are available from a paper by Pryor (1976), his sample (from the 1966–67 West Malaysia Family Survey) is limited to married women of reproductive age. The following examination of the characteristics of women who migrated during the 1965–70 period is based on data from the 1970 census, the latest source of nationwide migration data. Our analysis is limited to persons aged ten and over who have been residing in their present location for less than five years and whose previous place of residence is another town, village, or administrative district in Peninsular Malaysia. Migrants from Sabah, Sarawak, and abroad are excluded, as are those who moved within the same town, village, or administrative district. Towns and districts with 10,000 or more persons are classified as urban; the rest are classified as rural. Table 7.6 compares the demographic and socioeconomic characteristics of the 1965–70 cohort of female rural-to-urban migrants with those of all women in urban and rural areas in 1970.

AGE AND MARITAL STATUS

Migrants have a younger age distribution than both the urban and rural female population. About 77 percent of the female rural-to-urban migrants above age ten in all three community groups were between 10 and 30 years old when they migrated. Only about 57 percent of the overall female population ten years old or over are in the same group. There is, therefore, a disproportionate number of young women in the migrant stream.

Slightly less than half the female migrants were married in 1970. There is a higher percentage of married female migrants than male migrants, however, because the age at marriage is higher for males than for females generally, but the migrant age distribution is more or less the same for both sexes. The largest proportion of single women is found among the Chinese migrants; nearly 52 percent of Chinese female migrants but only 44 percent of Malay female migrants are single. There is a higher percentage of widows among Malay and Indian migrants, however. Presumably older women migrate either because they have children or relatives living in the urban areas or to engage in petty trading in the urban marketplace. Such activity is fairly common among older Malay and Indian women who need a source of income to support themselves.

EDUCATION

About 22 percent of the female migrants aged ten and above lack formal education; by comparison, only about 6 percent of male migrants have no education. The proportion of migrant women without education is lower than the proportion of urban women, however, and less than half the proportion of rural women in the same category. There is also a higher proportion of migrant women with postsecondary education compared with all urban or rural women in 1970, although the percentage of migrants

Table 7.6 Percentage distribution of female rural-to-urban migrants (1965–70) and urban and rural women (1970), by selected demographic and socioeconomic variables

Characteristic	Migrants				All women	
	Malays	Chinese	Indians	Total	Urban	Rural
Age[a]						
10–19	43.2	44.6	50.1	44.5	34.9	36.1
20–29	33.8	36.0	21.3	33.1	23.4	20.8
30–39	11.1	9.3	8.8	10.1	15.9	16.0
40–49	5.3	3.5	5.0	4.8	10.7	11.6
50–59	2.8	3.1	13.8	4.1	7.7	8.1
60+	3.9	3.5	1.3	3.4	7.5	7.5
Marital status						
Never married	43.8	51.9	46.3	47.4	45.1	37.1
Married	46.8	45.7	46.3	46.2	45.0	51.6
Widowed	8.3	2.1	6.3	5.6	9.0	9.9
Divorced/separated	1.1	0.3	1.3	0.8	0.9	1.3
Level of education						
No schooling	20.8	22.8	28.8	22.3	29.5	47.2
Some primary	26.3	30.1	27.5	28.1 }	42.7	42.1
Completed primary	24.4	22.8	20.0	23.3		
Some secondary	21.1	15.2	20.0	18.5	16.4	7.8
Completed secondary	5.3	4.5	2.5	4.8	9.9	2.5
Postsecondary	2.2	4.5	1.3	2.5	1.5	0.4
Activity						
In labor force						
Employed	21.6	32.5	15.0	25.3	21.0	30.9
Unemployed	2.8	3.1	1.3	2.7	3.0	1.9
Not in labor force						
Looking after house	52.9	42.9	66.3	50.3	48.5	45.5
Student	19.4	13.5	8.8	15.9	20.1	15.2
Other	2.8	8.0	7.5	5.3	5.8	4.7
Not stated	0.6	na	1.3	0.4	1.5	1.8
Distribution of labor force by:						
Industry						
Agriculture, fishing	2.3	na	na	1.0	3.3	28.9
Agricultural processing	2.3	2.9	7.7	2.9	6.6	40.4
Mining	na	na	na	na	0.7	1.8
Manufacturing	15.9	34.0	na	23.8	17.4	4.9
Construction	na	na	na	na	1.3	0.2
Utilities	na	na	na	na	0.3	na
Commerce	6.8	8.7	7.7	8.3	11.1	3.6
Transport, communication	2.3	na	na	1.0	1.4	0.1
Service	54.5	40.8	76.9	49.0	41.0	7.1

Table 7.6 *(continued)*

Characteristic	Migrants				All women	
	Malays	Chinese	Indians	Total	Urban	Rural
Other	12.5	5.8	na	8.3	6.3	8.5
Not stated/looking for job	3.4	7.8	7.7	5.8	10.6	4.4
Occupation						
Professional, technical	20.5	6.8	7.7	12.6	12.0	2.6
Administrative	na	na	na	na	0.2	na
Clerical	5.7	4.9	na	4.9	11.7	1.1
Sales	5.7	5.8	na	5.8	8.5	3.4
Service	35.2	30.1	76.9	35.4	22.3	3.6
Agriculture	3.4	2.9	7.7	3.4	9.0	69.1
Production, transport	14.8	36.9	na	24.8	20.2	7.2
Other	11.4	6.8	na	8.3	5.5	8.5
Not stated/looking for job	3.4	5.8	7.7	4.9	10.6	4.4

a. Migrants are grouped according to age at time of migration. However, their distribution with regard to the other demographic and socioeconomic variables is that at the time of the 1970 census.

na—not available.

Sources: Tabulations from 1970 Population Census Sample Tape; Chander (1977).

who have completed secondary school falls between the percentages for urban and rural women. On average, it appears that migrant women are better educated than nonmigrant women in the urban or rural areas, indicating a rural-to-urban brain drain similar to that observed in many other developing countries among male (and sometimes female) migrants. It is possible, however, that some of the female migrants with postsecondary education may be enrolled in universities or technical colleges in the urban areas and their migration may not yet be permanent.

Chinese female migrants are the best educated and Indian migrants the least well educated. The proportion of migrants with postsecondary education is highest among the Chinese and lowest among the Indians; the proportion of migrants with no education is lowest among the Malays.

WOMEN IN THE LABOR FORCE

Half of all female rural-to-urban migrants reported their main activity as "looking after house" even though they are better educated than the average woman. This is slightly more than the percentage of urban and rural women who claim to be housewives and implies that the majority of female rural-to-urban migrants do not move autonomously for economic reasons but with their families. Only 25 percent of the migrant women are employed whereas 3 percent are unemployed and 16 percent are students (Table 7.6). The percentage employed is slightly higher among migrant women than among urban women. It is highest in the rural areas where many women are employed in agriculture. There is little difference in the unemployment rates of migrant women and all urban women. A higher percentage of all urban women compared to migrant women are classified as students.

There is also variation in the activity of female migrants in the three community groups. A higher proportion of Chinese female migrants are employed. This is not surprising considering that Chinese female migrants are better educated and that, for many of them, migration may be related to employment opportunities. The proportion of students is highest among the Malays, a reflection of the increasingly large numbers of rural Malay girls who are being given opportunities for higher education in institutions concentrated in the cities. Indian female migrants have the highest proportion "looking after house" and the lowest proportion of students among the three community groups. This pattern is consistent with the lower level of education of Indian migrants compared with Malay and Chinese migrants.

Among the female migrants who were in the labor force in 1970, nearly half were employed in the service sector and one quarter were employed in manufacturing. Because the service sector includes government service, the distribution of migrants by occupation may give a better indication of the types of jobs usually held by female migrants. According to the classification by occupation, 35.4 percent of female migrants are service workers: domestic help, waitresses, hairdressers, and members of the police and armed forces. Some 60 percent of all female service workers in the urban areas are employed as domestic help, however, and the proportion among female rural-to-urban migrants is likely to be about the same or even higher. The proportion of service workers is certainly higher among migrant women than among all urban women: 35.4 percent of employed migrants compared to 22.3 percent of employed urban women. Although their number is small, the Indian female migrants in the labor force are very much concentrated in the service sector. The largest proportion of employed Malay female migrants are also in this sector.

Compared to Malay and Indian female migrants in 1970, a higher proportion of Chinese female migrants was employed as production workers in manufacturing. The implementation in 1970 of the government's New Economic Policy, which requires private industry to employ a quota of Malays, is likely to have increased the proportion of Malay female migrants employed in the manufacturing sector, however—especially with the recent active recruitment of Malay girls from rural areas for factory employment.

Over 20 percent of Malay female migrants in the labor force are professional or technical workers, compared with about 7 percent among Chinese and Indian migrants and 12 percent among all urban women. This category includes teachers, nurses and other medical workers who are mostly government employees, as well as other professionals who have college and university degrees. About 60 percent of female professional and technical workers in urban areas are schoolteachers; approximately 20 percent are nurses.

The labor-force participation of female rural-to-urban migrants in Peninsular Malaysia differs from that in many other countries where migrant women are poor and take menial jobs to support themselves and their families. About half the Malaysian migrant women appear to be housewives who accompany their husbands to the cities; these women are not economically active and may even employ "mother's helpers," usually teenage girls from their own villages, to help them with housework and child care. Among the migrants who are in the labor force, 12 percent (20 percent among the Malays) hold professional jobs, an indication of their high level of education. The largest proportions, however, are still employed in the service and manufacturing sectors (35 and 25 percent respectively).

This profile of the female rural-to-urban migrant in Peninsular Malaysia applies to the 1965–70 female migrant cohort for whom data are available from the 1970 census. Characteristics of the more recent female migrants may differ from those of the 1965–70 cohort as more Malay women move into the cities to take jobs in industry. An analysis of the characteristics of migrants who moved to the cities after 1970 will have to await data from the 1980 census.

CAUSES AND CONSEQUENCES

Some insights into the causes of female rural-to-urban migration in Malaysia were given by Provencher (1975) in his paper on Malay perceptions of migration. In the past, young Malay women were kept in the house in the rural areas to ensure their virtue and also because their labor in agricultural and household work was needed. Moreover, there was little opportunity for young unmarried women to find work in the towns and cities unless they were well educated. There was also some apprehension among rural parents that unless the girls in the cities were properly supervised, they would lapse into evil ways and have trouble finding a respectable husband. These attitudes help to explain the small proportion of Malay female migrants prior to 1970.

While young Malay women are discouraged from venturing outside the village, older married women have traditionally been mobile for both economic and social reasons. These women traveled between villages and

towns to buy and sell produce and handicrafts and to visit friends and relatives. The large percentage of widows among Malay migrants in the 1965–
70 rural-to-urban migration cohort confirms the higher mobility of older
women and may also imply that short-term visits sometimes become permanent moves.

Unlike young women, young Malay men are encouraged to *merantau*—
that is, to undertake a long journey or period of wandering in order to gain
experience in the world. This custom is likely to result in permanent
migration when the young man finds a job or decides to marry and settle
down away from his home village.

With these different attitudes toward the movement of male and female
young adults, it is not surprising that migrants in Peninsular Malaysia
have been predominantly male. The situation in the rural and urban
areas, which has been traditionally unfavorable to female rural-to-urban
migration, is now beginning to change, however.

According to Provencher, the use of machines and other laborsaving
techniques in rice-growing and rubber-tapping in recent years has meant
that the demand for female agricultural labor has declined. This development may enable them to stay in school longer until they qualify for upper
secondary or postsecondary education, which then requires them to move
to educational institutions in the towns and cities. Women who attend
school in town find that they have the necessary education for urban work
and tend to remain and seek employment there.

In the past, employment opportunities for young women in urban areas
were extremely limited. Today, however, the creation of jobs in government and industry together with the higher educational qualifications of
the rural young women have made urban employment available to them.
A number of government programs implemented after 1970 may have
encouraged the migration of women to the cities. One of these is the New
Economic Policy, which has two broad objectives: the elimination of poverty irrespective of race and the restructuring of society to eliminate identification of race with economic function. This policy calls for a correction of
regional and racial imbalances in income and opportunities in social and
economic development and has been translated into programs of both
rural and urban development. While efforts are made to modernize the
rural sector and increase the income of the predominantly rural Malay
population, expansion of the urban economy is also considered essential in
order to provide opportunities for rural Malays to move to the cities and
thus to higher-paying jobs.

A related policy is to give more urban jobs to Malays by establishing a
quota system in industry and business and creating jobs in both public and
private sectors. Because 85.2 percent of the Malays still resided in rural
areas in 1970, Malay labor would have to come from the countryside in

order to fill the quota (not less than 30 percent Malays in any business or industry). It has been pointed out that these policies are especially timely because they were implemented in a period when educated rural young women were eager to take advantage of their education to obtain employment and, moreover, social restrictions on young women were beginning to weaken due to exposure to modern ideas (Provencher 1975). Economic development—especially the growth of multinational electronics and other light manufacturing industries located near metropolitan centers—has resulted in the creation of thousands of urban jobs in manufacturing and service. These opportunities, together with the preference for female labor in many assembly-line industries, have further encouraged young women to migrate from rural areas to the cities to seek employment. It is estimated that there are now more than 30,000 young rural Malay women working in urban factories.

The increase in the number of young Malay women in the cities after 1970, although not yet well documented, is beginning to arouse concern in some circles about the social consequences of migration for the women themselves and for the society. Provencher (1975:6) notes that "young unmarried Malay women living by themselves in cities indicate revolutionary changes in Malay values and Malay social organization." The older generation of Malays is concerned that the women may succumb to ideas that are contrary to traditional Malay culture. They wonder, too, how these changes will affect the next generation, for women are regarded as the primary force in the socialization of children and as the guardians of Malay tradition.

There is also concern about how rural women will adapt to city life. Social practices in the city are often different from those in the village—for example, young men and women can socialize together and go out more freely in the cities than in the rural areas, where such practices excite gossip. Urban life is also thought to be more socially isolated than village life. These aspects of urban life can be problematic for female migrants who are on their own for the first time. Moreover, they face problems related to housing and job security (see Chapter 11). Because of the high cost of living in the cities compared to their wages, many young women live in crowded housing conditions. Job security is another serious problem; workers who fail to maintain a set level of productivity are usually replaced.

Much of the preceding discussion applies mainly to female migration among the Malays. Little information is available on the causes of migration among Chinese and Indian women. Because the Chinese and Indians have their own social values, and because government policies are often devised to benefit Malays specifically, there are reasons to expect that female rural-to-urban migration among the Indians and Chinese may differ from the Malay situation. The socioeconomic characteristics of Chinese female migrants in 1965–70 (Table 7.6) indicate that more than half of them were young single women. They are also disproportionately employed in manufacturing and as service workers, indicating that many of them migrated because of employment opportunities in these sectors of the urban economy. A higher proportion of Chinese migrant women than Malay migrant women were employed in industry before 1970. With the new economic policies established after 1970, this situation is likely to have changed. The number of Indian female migrants to urban areas in 1965–70 is quite small compared with Malay and Chinese migrants. More than 80 percent of them are not economically active, suggesting family reasons for migration. What we need now, however, is more information on the causes and consequences of their migration.

PRIORITIES FOR RESEARCH AND ACTION

The preceding examination of female rural-to-urban migration in Peninsular Malaysia suggests several directions for research and action. We propose that priority be given to the following three topics in research.

First: national trends and patterns of recent female migration in the peninsula. Our examination of data and the literature suggests that the pattern of female rural-to-urban migration may have changed substantially since 1970. When data from the 1980 census become available, it will be possible to document the changes that have occurred during the 1970s. The question on the main reason for migration that has been added to the 1980 census will provide additional information on internal migration. Future censuses will need to ask more questions of migrants, however, in order to determine when they migrate and their socioeconomic and demographic characteristics before and after migration to their current place of residence. In addition to the question on duration of residence at present locality that was asked in the 1970 census, questions on premigration marital and occupational status can be asked of those who have been living at their present location for less than ten years. The additional data will provide essential information on nationwide patterns of both female and male migration.

Second: characteristics of female migrants, their motivations for migration, and their adaptation to urban life. Detailed studies of recent female rural-to-urban migrants, and the causes and consequences of their migration to cities, are important for planning. Certain questions need to be answered: What proportion of women migrants migrate on their own, without their families? Why do they migrate? How many come for secondary and university education and then stay on to work in the cities? How many return to their home village or to other rural areas and why? A group of local scholars is presently coordinating research efforts on these topics. Comparative studies could also be carried out on urban-to-urban and urban-to-rural female migrants if their numbers are significant. Third: the effect of the government's development and labor-force policies on female migration. We have discussed some of the Malaysian government's policies on urban employment and work-force quotas that may have had an effect on female migration. What we need now is a detailed study of the extent to which these policies have influenced female migration.

Research on these three topics should not be limited to any one of the three major ethnic groups in Malaysia; rather, an effort should be made to examine ethnic differentials in trends and patterns. A good strategy would be to design comparative research efforts so that the results from careful studies of each of the three ethnic groups may be compared. In addition to these research priorities, we would also suggest two action-oriented priorities.

First: programs for urban migrant women. Services for urban migrant women appear to be lacking, primarily because female migration to cities has not been significant until recently. A survey of services available for urban women needs to be carried out. Social services available to all urban women may need to be supplemented by special services for migrant women, such as counseling on employment, assistance in obtaining housing, and other adjustments to city life.

Second: a periodic national migration study. Our report would have been more timely if there had been an intercensal survey or a national migration survey in mid-decade. Because of the rapid social and economic change that is taking place and the influence of new economic policies on population distribution, there is a need to monitor migration patterns at shorter intervals rather than be limited to the decennial census.

REFERENCES

Ariffin, J.
  1978   Industrial development in Peninsular Malaysia and rural-to-urban migration of women workers—impact and implications. Paper presented at the 10th International Congress of Anthropological and Ethnological Sciences, session on Development and Women, New Delhi.

Blake, M. L.
  1975   *Towards a Better Deal for the Young Worker.* Kuala Lumpur: Federation of Family Planning Associations.

Chew, S.
  1977   Employment and unemployment in Penang. Unpublished manuscript, Faculty of Economics and Administration, University of Malaya, Kuala Lumpur.

Chander, R. (ed.)
  1977   *1970 Population Census General Report.* Vol. 1 and 2. Kuala Lumpur: Department of Statistics.

Hirschman, Charles
  1976   Recent urbanization trends in Peninsular Malaysia. *Demography* 13(4): 445-62.

Narayanan, Suresh
  1977   *Urban Inmigration and Labor Absorption: A Study of Metropolitan Urban Selangor.* CAMS Discussion Paper 77-09. Quezon City, Philippines: Committee on Asian Manpower Studies.

Provencher, Ronald
  1975   *Shifts in the Cycle of Experience: Malay Perceptions of Migration.* (Mimeographed.) De Kalb: Northern Illinois University.

Pryor, Robin
  1976   *Demographic Sample Data on Malaysian Internal Migrants, 1967 and 1969.* Working Papers in Demography, No. 4. Canberra: Australian National University, Department of Demography.

Young, M. L.
  1977   Migration and employment: a case study of a rural settlement within a development scheme in Peninsular Malaysia. Paper presented to the UNCRD Colloquium on Rural-Urban Relations, Nagoya.

Chapter 8

Female Migration in Thailand

Fred Arnold
Suwanlee Piampiti

The rapid growth in the rate of female migration in Thailand has brought
to light the need to conduct more research in this area and to devise appropriate government policies. Although males continue to dominate overall
migration, the gap is closing rapidly. Moreover, women outnumber men
by a large margin in recent migration streams to Bangkok metropolis. Our
purposes in this chapter are to review past and current research in female
migration in Thailand and to outline policies that influence this component of mobility. We begin by placing female migration in the context of
overall migration and urbanization patterns in Thailand. Subsequent sections cover characteristics of female migrants, motivation for migration,
and adjustment problems. The final section discusses current policies for
female migrants and makes recommendations for implementing new programs in this area.

DATA SOURCES

Prior to the mid-1950s, analysis of internal migration in Thailand was
largely speculative because of a dearth of reliable migration data. Although the census of population has been carried out periodically since
1911, it was not until 1960 that information relevant to the migration of
Thailand's population was tabulated. In the 1947 census, data were collected on place of birth but no tabulations relating to this variable were
made. Population registration records also have a long history since the
implementation of a compulsory civil registration system in 1917, but the
law is not strictly enforced and registration information is too incomplete
to be useful for the scientific study of migration patterns. Not until 1954,
when the National Demographic and Economic Survey was conducted,
was a serious attempt made to examine patterns and distances of population movements (Wichiencharoen 1960). During this period, policy-makers and the public began to take an interest in the issue of migration since a

sizable number of migrants from the northeast were moving to Bangkok daily or passing through Bangkok on the way to other changwats (provinces). This migration stream was examined by Textor (1961), who undertook a 1955 study of northeastern farmers who periodically migrated to Bangkok and became pedicab drivers, and by Meinkoth (1962) who conducted a 1957 study on reasons for migration and the characteristics of migrants from the northeast to Bangkok.

In the next 15 years, data on migration in Thailand increased substantially with the availability of data from two censuses and the Longitudinal Study of Social, Economic, and Demographic Change. In the 1960 and 1970 censuses, two questions provided information for a direct measure of migration—namely, place of birth and migration within the five years prior to the census. The National Statistical Office produced tabulations on place of birth by place of residence and on place of current residence by previous place of residence within the five years prior to the census, crosstabulated by age and sex. We will use the census data for 1960 and 1970 to examine changing patterns of internal migration in Thailand.

PATTERNS OF MIGRATION: 1960 AND 1970

THE VOLUME OF MIGRATION

In 1960, approximately one in eight persons in Thailand was a lifetime migrant. By 1970, the number was one in seven. Table 8.1 shows the percentage distribution of persons who were born in their changwat (province) of present residence, as well as the percentage of persons born in one changwat but living in another on the census date. By far the highest proportion of lifetime migrants was found in the capital of Bangkok–Thon Buri; the south had the lowest percentage of lifetime migrants in both 1960 and 1970.

Changes in migration patterns can be seen more clearly by examining the volume of recent migration. For five-year migrants, both the volume and rate of internal migration in Thailand increased substantially from 1955–60 to 1965–70. In 1955–60, approximately 844,000 persons, or 3.8 percent of the population aged 5 and over, changed their changwat of residence. By 1965–70, the number had risen to 1,800,000, or 6.3 percent of the comparable population. As we will see, the reasons for this substantial increase are manifold.

THE CHANGING COMPOSITION OF MIGRATION

Between 1960 and 1970 the total population increased by 31 percent while the number of recent (five-year) migrants increased by 125 percent. This rapid growth in the volume of migration was accompanied by a notable shift in the sex composition of migrants:

Table 8.1 Place of birth by region of residence: 1960 and 1970

Residential status	Region of residence (%)					
	Whole kingdom	Bangkok–Thon Buri	North	Central[a]	Northeast	South
1970						
Living in changwat of birth	85.9	67.4	86.9	84.6	89.7	89.2
Living in other changwat	13.1	27.2	12.6	14.4	10.0	9.9
Foreign-born	1.0	5.4	0.5	1.0	0.3	0.9
Total	100.0	100.0	100.0	100.0	100.0	100.0
1960						
Living in changwat of birth	87.3	66.7	90.9	88.0	88.3	90.6
Living in other changwat	10.8	22.8	8.5	10.3	10.9	7.7
Foreign-born	1.9	10.5	0.6	1.7	0.8	1.7
Total	100.0	100.0	100.0	100.0	100.0	100.0

a. Excluding Bangkok–Thon Buri.

Sources: Thailand, CSO (1962: table 5); Thailand, NSO (1973: table 8A).

	Population (in thousands)		% Change (1960–70)	% Change in Number of Five-year Migrants (1960–70)
	1960	1970		
Both Sexes	26,259	34,397	31.0	124.8
Male	13,154	17,124	30.2	111.6
Female	13,105	17,273	31.8	142.3

These data clearly indicate that overall migration in Thailand is rapidly increasing. Although the change in migratory behavior has been particularly dramatic for females, male migrants outnumbered female migrants in both census years.

During the 1955–60 period, migration was highly concentrated in the 10–39 age range, with peak rates for both males and females at ages 20 to 29. Males had higher migration rates than females at all ages, but the sex difference in migration was greatest at ages 20 to 29, when the rate was 72 per thousand males and only 44 per thousand females.

While migration rates had increased substantially for both males and females by 1965–70, the sex differential narrowed considerably. The pattern of migration by age is quite similar for the two periods, however. For both periods, migration rates reached a peak in the age group 20–29 for both sexes.

From 1965 to 1970, males were more likely to migrate than females in every age group except those aged 10 to 19, where the rate for females was 63 as opposed to 60 for males. At ages 5 to 9, of course, there is little difference in male and female rates of migration because most of these children migrate with their parents. At ages 10 to 19, the higher rate of migration for females doubtless reflects the greater incidence of marriage among females,[1] the tendency for young wives to move with their husbands in an older age group, and the demand in cities for domestic servants and other kinds of female labor.

Historically Bangkok has dominated the urban scene in Thailand and over the years its dominance has increased. Apart from being the capital of the country, Bangkok functions as Thailand's commercial, educational, and communications center. Registration figures from the Ministry of the Interior indicate that there were 4.5 million persons residing in the Bangkok metropolis in 1977 and that Bangkok was 43 times the size of the next largest city, Chiang Mai (Thailand, MI, 1978). Thus Bangkok is one of the most striking examples of urban primacy in the world.

Although Bangkok must figure prominently in any analysis of urbanization, it is important to note that smaller cities throughout the country have begun to play a major role in Thailand's urban development. Between 1947 and 1970, the number of places of moderate size (20,000 to 100,000 population) increased from 5 to 36 (Goldstein n.d.). The central region contained 71 percent of the urban population in 1970, but eight of the top ten cities were outside the central region. Although the remaining 29 percent of the urban population was shared almost equally among the other three regions, the level of urbanization in these regions varied substantially because of the uneven distribution of the total population by region. Only 3.7 percent of the population in the northeast lived in municipal areas, compared to 5.9 percent in the north and 10.7 percent in the south (Arnold et al. 1977). Although all but one province experienced an increase in its municipal area population between 1960 and 1970, the rate of growth was quite variable. Over this same period, the municipal population grew by more than 45 percent in 15 provinces, 35 to 45 percent in 6 provinces, 15 to 35 percent in 33 provinces, and less than 15 percent in 14 provinces (Piampiti 1976a).[2] Moreover, migration to urban places varied considerably in different areas. The influence of migration on urban growth and urban characteristics is explored in the next section.

MIGRATION TO URBAN AREAS

The rapid growth of urban areas in Thailand can be traced to two causes: an excess of births over deaths in the cities and large-scale migration to urban areas. Between 1970 and 1975, 40 percent of urban growth was due to migration and the rest was due to natural increase (Goldstein n.d.). Although migration from rural to urban areas is substantial and has provided the focus for several migration studies, this component of migration is only a small part of overall migration in Thailand. For females who moved between 1965 and 1970, rural-to-urban migration constituted only 12.0 percent of all migration while urban-to-urban migration provided an additional 11.1 percent of all migration. By far the most prominent type of migration took place among rural areas (71.0 percent); the migration stream from urban to rural areas (5.9 percent) accounted for the remaining flow (Arnold and Boonpratuang 1976). It should be noted that the size of the urban-to-rural female migration stream was half as large as the rural-to-urban stream, indicating a sizable volume of return migration as well as out-migration on the part of women born in municipal areas. Moreover, there is a considerable volume of short-term circular movement back and forth between rural and urban places, particularly to and from Bangkok (Goldstein and Pitaktepsombati 1974).

Migration to the cities is particularly important, though, in terms of its size relative to the urban population base and its potential for creating or exacerbating a whole range of social and economic problems. The Longitudinal Survey, conducted in 1970, found considerable residential instability among young women and men in urban places—over half those aged

20 to 34 had changed their residence within the previous five years (Gold-stein et al. 1974). The 1970 census also indicated a large volume of migration to Bangkok from other areas. More than 25 percent of both women and men in Bangkok in 1970 were born elsewhere in Thailand; women were somewhat more likely than men to have moved to Bangkok and somewhat less likely to have left the capital city for other provinces. Further, over half of all women aged 20 and over living in Bangkok–Thon Buri were born outside their changwat of 1970 residence. Recent (5-year) female migration to Bangkok was similarly strong in 1970—one in five females aged five years or over had migrated since 1965 (Thailand, NSO, 1972). These proportions include women who had moved from Bangkok to Thon Buri and vice versa.

Between 1955–60 and 1965–70, there was a striking change in the sex composition of migration to the capital. From 1955 to 1960, some 70,000 males and 60,000 females migrated to Bangkok metropolis, whereas from 1965 to 1970 there were 145,000 male migrants and 153,000 female migrants. The impact of the shifting sex composition of migrants is clearly visible in the sex ratios of residents of Bangkok metropolis in the last two census years. The sex ratio of 103.9 in 1960 dropped to a level of 97.7 in 1970 and the largest declines were registered in the prime migration ages (see Chapter 12). More recent data from the 1976–78 annual rounds of the Survey of Migration in Bangkok metropolis indicate that female dominance of migration to Bangkok is becoming stronger. The sex ratio of migrants to Bangkok metropolis decreased from 87.9 in 1976, to 74.7 in 1977, to 68.0 in 1978 (Thailand, NSO, 1977–79).[3]

Although the increase in female migration from 1960 to 1970 was registered in all but a few remote provinces (Sternstein 1976), males continued to dominate the migration streams from the South and Central Regions until recently (Table 8.2). In 1975–77, however, substantially more females than males moved to Bangkok from every region. Every region experienced a steady decline in the sex ratio of migrants to Bangkok throughout the period, but the decline was most dramatic in the northeast,

Table 8.2 Sex ratio of migrants to Bangkok metropolis: 1955–77

Region	1955–60	1965–70	1975–77
Central	113.8	101.0	80.8
North	92.0	79.1	70.7
Northeast	123.6	84.7	57.3
South	136.2	107.6	83.5

Sources: Piampiti (1976a); Thailand, NSO (1979).

where the sex ratio of migrants was cut in half. Overall the rapid change in the sex ratio of migrants to Bangkok over the past 20 years from a male-dominated flow in 1955–60 to a 3:2 preponderance of women in recent years is one of the most striking features of migration patterns in Thailand in recent history.[4]

Female migration to urban areas is particularly high among young adults, as shown by the results of the 1970 Longitudinal Survey (Table 8.3). About 30 percent of women aged 15 to 24 had moved to urban areas (from rural areas or other urban areas) between 1965 and 1970. This proportion dropped to one in six at ages 25 to 34 and less than one in ten at age 35 and over. At every age female migration rates were higher for urban destinations outside Bangkok than for Bangkok itself. Goldstein and Pitak-tepsombati (1974:35) attribute the high migration rate to provincial urban places to "the possibility that these smaller places are increasing their attractiveness to migrants, both because of the earlier very rapid growth of Bangkok and because of the increase in opportunities available in smaller urban places." The concentration of advanced educational facilities in Bangkok until recently may be responsible for the close migration rates between Bangkok and provincial urban places at ages 15–19 and 20–24.

Even though female migration rates were particularly high in provincial urban places, male migrants outnumbered female migrants in urban areas outside Bangkok–Thon Buri (Tables 8.3 and 8.4). Migration to municipal areas in the Central Region outside the capital city was dominated by males, particularly at ages 20 to 49, with sex ratios over 150. Although the north sent many more females than males to Bangkok, migrants in municipal areas in the North Region itself were predominantly male.

Table 8.3 **Percentage of females classified as five-year migrants by age and 1970 residence**

Age	Total urban	Bangkok	Provincial urban places
< 15	11.7	7.5	17.5
15–19	28.1	26.7	30.4
20–24	30.0	27.0	35.5
25–34	16.1	11.9	22.5
35–44	9.9	6.1	15.0
45–64	8.9	6.2	11.8
65+	7.4	3.4	12.4
All ages	15.8	12.7	20.2

Source: Goldstein et al. (n.d.:134).

Table 8.4 Sex ratio of migrants in municipal areas by age and region: 1965—70

Age	Region			
	North	Central[a]	Northeast	South
5—9	104.2	105.7	101.8	100.8
10—19	93.2	101.1	91.0	84.9
20—29	134.1	154.0	117.0	102.9
30—39	144.4	160.1	141.7	144.9
40—49	155.0	160.1	148.6	154.1
50—59	140.5	130.4	132.2	128.5
60+	78.6	108.0	85.7	83.1
All ages	119.2	130.3	108.0	105.9

Note: Sex ratio = M/F X 100.

a. Excluding Bangkok—Thon Buri.

Source: Piampiti (1976a: table 25).

In many countries it has been observed that migration to large cities proceeds in a stepping-stone fashion from rural villages to small urban areas and eventually to large cities. This pattern is not commonly followed for migration to Bangkok, however, which is composed principally of single moves directly from villages to Bangkok (Goldstein n.d.). But this does not imply that migrants to Bangkok had had no previous contact with the capital city. As explained in Chapter 12, Piampiti found that although 90 percent of female migrants to four districts in Bangkok metropolis were making their first move, 70 percent had in fact visited Bangkok previously.

In recent years a disproportionately large number of female migrants to Bangkok have come from the northeast, at least partially in response to chronic drought in that region. The 1977 and 1978 Surveys of Migration in Bangkok metropolis indicate that nearly half of all female migrants to Bangkok moved from the northeast and about a third from the central plains, followed by the north with 11 percent, and the south with 6 percent (Thailand, NSO, 1978, 1979). The number of female migrants to Bangkok is particularly high during the agricultural slack season when employment opportunities in rural areas are limited.

There appears to be a great deal of uncertainty involved in these moves, as evidenced by the large proportion of women in several studies who did not know how long they expected to remain in Bangkok. The most recent Survey of Migration in Bangkok metropolis found that about half of the women who move to Bangkok cannot fix the length of time they expect to stay; only about one-third intend to stay forever, and the rest expect to stay for varying lengths of time but mostly for less than a year (Thailand,

NSO, 1978, 1979). Therefore migration of women to Bangkok cannot generally be characterized as a deliberate, permanent move. In fact there appears to be a substantial element of chance involved. If things go well in the city and a woman adjusts well to a life-style that is often radically different from her previous experience, she may spend considerable time in Bangkok or even make it her permanent home. If not, she can always leave Bangkok and return to her previous place of residence.

CHARACTERISTICS OF FEMALE MIGRANTS

The Survey of Migration in Bangkok metropolis has painted a picture of the typical migrant to Bangkok as a "young, unmarried male or female from a village in the northeast who moves to Bangkok without any other family members to seek employment as a laborer or service worker" (Thailand, NSO, 1979:35). Although migration from one rural area to another constitutes the majority of moves in Thailand, we know vastly more about the migrants who have moved to urban areas. Therefore the findings cited in this section give particular emphasis to the characteristics of migrants to the cities, especially Bangkok.

SOCIODEMOGRAPHIC CHARACTERISTICS

Peak migration rates appear to be somewhat earlier for females than for males—particularly in Bangkok, where 57 percent of female migrants are under age 20 compared to 47 percent of male migrants (Thailand, NSO, 1979; Arnold and Boonpratuang 1976).[5] The youth of female migrants to Bangkok is partially responsible for the fact that the overwhelming majority have never been married. Over 70 percent of female migrants to Bangkok 15 years of age and over were reported to be single in the 1978 Survey of Migration in Bangkok metropolis (Thailand, NSO, 1979). This finding contrasts sharply with the pattern found for all migrants in Thailand (including intraprovincial migrants) in the 1970 census. Overall 61.8 percent of female migrants enumerated in the census were currently married and only 29.2 percent had never been married (Arnold and Boonpratuang 1976:56-57). At every age up to 50, female migrants were more likely to be married than female nonmigrants; differences were especially great at ages 15 to 24. It appears that marriage itself is a primary motivation for moving at these ages and that married women are more likely to move than unmarried women. At ages 30 and over, migrant women were more likely than nonmigrant women to be widowed, divorced, or separated, indicating that marital dissolution may affect migration patterns.

The proportion of women who migrated between 1965 and 1970 increased steadily with higher educational attainment from a level of 9.3 percent for women with no education, to 10.4 percent for women with a primary school background, to 18.5 percent for women who attended secondary school, to a high of 21.8 percent for those who went to college. Although a substantially higher proportion of migrants than nonmigrants had a secondary school education or higher, female migrants below age 40 were also more likely to have received no formal education than were nonmigrants (Arnold and Boonpratuang 1976). This finding suggests that female migration consists disproportionately of at least two contrasting types of women: those with more than average education who move in order to attend school or after their schooling is complete, and young women with no formal schooling. However, studies of migration to Bangkok have consistently shown a very low proportion of women (less than 3 percent) with no formal education and a high proportion who have gone beyond primary school (Thailand, NSO, 1977–79).

The pattern of school attendance of migrant and nonmigrant women highlights the role that education plays in the migration process. From ages 7 to 13, female migrants were less likely to be attending school than female nonmigrants. This result may be a function of two separate factors: the reluctance of families to move while their children are attending school and the disruptive effect of moves on children's schooling. After age 13, there is a shift in the pattern of school attendance and migrant women attend school to a greater degree than women who had not migrated. This crossover point corresponds roughly to the age of entrance into secondary school. Because of the uneven distribution of secondary schools and universities in Thailand, women who want to continue their schooling are likely to have to move. In fact, the census data tend to downplay the role of education in the mobility process because many students were enumerated at their parents' homes to which they had returned for the summer vacation.

ECONOMIC CHARACTERISTICS

The Longitudinal Survey found that young female migrants consisted disproportionately of those who were economically active, but this relationship did not hold true for women aged 25 and over. According to Goldstein et al. (1974), this pattern indicates that migration of women over 25 is more closely associated with marriage and family movement. For Bangkok metropolis, however, labor-force participation rates for female in-migrants are higher than for the total female population at all ages, although the relationship is particularly strong at ages 11 to 19 (Thailand, NSO, 1977). The majority of female migrants to Bangkok (57.6 percent) worked both before and after they moved, 19.2 percent did not work in either place, while 13.0 percent started working only after they moved, and 10.1 percent stopped working after they moved (Thailand, NSO, 1979).

Because most migration takes place within rural areas, it is not surprising to find that 72.2 percent of economically active female migrants enumerated in the 1970 census were engaged in agriculture compared to 86.1 percent of economically active nonmigrant women (Arnold and Boonpratuang 1975). Nevertheless, women who worked on farms were least likely to have moved in the five years before the census (only 8.3 percent). Women who were employed as transport equipment operators (38.0 percent) or service workers (31.5 percent) were most likely to have moved in the five-year period, while sales workers tended to be rather sedentary (12.4 percent). The Longitudinal Survey found that service workers in urban areas were even more likely to be recent migrants. Nearly 55 percent of female service workers in Bangkok (46 percent after age was standardized) and 52 percent of those in provincial urban places (40 percent after standardization) were classified as migrants, while no more than 17 percent of any other occupational group had migrated in the preceding five years (Goldstein n.d.:168). In fact, fully 70 percent of young female service workers (age 11 to 24) were migrants. These observations led Goldstein et al. (1974) to the conclusion that women who migrate to urban areas often come with no assurance of employment and consequently enter into employment in the tertiary sector.

More recently, the Survey of Migration in Bangkok metropolis has found that well over half of female migrants to Bangkok take jobs as service, sport, and recreation workers while more than one-quarter become crafts workers, production process workers, and laborers (Thailand, NSO, 1979). Although 84 percent were farmers before coming to Bangkok, fewer than 1 percent were able to work on farms in Bangkok metropolis (even though 13 percent of all women in Bangkok metropolis were farmers).

Although large numbers of women migrate to Bangkok with no assured employment, very few remain unemployed. The unemployment rate of female migrants to Bangkok metropolis is marginally higher than it is for all women in Bangkok (1.3 percent versus 0.9 percent), but both of these unemployment rates are usually low (Thailand, NSO, 1979). Those who are unable to find work may return home, of course, so these figures may underestimate the extent of the problem. Many women who moved to Bangkok relied on friends or acquaintances to help them find work (40.4 percent), but one-third of the women had no contact at all for seeking work (Thailand, NSO, 1979). Only 2.6 percent of the migrant women relied on the Labor Department for help in seeking employment, compared to 7.3 percent of male migrants. Evidently the services of the Labor Department are not geared for women.

Although unemployment does not appear to be a major problem among female migrants to Bangkok, this does not mean that these women are taking jobs that make full use of their capabilities. In fact, it has been estimated that a startling 76.9 percent of women who migrate to Bangkok metropolis and join the labor force are inadequately utilized; this figure rises to 91.9 percent for women who migrate from nonmunicipal areas (Table 8.5). Relatively few are underutilized in relation to skills or hours of work or periods of unemployment. However, 57.4 percent of economically active nonmigrant women in Bangkok could be classified as inadequately utilized by income, while 71.7 percent of all migrant women and 85.5 percent of women who migrated from nonmunicipal areas fell in that category. Thus, while outright unemployment does not seem to be a matter of great concern, low income of migrant women is a problem of major dimensions.

Even though the income of migrants to urban areas may be inadequate, it may still be higher than what they were accustomed to receiving previously. Piampiti (1976b) found that women who migrated to municipal areas in the south were able to increase their median income by more than 50 percent—from 1,100 baht per month before they moved to 1,700 baht per month after migration. Moreover, migration to urban areas seems to be accompanied by an improvement in living conditions. More than 60 percent of female migrants to Bangkok metropolis and to municipal areas in the south reported that their living conditions had improved after the move; fewer than 5 percent thought their living conditions had deteriorated (Piampiti 1976b).

This profile of migrants throughout Thailand and to municipal areas in particular indicates that women who migrate are selected not at random but on a number of different characteristics. Examination of these characteristics yields clues about what motivates women to migrate. Reasons for migration can also be elicited more directly through interviews with migrant women, although it is difficult to untangle the complex motivations

Table 8.5 Labor utilization of women 11 years old and over in Bangkok metropolis: 1975

% of labor force	Non-migrants	Migrants	Migrants from municipal areas	Migrants from other areas
Total labor force	100.0	100.0	100.0	100.0
Adequately utilized	37.4	23.1	38.0	8.1
Inadequately utilized	62.6	76.9	62.0	91.9
By unemployment	3.5	4.5	3.3	5.7
By hours of work	1.4	0.7	0.7	0.7
By income	57.4	71.7	58.0	85.5
By mismatch	0.3	0.0	0.0	0.0

Source: Thailand, NSO (1976).

for moving from a single question. The next section explores the major reasons for moving and the factors that may facilitate or impede migration.

MOTIVATION FOR MIGRATION

Most migration is motivated by a combination of unfavorable conditions at the place of origin (push factors). After reviewing the migration literature in Thailand, Prachuabmoh and Tirasawat (1974) concluded that push and pull factors are both important. Certainly there are many documented cases in which migration in Thailand has been precipitated by such factors as poverty or severe drought. But Chamratrithirong (1976) argues that although push factors account for a great number of out-migrants from the poorer provinces, migration rates seem to be influenced more by physical and cultural facilitating factors than by push factors. Based on a macrolevel analysis of the 1970 census, he found that both female and male migrants to Bangkok in particular were more likely to come from more developed, more modern provinces. Socioeconomic development was found to be positively (and statistically significantly) related to female in-migration, out-migration, gross-migration, and migration to Greater Bangkok. He concludes that the data support Davis' thesis of relative deprivation since migration is usually not directly stimulated by poverty. Arnold and Cochrane (1980) arrived at similar results in their recent study of motivations for migration in Thailand. In addition, they found that male and female migration streams respond to per capita income and unemployment differences among provinces in the same way, but that women are less responsive than men to differences in the scarcity or availability of farmland.

Studies that have been conducted in Bangkok and municipal areas in southern Thailand have asked women directly about their reasons for moving. In each case, economics has played a dominant role in migration decisions. Bangkok in particular seems to attract women who are looking for work. Over 56 percent of migrants ten years old and over surveyed in 1978 said they came to Bangkok to look for work, and the proportion approached two-thirds for women aged 10 to 19 (Thailand, NSO, 1979). An additional 12.1 percent had come to change jobs or were officially transferred to Bangkok. In all, 68.4 percent of women gave job-related reasons for their move. The next largest group (22.2 percent) had migrated along with the head of the household and gave no separate reason for their move. An additional 8.1 percent came to continue schooling in Bangkok, which until 1964 was the only city in Thailand with universities.

Piampiti's study of female migrants to Bangkok aged 15 and over (see Chapter 12 of this volume) also found that most women move for economic reasons. But she found a substantially larger proportion who cited education as their main reason for coming (37.5 percent) and a substantially smaller proportion who were simply following their husband or other relatives (12.2 percent). Another study, also conducted by Piampiti (1976b), of female migrants to urban areas in southern Thailand found economic factors to be somewhat less salient (cited by about one-third of the women). Education was again an important motive for migration (29.0 percent), and about 23 percent of the women said they were following their husband. All the studies conducted to date show that, by and large, women who move to urban areas are not simply moving with their husbands. In fact, in no study did the proportion of women who have this reason as the principal cause of their move exceed 23 percent. This fact underlines the importance of studying female migrants in their own right —as individuals who make their own migration decisions and who have their own reasons for leaving their former place of residence. Economics is an important motive for their moves, but they do not seem to be putting an excessive strain on the labor market in urban areas. Although the labor market has proved itself capable of absorbing large numbers of new migrants, these women are often willing to accept low-paying jobs in the service sector and they may consequently have a depressing effect on wages in the cities.

A number of factors may facilitate migration or make it more difficult, including the availability of resources for the move, the cost of traveling over long distances, and family relationships. Certainly the road from the village to Bangkok is often quite long. The system of major highways is good and bus transportation is cheap and efficient, but long distance can still be a deterrent to migration. Chamratrithirong (1976) found that the correlation between five-year migration rates to Greater Bangkok and the logarithm of the distance to Bangkok decreased slightly from -0.90 in 1960 to -0.84 in 1970, however, suggesting that the significance of distance has lessened somewhat. His results also led to the conclusion that improvements in transportation may be more important in the migration decisions of females than males and that males may be more adventurous in deciding to migrate whereas females may rely more strongly on such issues as ease of moving. Nevertheless, his data do not fully support the thesis that women move shorter distances than men. In fact, he suggests that since intervening opportunities are greater for males than for females, women often have to move longer distances.

A woman's family may also be instrumental in encouraging or discouraging her plans to move. Although little direct information is available on the family's influence on migration decisions, some indirect information was collected from nonmigrants in a village in Ayutthaya (a province close to Bangkok). Nonmigrants who had had someone in the household move to Bangkok were asked to cite good points and bad points about the move. Economic considerations figured heavily in their answers (Piampiti 1978). Over half said the move was good because the migrants send money to help the family; 44 percent said that the burden of raising children is reduced when they leave. On the other hand, they lose the benefits of their children's labor. Over 25 percent felt that there were not enough people to help with the farming; 21 percent said there were not enough people to help with the housework. An additional 18 percent considered the move disadvantageous because they themselves had to send money to those who had gone to Bangkok—evidently the financial flow operates in both directions. Most of the rest said they were lonely or worried about those who had left. It is not clear whether or not the respondents were generally supportive of the move or in fact whether the opinions of other family members had a major influence on migration decisions. It is clear, however, that migration can shape not only the lives of the migrants themselves but also the lives of those who remain behind.

ADJUSTMENT PROBLEMS OF FEMALE MIGRANTS

There is very little direct information on how well migrant women adjust to their new environments, but once again a lot can be inferred from related data. The fact that unemployment among migrant women is low, for example, suggests that severe economic problems may not be prevalent. Their low income, however, indicates that economic hardship is a fact of life for most of these women. Additional information on the type of move and the degree of contact with their original community is also indicative of their ability to adapt to new circumstances.

The degree to which migrants are cut off from their former communities depends on whom they move with, whom they rely on after the move, and how much contact they continue to have with their original community. The 1978 Survey of Migration in Bangkok metropolis found that 63.5 percent of female migrants moved alone, 26.2 percent moved with the whole family, and 14.7 percent moved with some family members. Piampiti (see Chapter 12) found an even higher percentage of female migrants to Bangkok (aged 15 and over) who had moved alone (70 percent), but she also noted that a similar percentage had visited Bangkok previously and hence had some idea of what to expect. She also found that migrant women relied heavily on family and friends who had migrated earlier, so that they were not all alone in the big city.

There is some evidence that women who move to Bangkok keep in frequent contact with those at home, expecially if they have moved from nearby provinces (Piampiti 1978). Such contact might ease the transition from rural life to urban life, but on the other hand it may create homesickness and impede adaptation to Bangkok. A woman's financial ties to her family back home also appear to be quite strong. About 45 percent of employed female migrants who lived in Bangkok for less than two years reported that they had sent money home; the average amount of money sent was the baht equivalent of $5 to $25 each time (Thailand, NSO, 1979). This financial support was confirmed by nonmigrants in Ayutthaya who reported that 35 percent of those in their families who moved to Bangkok sent remittances home regularly and another 29 percent sent remittances occasionally (Piampiti 1978).

Direct evidence on the adjustment of female migrants is available for urban areas only. The Survey of Migration in Bangkok metropolis elicited more positive ideas about Bangkok than negative ideas from female migrants (Thailand, NSO, 1979), although it is always possible that the respondents were reluctant to criticize their new homes in the presence of a local interviewer. Working conditions (including income and security) were praised by 21 percent of the women, but 12 percent registered complaints about working conditions. Living conditions seemed to be most satisfactory; 24 percent of the women spontaneously said they were favorable to housing and public utilities and only 5 percent criticized these aspects of life in Bangkok. As might be expected, the women were least favorable toward the environment (including safety and traffic); only 1 percent mentioned the environment in a positive light and 12 percent cited it as a negative aspect of life in Bangkok. More than 50 percent expressed no positive ideas about Bangkok (or their answers were unknown) while over 70 percent expressed no negative ideas. This result may suggest that the respondents had not formed strong opinions either way or that the survey was unsuccessful in eliciting their feelings. Presumably the answers to these questions would be very different for women who moved to rural areas or to other cities. In fact, women who migrated to municipal areas in the South Region reported having more problems adjusting to the dialect and the food than to any of the conditions mentioned above (Piampiti 1976b).

The high rate of residential instability for women in the Bangkok area and the fact that most female migrants to Bangkok come from rural areas outside the Central Region in Thailand suggest that government policies may be needed to monitor the flow of migrants and help female migrants adapt to their new environment. The new services should be based on the adjustment problems that female migrants encounter. The next section reviews the development of government policies and programs that affect migration in general and female migration in particular.

POLICIES AND PROGRAMS

Population policy in Thailand was first incorporated in the Third National Economic and Social Development Plan, but that plan emphasized only family planning programs to reduce the population growth rate to a target level. The issues of population redistribution and urbanization have just recently become a matter of official concern due to the uneven geographic distribution of the population, particularly its heavy concentration in Bangkok metropolis. The rapid pace of metropolitan growth and its significance for the country's social, economic, and demographic conditions emphasized the need to consider the role of migration in relation to national development. Hence, for the first time, planning for population redistribution and human settlement was included in the Fourth Plan, covering the period 1977–81.

Although population redistribution policies had never been adopted in the former plans, other policies for national development such as the development of essential infrastructure, communication, and transportation systems in rural areas had an incidental impact on migration. These policies helped stimulate the heavy flow of migrants to the capital city. The development of a better system of transportation and communication helped reduce the physical and social distance and thus encouraged rural-to-urban movement. Furthermore, the development of rural communities stimulated not only return migration but possibly also urban-to-rural movement of persons of high socioeconomic status who took advantage of the new opportunities in rural areas (Prachuabmoh and Tirasawat 1974).

These changes, coupled with the high birth rate during the past decade, caused a high population concentration in Bangkok metropolis, which was inevitably faced with problems as severe as those found in any major city. The Fourth Plan thus redirected migrants to intermediate urban growth poles and encouraged them to move from Bangkok metropolis—a strategy of decentralized urbanization. The plan calls for the control of urban land on the periphery of Bangkok metropolis. In urban centers outside Bangkok, the plan calls for the development of urban infrastructure, the creation of employment, and the integration of rural and urban development (Thailand, NESDB, 1978:228).

In many countries, programs designed to control migration into metropolitan areas have entailed stopping the flow of migrants at the source, redirecting the flow to rural frontier areas or intermediate urban growth poles, returning the rural-to-urban migrants to their home towns, or accommodating existing patterns of rural-to-urban migration (Simmons et al. 1977). The policies adopted so far in Thailand, however, as in many other countries, have been distinctly concerned with places rather than people. There has been no attempt to accommodate existing patterns of rural-to-urban migration by providing services that will improve the lot of migrants. Yet current patterns of female migration to the city will ultimately necessitate programs of assistance for urban migrant women.

Urbanward migration—especially to large cities—often ends in substantial economic improvement: Earnings improve, poverty and unemployment are reduced, occupational status is enhanced. Female migrants

in Bangkok metropolis were also found to be content with their experiences, since migration had enabled them to better themselves both economically and socially. Nevertheless, migrants were found to cluster at the
lower end of the socioeconomic scale because their occupational choices
are limited by their meager education.

The large proportion of women employed in the service category is
important because most of them are domestic workers, restaurant workers, bar girls, masseuses, prostitutes, and the like. Since women generally
move to Bangkok at the persuasion of their friends or acquaintances, the
newcomers tend to acquire the same type of work and life-style as their
friends. But in some cases they are deceived into coming by false pictures
of modern life in the mass media. Thus many women move to the city with
high aspirations but end up as bar girls or prostitutes. As Karnasuta points
out, there is a problem of rural women migrating to urban areas and taking up these careers in order to support their family, since their original
agricultural occupation provided little income. The primary cause of their
problems was found to be a lack of earning opportunities, which stemmed
from the social view of female inferiority and the insufficient provision by
the government of education and training opportunities, both in quantity
and quality (Karnasuta 1978:685). Government programs should be developed to solve this problem.

More information—on female migration patterns, on the sources of
information for migrants, on the adjustment of female migrants and the
problems they face—is needed to guide the formulation of policy. Yet previous research findings and humanitarian considerations suggest a number of approaches to policy-making that can be recommended in spite of
inadequate data. First of all, programs dealing with female migration and
women in the cities should encompass both rural and urban areas. Although rural development might provide more job opportunities in nonmunicipal areas and thereby reduce the pressure for women to migrate,
the relationship between rural development and migration is not certain
and the *type* of development is crucial (Rhoda 1979). Agricultural mechanization, for example, might reduce the need for farm labor and thereby
encourage out-migration. But the provision of supplementary jobs (such
as handicrafts) for rural women, particularly during the agricultural slack
season, could counter the pressure for them to seek employment in the
cities.

Providing better information about migration and working in the cities
would undoubtedly help women make more rational decisions about
moving. This information could be imparted in adult education courses,
through special information campaigns, or as part of the basic school cur-
riculum. Although efforts to expand educational opportunities for women
might reduce migration at young ages by encouraging women to stay in

school longer, it should be recognized that increased education is associated with higher migration rates. Nevertheless, women with more education are better able to cope with moves away from their parental place of residence, so the possible effect on migration rates should not be considered a drawback to increasing educational opportunities. Strict enforcement of child labor laws might also limit the migration to the city of young women less able to cope with the radical change in environment.

Both governmental and private agencies can do more to assist women who migrate to the cities. The Labor Department, for example, is currently assisting more male migrants than female migrants to Bangkok in obtaining employment. The department might take a more active role in assisting bar girls, massage parlor girls, and prostitutes to secure other types of employment. Other government agencies could help them to return home or migrate to another area if they wish to do so. Private agencies, such as the National Council of Women and the Council on Social Welfare of Thailand, could deal more effectively with the problems of female migrants if they assigned staff to focus on this area of concern.

To provide a framework for public policy on women in the cities, the Thai government should develop specific programs for future Economic and Social Development Plans—programs designed explicitly for women, for example, or programs that might affect their welfare. The specific recognition of problems faced by women in the cities will stimulate government agencies to establish programs for them.

NOTES

1. At ages 15 to 19, for example, the incidence of marriage was five times greater for females than males.

2. The 1970 census indicated that the population in municipal areas constituted 13.2 percent of the total population in April 1970 whereas registration figures for December 1970 show a level of 14.7 percent. The lower census figures may have resulted from a serious underenumeration in municipal areas in the 1970 census (Arnold and Phananiramai 1975). Goldstein and Goldstein (1978) have shown that the level of urbanization is strongly influenced by the definition of the urban population that is used. For example, the level of urbanization of 14.7 percent in December 1970 would increase to 20.8 percent if large sanitary districts were included as urban and to 24.9 percent if all sanitary districts were included as urban. Whatever definition is accepted, it is clear that Thailand can still be characterized as a rural country with most of the population living in small villages.

3. The Surveys of Migration to Bangkok Metropolis interview persons who have moved to Bangkok within the past 24 months. The surveys conducted before 1977 underrepresented short-term migrants; this bias should be taken into account in interpreting annual changes in the characteristics of migrants.

4. In interpreting the sex ratio of migrants to urban areas, it is important to note that in developing countries underenumeration of male migrants in metropolitan areas tends to be greater than underenumeration of female migrants. Women often migrate to the cities if they have friends or relatives to live with. Men are more likely to lead a solitary existence or have unstable residences, however, and thus may be omitted from surveys.

5. Age and other characteristics of migrants refer to the time of the census or survey rather than to the time of migration. Since some of these characteristics (such as marital status and occupation) may have changed after migration, the results should be interpreted cautiously.

BIBLIOGRAPHY

Arnold, Fred, and Supani Boonpratuang
1975   *1970 Population and Housing Census: Economic Characteristics.* Subject Report No. 1. Bangkok: National Statistical Office.
1976   *1970 Population and Housing Census: Migration.* Subject Report No. 2. Bangkok: National Statistical Office.

Arnold, Fred, and Susan H. Cochrane
1980   *Economic Motivation versus City Lights: Testing Hypotheses about Inter-Changwat Migration in Thailand.* World Bank Staff Working Paper No. 416. Washington, D.C.: The World Bank.

Arnold, Fred, and Mathana Phananiramai
1975   *Revised Estimates of the 1970 Population of Thailand.* Research Paper No. 1. Bangkok: National Statistical Office.

Arnold, Fred, Robert D. Retherford, and Anuri Wanglee
1977   *The Demographic Situation in Thailand.* Papers of the East-West Population Institute, No. 45. Honolulu: East-West Center.

Chamratrithirong, Apichat
1976   Fertility, nuptiality and migration in Thailand, 1970 census: multiphasic response theory. Unpublished doctoral dissertation, Brown University.

Fawcett, James T.
1980   A value-expectancy approach to migration decisions. Paper presented at the annual meeting of the Population Association of America, Denver, 10–12 April.

Goldstein, Sidney, and Alice Goldstein
1978   Thailand's urban population reconsidered. *Demography* 13:239–58.

Goldstein, Sidney, and Pichit Pitaktepsombati
1974   *Migration and Urban Growth in Thailand: An Exploration of Interrelations Among Origin, Recency and Frequency of Moves.* Institute of Population Studies, Paper No. 14. Bangkok: Chulalongkorn University.

Goldstein, Sidney, Visid Prachuabmoh, and Alice Goldstein
1974   *Urban-Rural Migration Differentials in Thailand.* Institute of Population Studies, Research Report No. 12. Bangkok: Chulalongkorn University.

Goldstein, Sidney, et al.
  n.d.   *Urbanization, Migration, and Fertility in Thailand.* Report submitted to the Center for Population Research, National Institute of Child Health and Human Development. Providence, R.I.: Population Studies and Training Center, Brown University.

Karnasuta, Kattiya
  1978   Development planning for women in Thailand. *Thai Journal of Development Administration* 18:679–704.

Meinkoth, Marian R.
  1962   Migration in Thailand with particular reference to the northeast. *Economic and Business Bulletin* 14:3–45.

Morrison, Peter A.
  1972   *Future Urban Growth and the Nonmetropolitan Population: Policies for Coping with Local Decline.* Santa Monica: Rand Corporation.
  1973   *How Population Movements Shape National Growth.* Santa Monica, California: Rand Corporation.

Piampiti, Suwanlee
  1976a   Internal migration. In *Population of Thailand.* Bangkok: United Nations, ESCAP.
  1976b   *Effects of Migration on Urban Development in the Southern Region of Thailand.* Research Report No. 9. Bangkok: SEAPRAP.
  1978   *Out-Migration from Ayutthaya.* Bangkok: School of Applied Statistics, National Institute of Development Administration. (In Thai.)
  1979   Policies and programs for female migration in Thailand. Paper presented to the Working Group on Women in the Cities, East-West Population Institute, Honolulu, 5–23 March.

Prachuabmoh, Visid, and Penporn Tirasawat
  1974   *Internal Migration in Thailand, 1947–1972.* Paper No. 7. Bangkok: Institute of Population Studies, Chulalongkorn University.

Rhoda, Richard E.
  1979   *Development Activities and Rural-Urban Migration: Is It Possible to Keep Them Down on the Farm?* Washington, D.C.: Office of Urban Development, Bureau for Development Support, Agency for International Development.

Simmons, A., S. Diaz-Briquets, and A. A. Laquain
  1977   *Social Change and Internal Migration: A Review of Research Findings from Africa, Asia, and Latin America.* Ottawa: International Development Research Centre.

Sternstein, Larry
  1976   Migration and development in Thailand. *London Geographical Review* 66: 401–19.

Textor, R. B.
  1961   *From Peasant to Pedicab Driver.* Southeast Asia Studies, Cultural Report Series, No. 9. New Haven: Yale University.

Thailand, Central Statistical Office (CSO)
  1962   *Census of Population, 1960.* Bangkok.

Thailand, Ministry of the Interior (MI)
1978 *Reports on Population Registration Records by Changwat.* Bangkok: Department of Local Administration.

Thailand, National Economic and Social Development Board (NESDB)
1978 *The Fourth Plan.* Bangkok: Office of the Prime Minister.

Thailand, National Statistical Office (NSO)
1972 *1970 Population and Housing Census: Changwat Phra Nakhon and Changwat Thon Buri.* Bangkok.
1973 *1970 Population and Housing Census: Whole Kingdom.* Bangkok.
1976 *The Utilization of Labor in Thailand, 1975.* Bangkok.
1977–79 *The Survey of Migration in Bangkok Metropolis.* Bangkok: National Statistical Office.

Wichiencharoen, Adul
1960 Movements of population within Thailand. *Journal of Public Administration* 1(2):29–35.

Chapter 9

The Migration of Women in the Philippines

Elizabeth U. Eviota
Peter C. Smith

This chapter has two goals: first, to describe contemporary patterns of female migration in the Philippines; and second, to review policy-making and planning in the Philippines as they relate to women and particularly to female migrants. Survey and census data reveal a pattern of female migration that is exceptional in Asia. Women are numerically dominant in almost all kinds of contemporary Philippine migration, and they constitute a large majority in the recent urbanward migration of teenage and young-adult cohorts. In fact, the contemporary sex composition of Philippine migration more readily invites comparison with that of Latin America than with the other countries of Asia represented in this volume.[1]

Employing historical evidence on migration, most of it indirect, we show that the contemporary pattern is not a traditional one in Philippine society; rather, it is an emergent phenomenon. Data for the earlier years of this century suggest that the major migration prior to mid-century was male-dominant—a frontierward (rural-to-rural) movement of a kind that has commonly involved males in many other settings. But even the smaller urbanward migratory streams of a few decades ago comprised mainly men. The transformation of the migration system to its current female-dominant form seems to have begun in the interwar years; by the postwar period this new pattern had become very evident.

We also examine contemporary and historical data on women's occupations in urban areas, which show that there has been concomitant transformation of women's economic roles. Data from the turn of the century indicate that most occupations were filled predominantly by men, whereas more recently women have come to participate in or even dominate many occupational categories. These demographic patterns raise an important question: what is the impetus for these changes? Are certain occupations in the cities now filled by women because migration has increased the availability of women workers in urban areas? Or have women increasingly been attracted to the cities because the job market there has opened up for them? Is demand influencing supply, or the reverse? These alternate views of the same issue have quite different policy implications.

The final section of this essay reviews Philippine policies and programs aimed directly or indirectly at women or migrants. We conclude that despite the demonstrated importance of women in the Philippine migration system there is little official recognition of these patterns in the government's programs. It remains to be seen whether the growing volume of rhetoric and preamble is a genuine response to Philippine realities or merely a defensive reaction.

MIGRATION IN THE PAST

Until recently, the history of migration in the Philippines has been a chronicle of long-distance migrations to national frontiers. The most important shifts of population have resulted from the stimuli of population pressures in areas of origin and the opening of new lands for subsistence or market agriculture in areas of destination. Like frontier migrations elsewhere, the major Philippine migrations of the past century or so have been dominated by men.

Frontierward movement is evident as early as the nineteenth century, when it was stimulated by the economic development policies of the Spanish colonial regimes.[2] There is little quantitative information about that epoch, but nineteenth-century sex ratios for the major receiving regions in comparison with the major source areas make it clear that these early migrations were primarily male. Sex ratios on the frontiers were uniformly high; sex ratios in the sending areas were uniformly low.[3] The expansion of this frontierward migration in the twentieth century is easier to document. The most prominent features of twentieth-century migration are outlined here to provide an empirical backdrop for our later discussion of female migration and its place in the national migration pattern.

The total volume of migration—intraprovincial, interprovincial, and interregional—has certainly been substantial. In 1970 one in four persons nationwide was living away from his or her place of birth, and in the principal destination regions this figure was substantially higher (NCSO 1974: tables IV–9, IV–11). Migrants constituted 30 percent of Mindanao's population and 40 percent of Manila's population.

One of the outstanding characteristics of the Philippine migration system has been its long-distance orientation. Nationwide, nearly twice as many people migrated to another region as migrated within their provinces of birth. It is also evident that this long-distance migration has focused upon particular regions of destination, especially northern and southern Mindanao. The system's long-distance feature is evident in the fact that no fewer than half of all interregional lifetime migrants recorded in the 1960 census had also moved from their zone of birth.[4] Long-distance transfers have significantly redistributed the population; the population of the central or Visayan zone has declined proportionally while the southern (Mindanao) zone's share of the population has increased.

As we have already noted, the male-dominated frontier movements have not persisted. The proportion of female migrants has begun to grow. Some women began to migrate to frontier settlements independently of men, whereas many others were wives of the earliest settlers (Simkins and Wernstedt 1971). In recent years women have constituted the majority of young frontier migrants.

Limited data make it much more difficult to describe the internal migration from rural to urban areas in the early decades of the twentieth century. In general, though, urbanward flows of population do not seem to have been an important component of the total migration system. Pernia (1977: chap. 3) has estimated that the contribution of migration to urban growth was actually negative in the period from 1903 to 1939 and migrants accounted for only 15 to 20 percent of the urban growth between 1939 and 1960. He attributes most of the urban growth of those early decades to reclassification of areas from rural to urban status and to natural increase within cities.

But the migration system has undergone a transformation in recent decades. The frontier exodus has ended, and in its place we find a predominance of urbanward movement—mainly young and mainly female.

THE NEW MIGRATION PATTERN

By the 1960s the pattern of migration had gained diversity. No longer dominated by the major frontier movements, the national migration system included growing numbers of people moving in new directions, and the interregional flows were supplemented by important shifts of population within regions and provinces. Among these migrations were rural-to-urban shifts both within and across provincial boundaries.

But migration continued to be dominated by the young and, for the first time, by younger women. This pattern, which persists today, is demonstrated by indexes of age and sex composition among recent migrants, shown in Table 9.1 separately for rural, urban, and metropolitan destinations. In general, female migrants to both urban and rural destinations tend to be 15 to 34 years of age whereas male migrants tend to be somewhat older. Among women, short-distance migrants tend to be younger than long-distance movers. The sex ratios in these recent streams are especially interesting. The more urban the destination, the more likely the migrant is to be female. More than two out of three urban migrants in the 1960s who were 15 to 19 years old in 1970 were female, and the percentage of females was even higher among metropolitan migrants.

It is likely that most female migrants over age 30 at the time of migra-

Table 9.1 Indexes of age selectivity by sex and sex ratios, among migrants in the 1960s, by type of destination and distance of move

Measure and group	Destination Manila		Destination other urban		Destination rural	
	From another province	From same province	From another province	From same province	From another province	From same province
Age-selectivity indexes—male						
10–14	−37.87	9.85				
15–19	17.85	−4.15				
20–24	55.85	−13.00	31.8		12.1	4.3
25–29	34.41	−8.01	41.9	14.7	34.9	15.0
30–34	−0.97	22.58	23.7	28.9	34.0	17.5
35–39	−17.04	3.97	0.0	16.7	12.4	11.2
40+	−38.55	−16.83				
Age-selectivity indexes—female						
10–14	−35.92	11.35				
15–19	57.38	−18.13				
20–24	46.45	−14.68	26.3	23.1	25.3	3.0
25–29	6.17	−1.95	38.3	8.6	36.2	30.7
30–34	−18.70	5.91	23.7	15.3	18.2	26.0
35–39	−37.06	11.71	1.0	5.0		10.1
40+	−45.17	14.28				
Sex ratios						
10–14	728	1,006	822	818	1,030	1,090
15–19	442	936	473	471	835	757
20–24	675	879	671	557	859	675

Sex ratios *(continued)*

25–29	957	963	935	769	1,031	908
30–34	935	987	1,084	1,029	1,215	1,010
35–39	1,019	977	1,154	1,157	1,259	1,160
40–44	1,050	919	1,056	983	1,182	1,084
45–49	929	966	1,006	988	1,168	969
50–54	534	926	836	940[b]	1,231	875
All ages[a]	699	949	784	744[b]	1,027	906

a. Ten years and older.

b. Based on fewer than 1,000 cases.

Source: NCSO (1979: table IV-10).

tion were moving with husbands and families, but a high percentage of the younger female migrants must have been single—migrating in a fairly autonomous fashion.[5] The character of the entire metropolitan migration stream—indeed, of the entire metropolis—has been strongly influenced by this youth cohort of female migrants.

The recent pattern of female-dominant migration in the youth cohort is remarkably widespread. It is found in a variety of interregional and rural-to-urban streams involving varying distances of migration (Table 9.2). Urbanward migration everywhere is uniformly more female in composition than is migration to rural destinations. Significantly, this is true regardless of the destination: less or more developed; sending area or frontier. That rural, short-distance migration tends to be more equally divided between men and women suggests that it is associated with family or marriage. Migration over longer distances tends increasingly to be female, with the exception of migration to the frontier provinces where the older pattern of male-dominant pioneering apparently lingers. Some of the lowest sex ratios are found in urbanward migration streams over intermediate distances.

Other indications of the importance of young female migrants are provided by other data not shown here. First, the prevalence of migrants is very high among the young. In 1970, lifetime migrants made up nearly

Table 9.2 Sex ratios among persons 15-24 years old, by type of migration during the 1960s and area of destination

Area of destination	Type of migration			
	All types	Intra-municipality	Other intra-provincial	Inter-provincial
Frontier				
Urban	785	836	556	706
Rural	952	960	816	976
Less developed				
Urban	842	923	428	603
Rural	997	1038	723	650
More developed				
Urban	807	896	422	570
Rural	954	989	660	762
Metropolitan				
Manila	778	916	935	553
Urban Rizal	731	887	754	557

Source: NCSO (1974).

one-third of the age group among females and more than one-fourth among males. The prevalence of migrants is highest among females in all categories of current residence and type of migration. Second, although urbanward streams are important for both sexes, women are at the forefront in this respect. Among recent (five-year) migrants in 1970, some 57.6 percent of the females had urban destinations compared with 48.7 percent among the males.

URBANIZATION AND FILIPINO WOMEN

One of the most important characteristics of female urbanward migration in the Philippines is that is it not entirely or even primarily a migration to the largest metropolitan area. Only one-third of the urbanward total was found in the Manila metropolitan area in 1970, much of this in cities outside though near Manila itself. On the other hand, six out of ten of the female migrants moved to a large city. The remainder moved to municipal *poblaciónes* (small towns) and smaller chartered cities. A disaggregation of these migrants into long and short-distance (interprovincial and intraprovincial) migrants shows that the streams to big cities, including Manila, were dominated by women moving long distances across provincial boundaries, whereas the streams to the smaller cities and *poblaciónes* were dominated by persons moving within the same province.

That the inflow to cities is largely a new phenomenon is indicated by the 1939–70 trend in big-city sex ratios. A scatterplot of sex ratios at ages 15–19 and 20–24 in the 50 largest cities (Figure 9.1) illustrates the variety of patterns. Most of the large cities have seen declining sex ratios in the important 15–19 and 20–24 age groups, and in most cities the 1970 sex ratios indicate a predominance of women. The transformation of sex composition at ages 20–24 is especially prominent. The high prewar ratios in many cities have entirely disappeared, for reasons that vary from city to city. The sharp decline in the Olongapo City sex ratio, for example, is surely related to the entertainment and service industry that has grown up around the nearby U.S. naval base. Other cities that have seen sharp declines are frontier settlements that have recently matured and stabilized (Zamboanga, Davao, Cotabato).

The forces underlying the historical evolution of these urban sex ratios are too complex to examine here in detail. It is useful, though, to look briefly at the 1970 pattern of variation across major cities. We examine two indexes of female migration: first, the prevalence of ten-year (1960–70) migrants among females ten years old and over in 1970, and second, the sex ratios among migrants of ten and over in 1970. Correlations of both migration indexes with selected social and economic indicators are given in Table 9.3.

Figure 9.1 Postwar sex ratio changes in the 50 largest Philippine cities: 1939—70

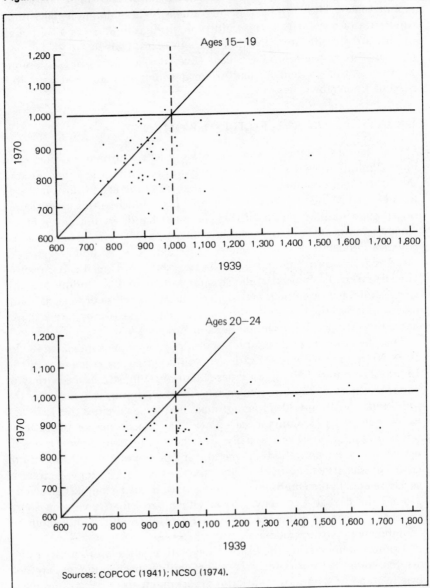

Sources: COPCOC (1941); NCSO (1974).

Table 9.3 Zero-order correlations between two indexes of female migration and selected social and economic characteristics of females: 50 largest cities in 1970

Social or economic characteristic	Index of female migration in the 1960s	
	Prevalence	Sex ratio
% single, ages 20–24	0.195	-0.619[b]
% literate, ages 15–19	0.291[a]	-0.449[b]
% attending school	0.377[b]	-0.076
% economically active	0.030	-0.306[a]
% economically active in service occupations	0.609[b]	-0.539[b]

a. Significant at the 0.05 level.
b. Significant at the 0.01 level.
Source: Calculated from NCSO (1974, reports by province).

Examination of individual cities indicates that female-dominant streams are found throughout all the cities of Luzon and in most Visayan and Mindanao cities. In most cases women predominate in recent migration to surrounding provincial areas as well, although there are ten cities in provinces of heavy male in-migration that nevertheless attract more women than men. Only 11 among the 50 largest cities draw males disproportionately. The ten cases involve primarily the lingering frontier area of Mindanao (notably the cities of Cagayan de Oro and Davao); of the latter 11 cases, six are in Mindanao and five in the Visayas (especially Bacolod and Negros Occidental).

Correlations between these city sex ratios, the prevalence of female migrants, and socioeconomic variables (Table 9.3) suggest some of the forces that may be at work. The data indicate that the cities most attractive to migrants have tended to draw those of both sexes; as a result, male and female migration prevalences are highly correlated across cities ($r = 0.967$). Nevertheless, the sex ratio among migrants does have substantial variability (standard deviation $= 130.1$), and the prevalence of female migrants and the sex ratio among migrants are virtually uncorrelated across cities ($r = 0.013$). Clearly these two migration indexes measure quite different aspects of the female migration pattern: the prevalence of female migrants and the degree of female dominance in the total migration stream.

What kind of city attracts disproportionate numbers of females? Some indication is provided by the correlations across cities on certain female social and economic characteristics. The percentage economically active and the prevalence of migrants are uncorrelated, yet the same economic variable is significantly correlated with the migrant sex ratio. Thus a high proportion of economically active women is found in cities where females are the prevalent migrants. This finding suggests indirectly that economically active migrant women tend to be single or otherwise independent—an inference that is supported by the correlation between the female percentage single and the migrant sex ratio (-0.619). Note that both migrant prevalence and the migrant sex ratio are associated with the proportion of economically active women in service occupations. The services category is largest where female migrants are most prevalent and also where the proportion female among migrants is highest. We will have a further look at this result later in the analysis.

Another reason for female migration to cities is schooling, for the correlation between the percentage in school and migrant prevalence is positive. The correlation is positive for males as well ($r = 0.338$), however, and the schooling variable is uncorrelated with the migrant sex ratio. Educational opportunity seems to be a major stimulus for both sexes.

Finally, urban literacy is correlated with both female migration indexes. The highest literacy is found where both the prevalence of migrants and the proportion female among migrants are highest. The reason for this result is unclear. Perhaps women are attracted (more than men) to areas of high literacy, but if literate women are being drawn to cities disproportionately it would lead to the same result.

This brief analysis needs to be extended to additional variables describing both of the sexes, but even the few results just described suggest an important conclusion: Many Philippine cities have recently been attracting disproportionate numbers of single, literate women whose urban lifestyles involve a high level of economic activity, especially in the urban service economy. The occupational data examined later corroborate this conclusion.

Despite the spatial ubiquity of female urbanward migration, the primacy of Manila in the national life of the Philippines and in the national migration system should not be understated. Already important administratively and culturally by the end of the Spanish era, Manila's significance grew in the twentieth century. It has emerged as the single most important destination for migrants. Early twentieth-century migration to the metropolitan city was dominated by men, but more recently women have moved to Manila in disproportionate numbers. This transition is indicated by the following series of sex ratios (males per 100 females) for Manila:

Ages	1903	1918	1939	1970
15–19	1,414	1,356	921	759
20–24	1,592	1,551	1,109	855

In the 1960s, when the metropolitan area contained 13.0 percent of the national population, more than one in three (35.9 percent) of the women who changed their province of residence moved there. We will see later that the effect of this disproportion in numbers is heightened by the proportions of educational and other resources these young women represent.

Just as Manila is central in the national migration pattern, migrants have a significant place in Manila's population composition. Table 9.4 shows that little more than half the metropolitan population in 1970 had been born in the metropolitan region. The migrant share of population is especially high among women in central Manila, where nearly six out of ten 1970 residents were born elsewhere. Even more significantly, one in four males ten years old or more in 1970, and a higher fraction of women, had migrated to the metropolitan area within the preceding decade. The data suggest also that for both sexes the greatest recent in-migration has been to the suburban towns, where among females nearly four in ten were migrants. The sex ratios indicate that the proportion female is greatest both among the most recent arrivals and among those moving to central Manila.

In subsequent sections of this study we examine two prominent social changes of the twentieth century and their links with female migration to cities. First, we look at the phenomenal growth of education and the selectivity on educational attainment so evident among recent female migrants. Then we consider the realm of women's occupations—the pattern of migrants' previous occupations and the occupational niches that migrants of each sex find for themselves in the cities.

THE IMPACT OF EDUCATION AND LITERACY

The growth of education is probably the single most important social change in the Philippines in the present century, and its importance is especially pronounced for women. Two major changes have occurred. First, the mean level of educational attainment has risen across the population as a whole, so that in a recent cohort the average adult had about ten years of schooling and nearly all adults were literate; second, sex differentials in educational attainment and literacy have been reduced substantially (Smith and Cheung 1981).

In contrast to this picture of convergence, urban/rural differentials in education have persisted and a pronounced selectivity of the well-educated into rural-to-urban migration streams is exacerbating the problem. Table 9.5 classifies the educational attainments of men and women by their current residence and migrant status. It is evident that the urban and especially the metropolitan sectors are drawing the educated population away from the rural areas. The percentage who completed at least some high school is almost as high among male rural-to-urban migrants as among

Table 9.4 Percentages in selected migration statuses and sex ratios in each migration status: sectors of the Manila metropolitan area in 1970, by sex

Index and migration status	Metropolitan area							
	Total		Manila City		Suburbs		Fringe	
	Male	Female	Male	Female	Male	Female	Male	Female
Percentage in selected migration statuses								
Native-born[a]	58.6	54.4	62.0	42.9	94.2	85.9	69.1	66.9
Migrants, 1960–70[b]	25.7	30.4	18.9	24.0	32.0	38.0	23.9	25.9
Migrants, 1965–70[c]	13.7	17.5	9.7	13.5	16.8	21.6	13.7	15.4
Sex ratio								
Native-born[a]	1,013		1,347		1,017		1,006	
Migrants, 1960–70[b]	754		699		737		857	
Migrants, 1965–70[c]	723		650		702		846	

a. All ages; includes those whose place of birth was not stated.
b. Population ten years of age and over.
c. Population five years of age and over.
Source: Flieger et al. (1977: tables 17–19).

urban natives, for example, and is twice as high as in the stay-behind rural population. Of importance here is the usual location of post-primary school facilities in urban places.

Two observations summarize these data. First, the educational attainment of migrants tends to be intermediate between that of rural stayers and urban natives. Second, the pattern of educational selectivity is much stronger for women than for men, particularly among women moving from the rural areas to the metropolis. These patterns among females have important implications for the individual migrants, some of which are explored below in connection with data on occupations. But there are dramatic implications for the sending and receiving communities as well.

URBAN JOBS AND URBANWARD MIGRATION

The character of the metropolitan economy has undergone momentous change in the past 75 years in response to a variety of forces, including technological changes and the evolution of a Philippine role in the international trade system. One of the most important social consequences of Philippine economic development is the rise of a westernized and capitalist middle and upper class and a service economy organized around it. Some occupations have expanded while others have declined. Although we can-

Table 9.5 Educational attainment among persons 15 years old and over, by place of residence, migrant status, and sex: 1973

Area and migrant status	Female (%)			Male (%)		
	No schooling	Elementary (grades 1–7)[a]	At least some high school	No schooling	Elementary (grades 1–7)[a]	At least some high school
Rural						
Native (nonmigrant)	14.5	61.7	23.8	11.7	61.8	26.5
In-migrant from other rural area	7.0	68.7	24.4	7.1	72.5	20.4
In-migrant from urban area	10.5	55.5	33.9	15.5	40.9	43.6
Urban (excluding metropolitan)						
Native (nonmigrant)	8.1	42.4	49.4	5.4	41.1	53.6
In-migrant from other urban area	4.1	30.2	65.7	1.8	30.0	68.3
In-migrant from rural area	7.9	42.3	50.7	5.9	41.0	53.0
Metropolitan						
Native (nonmigrant)	3.5	24.6	71.7	2.3	20.7	77.0
In-migrant from urban area	1.4	31.8	66.8	0.7	21.9	77.5
In-migrant from rural area	1.4	46.3	52.3	0.9	27.5	71.6

a. Includes persons for whom no information on educational attainment was available.

Source: Based on Pernia (1977: app. table 11).

not describe these changes here, it is important to recognize certain critical aspects of the urban labor market as they bear upon women's work in the city. We illustrate changes at the two extremes of the distribution: professional and technical occupations at one end and service occupations at the other.

The professional ranks (Table 9.6) at the turn of the century were very limited for both sexes. Males were widely distributed in the various professional occupations, but women were virtually confined within two categories: "professors and teachers" (mainly elementary and secondary school teachers) and "nurses, etc." (encompassing a variety of subordinate roles within the medical profession). These were the only professional occupations having anything near proportionate representation by women.

In the ensuing decades women began to find their way into other professional occupations, but they continued to be concentrated in teaching and nursing. Only one professional female out of five in 1970 was not in one or the other of these fields, and professions other than these two had a combined sex ratio indicating about three men for every woman.

At the other end of the occupational continuum—the "services, sports, and related occupations"—we find dramatic improvement in the sex ratio overall but little change in the distribution of women's occupations. In 1903, some 93.0 percent of all female service workers were domestics; this figure was roughly maintained through 1970. The most important change within the services category came in the remarkable transformation of the sex ratio among servants and household help. By 1970 nearly nine in ten persons in the domestic help categories were women, in contrast to the more balanced sex composition of the occupation earlier in the century. Thus women in the services category have continued to be concentrated in these low-pay, subordinate occupations. The domestic jobs are now dominated by women, whereas the remaining service occupations are more nearly balanced in their sex composition or are dominated by men.

With this information as background, we turn now to evidence showing the most common urban occupations of migrant and urban-born men and women. It will be apparent that the evolution of the urban labor force and the transformation of the migration system are closely related developments. The broad outlines of the occupational distribution in 1973 are indicated in Table 9.7. We focus on the major differences between the urban-born of each residence category and those who were migrants from another residential sector. Two prominent patterns among females should be highlighted. First, the professional, clerical, and sales categories (essentially the white-collar occupations) employed the majority of native urban women who were working (62.2 percent) but little more than one-third of the working women who had come to the urban sector from the rural sector. Second, and in contrast, the service occupations employed only 16.6 percent of urban-born working women in the urban sector, but they em-

Table 9.6 Selected indicators of changing participation in the Manila work force among persons 15–24 years old: 1903–70

Occupation	Percentage distributions						Sex ratios[a]		
	Female			Male					
	1903[a]	1939	1970	1903[a]	1939	1970	1903[a]	1939	1970
All occupations	100.0	100.0	99.9	99.9	100.1	100.0	2,674	1,644	1,813
Professional, technical, and related	1.0	7.3	5.8	1.6	4.3	1.5	4,686	963	456
Service, sport, and related	40.8	52.9	31.2	35.7	20.6	4.7	1,498	639	273
All other	58.2	39.8	62.9	62.6	75.2	93.8	2,878	3,102	2,692
Professional, technical, related	100.0	99.9	100.0	100.0	100.0	100.1	5,247	963	666
Professor, teacher	52.4	31.8	56.7	8.4	5.2	6.0	838	157	69
Nurse, midwife, medical not elsewhere classified	45.8	33.5	21.9	0.1	17.8	3.0	17	511	91
All other	1.8	34.6	21.4	91.5	77.0	91.1	26,672	2,141	2,837
Service, sport, related	100.0	100.0	99.9	100.0	100.1	99.9	2,449	639	256
Servant, houseboy, housegirl	31.8	82.7	90.2	21.3	54.8	46.5	1,637	423	
Cook	3.2	1.8	2.7	5.3	7.2		4,035	2,617	132
Launderer	58.0	6.5		2.9	2.0		123	200	
Waiter/waitress	0.0	2.9		0.0	12.6	11.1		2,789	1,039
All other	7.0	6.1	7.0	70.5	23.5	42.3	21,541	2,446	1,537

Note: Percentages may not sum to 100.0 because of rounding.

a. All ages.

Sources: USBOC (1905); COPCOC (1941); NCSO (1974).

Table 9.7 Occupational distributions among persons, by place of current residence, migrant status, and sex: 1973

Current residence and migrant status	Female (%)						Male (%)					
	All occupa-tions	Prof., clerical, sales	Farm-ing, mining	Trans-port, commu-nication	Crafts	Ser-vices	All occupa-tions	Prof., clerical, sales	Farm-ing, mining	Trans-port, commu-nication	Crafts	Ser-vices
Rural	100.0	29.0	39.2	0.5	24.1	7.2	99.9	5.7	78.0	6.3	7.7	2.2
Native (nonmigrant)	99.9	29.3	38.9	0.3	24.9	6.5	100.1	5.7	79.2	6.0	7.1	2.1
In-migrant from other rural area	100.0	15.0	56.5	2.7	7.5	18.3	100.0	3.5	76.0	7.2	12.1	1.2
In-migrant from urban or metropolitan area	100.1	41.0	24.2	1.4	23.9	9.6	99.9	10.4	56.1	11.5	16.1	5.8
Urban (excluding metropolitan)	100.0	55.6	7.3	0.7	9.7	26.7	99.9	23.8	37.8	15.0	16.8	6.5
Native (nonmigrant)	99.9	62.2	8.9	1.0	11.8	16.0	100.0	22.5	39.2	15.2	17.5	5.6
In-migrant from other urban area	100.0	54.4	1.3	0.0	10.0	34.3	100.0	45.7	18.6	11.8	18.5	5.4
In-migrant from rural area	100.0	39.2	4.7	0.0	4.5	51.6	99.9	21.6	38.7	15.5	13.2	10.9
Metropolitan	100.0	47.8	0.1	1.7	10.2	40.2	100.0	40.4	3.3	18.2	27.6	10.5
Native (nonmigrant)	100.1	72.9	0.3	2.5	17.2	7.2	99.9	41.7	2.8	18.4	28.6	8.4
In-migrant from non-metropolitan urban area	99.9	49.8	0.0	1.4	8.1	40.6	100.0	44.3	2.3	16.3	24.5	12.6
In-migrant from rural area	100.0	18.7	0.0	1.2	4.3	75.8	99.9	30.4	6.2	20.6	29.9	12.8

Note: Percentages may not sum to 100.0 because of rounding.

Sources: 1973 National Demographic Survey; Pernia (1975).

ployed fully half the working in-migrants from rural origins. Moreover, both of these native/migrant differentials are even sharper in the metropolitan region. The metropolitan differentials between the native-born and migrants are remarkable. Nearly three in four employed native urban women are in white-collar occupations, compared with fewer than one in four among migrant women. Similarly, only one in 14 is in a service occupation, compared with three of four among migrants. There are native/migrant occupational differences among men as well, but they are not nearly so important. Men are more widely dispersed across the occupational groups, and as migrants they are less sharply segregated.

These observations are borne out by detailed tabulations of occupation and other characteristics. In Table 9.8 we present a detailed occupational classification, with the adult urban population of each sex divided into urban-born and migrant groups. The latter group is disaggregated to distinguish recent migrants and, among these, persons who might be considered typical of modern migrants—those young (under 30 years of age) and still single in 1973.

Among females with occupations, we note that the professional ranks are disproportionately the preserve of the urban-born. One in five is a professional, and 56 percent of all professional women are urban-born. Among males the urban-born are also prominent, but lifetime migrants play a significant role as well. The urban-born are also prominent in the clerical and sales occupations but are otherwise fairly equally distributed across occupations. The single significant exception is the "service and sports" occupations, which are poorly represented by both sexes; these occupations are dominated by migrants.

Seven of ten females in the services category are migrants; and more than half of these, 39 percent of the women in the category, are young, single, and recent migrants. Among men a similar though somewhat less remarkable pattern is found. Nearly six out of ten males in the service occupations are migrants; these men tend to be long-term rather than recent migrants, older and married rather than young and single. (A more refined occupational classification might show that men and women tend to work in different occupations within the services category.)

Finally, nearly all the females in the services were domestics, whereas fewer than half the males are in this category. Remarkably, of female domestics in urban areas in 1973, 41.3 percent were young, recently arrived, and single.

These data present a picture of extreme occupational differentiation—by sex and migrant status and by age and marital status. What these tables do not tell us is the meaning of these prominent patterns for the life chances of the people involved. Particularly in the case of young, single females—so large a component of recent urbanward migration—two questions need to be answered. First, looking back to the rural preparation of

Table 9.8 Detailed occupational characteristics of urban residents, by sex and

| Occupation | Female | | |
	All persons 15+	Urban-born	Lifetime rural-to-urban migrants
Percentage distribution by occupation			
All occupations	**100.0**	**99.9**	**100.0**
Professional, technical, administrative	**19.3**	**22.6**	**16.3**
Professor, teacher	12.7	15.6	10.0
All other	6.6	7.0	6.3
Clerical, sales	**37.5**	**43.2**	**32.1**
Working proprietor, trader	10.9	11.0	10.7
Sales person, vendor, etc.	14.8	16.5	13.3
All other	11.8	15.7	8.1
Transport, communication	**1.0**	**1.5**	**0.5**
Crafts, general labor	**10.7**	**11.2**	**10.2**
Tailor, dressmaker, etc.	5.5	6.0	5.1
All other	5.2	5.2	5.1
Service, sport	**29.3**	**18.9**	**38.7**
Housekeeper, cook, maid, etc.	26.1	16.3	35.1
All other	3.1	2.6	3.6
Agriculture, mining	**2.3**	**2.4**	**2.2**
Percentage distribution by migration experience			
All occupations	**100.0**	**47.7**	**52.3**
Professional, technical, administrative	**100.0**	**55.9**	**44.1**
Professor, teacher	100.0	58.9	41.1
All other	100.0	50.4	49.6
Clerical, sales	**100.0**	**55.2**	**44.8**
Working proprietor, trader	100.0	48.5	51.5
Sales person, vendor, etc.	100.0	53.2	46.8
All other	100.0	63.8	36.2
Transport, communication	**100.0**	**71.4**	**28.6**
Crafts, general labor	**100.0**	**50.0**	**50.0**
Tailor, dressmaker, etc.	100.0	51.7	48.3
All other	100.0	48.1	51.9
Service, sport	**100.0**	**30.9**	**69.1**
Housekeeper, cook, maid, etc.	100.0	29.8	70.2
All other	100.0	40.0	60.0
Agriculture, mining	**100.0**	**50.0**	**50.0**

Note: Percentages may not sum to 100.0 because of rounding.
Source: 1973 National Demographic Survey.

migration status: 1973

		Male				
Recent migrants				Lifetime rural-to-urban migrants	Recent migrants	
All	15–24 and single	All persons 15+	Urban-born		All	15–24 and single
100.0	99.9	100.0	100.0	100.1	99.9	100.0
10.3	4.1	12.6	11.2	13.9	9.3	4.3
7.2	2.8	1.7	1.5	2.0	1.8	1.6
3.1	1.3	10.9	9.7	11.9	7.5	2.7
25.2	15.0	22.1	24.0	20.3	16.1	17.7
7.0	0.6	5.7	5.7	5.6	3.1	0.0
12.8	10.0	7.1	7.7	6.5	6.5	10.2
5.4	4.4	9.3	10.6	8.2	6.5	7.5
0.7	0.6	17.8	17.5	18.1	20.0	20.9
7.2	5.6	25.2	25.2	25.2	28.2	27.8
3.1	1.3	1.9	1.6	2.2	2.5	3.7
4.1	4.4	23.2	23.6	23.0	25.7	24.1
54.1	74.0	8.9	7.8	9.8	11.3	17.1
50.2	70.8	1.5	1.1	1.8	2.8	7.5
3.9	3.1	7.3	6.7	7.9	8.5	9.6
2.4	0.6	13.4	14.2	12.7	15.0	12.3
25.8	15.2	100.0	46.7	53.3	20.2	5.3
13.9	3.2	100.0	41.4	58.6	14.9	1.8
14.7	3.4	100.0	40.3	59.7	21.0	4.8
12.2	2.9	100.0	41.6	58.4	14.0	1.3
17.4	6.1	100.0	50.8	49.2	14.8	4.2
16.7	0.9	100.0	47.3	52.7	10.9	0.0
22.3	10.3	100.0	50.8	49.2	18.7	7.5
11.8	5.7	100.0	53.0	47.0	14.2	4.2
19.0	9.5	100.0	45.8	54.2	22.7	6.2
17.4	8.0	99.9	46.6	53.3	22.7	5.8
14.7	3.4	100.0	38.2	61.8	26.5	10.3
20.4	13.0	100.0	47.3	52.7	22.4	5.4
47.7	38.6	100.0	41.3	58.7	25.7	10.2
49.5	41.3	100.0	35.2	64.8	37.0	25.9
32.3	15.4	100.0	42.5	57.5	23.4	6.9
27.1	4.2	100.0	49.5	50.5	22.6	4.8

these young people for life as urban migrants, we wonder what characteristics matter for occupational placement and urban chances generally. Second, looking ahead, it is important to determine the occupational futures
of migrants in these various occupational niches and whether prospects
differ by sex, education, or other characteristics.

On the second issue our data fail us, for we have only cross-sectional
information. Recently migrated young single women may appear disproportionately in the domestic services simply because they are recent arrivals. Their future may include steady movement out of this migrant en-
clave to a wider range of economic possibilities—through future education
perhaps, or through marriage, or simply by acquiring a better grasp of the
workings of the urban labor market. Alternatively, the domestic occupations may represent an economic dead end into which the surplus labor of
women is drawn. Data on the subsequent life cycles and careers of domestic servants are sorely lacking.

On the first question—whether the occupations of migrants depend on
background characteristics other than sex (which surely does matter)—the
evidence suggests that educational preparation counts for little, at least
until a fairly high level of education is attained. Distinguishing females
with advanced education (six or more years of formal schooling), we find
that more than four in five among the recent, young, and single migrants
in the services category had at least this level of education. Of those with
considerable education just over half are in the services.

It is the contrast of this pattern with the case for male migrants that is
most disturbing. Among well-educated males, 28.7 percent are in white-
collar occupations, another 20.5 percent are in transportation and communications (especially truck and jeepney drivers and refuse collectors in the
informal sector), and 28.3 percent are in crafts (especially mechanics,
machine operators, and carpenters).

The picture improves among female migrants with some exposure to a
college education. Three of four are in white-collar employment, primarily
in the clerical and sales categories. Nevertheless, nearly one in five, even
among college women, are in the services.

POLICIES AND PROGRAMS

Despite the volume and economic significance of female migration in the
Philippines, there are no government policies or programs that reflect an
understanding of female migration patterns. Moreover, research on female migrants is scarce and focuses mainly on the adaptation of married
women migrants as members of households. In this final section, therefore, we discuss what the government and the private sector are doing to
influence the movement of persons in general.

In the early 1970s, the government initiated a variety of programs related to migration (Ocampo 1976; Cariño 1976). Cariño (1976:260–63) describes these programs as follows:

1. *Programs and activities that encourage people to stay where they are.* There are programs for building local institutions [for] strengthening the capabilities and increasing the resources of local governments, in order to keep people in the rural areas. Examples are the management and training assistance given by the government, community programs which give grants-in-aid and technical assistance to the barrios (localities), and revenue-sharing schemes which allocate to less developed areas some share of tax revenues. There are also programs to extend or transfer technology to the rural areas, including rural electrification, the installment of improved water-supply systems, projects in agricultural extension like the introduction of high-yielding varieties of rice and other crops, and the establishment of barangay [village] secondary schools.

2. *Programs and activities that discourage people from moving to certain areas.* An example is the "Libre ang Pilipino" program through which children of bona fide Manila residents enjoyed free access to the public schools of the city.

3. *Programs and activities that encourage people to move to rural areas.* An example was the government effort to transfer farmers to Mindanao through various subsidized resettlement projects.

4. *Programs and activities that encourage people to move to smaller urban areas.* The recently adopted regional approach to development exemplifies this category. Regions were delineated and regional capitals were selected as sites for regional offices and as secondary growth centers that could serve as "counter-magnets" and rechannel movement away from the primate city.

5. *Programs and activities that cope with the problems brought about by internal migration.* Some examples are programs that deal with problems of urban growth, such as inadequate urban services (e.g., garbage disposal, water, electricity), housing shortages, slums and squatting, crime, and the poor quality of education.

6. *Institutional supports for programs and activities that influence internal migration.*

As this scheme implies, most migration policies in the Philippines are intended to have a broad impact; rarely do they distinguish among types of migrant. The most common type of policy is directed at regional restrictions on migration.

To deal with urban slum dwellers and squatters, for example, the government has initiated a resettlement scheme providing subsidized home-sites and housing. The major goal of the program is to relieve congestion in the Manila metropolitan area. The program has had limited success in resettlement areas like Carmona and Sapang Palay, however, because of limited availability of jobs as well as inadequate housing, services, and environmental amenities at the resettlement sites.

Since the desire for work or an increase in pay is a decisive influence in the migration process, there are labor programs to create appropriate jobs and give job-seekers access to them. But these are small-scale programs having little overall effect.

Another policy instrument involves government sanctions to regulate polluting and hazardous industries within a 50-kilometer radius of Manila. The government offers infrastructure facilities to firms willing to locate outside this radius. There is also a program to disperse government offices into frontier regions. The measures being taken include the decentralization of offices, the building of secondary growth centers in other regions, and the location of colleges and universities in areas outside metropolitan Manila.

The arguments for and against these policies have centered on whether they are equitable for in-migrants and whether they exploit the country-side. The apparent difficulties of these schemes suggest the complexities of migration-related government action. Thus policies to reduce congestion in cities can simultaneously draw people to the same cities.

Insofar as these policies affect the movement of all persons, they can have indirect consequences on women's lives. As we have illustrated in the preceding section, however, programs and policies have not been responsive to the changing composition of Philippine migration—that is, to the new importance of young females. In the absence of explicit programs and policies, therefore, we turn to programs directed toward women generally. In response to the designation of 1975 as International Women's Year, the Philippine government established a National Commission on the Role of Filipino Women (NCRFW). The commission's professed goal, derived from the National Economic and Development Authority's (NEDA) Five-Year Philippine Development Plan, 1978–1982, is to achieve a "much improved quality of life for every Filipino."

Although the NCRFW bases its rationale for program expenditures on current policies in the national development plan, it is notable that the national plan makes no mention of women as a focus of concern. This absence of an affirmative statement on behalf of women reflects the common notion among development planners in government of the current role of Philippine women: that women's participation is already at a high level and, consequently, the proper course is merely to sustain that participation. Further, the basic concern of the government, frequently reiterated, is maximum feasible economic growth, the achievement of which is assumed automatically to benefit both women and men. To quote a common slogan, women and men are "partners in progress."

A coordinated national plan of action on the role of women in Philippine development has not yet emerged from the NCRFW nor, for that matter, from any other government agency. Nevertheless, both the government and the private sector have made limited efforts at dealing with the situation of women locally. These efforts can be classified into four types: those concerned with legal reforms, those concerned with the education of women and their employability, those directed to improving their material welfare, and those that attempt to enhance women's participation in decision-making.

LEGAL REFORMS

Legislative reforms have been proposed by the University of the Philippines Law Center and the NCRFW. These reforms are directed toward changing laws that discriminate against women. They are meant to ensure equality either in the maintenance or in the dissolution of the marital bond, in childrearing and support of the family, and in the inheritance, acquisition, and disposition of property. The Bureau of Women and Minors in the Ministry of Labor and the NCRFW have proposed amendments to the labor code to remove barriers to the employment of women. These amendments cover equality in the terms and conditions of employment, including equal pay for equal work.

EDUCATION

Public and private efforts have been made to improve the quality of women's education. The Ministry of Education and Culture (MEC) and the NCRFW have given priority to providing learning modules on equal rights, which will soon be included in the elementary and secondary level courses. The National Federation of Women's Clubs has initiated training for women through child-care centers, nutrition and nursery classes, consumer affairs groups, community beautification and cleanliness campaigns, food production efforts, literacy programs, and home industry projects. The NCRFW itself conducts open forums and public information classes to educate women, leadership training seminars to help rural women, and managerial skills workshops. It also offers a scholarship program and assistance to minority women.

EMPLOYMENT

Employment programs for women are of two kinds: those that aim at increasing women's productivity by involving them directly in market activity and those that look after the welfare of working women. The first type of program trains women by organizing them into productive units and providing them with training in skills and with technical, financial, and institutional supports for production and marketing. Philippine Business for Social Progress (PBSP), a private foundation, has been particularly active in supporting women in food processing, swine and poultry raising, and handicraft and cottage industries. The NCRFW has also initiated a program encouraging women to engage in income-generating activites. The Foundation for the Advancement of Filipino Women (FAFW), another private foundation, funds income-generating and health projects. Other agencies place emphasis on leadership skills in their training and employment programs. Most of these agencies coordinate with nongovernmental organizations to implement their projects at the local level.

The other type of employment program, which oversees the welfare of working women, is directed primarily by the Women's Division of the Ministry of Labor. This division monitors the labor standards applied to women workers, conducts discussion groups with women workers, undertakes information drives on worker rights, and provides guidance, counseling, and referral services. It has been active in helping women in service occupations, especially "hospitality girls," waitresses, and unorganized women workers. One program of "mass lifelong education" reaches out to working women in rural and depressed areas.

PARTICIPATION IN DECISION-MAKING

PBSP has emphasized organizing women and involving them in decision-making. It stresses training in leadership and organizational skills that will enable women to manage business and community projects. The Young Women's Christian Association (YWCA) gears its projects toward widening income-earning opportunities by holding seminars where women can develop social graces, management potential, and leadership skills. The Civic Assembly of Women of the Philippines (CAWP) holds leadership training seminars for rural women. The Kapisanang ng Kabataan Barangay (associations of village women) provide channels for women's participation in public affairs.

WHERE THE PROGRAMS FAIL

The task of programs for women is to improve the quality of women's lives. In this respect, all these programs are valuable, though they are organized on too small a scale to influence more than a fraction of their target population. But their main shortcoming is the traditional conception of women's economic and social roles on which they all seem to be based. Most of these programs attempt to enhance women's abilities as secondary earners in households headed and supported by their spouses. As a result, many of the training programs aim to inculcate skills that are judged to be compatible with responsibilities in the home, whereas training programs for men are frequently directed to developing skills marketable outside the home. Programs with this rationale offer inadequate alternatives to women's traditional roles and poorly prepare them for formal-sector employment.

Migrant women are particularly disadvantaged because of their inability to find economic opportunities in the urban economy. The number of migrant women is growing, yet no program has addressed their problems directly. More remarkable still is the absence of programs for single women and women who are heads of households, whether in urban or in rural areas. Where migrant women are concerned, the most useful option for programs may lie in providing support services. Other programs might focus on making educational opportunities more accessible to women and teaching them skills that will develop their economic potential in an urban setting.

NOTES

1. The similarity extends to patterns of female economic activity in urban areas as well (Durand 1975:69), as discussed below.

2. For a survey of the shift from mercantile to development policies in the late eighteenth century, see de la Costa (1967). Support for the empirical statements in this paragraph is found in Larkin (1972), McLennan (1979), Owen (1976), and Cruikshank (1975).

3. For example, in the census of 1903 sex ratios were lower on the long-settled east coast of Cebu than on the newly settled west coast, lower in the Visayan Islands than in Mindanao, and lower on the Ilocos Coast than in bordering areas of the Central Plain and in the Cagayan Valley (unpublished analysis).

4. See BCS (1963:vol. 2, app.). Throughout this analysis the term "zone" denotes the three broad regions of the country: Luzon, the Visayas, and Mindanao.

5. We use the term "autonomous" in the same sense as Thadani and Todaro in Chapter 3 of this volume.

REFERENCES

Bureau of Census and Statistics (BCS)
    1963   Census of the Philippines 1960: Population and Housing. Manila.
Cariño, Benjamin
    1976   Managing migration streams and population redistribution: alternative strategies and research needs. In Rodolfo A. Bulatao (ed.), Philippine Population Research. Makati: Population Center Foundation.
Commonwealth of the Philippines, Commission of the Census (COPCOC)
    1941   Census of the Philippines: 1939. Vol. II. Manila: Bureau of Printing.

Cruikshank, Robert Bruce
   1975   A history of Samar Island, the Philippines, 1968–1868. Unpublished doc-
          toral dissertation, University of Wisconsin at Madison.

de la Costa, Horacio (ed.)
   1967   *Asia and the Philippines: Collected Historical Papers.* Manila: Solidaridad Pub-
          lishing House.

Durand, John D.
   1975   *The Labor Force in Economic Development: A Comparison of International Census
          Data 1946–1966.* Princeton: Princeton University Press.

Flieger, Wilhelm, et al.
   1977   *Geographical Patterns of Internal Migration in the Philippines: 1960–1970.* Mono-
          graph No. 5. Manila: National Census and Statistics Office.

Larkin, John A.
   1972   *The Pampangans: Colonial Society in a Philippine Province.* Berkeley: University
          of California Press.

McLennan, Marshall
   1969   Land and tenancy in the Central Luzon Plain. *Philippine Studies* 17(4):
          651–82.

National Census and Statistics Office (NCSO)
   1974   *1970 Census of Population and Housing: Final Report.* Vol. II. Manila.

Ocampo, Romeo
   1976   Policies and programs that influence spatial mobility. Paper read at the
          Seminar Workshop on Migration, Makati, Rizal. 19 March.

Owen, Norman G.
   1976   Kabikolan in the nineteenth century: socioeconomic change in the provin-
          cial Philippines. Unpublished doctoral dissertation, University of Mich-
          igan.

Pernia, Ernesto M.
   1975   *Philippine Migration Streams: Demographic and Socioeconomic Characteristics.*
          UPPI Research Note No. 5. Manila: University of the Philippines Popula-
          tion Institute.
   1977   *Urbanization, Population Growth, and Economic Development in the Philippines.*
          Westport, Conn.: Greenwood Press.

Simpkins, Paul D., and Frederick L. Wernstedt
   1971   *Philippine Migration: The Settlement of the Digos-Padada Valley, Davao Province.*
          Southeast Asian Studies, Monograph Series, No. 16. New Haven: Yale
          University Press.

Smith, Peter C., and Paul P. L. Cheung
   1981   Social origins and sex-differential schooling in the Philippines. *Comparative
          Education Review* 25 (February):28–44.

United Nations Bureau of the Census (USBOC)
   1905   *Census of the Philippine Islands, Taken Under the Direction of the Philippine Com-
          mission in the Year 1903.* 4 vols. Washington, D.C.

Chapter 10

Urban Migrant Women in the Republic of Korea

Sawon Hong

Urbanward migration has become a sociopolitical issue in the Republic of Korea because of its rapid increase over a short period of time. Although rural-to-urban migration has stimulated economic growth and increased overall productivity through the relocation of labor, new social and economic problems such as urban unemployment and a scarcity of young labor in rural areas have resulted. One interesting aspect of this migration, as far as women are concerned, is that a large proportion of migrants are single women who migrate alone in search of jobs or education and live and work outside the home. This pattern represents a distinct departure from past tradition in which women were closely tied to the family and were unlikely to move or to live alone. This change is likely to have ramifications for women's status in Korea.

This essay examines the characteristics of urban migrant women in Korea and seeks to identify their socioeconomic needs. It also describes existing policies and programs relevant to these women and discusses their adequacy in meeting the migrants' basic needs. I conclude by offering recommendations regarding the improvement of policies and programs and pointing out further research issues relating to female migration in Korea.

Data on female migrants in Korea are scattered and fragmentary. For this reason, the conclusions offered here are presented in only the most tentative spirit. The main sources of data used in this chapter are the 1966, 1970, and 1975 censuses. These censuses provide general information about internal migration in Korea but only at the macrolevel. Additional data come from a national sample survey conducted in 1977 by the Economic Planning Board (EPB) and the Korea Development Institute, which provides detailed information about recent migrants,[1] and other surveys that offer some information about the lives of migrants in the cities. In the following analysis, the term "migrants" refers only to rural-to-urban migrants (unless otherwise specified) who moved during the five-year period before the census or survey date.

BACKGROUND

Rapid economic development in the early 1960s has stimulated a great increase in the rate of urbanization. The proportion of the population living in urban areas doubled between 1955 and 1975 (from 24.8 percent to 48.4 percent). The urban population has grown at an average annual rate of 5.8 percent since 1955, while the rural population has grown by only 0.5 percent a year (Hong 1978:21). During the most intensive period of urbanization (1966–70), the urban population increased at an average annual rate of 7.0, while the rural population decreased by 1.2 percent a year on the average. More than 70 percent of the increase in the urban population during the 1960–70 period was due to rural-to-urban migration.

Both male and female rural out-migrants outnumbered urban out-migrants in all three periods (Table 10.1). During the period 1965–70, there were more than twice as many rural out-migrants as urban out-migrants. The direction of migration is the same for both sexes: During 1961–66, the largest migration stream was rural-to-rural, but during 1965–70 and 1970–75 the predominant migration pattern was from rural areas to cities other than Seoul. Although the rural-to-Seoul migration stream has always been smaller than that from rural to other urban areas, the gap has become greater in recent years. One notable change during the 1961–75 period is that the proportion of migrants going to Seoul increased up to 1970 and then slowed down—from 27.1 percent in 1961–66, to 31.7 percent in 1965–70, to 26.1 percent in 1970–75. This slowdown during the 1970s indicates that with the emergence of alternative industrial areas a

Table 10.1 Number of migrants (in thousands) by sex and migration stream: 1961–66, 1965–70, and 1970–75

Migration stream	1961–66		1965–70		1970–75	
	Male	Female	Male	Female	Male	Female
Rural-Seoul	193.2	228.9	384.0	429.4	288.0	359.0
Urban-Seoul	123.4	129.8	181.5	196.4	191.6	214.5
Rural-urban	239.6	251.5	502.4	511.0	517.6	589.7
Urban-urban	220.7	256.4	221.3	192.7	214.8	240.0
Rural-rural	245.4	283.2	315.5	333.0	265.6	297.6
Urban-rural	100.2	98.5	125.9	119.6	156.0	174.4
Seoul-rural	22.9	32.6	72.9	68.8	108.3	119.5
Seoul-urban	33.8	32.7	52.7	53.6	144.4	152.0
Total	1,179.2	1,307.6	1,856.2	1,904.5	1,886.3	2,146.7

Sources: EPB (1968:210–18; 1973:170–73; 1978:32–35).

considerable proportion of migrants began to move into cities other than Seoul.

There were more female than male migrants in all three periods. Among rural-to-urban migrants (including those moving to Seoul), 53 percent were women during 1961–66. During 1965–70 and 1970–75 the percentage who were female was 51 and 54 respectively.

Several generalizations follow from these findings: The number of migrants has increased steadily since the early 1960s; more people move from rural areas than from cities; rural out-migrants go to cities much more than to other rural areas; all these patterns are the same for both sexes for all three periods; in most migration streams, females outnumber males by a small percentage. In summary, then, women move as much as men and are thus as important as men for migration studies. Virtually all Korean migration research has focused on male heads of household, however, primarily because of the availability of data for this migrant group.

CHARACTERISTICS OF FEMALE MIGRANTS

AGE AND MARITAL STATUS

More than 60 percent of the women who migrated between 1961 and 1975 were 10 to 29 years old (Table 10.2). Compared to rural nonmigrants, migrants include a smaller proportion of young persons and a smaller proportion of those in older age groups. The age at migration is lower than shown by the data because the age shown is at the time of the survey or

Table 10.2 Percentage distribution of female rural-to-urban migrants and rural nonmigrants by age: 1961–66, 1965–70, and 1970–75

Age group	1961–66		1965–70		1970–75	
	Mi-grants	Nonmi-grants	Mi-grants	Nonmi-grants	Mi-grants	Nonmi-grants
< 10	11.4	19.6	9.6	18.4	7.4	13.2
10–19	31.4	24.3	33.1	26.1	37.3	28.9
20–29	33.3	13.2	31.6	12.1	32.8	12.2
30–39	11.8	14.1	13.1	14.2	10.0	13.4
40–49	5.2	11.6	5.4	11.4	5.2	12.7
50+	7.5	17.1	7.1	17.8	7.3	20.4
Total	100.0	100.0	100.0	100.0	100.0	100.0
No. (in thousands)	480.5	7,403.0	949.4	7,400.4	948.7	6,962.2

Sources: EPB (1968:213–18; 1972:26–28; 1973:170–72; 1977:26–28; 1978:34–35).

census and not at the time of migration. The age distribution of female migrants reflects the greater propensity of younger women to migrate, probably for employment reasons or educational opportunities.

There are no data showing the marital status of migrants at the time of migration. Although available data tell us the marital status at the time of the census or survey, that date can be as much as five years after migration. We can only assume that the proportion of single persons was higher at the time of migration than at the time of the census or survey. Among females over 15 years of age, more married women than single women migrate to cities other than Seoul, but about the same number of married and unmarried women move to Seoul.

EDUCATION LEVEL

There are no data on migrants' educational attainment at the time of migration. It is clear, however, that except for a few migrants who continue with their education after migration (only about 4.6 percent of the total rural-to-urban female migrants)—the educational level of most migrants does not change after migration. Therefore the data on education at the time of the census or survey can be considered reasonably adequate.

Compared with nonmigrants, more migrants to Seoul and other cities are classified as attending college or university. This finding indicates the better facilities for higher education in the cities and suggests that these facilities constitute an urban pull. Female migrants to the cities have more education than rural nonmigrants. Only ten percent of migrants who moved during 1970–75 had no schooling at all, and 12 percent had a high school education or more. Among female rural nonmigrants, by contrast, 39 percent had no schooling and only 3 percent had at least a high school education. Thus higher education appears to promote geographic mobility.

Although migrants are generally better educated than rural nonmigrants, their educational level does not compare favorably with urban residents. The proportion of high school graduates among female migrants in 1970–75 is 13 percent and 10 percent for migrants to Seoul and urban areas, respectively, compared with 21 percent for Seoul residents and 14 percent for urban residents. Unmarried migrants also have much lower school enrollment rates than nonmigrants. This rate is especially dramatic in the case of females in the 15–19 age group: Nearly 44 percent of nonmigrants are enrolled in school compared with only 13 percent of migrants (D. Y. Kim 1978:22).

EMPLOYMENT STATUS

Statistics on the employment status of the migrants at the time of moving are not available from the census. A survey by the EPB indicates that employed women are less likely to migrate: 33.3 percent of rural nonmigrant women are employed, but only 14.1 percent of female migrants to cities were employed prior to migration.

A sample survey of rural migrants to Seoul shows that among the heads of migrant households, only 12 percent already had jobs arranged prior to their migration; 21 percent migrated without jobs but with the hope of getting help from relatives already in cities; and 61 percent migrated without a job or specific plans on how to get one.[2]

Between 1960 and 1974 the female work-force participation rate rose from 19 to 30 percent in urban areas. The biggest increase was among young, single women under the age of 24 (S. K. Kim 1976:45). Beyond the age of 25, female labor-force participation rates drop dramatically for female migrants (from 55 percent to 17 percent) but very little for nonmigrants (from 40 to about 36 percent; Kim and Lee 1976:28–29).

There are also differences between migrants and urban residents regarding employment status. More urban residents are in white-collar jobs whereas there are more blue-collar and service workers among migrants (see Table 10.3). More employed female than male migrants are concentrated in the production and service occupations. Since this concentration persists across all age groups, it reflects the lower occupational mobility of Korean women. Participation in modern production amd clerical jobs has been open primarily to unmarried women. Some 84 percent of single working women are in production, clerical, or service jobs, compared to only 28 percent of married women. Some 43 percent of married working women are in agriculture and another 24 percent are in shop sales, usually of the small, family-managed variety (Repetto 1978:59).

REASONS FOR MIGRATION

Prior to 1960, most urban job opportunities were in the service sector. It was only after 1960 that migration, especially rural-to-urban migration, became heavily influenced by urban-centered industrial development. These employment opportunities, together with the sociocultural attractions of the city, have been the principal motives stimulating rural people to migrate.

The influences of socioeconomic development and western culture have deeply affected both rural and urban Korea. As elsewhere, the impact of modernization in urban areas has been both wider and deeper than in the countryside. These changes have created large social and economic differentials between urban and rural areas. Family structure, female employment patterns, and consumption levels differ substantially between urban and rural residents. A recent survey by the Korean Chamber of Commerce and Industry (KCCI 1977) revealed that Seoul alone accounts for 32 percent of the gross national product, 26 percent of all manufacturing plants, 27 percent of all export firms, 45 percent of all banking insti-

Table 10.3 Percentage distribution of employed females 15 years old and over, by migration status and occupation: urban Korea, 1965–70 and 1970–75

| | 1965–70 | | | | 1970–75 | | | |
| | Seoul | | Other cities | | Seoul | | Other cities | |
Occupational group	Migrants	Nonmigrants	Migrants	Nonmigrants	Migrants	Nonmigrants	Migrants	Nonmigrants
Professional	2.4	7.2	3.0	4.2	2.1	7.0	2.4	4.2
Administrative	0.1	0.5	0.1	0.2	0.1	0.4	0.0	0.2
Clerical	5.2	13.6	3.6	6.6	8.5	15.5	5.0	7.9
Sales	9.7	24.2	14.3	23.9	9.2	22.0	10.0	22.3
Service	44.1	22.5	33.1	17.6	34.0	21.1	20.4	18.1
Farming	0.6	2.0	5.0	17.8	0.6	2.5	3.7	14.9
Production	37.4	29.6	40.6	29.8	45.5	31.5	58.6	32.3
Others	0.3	0.2	0.3	0.1	0.0	0.0	0.0	0.0
Unknown	0.1	0.2	0.1	0.1	0.0	0.0	0.0	0.0
Total	100.0	100.0	100.0	100.0	100.0	100.0	100.0	100.0
No. (in thousands)	143.7	196.7	137.1	416.5	144.9	481.4	211.9	784.1

Sources: EPB (1972, 1978).

tutions, and 51 percent of all colleges and universities. The rapid and pervasive development of a national communications system ensured that these important differentials are perceived by all sectors of the population. This development, together with the greater physical and social mobility (particularly of women) in postwar Korea, has encouraged migration on a large scale.

Although data on the motivation to migrate are limited to the 1961–66 period, it is quite likely that similar reasons persist even now. As Table 10.4 shows, more than half the female migrants leave their villages to accompany their families whereas about 30 percent of males give this reason. Moreover, about half of male migrants leave for better economic opportunities, especially employment, while only one-quarter of women migrate for economic reasons. Economic opportunity is the most important motivation for men to migrate. More men than women also migrate for higher education.

Thus, relatively speaking, women are in a more dependent position than men in terms of migration. This point is supported by recent EPB data indicating that more than 78 percent of all married female migrants and 48 percent of all single female migrants moved with their families (Table 10.5). Although the data in Tables 10.4 and 10.5 are not precisely comparable, they present strong evidence that married women migrate mainly to be with their families. Married women who migrate without families (22 percent) are assumed to be joining husbands or preceding

Table 10.4 Percentage distribution of rural migrants five years old and over, by sex and reason for migration: 1961–66

Reason	Female		Male	
	Rural-to-urban migrants	All rural migrants	Rural-to-urban migrants	All rural migrants
Seeking job	11.7	10.8	20.2	24.3
Job transfer	14.3	12.0	28.9	26.3
Education	11.6	8.8	16.7	12.4
Housing	5.6	4.5	3.3	3.3
Health	6.6	0.4	0.3	0.3
Family	54.5	60.0	29.8	32.0
Others	1.7	3.1	0.9	1.3
Unknown	0.4	0.4	0.1	0.2
Total	100.0	100.0	100.0	100.0
No. (in thousands)	480.5	763.6	432.8	678.3

Sources: EPB (1968:269, 272).

Table 10.5 Percentage distribution of rural-to-urban female migrants 15 years old and over, by marital status and migration unit: 1977

Marital status	Unit of migration		Total
	Family	Individual	
Currently married	78	22	100
Divorced, separated, widowed	78	22	100
Single	48	52	100

Source: EPB, unpublished survey data, 1977.

them. Most unmarried female migrants who migrate without their families are probably doing so in response to employment and, to a lesser degree, educational opportunities.

THE MIGRANT WOMAN IN THE CITY

Although migrants seem to be in a better socioeconomic position today than before migration (materially and in other ways), they are usually poorly prepared in terms of experience or training for life and work in the urban setting. Many migrants had few economic resources for establishing themselves in the new urban environment. Moreover, Korean cities have been rather ill-equipped to house migrants and respond to their needs. The socioeconomic deprivation of migrants relative to the general urban population may also confuse and alienate them. The process of adapting to the new, more complex life-style undoubtedly carries a psychological cost, a cost that is likely to be especially severe for single female migrants.

Not much is known about the urban life of migrants in general: their most serious problems, whether they reside in the undesirable urban periphery, how they adjust to urban life. No study has been carried out to investigate these issues. We can only derive fragments of information about them from a few studies of limited scope conducted for other purposes. The following sketches have been drawn from these sources.[3]

Married and unmarried women form two quite distinct categories of female migrants. Very few migrants are divorced or widowed women. Because married and unmarried female migrants have different characteristics and needs, the two groups of women are treated separately throughout the remainder of this study.

Migrant households are likely to be nuclear with no older relatives to assist with domestic work or babysitting. They are usually forced to change their urban residence at least once in search of adequate housing, with an average length of stay in their initial housing of only one year. EPB data show that only 23 percent of migrant households own their houses, compared to 67 percent of nonmigrants. This finding is consistent with the generally lower socioeconomic status of migrant families, who also have to face the cost of relocation at the beginning of their urban residence. Since it is known that private, governmental, and voluntary services tend to be less available in urban, low-income areas, it may be inferred that migrant families lack adequate services in addition to their other problems.

According to EPB data, 72 percent of all migrant women who were housekeepers at the time of migration continued to be so, while 26 percent moved from full-time housekeeping to employment outside the home. Thus while there is substantial role continuity for women migrating with families, many do enter the labor force full time after migration. Many migrants save and gradually improve their financial well-being. It is likely, however, that migrants have more economic difficulties, at least in the first few years of their lives in the city, than urban residents.

According to EPB data, more than 69 percent of all migrant women are single. Among these unmarried women, more than 67 percent are employed and 17 percent are students. They are young women with less education than their urban counterparts. Although not all are rural-to-urban migrants, more than half are from villages. These migrants, in common with all employed unmarried workers in urban areas, are concentrated in the production and service sectors, especially in light industries such as electronics and textiles. Because of their meager education they usually work in low-skilled, low-paid jobs.

Nearly one-third of all unmarried female migrants live in a dormitory or similar accommodation provided by the factory; another 40 percent or so live with their family; the remainder have to provide for themselves. The combination of low wages and the urban housing shortage undoubtedly leads to housing problems for the last group. The surveys also suggest that these women are in need of better health care and working conditions: 34.7 percent of the respondents considered themselves to be in poor health; another 37 percent reported fatigue due to overwork or general stress.

The process of modernization has also led to an increase in premarital sexual activity among Korean youth. Young, poorly educated, basically rural, living alone or with little supervision, migrant women are particularly vulnerable to the problems of premarital pregnancy. A 1977 survey (Nurses Association News, 11 August 1977) found that 47 percent of single female workers have had premarital sexual experience. The incidence of premarital pregnancy is at least 16 percent for currently married women aged 15 to 49 (Hong 1978).

Another problem faced by women workers in Korea—married and unmarried—is wage discrimination. Women are systematically discriminated against in terms of wages paid at all levels. Only 5 percent of all women are paid more than ₩70,000 per month, for example, compared to about 45 percent of men. Moreover, about 43 percent of all employed women, but only 11.6 percent of employed men, earn less than ₩30,000 per month, which is the government's minimum wage (Hong 1979).

Despite the problems mentioned, the majority of these young women still want to live in cities. This desire is reinforced by the fact that 66.9 percent of their parents think it is a good thing for their children to live in cities, although only 31.5 percent agreed with their daughters migrating to cities initially (D. H. Kim et al. 1974:17–18).

Although physically separated from their families, these women attempt to maintain contact. Even with their low salaries, 55 percent of single workers living alone send money home (although not regularly); more than 60 percent of them visit their families one to five times a year; and 83.2 percent of them were visited by their parents (D. H. Kim et al. 1974:28–29).

BASIC NEEDS OF FEMALE MIGRANTS

Two points need to be made before attempting to identify the needs of female migrants. First, one must not assume that all migrants are poverty-stricken and living in a generally deprived state. Some migrants probably have at least as much access to income and services as nonmigrants. Moreover, there are advantages in the urban area that, in the minds of the migrants themselves at least, help to compensate for the disadvantages. Thus, although not all aspects of city life are favorable, we must not conclude that migration automatically makes people worse off than they were before (Browning 1971). Second, many of the migrants' problems tend to be common to both men and women or to a family unit. Thus it would be misleading to discuss them only in relation to a certain category of migrants. This reservation is important because it would be wrong to consider a number of special problems just for women in cases where the need is much broader.

Table 10.6 summarizes migrants' needs by sex and marital status. As before, our focus is on female migrants (married and unmarried). Married migrant women can be further subdivided into employed and unemployed categories since employment adds a new dimension to a woman's life-style and needs. What are the characteristics of the married migrant? She is young (usually 19 to 34 years old), has fewer then average children, is in the lower socioeconomic group, lives in a low-income environment in a nuclear family, and receives lower wages than her male counterpart. An unknown number of these women will seek work, and even fewer will actually take full-time employment. An unknown number will find part-time or casual employment.

Table 10.6 Basic needs of migrants

Service	Female			Male		Government programs?
	Unmarried	Married		Unmarried	Married (head of household)[a]	
		Employed	Unemployed			
Day care		x				Yes, limited
Job counseling and job location	x	x		x	x	Yes, limited
Adult education and vocational training	x	x	x	x	x	Yes, limited
Working conditions monitoring	x	x		x	x	Yes
Wage and job discrimination	x	x		x	x	Yes
Unemployment benefits/ provision of day work	x	x		x	x	Some day work
Housing	x	x	x	x	x	Limited
Personal counseling and services, including family planning	x			x		None in practice
Family health care, including family planning		x	x			Mainly family planning
Delivery of social services (education, general health)		x	x	x	x	Unevenly implemented and distributed
High school or college placement	x			x		No

a. Represents the family as a unit.

From this outline one can readily determine that married female migrants who work, or who wish to work, require certain services: day-care facilities to look after their children, job counseling and assistance in locating a job, either adult education (for improved literacy or other skills) or vocational training to provide immediate job-related skills, the monitoring of general working conditions to protect their health and avoid exploitation, protection against job and especially wage discrimination, and either unemployment benefits or the provision of publicly funded day work. Regarding social services, these migrants are particularly in need of family health care, including contraceptive services, as well as improved environmental conditions. Married female migrants who do not work do not, of course, need these employment services. Their needs for other social services, however, remain essentially the same as those of their employed sisters. As indicated in Table 10.6, the needs of married males, treated here as heads of household, are very similar to those of their wives. The major exception is their greater freedom from wage discrimination.

Unmarried migrants are usually young (in the lower half of the 15–19 age group), are relocated in the urban environment without their families, and live either in factory-provided dormitories (about 30 percent) or find their own housing (about 30 percent). They are not as well educated as their urban counterparts and have little upward mobility. They work for low wages and are subject to wage and, to a lesser degree, job discrimination. They are as likely as not to be sexually active and at risk of pregnancy; they are looking toward marriage and tend to drop out of the labor force following marriage. And, finally, they may suffer from poor working conditions and have access to few social services.

These women have the same employment-related needs as the employed married female migrants. Since they often work in large production facilities or in some demimonde job (in bars and nightclubs), their need for safe and nonexploitative working conditions is probably greater than that of married migrant women. Because those who must find their own housing are likely to have to do so alone, and with very few options owing to their low income, they might be more needy in this respect also. Because of their rural background and general lack of social preparation for the rapid pace and complexity of urban life, these single migrants need personal counseling, especially in regard to their relationship with males. Access to contraceptive counseling and services, legal abortion, and marriage counseling should be part of this service.

A final category of need has been included in Table 10.6—high school or college placement—because a large proportion (11.6 percent) of single women migrants come to the cities in search of educational opportunities. Nevertheless, this need cannot be given a high priority in Korea because the rural areas are already well served with educational institutions and the situation is constantly improving. Moreover, the government is trying to discourage migration to the cities, especially to Seoul. Notwithstanding these efforts, programs for general or vocational training at night or part time should be provided. To the extent possible, it would be desirable to arrange for high school and college work to be taken on this basis also.

The needs of unmarried males are nearly identical to those of unmarried females. Here again the major exception is in wage and job discrimination. The greater vulnerability of single women to various forms of exploitation makes their needs for counseling and housing greater than that of males, however.

POLICIES AND PROGRAMS FOR MIGRANTS

Very few policies and programs relate specifically to women, and practically none to female migrants. The general policies and programs that do exist are listed in Table 10.6 and described in the following paragraph.

DAY-CARE SERVICES FOR WORKING MOTHERS

These services are provided by private and voluntary agencies under the license and supervision of the Ministry of Health and Social Affairs (MOHSA). The present network of 615 centers—mainly urban and each serving about 41,000 persons—also provides food supplements and some family planning and nutrition education (MOHSA 1977). They are useful programs but still inadequate.

JOB COUNSELING AND JOB LOCATION

Only a few public or voluntary service agencies offer these services. Out of 168,000 job referrals in 1977 for which there were data, 90 percent were arranged through commercial employment offices.[4] Of this number 83 percent of the job seekers were placed in jobs as domestic servants, bar hostesses, and the like. That these offices are not always reliable may be inferred by the fact that in 1977 alone five such offices were forced to close by the authorities, 18 licenses were suspended, and 73 persons were indicted.

As of 1976, there were 28 women's vocational guidance centers, all located in major cities, and ten of them in Seoul (MOHSA 1977:262–63); some provinces do not have even one center. All provincial or city governments have women's sections that provide employment consultation for women. For all of Korea, 347 staff members provided consultation service for about 216,605 cases in 1976. Of this number, 3.2 percent of the consultations were for vocational guidance and about 30 percent were actual job placement (MOHSA 1977:264–65). In addition, Administration of Labor

Affairs (ALA) local branch offices (two in Seoul and Pusan and 34 local offices) provide job placement services. Despite this good beginning, the number is still low in relation to the need.

A national monitoring system is needed to determine job market information by community: the kinds and locations of jobs needed. This system would provide a link between available jobs and available workers and widen the labor employment market, which is now concentrated in only a few places. Furthermore, agencies providing these services must make the public fully aware of them.

ADULT EDUCATION AND VOCATIONAL TRAINING

The MOHSA and several women's organizations offer informal educational programs for all women. Although the degree to which these programs affect migrants is not known, they are available to everybody and could therefore benefit migrant women. But more classes, more flexible time schedules, and more practical curricula are needed. Moreover, vocational and technical training for better job skills should be provided equally to women. So far, the most highly skilled jobs—and the training needed to get them—have been limited to men. The teaching of these skills to women should begin at a young age.

With respect to research, it is important to know what kind of workers the society needs, the general and vocational education needed to train them, and the needs of the migrants themselves. This information would provide the basis for appropriate education programs and for labor-force planning.

THE MONITORING OF WORKING CONDITIONS

The ALA Office on Women and Minors is charged with the responsibility of administering the family planning program in industry. It is also expected to supervise industries with large numbers of women to ensure conformance with the (not very rigorous) law governing the conditions of work, to encourage employers to improve working conditions for women, and to recommend policy on women's working conditions. The service is reasonably effective for the large industries, given the liberal nature of the law.

PROTECTION AGAINST WAGE AND JOB DISCRIMINATION

Programs are badly needed to protect all women workers against wage and job discrimination. Enforceable policies must be established to reduce, and eventually eliminate, such discrimination. It is especially critical for the government to set an example for the private sector. Aggressive affirmative action programs will help to ensure that these programs are taken seriously.

UNEMPLOYMENT BENEFITS AND THE PROVISION OF TEMPORARY WORK

Since women are presumed to be the responsibility of a male—father, husband, or brothers—there is little in the way of unemployment benefits. Some larger cities like Seoul do provide a limited amount of temporary day labor in which women participate. In fact, there is a general need for all workers to enjoy basic social security benefits, which are, as yet, poorly developed in Korea. Although there is now movement in this direction (homes for the aged, for example, and mother and child welfare institutions), it will be years before these benefits become widespread.

HOUSING

As in major cities everywhere, especially those in Asia, the supply of housing (both number and quality) is inadequate. Urban low-income housing is provided by the government, but this effort meets only a small proportion of the real need. Given the enormous investments that would be needed to construct decent housing, it is unrealistic to exhort the government to undertake this task. It would be more practical for the government to concentrate on the general improvement of environmental and sanitary conditions for urban low-income areas and to monitor the condition of housing in these areas, especially housing owned by absentee landlords. Moreover, the government could work with at least the larger industries to guarantee and, if necessary, to subsidize low-interest mortgages for low-income workers in the manner of the Federal Housing Administration in the United States.

In the case of unmarried female workers, it is not known whether the factory-provided facilities are adequate in terms of number, cost, and living conditions. Nor is it known just what conditions are experienced by the unmarried women who have to make their own housing arrangements.

PERSONAL COUNSELING AND SERVICES

As indicated above, some counseling services are provided in the major cities, although these are few in number and tend to relate to employment. Very few young women use these services. To fill the gap, government and private organizations like the ALA and the YWCA should provide such services within the larger industrial enterprises and in other accessible locations.

As a result of an active ALA program, contraceptive counseling and services are now widely available to married workers in the medium- and large-scale industries. Because of government and social conservatism, however, these services have not always been offered to unmarried workers. A greater effort should be made to provide access to these services for unmarried workers in a sufficiently discreet way to ensure access.

HEALTH CARE

Although the larger factories (more than 500 employees) provide in-plant clinics, these facilities usually give no more than first aid services. A new national medical insurance scheme is beginning to cover workers in these larger establishments, however. The Korean government, with its traditional nonwelfare orientation, has energetically promoted population control services in interests of economic development while simultaneously ignoring family health care services. Although there is evidence that this attitude is changing, the country still has a long way to go. The middle and upper classes have had the option of private medicine, an alternative essentially denied to the lower-income population, which includes migrants. Since most classes are unable to obtain these services commercially, the government should concentrate its growing interest in such services on the low-income areas, including those inhabited by migrants. The medical insurance scheme should also be made available to workers in smaller factories.

DELIVERY OF SERVICES

Although it is not strongly welfare oriented, the Korean government has stated its intention to provide a wide variety of services, including primary health care, public education, low-income housing, and environmental maintenance. The urban low-income areas are typically less well served by such services than the wealthier areas. Although there may be practical reasons for this neglect, the fact remains that it is the low-income residents, including migrants, who are most in need.

As the preceding analysis documents, female migrants (and migrants generally) tend to be poorly served by government policies and programs. This is especially true of the following high-priority needs: job counseling and job location, adult education and vocational training, wage and job discrimination, monitoring of housing and the environment, and basic health care.

Although a number of policies do provide needed services to women, many of them are poorly implemented, and many urban residents, especially those with low incomes, lack access to them. It may thus be concluded that the government should move forward on two fronts: implementing existing policy and initiating new programs designed to meet basic needs. Although the government cannot be expected to undertake the delivery of a large number of existing or new services, it should encourage the Korean private sector—especially the production and services industries that profit from the labor of these women—to provide the services that are related to employment.

While the government is beginning to provide services to the urban low-income population, including migrants, it is also trying to discourage further urban growth through migration. Some of these policies may affect migration:

1. Differential education fees: Fees for public school education vary with the size of the city; the largest cities charge the highest fees. The fees are the same for residents and nonresidents alike. Since the difference between the highest and lowest fees is not great, this policy probably does little to restrict migration.

2. Differential resident taxes: Resident taxes, like education fees, vary by the size of the city; they are highest in the largest cities. Again the differences in taxation levels are probably not so great as to discourage migration significantly. Moreover, both residents and migrants who have very low incomes are exempted from paying the taxes.

3. Mother and child welfare institutes: The Ministry of Health and Social Affairs, in collaboration with the city government, operates a small network of such institutes in urban areas. The institutes provide a variety of basic services. Eligible women must be low-income widows with more than two children under the age of 13. A further restriction is that the woman must have been a resident in the city for more than three years. Given the small number of women eligible for such services, this policy too is unlikely to deter rural-to-urban migration.

RECOMMENDATIONS

It is customary for policy papers to make recommendations for new policies, programs, and further research. This custom has its drawbacks, however. Researchers are poorly equipped to make usable recommendations to bureaucracies; bureaucracies are poorly equipped to use the recommendations; and clients are poorly equipped to articulate their common needs. There also appear to be three major impediments to effective socioeconomic programs for women in Korea:

1. Until quite recently, Korean public policy has not been service or welfare oriented—a characteristic that has hindered the development of socioeconomic services for disadvantaged groups.

2. The government and public opinion, which is generally male-dominated, are not concerned about the problems of women, including female migrants and other disadvantaged women.

3. Even if the women are able to define their fundamental needs, they are fragmented into subgroups and lack the organizational base and leadership for bringing those needs to the attention of policy-makers.

Government policy vis-à-vis social services is gradually changing, however, and, even more gradually, women's concerns are beginning to be heard. Even so, a great deal more will be needed before government and voluntary agencies understand these needs and deliver the relevant services. Clearly the government should make a much greater effort to help female migrants create the organizational base and leadership needed to link them as clients to the public bureaucracy. Service programs are invariably conceptualized, decided upon, and imposed by people in the bureaucracy who know little of the clientele. Usually they are men who live and work in different worlds. It is difficult for the public system to deliver relevant services for these reasons alone, not to mention the massive organizational problems of training, motivation, accountability, and the myriad other constraints that have made the word bureaucracy synonymous with low efficiency.

Korean women themselves must be helped to consider and articulate their needs. This task can be accomplished through more government programs to foster, strengthen, and make greater use of female-oriented community organizations such as women's clubs.

The problem of providing linkage organizations is somewhat different for unmarried migrants since they are not part of a community, unless they live with their families. In these cases, the trade unions, which are present in all major industries, should be encouraged by the government to take a much more active role in understanding the needs of these young women and helping them articulate their needs to employers and public policymakers.

Current government policy does encourage working through such groups as the national Women's Clubs. At the present time, however, the government tends to use these agencies as an arm of the bureaucracy extending downward to the people. This strategy should be turned around so that these organizations become focal points for local concerns: an arm of the people extended upward to the government. This turnabout will provide a far more realistic indication of actual needs and will make the people in need the prime movers rather than the government.

Experience with health and other services in a number of countries (including Korea with the New Community Movement) has shown that the resource supply system of the public bureaucracy works best when demands originate from the bottom up with the personal commitment this action implies. Something even more fundamental, however, is needed before women's needs are truly taken seriously. What is lacking is a national will to improve women's status. This movement must secure the support of national leaders and opinion-makers, especially those in the educational establishment and the media. Without this fundamental backing, all the policies, programs, plans, and infrastructure can never be more than partly effective, and experience suggests that the leadership will provide this support only when women have achieved an awareness of themselves and are able to express their needs to the leadership in unequivocal terms.

NOTES

1. This survey was carried out in March 1977 in order to formulate a system of "social indicators" for Korea. About 9,800 households were sampled throughout the country. Data were not yet fully published as of January 1980.

2. *Hankuk Daily Newspaper*, "70% of the Slum Residents Are Rural Migrants," 20 November 1970. The survey was carried out by a group of students from Seoul National University in May–June 1970. 136 household heads in two slum areas in Seoul were studied.

3. The surveys used for this section were those conducted by (1) the Research Institute of Public Affairs, *A Study for Reservation and Utilization of Women Labor Forces, 1972* (conducted in December 1972 using 463 female workers employed in 20 export-oriented manufacturing factories in eight cities); (2) the Federation of Korean Trade Unions (a survey on unmarried working women in spring 1977); and (3) Dae-Hwan Kim et al., *A Study on the Female Rural Migrants' Adjustment to Urban Life*, Ewha Women's University, 1974 (conducted in September 1973 with sample of 356 women who migrated to Seoul from rural areas).

4. *Hankuk Daily Newspaper*, "Commercial Employment Offices Will Be Closed," 13 December 1977.

REFERENCES

Browning, Harley
    1971   Migrant selectivity and the growth of large cities in developing societies. In *Rapid Population Growth: Consequences and Policy Implications*. Baltimore: Johns Hopkins University Press.

Hong, Sawon
    1978   *Population Status Report: Korea.* Seoul: Development Institute.
    1979   Women in development planning—the case of Korea. *Korea Journal*, 19(7): 9–26.

Kim, Dae-Hwan, et al.
    1974   *A Study of the Effects of Rural Out-migration on Rural Development and Their Measures.* Seoul: Ministry of Science and Technology.

Kim, Dae Young
    1978   *Migration and Korean Development.* Working Paper 7805. Seoul: Development Institute.

Kim, Dae Young, and Hyo-Koo Lee
    1976   *Characteristics of Internal Migration in Korea, 1965–70.* Seoul: Development Institute.

Kim, Soo Kon
    1976   *Labor Force Behavior and Unemployment in Korea.* Seoul: Development Institute.

Korea Economic Planning Board, (EPB)
    1968   *1966 Some Findings from the Special Demographic Survey.*
    1972   *1970 Population and Housing Census Report,* Vol. 1: Whole Country.
    1973   *1970 Population and Housing Census Report,* Vol. 2: Internal Migration.
    1977   *1975 Population and Housing Census Report,* Vol. 1: Whole Country.
    1978   *1975 Population and Housing Census Report,* Vol. 2: Internal Migration and Housing.

Korea Chamber of Commerce and Industry (KCCI)
    1977   *A Study on the Relative Economic Importance of Seoul.* Seoul.

Ministry of Health and Social Affairs (MOHSA)
    1977   *Yearbook of Public Health and Social Statistics 1977.* Seoul.

Repetto, Robert
    1978   *Economic Development and Fertility Decline in the Republic of Korea.* Working Paper 7805. Seoul: Development Institute.

PART 3

WOMEN MIGRANTS IN ASIAN CITIES: CASE STUDIES

Chapter 11

Migration of Women Workers in Peninsular Malaysia: Impact and Implications

Jamilah Ariffin

The massive influx of young single Malay women from the traditional rural sector into the modern urban industrial sector is a recent but nevertheless significant feature of the Malaysian scene. Before 1970, it was uncommon to hear of autonomous migration of single Malay females or to see Malay girls working in modern factories. This chapter describes the relationship between industrial development in Peninsular Malaysia after 1970 and the massive exodus of young single women from the countryside to the urban industrial centers. It also discusses the impact and implications of this rural-to-urban migration on the migrants in particular and Malaysian society in general.

The analysis draws upon empirical data obtained from an ongoing investigation of 1,278 migrant Malay female workers employed in 1977 as production operators in 120 factories located in 11 major urban industrial areas in Peninsular Malaysia.[1] This study has three major objectives: to explore the causes of rural-to-urban migration of Malay women to urban industrial centers of Peninsular Malaysia; to trace the adaptation of migrants to work and life in the urban environment; and to gauge the changes in their outlook and values.

The overall study consists of four separate surveys that complement each other. First, a sample survey of female Malay migrant workers was carried out in the three prominent free trade zones of Malaysia: Bayan Lepas free trade zone in Penang, Batu Berendam free trade zone in Malacca, and Sungai-Way free trade zone in Selangor. All factories in each area were asked whether they had Malay female migrant workers on their production lines. On the basis of the information received, two-thirds of the electronics factories in each free trade zone were selected and from each factory a sample of Malay female migrant workers was obtained by random selection.

Using a similar approach, a sample of Malay female migrant workers presently employed in "female-dominated" factories in the four major industrial estates of Malaysia was also obtained. These industrial estates are Tampoi-Larkin industrial estate in Johor Baru, Senawang industrial estate in Seremban, Prai industrial estate, and Tanjong Kling free trade zone in Malacca.

In order to investigate the adaptation of Malay female migrants to urban living and to trace changes in their outlook, an intensive, longitudinal study of a sample of girls presently residing in three urban industrial communities was carried out as well. These communities are located on the outskirts of three industrial areas: Shah Alam industrial estate, Sungai-Way free trade zone, and Selayang Baru industrial site. Using the criteria of residential location in these communities and employment on these industrial sites, a sample consisting of migrant workers employed by multinational companies, joint-venture companies, and locally owned companies was obtained.

Finally, three different types of garment factories were included as case studies: one owned by an Australian multinational company and located near the Datuk Keramat area in Kuala Lumpur, another a joint-venture company in Petaling Jaya, and the third a locally incorporated company in Petaling Jaya. In all three cases all Malay female migrant workers were included in the sample.

THE PULL FACTORS

Analysis of the relationship between rapid industrial development after 1970 and the rural-to-urban migration of Malay female workers reveals that changes in the migration pattern by sex result from selectivity in the pull factors of urban industrial development. This selectivity is the outcome of an interplay between the industrialization program and the New Economic Policy of Malaysia.

For the purpose of this chapter a brief note on the differences in the pattern of industrialization before 1970 and after 1970 is sufficient background. (For a brief account of industrialization policies and patterns, see Lim 1973.) Before 1970, most manufacturing industries were engaged in import substitution. The majority were small-scale enterprises employing fewer than 500 workers; most were owned by locals (mainly Chinese) and run on a family basis. There were very few multinational corporations. This pattern changed significantly after 1970.

A large proportion of manufacturing industry is now composed of export-oriented and labor-intensive concerns. These changes are in line with the new industrialization program, which aims at expanding the industrial and service sectors in order to create more jobs. The prime objective is the eradication of widespread unemployment and underemployment, which is prominent in the urban areas and most observable among youth between the ages of 15 and 19.[2] There are more unemployed males than females within this age group. Underemployment is a prominent feature of the labor force in the countryside as well.

Another industrial strategy adopted by the government as a means to achieving its industrial objectives is the encouragement given to multinational corporations to set up their plants in Malaysia. This encouragement is offered in the form of incentives: tax holidays, pioneer status privileges, and the establishment of free trade zones. As a result of these incentives, by 1974 many of the large-scale enterprises in Malaysia were owned by multinational corporations.

Of the types of manufacturing industry given special industrial incentives, the electronics industry heads the list. It is expected that each electronics factory will employ no fewer than 750 employees. Multinational corporations have been encouraged to set up electronics factories in Malaysia on this basis, and their rate of growth is certainly impressive. In 1970 there were 41 firms employing 3,200 workers, but by 1976 this number had increased to 138 with a total of 47,000 workers. Most of these factories are located in the free trade zones, which are near the cities on the west coast of Peninsular Malaysia.[3]

Whether it was envisaged by the Malaysian government or not, these electronic firms and similar concerns like the textile and garment industries employ more female than male workers; for example, according to a recent survey of the labor force of industries in West Malaysia, female workers constitute 55.5 percent of the labor force for the electronics industry, 56.5 percent for textiles, and 89.5 percent for the garment industry.[4]

The New Economic Policy, introduced in 1970, is intended to reduce poverty irrespective of race and to restructure Malaysian society in order to eliminate the identification of race with economic function. Among other things, it categorically implies that the intake of workers must reflect the racial composition of the society; thus not less than 30 percent of the work force in every industry must be Malay.[5] Since its implementation, reports on the composition of the labor force of manufacturing firms show that more than 50 percent of their unskilled workers are Malays. In the case of firms employing many females, the majority of the Malay women workers are migrants from rural areas. This is because the majority of Malays are in the rural areas and there are not enough Malay girls in the urban population to fulfill the quota imposed by the government policy. In the initial stages of its industrial development in Penang, for example, the state government, in collaboration with the industries, had to take deliberate steps to recruit Malay girls from as far away as the east coast of Malaysia (Von Der Mehden 1973). My survey data seem to support this finding, since they indicate that 69 percent of the female factory workers interviewed are interstate migrants.

THE PUSH FACTORS

So far we have seen how the interplay of the industrialization program and the New Economic Policy has acted to induce the migration of Malay girls from the rural sector. Now we analyze the factors that prompt girls to leave their rural villages and take up jobs as factory workers in the urban industrial centers. The two most frequently given reasons for migration are economic motives and personal motives (Table 11.1). Many studies on the causes of rural-to-urban migration stress that the main motive is to improve one's economic situation (Borowski 1967). This finding is supported by the data reported here, which show that 74 percent of the respondents cited as the most important reason for migrating the desire to improve their economic position and that of their families.

Economic Motives

The economic motive seems to be very strong indeed. In response to the question "What do you hope to achieve from migrating to the city?" more than half the sample of girls (56 percent) mentioned that they wanted to obtain a job and achieve a better living standard than the one they experienced in their villages.

The data relating to their background reveal the rationale behind this motive. Most of the respondents come from poor families with low incomes; moreover, these incomes are shared by many siblings. The majority of their fathers are small-scale farmers or low-level government employees. Twenty percent of their fathers are heads of households and earn a monthly income of less than 100 Malaysian ringgit; 51.3 percent receive less than 250 ringgit. These incomes are in or around the poverty-income bracket by Malaysian standards, especially when we consider the government figures for 1976, which place the per capita income at 2,206 ringgit.[6] Their poverty is made worse by having to support a large number of children. The data reveal that 52 percent of the girls have more than six brothers and sisters while only 6 percent come from small families with fewer than three siblings.

The survey findings also indicate a significant force behind the respondents' decisions to migrate to urban areas and find work in the factories. This force is the achievement of academic qualifications. Virtually all the girls have had some formal education. Almost half have middle-range educational qualifications while more than a quarter have prematriculation qualifications. Until a short time ago, these qualifications easily provided access to jobs in the nursing, clerical, and teaching professions, which are considered respectable and suitable pursuits for women. (This is also true in other developing societies; see Youssef 1976.) In Malaysia today, however, due to the limited job opportunities in general and especially in these fields, girls with these qualifications are forced to seek employment as

Table 11.1 Percentage distribution of respondents by reasons for moving

Subsample by research site	Reason for moving				Objective		
	Improve living standard	Personal reasons	Freedom and independence	Other[a]	Obtain job/improve living standard	Send money home	Other[b]
Datuk Keramat (N = 36)	91.7	0	19.4	8.3	75.0	5.6	0
Shah Alam (N = 30)	80.0	0	40.0	20	50.0	0	10.0
Sungai Way-Subang (N = 140)	68.6	10.7	24.29	20.7	51.5	17.1	6.4
Selayang Baru (N = 33)	39.4	36.4	0	24.2	33.3	9.1	45.5
Petaling Jaya (N = 136)	82.4	8.8	12.5	8.8	56.6	22.1	6.6
Johor Baru (N = 134)	76.9	17.2	21.6	5.9	56.8	16.4	1.5
Penang (N = 134)	75.6	17.4	15.0	5.2	53.8	24.4	6.8
Seremban (N = 166)	83.8	4.4	7.5	11.8	80.6	5.6	6.3
Province Wellesley (N = 155)	64.5	29.7	33.6	5.8	42.6	19.4	4.5
Malacca (N = 114)	66.7	24.6	21.9	7.8	46.5	19.4	7.9
Total (N = 1,278)	74.2	15.8	18.7	9.7	55.5	16.9	6.8

a. Does not include "no answer."

b. Does not include "don't know/no answer."

unskilled factory workers. Since most of these factories are in urban areas and employment opportunities in the villages are limited, rural girls migrate to the urban industrial centers.

These complementary forces—the push of limited job opportunities in the rural areas and the pull of employment openings in the urban industrial areas—are acknowledged by the girls. Some 89 percent had no other occupational choice at the time they were offered their factory job. In reply to the question "If you could get factory jobs in the village, would you prefer to work in the city?", 61.7 percent said they would prefer to work in the village.

PERSONAL MOTIVES

The second most frequently quoted reason for migration is the intention to achieve individual freedom. Nineteen percent of those interviewed said they hoped to achieve freedom and "stand on their own feet". The breakdown by research site shows that between 7.5 and 40.0 percent of the respondents in the subsamples expressed this motivation.

This motivation may be due to the encroachment of modern, urban influences in the rural sector. Traditional village values are now being challenged through the mass media, modern education, governmental development programs, and return migration. One traditional village norm that is being challenged seriously is the concept of proper conduct for young unmarried women. Among other things, a village Malay girl is expected to be obedient to her parents and elders, docile in her manners, and efficient in carrying out her domestic chores. As soon as she reaches marriageable age, she is closely watched and chaperoned.[7] The village girl's outdoor activities, work-force participation, and freedom in general are restricted until she is married off by her parents. Until then, her relationships with men other than those of her own family are completely curtailed and her reputation rests with the general opinion of the village community.

CONSEQUENCES FOR THE MIGRANTS

The literature on rural-to-urban migration in the developing countries describes migrant adjustment to urban life as a problematic process (Stark 1976). This adjustment is heavily influenced by two basic tasks: obtaining a suitable job and finding accommodations. The close connection between rural-to-urban migration and unemployment has been documented in several studies (see Bhargava 1971; Bairoch 1973; Gugler 1976). The continuous inflow of migrants makes it difficult for the city to accommodate them with its available facilities—hence the mushrooming of slums and squatter settlements.

EMPLOYMENT CONDITIONS AND JOB ORIENTATION

The respondents in the present sample were unemployed for a very short time: 67.1 percent said they obtained their factory job in less than two weeks after their arrival. This is not surprising, as many multinational companies are eager to employ Malay workers in order to abide by the government's New Economic Policy.[8] In many of these factories, girls are initially employed on probation; for three months their capabilities are assessed by factory supervisors. Workers on probation are paid on a daily basis whereas permanent workers are paid monthly. As there is no minimum wage legislation their earnings vary considerably according to company policy. My research indicates that 90.5 percent receive a monthly income ranging from M$70 to M$200. By urban income standards this figure falls within the lowest category. (In 1970 the mean monthly income for urban households in Malaysia was M$435; see Malaysia 1973:3.)

Hours of work are related to shift duty. In many factories, especially electronics, work hours are divided into three shifts; each shift duty consists of about eight solid hours of work with a rest period of 15 minutes every three hours. Female factory workers work about six shifts a week. In many factories, especially in electronics, overtime work is compulsory.[9] In the electronics industry, where the majority of women are employed, there is no worker's union. Moves to unionize workers are actively opposed by employers and Malaysian government officials.

Permanent workers are entitled to certain social and medical benefits. In addition, many companies organize sports and games, excursions, and the company's annual dinner and annual beauty contest. For factory girls who come from rural villages where unmarried girls' outdoor activities are restricted, these are totally new experiences.[10]

In brief, the factory environment creates new situations to which rural girls must conform. Four situations are especially significant: the inevitability of working and mixing with men; earning money and learning to use it independently; working according to regulated hours and having leisure time during off-duty hours; and participating in westernized functions and urban outdoor activities. All these situations are not only foreign to rural village culture but also condemned by village society.

How do these girls view their employment conditions and how do they react? My analysis indicates that many of the girls are dissatisfied with the pay, the limited opportunities for job promotion, and the insecurity of tenure (Table 11.2). Nevertheless, many of them say that the prime reasons they stay at their present jobs are the pay and the economic freedom they derive from holding the job.

These seemingly contradictory findings can be understood when they are viewed against the reasons given for migrating in the first place—

Table 11.2 Percentage distribution of respondents by aspects of job satisfaction and dissatisfaction

Aspect of work	Very satis-fied	Quite satis-fied	Not satis-fied	Don't know	No answer	Total
Work arrangement	17.3	62.4	20.1	0.0	0.2	100.0
Work supervision	15.8	66.9	16.9	0.1	0.3	100.0
Cooperation of work mates	34.4	59.9	5.3	0.1	0.2	100.0
Pay	5.6	44.1	49.5	0.5	0.4	100.0
Opportunities for promotion	5.3	34.4	57.4	2.3	0.7	100.0
Job security	3.9	30.4	62.9	2.4	0.5	100.0
Mutual respect among work mates	24.0	66.9	8.5	2.2	0.4	100.0
Means to achieve wants	11.4	55.9	29.4	2.7	0.6	100.0
Means to achieve economic independence	18.5	68.4	12.0	0.6	0.6	100.0

namely, the economic motive of getting a job and the desire to achieve independence. Moreover, the girls realize that other jobs are not easy to come by. Nevertheless, dissatisfaction with certain aspects of their employment conditions may have prompted ideas about resigning. As many as 64.3 percent of the respondents said they had thought of resigning. But this does not mean that the girls thought their initial decision to migrate was in vain and they should return to their villages. Many of them stated a definite wish to stay in the urban areas. In response to the question "In the event of being retrenched by your employer, state your preference of action: find another job in the city, find a job elsewhere, or go home to your villages," 26.8 percent indicated that their first preference was to find another job in the city and their last preference was to go home, 29.5 percent preferred finding a job elsewhere before going home, and only 7.2 percent preferred to go home to their villages.

ACCOMMODATIONS AND LIVING CONDITIONS

Most of the companies do not provide housing facilities for their workers, and there were no government youth hostels in 1977.[11] The Ministry of Social Welfare, alarmed by unfavorable publicity about migrant female workers, has only recently embarked on a foster-parent adoption scheme (which was met with lukewarm support from the girls).

Due to their low incomes, the influence of their friends, and high housing rents, the majority of the girls stay in cheap housing in working-class residential areas. Either a group of girls rents a house and shares the expenses or they stay with landladies and pay for board and lodging. There are three prominent features about their living conditions.

First, when compared to the facilities in the rural villages (where, in 1970, only 32.3 percent of households had plumbing and only 24.6 percent had electricity; see Malaysia 1973:5), the girls' urban accommodations by these criteria have better standards. For example, 90.8 percent are staying in accommodations with plumbing and lighting.

Second, there is a high degree of overcrowding. In a small house consisting of three rooms, for example, it is very common to find as many as 15 occupants. This crowding can be considered extraordinary even by Malaysian standards, where figures from the population census indicate the average number of persons per dwelling to be 5.5 for rural areas and 6.8, 7.0, and 7. 5 for urban small, urban large, and metropolitan urban areas, respectively. As for those who stay with landladies, as many as 20 or 30 lodgers may be accommodated in a building converted into sleeping compartments by the use of curtains and the like.[12]

Third, there are no proper household amenities. In a majority of cases the amenities consist of bedding, a small kerosene stove, some utensils, and straw mats. They do not have proper kitchen facilities or a sitting room or bedroom furniture. Those lodging with landladies are usually provided with a sleeping place and allowed to use the kitchen and toilet facilities.

Although these living conditions are considered inadequate by urban standards, many of the girls are satisfied; in fact, as many as 83.4 percent expressed satisfaction with their living conditions. Having come from a background of poverty, they maintained that their standard of living had improved; as many as 71.0 percent indicated that it had improved slightly, while 10.9 percent said it had improved definitely and only 2.6 percent thought it had deteriorated.

BEHAVIOR

Having only meager household amenities and activated by their first taste of freedom, factory girls spend much of their leisure time outside their places of residence.[13] Being young, single, and strangers to the city, these girls are sought after by men. As mentioned earlier, male and female mixing is considered taboo in rural villages but in the urban environment there are ample opportunities to break this norm. Some 83 percent of the girls said that, by coming to the city, they had greater opportunities to mix with men.

Though evidence of adjustment difficulties is only impressionistic, my observations and those of others during the course of this research suggest that there are clear signs of social-psychological problems. The first indication is the frequent occurrence of mass hysteria among workers. Fully 60.5 percent said that mass hysteria had erupted at their workplace. These incidents are usually triggered by a few girls screaming that they are seeing ghosts, followed by uncontrollable fits of fainting. The situation in the factory then becomes chaotic as numbers of girls become hysterical. These outbreaks may be a symptom that the pressures of modern industrial work and living conditions are traumatic for many rural girls.[14]

IMPLICATIONS FOR MALAYSIAN SOCIETY

Only time will reveal the long-term implications of the migration of Malay females to the urban industrial centers. Nevertheless, on the basis of the preliminary findings of this research and my experience the following observations can be offered.

First, the migration is already regarded seriously by the mass media, local politicians, and the general public. Sensational news reports about the behavior of factory girls and their involvement with men in the unsavory activities of drug-taking, wild parties, and prostitution are a constant feature in local newspapers and magazines. On the basis of these reports some politicians have urged people in the rural areas not to allow their daughters to work in the factories. Members of the general public are beginning to form opinions about Malay factory girls; moreover, many of the factory girls are aware of their low status. More than half of the girls surveyed said they were sometimes looked down upon by the urban community. In brief, rural-to-urban migration of Malay factory workers is regarded as a social problem.

Second, this so-called social problem does not seem to be a temporary one for Malaysian society. The rural-to-urban migration of Malay female workers will continue so long as the present pattern of industrialization remains unchanged and the factories that employ a majority of female workers continue to expand operations. One of the latest reports on industry in Penang states that with the greater demand for electronics components and textiles, these industrial companies are expanding production. A newspaper report said that in November 1978 about 3,000 factory jobs were available for female workers in the Bayan Lepas industrial site in Penang.[15] It has been my observation, moreover, that a significant number of rural-to-urban female migrant workers want to remain in the cities. As many as 25.1 percent of the respondents said they would definitely remain in the cities, 34.1 percent were uncertain of their future plans, and only 7.7 percent expressed a definite wish to return to their village eventually.

Third, given the continuing expansion of industrial factories that employ female migrants and the expressed wish of many migrants to remain in the cities, it can be assumed that the massive influx of Malay female migrant workers will continue and eventually lead to the emergence of a new group of working-class Malays—namely, the female factory worker.

Fourth, since most of these migrants are young and single girls at the time of migration and have migrated on their own, without the company of their families, they are experiencing considerable independence in the cities. These circumstances may be significant in two ways. First, the girls are more likely to change their behavior, outlook, and values than if they were living in the urban areas with their elders. Second, since many of these young women are single and within the fertile age group, there is a high probability that they will marry and raise new members of the urban society. If these assumptions hold true, this train of events will create a new generation of urban-based Malays with new sets of behavior and values.

NOTES

This essay is a revised version of a paper presented at the 10th International Congress of Anthropological and Ethnological Sciences, New Delhi, December 1978. The research was financed by grants from the National University of Malaysia and the South East Asian Population Awards Program (SEAPRAP).

1. At the time of migration 98.4 percent of the respondents were unmarried and 1.6 percent were divorced or widowed women. At the time interviews were conducted, 93.1 percent of the respondents were single and 6.9 percent were married.

2. In 1975 the total number of people unemployed was 297,200, implying an unemployment rate of 7.0 percent. Labor-force surveys show that unemployment rates among youth in the 15–19 age category were high in 1974: 18.8 percent in urban areas and 15.6 percent in rural areas. See Malaysia (1973:31).

3. In other Southeast Asian countries these free trade zones are better known as "export processing zones." In 1977 there were only three gazetted free trade zones in Malaysia: Sungai-Way free trade zone in Selangor, Batu Beredam free trade zone in Malacca, and Bayan Lepas free trade zone in Penang.

4. These are unpublished figures obtained from the Federal Industrial Development Authority of Malaysia. For details, see Ariffin (1978a:4). Some unpublished figures were obtained from interviews with officials of the Ministry of Labor and Manpower Planning of Malaysia.

5. The New Economic Policy was introduced after the Malaysian race riots of 1969 and was aimed at correcting the grievances behind the riots. The NEP is designed to "eradicate poverty among all Malaysians irrespective of race and . . . restructure Malaysian society so that the present identification of race with economic function and geographic location is reduced and eventually eliminated." The 30 percent employment rate for the Malays was calculated on the basis that in 1970 Malays comprised 55.4 percent, Chinese 33.8 percent, Indians 9.1 percent, and others 1.7 percent of the labor force. The 30 percent rate of indigenous participation in commerce and industry is expected to be achieved by the year 2000. For details, see Malaysia (1976:chap. 1).

6. In Malaysia poverty is measured using the poverty-line approach. The poverty line is defined as the income needed to maintain a family in good health and provide

minimum conventional needs for clothing, household management, and transport. The poverty line for a family of five in 1970 was estimated by the Malaysian Social Welfare Department to be M$160 per month. In 1975 it was raised to M$210 per month. See World Bank (1976:15).

7. About a generation ago, as soon as a village maiden attained the age of 12 she would be secluded, never again to be seen or heard in public. Today, however, these restrictions are somewhat more relaxed.

8. Consistent with the current pattern of female employment in manufacturing industries in Malaysia, 58.9 percent of the girls in the research sample were employed with electronics firms, 12.9 percent with textiles, and 12.8 percent with garment manufacturers.

9. The payment for overtime work varies from company to company. For example, one factory in the survey paid one-fifth of the worker's daily wage while another paid one-sixth. In many electronics factories overtime work is compulsory and enforced during periods of high market demand for the factories' products. Electronics workers interviewed usually complained about night-shift duty because they are only given 36 hours off to adjust to new shifts. This compares unfavorably with hospital night-shift workers, who are given a rest period of four days (96 hours). For details, see Ariffin (1979).

10. As pointed out by Rachel Grossman and Linda Lim, women workers in electronics factories owned by multinational corporations are constantly exposed to westernized values and role models. In fact, according to these researchers, many multinational corporations in Southeast Asia in general and in Malaysia in particular manipulate their female workers to maintain submissive behavior. See Grossman (1979) and Lim (1978).

11. Of all the companies in the study, only two provide hostel facilities. In the case of government hostels it was only in 1978 that the first youth hostel for girls was established in Kuala Lumpur.

12. This finding is supported by the Federation of Family Planning Association of Malaysia's research.

13. Factory girls frequently buy their meals from roadside vendors and can be seen loitering around the shopping centers and cinema halls. This observation is also supported by the Federation of Family Planning Association's empirical study.

14. At one time in 1976 the situation was so bad that the government authorities in collaboration with the industries called for the services of a medical psychiatrist to investigate the matter. During my visits to the factories, I was informed by many managers that they often called upon the services of *bomohs* (traditional healers) to alleviate the situation.

15. *Business Times*, 17 November 1978, p. 15. An article in the *Straits Times*, 17 August 1978, succinctly described the situation: "3,000 jobs going at Bayan Lepas Penang, Wed.—About 3,000 vacancies for women production operators in electronics factories in the Bayan Lepas free trade zone are going begging because of labour shortage in Penang. As a result, the expansion programmes of several factories are being held up. The demand for factory workers at Bayan Lepas follows an up-turn in the electronics industry with most factories running on three daily shifts. A number of factories anxious to engage more workers has sent out recruiting teams to the northern states and the East Coast."

BIBLIOGRAPHY

Ariffin, Jamilah
1978a Penghijrahan buruh wanita ke sektor perkilangan. Paper presented at the Bumiputra Economic Convention, Universiti Kebangsaan Malaysia, March 1978.
1978b Rural-urban migration and the status of factory women workers in a developing society: a case study of peninsular Malaysia. Paper presented at the 1978 conference of the Sociological Association of Australia and New Zealand.
1979 The position of women workers in the manufacturing industries in Malaysia. Paper presented at the international seminar on Women in the Third World, Madras.

Bairoch, P.
1973 *Urban Unemployment in Developing Countries: The Nature of the Problem and Proposals for Its Solution.* Geneva: International Labour Office.

Bhargava, G.
1971 Implications of migration to towns. *Kurukshetra* 19(February).

Bogue, Donald J.
1963 Techniques and hypotheses for the study of differential migration. International Population Conference, London, 1961. Liege: International Union for the Scientific Study of Population.

Borowski, S.
1967 New forms and factors affecting rural urban migration in Poland. World Population Conference 1965. Vol. IV: *Migration, Urbanization and Economic Development.* New York: United Nations.

Boserup, Ester
1970 *Women's Role in Economic Development,* New York: St. Martin's Press.

Elizaga, J. C.
1965 Internal migration in Latin America. *International Social Science Journal* 17: 213–31.

Grossman, Rachel
1979 Women's place in the integrated circuit. Special joint issue of *Southeast Asia Chronicle* (No. 66) and *Pacific Research* (9(5–6)).

Gugler, J.
1976 Migration to urban centers of unemployment in tropical Africa. In A. H. Richmond and D. Kubot (eds.), *Internal Migration—The New World and the Third World.* Beverly Hills: Sage.

Heisler, H.
1974 Urbanization and the government of migration. In *Inter-relation of Urban and Rural Life in Zambia.* New York: St. Martin's Press.

Jansen, C.
1969 Some sociological aspects of migration. In J. A. Jackson (ed.), *Migration Sociological Studies 2.* London: Cambridge University Press.

Lim, Linda Y. C.
  1978   Women workers in multinational corporations. *Michigan Occasional Papers* 9:7.

Lim, Meng Seng
  1973   *Industrialization and Developing Countries.* Kuala Lumpur: Modern Education Publishers.

Malaysia
  1973   *Mid-Term Review of the Second Malaysia Plan 1971-1975.* Kuala Lumpur: Government Press.
  1976   *The Third Malaysia Plan 1976-80.* Kuala Lumpur: Government Press.

Ravenstein, E.
  1889   The laws of migration. *Journal of the Royal Statistical Society* 52:241–305.

Stark, Oded
  1976   *Rural to Urban Migration and Some Economic Issues: A Review Utilizing Findings of Surveys and Empirical Studies Covering the 1965-1975 Period.* Working Paper. Geneva: International Labour Office.

UNECA
  1969   Size and growth of urban population. In G. Breese (ed.), *The City in Newly Developing Countries.* Englewood Cliffs, N.J.: Prentice-Hall.
  1970   Migration, a sociological problem. In C. Jansen (ed.), *Readings in the Sociology of Migration.* Oxford: Pergamon Press.

Von Der Mehden, Fred R.
  1973   *Industrial Policy in Malaysia—A Penang Micro-Study.* Houston: Rice University, Program for Development Studies.

World Bank
  1976   *Malaysia: Second Plan Performance and Third Plan Issues.* Vol. 1. Washington.

Youssef, N. H.
  1976   *Women and Work in Developing Societies.* Westport, Conn.: Greenwood Press.

Chapter 12

Female Migrants in Bangkok Metropolis

Suwanlee Piampiti

In the process of national development the volume and rate of female migration within a country tend to increase. As the country becomes more industrialized and modernized, there is a shift of population from farm to urban areas accompanied by a fundamental change in the subsistence activities of women. As their educational level rises, so do their employment opportunities. Occupations that can be performed by women increase in number and importance, especially in the metropolitan areas. Increases in female education raise the demand for female labor, sometimes to the point where they can displace less educated men.

During the past decade, Thailand was one of the developing countries that experienced a substantial change in the roles of women. In Bangkok metropolis in 1960, for example, about 74 percent of employed females 11 years of age and over were employed in nonagricultural occupations. By 1970, this proportion had risen to 93 percent (Thailand, NSO, 1960 and 1970). In terms of education, the 1960 census reported that 50 percent of females six years of age and over had attained at least seven years of primary education whereas in 1970 the percentage was 59. These changes seem to be associated with increasing female migration rates in the whole country. Between 1960 and 1970, the number of male five-year migrants increased by 112 percent while that for females increased by 142 percent. (Five-year migrants are persons who moved to their present changwat, or province, within five years of the census date.)

The five-year migration streams were female-dominant to Bangkok only, however. Between 1955 and 1960, approximately 70,000 males and 60,000 females moved to the metropolitan area. The number of male migrants also exceeded the number of female migrants in every region— for example, the percentages of male migrants were 56, 59, 56, and 60 percent for the North, Central, Northeast, and South regions, respectively. In the later period, 1965 to 1970, male migrants still outnumbered female migrants except in Bangkok–Thon Buri, for the number of five-year migrants in the metropolis was composed of 145,000 males and 153,000 females, a reversal of the sex difference. In other areas, the difference between sexes had narrowed—the percentages of male migrants were 54, 55, 54, and 56 for the North, Central, Northeast, and South regions, respectively. Furthermore, it should be noted that the fraction of migrants with Bangkok as their destination was between 16 and 19 percent for males and females in both periods (Thailand NSO, 1960 and 1970:changwat series, table 9).

The substantial increase of female migrants to the metropolitan area is due to many causes other than the economic reasons cited in most studies. Friends, relatives, marriage, and education are also prominent. It is important to note, however, that in a developing country the underenumeration of migrants in metropolitan areas tends to be greater for males than for females. It is more likely that a man will lead a solitary existence, whereas a woman will usually go to the city only if there are friends or relatives to live with. Since the residences of men are sometimes unstable, male migrants can easily be missed in a census.

Nevertheless, the changes noted above lead to several significant points for study. In the past, most research on migration in Thailand has focused on male migrants because of their predominance in the stream. A study of pedicab drivers in Bangkok by Textor (1956) and another study by Meinkoth (1962) on migration from the northeast to Bangkok sampled only male migrants. In 1968 when the first comprehensive data on migration in Thailand were collected in the National Longitudinal Survey of Social, Economic, and Demographic Change, conducted by the Institute of Population Studies, respondents in the study were male heads of household. Since the movement of population has generally affected not only the migrants but also the areas of origin and destination, the increasing proportion of women will inevitably have demographic, economic, and social consequences. This study compares the characteristics of female migrants in Bangkok metropolis with female nonmigrants in both areas of origin and destination. As far as the available data permit, I wish to examine the effects of female migration on the socioeconomic conditions of migrants and on the areas of origin and destination.

SOURCES OF DATA

According to the registration records of Bangkok metropolis, in each year between 1970 and 1974 approximately 375,000 persons moved to the metropolitan area (Department of Policy and Planning, Bangkok Metropolis). Among 24 districts, the four that had the highest proportions of inmigrants—Phayathai, Bangkhen, Bangkapi, and Ratburana districts—

were selected as sample areas. Registration records from these districts were used as the sampling frame.

Although residents of Thailand are required to register changes of dwelling within a fortnight of a move,[1] the completeness of registration data on migration is unknown for it has never been estimated in any study. The Survey of Population Change in Thailand did find that the completeness of birth and death registration in Thailand was about 85 percent in 1974–75. Estimation of the completeness of migration registration is more complicated, though, for it involves various types of movement coupled with the negligence of residents in reporting themselves.

Nevertheless, registration data are one of the major sources of information for studies of migration. In this study the names and addresses of women aged 15 years and over who had registered their moves into the four sample districts between January 1974 and December 1975 were listed as the sampling frame. From 12,080 listed names, 1,250 female migrants were systematically selected along with their names and addresses. Various problems arose when it came to finding these women, however, including further moves by the women or inability to find the addresses listed. In these cases, women in the same household or next-door neighbors were substituted if they had moved to Bangkok during the survey period and were 15 years old or more. (Migration rates tend to rise after age 15 and reach a peak at ages 25 to 29; moreover, women below age 15 are more likely to be children who simply moved with their parents rather than making the decision to migrate themselves.)

The four sample districts have certain characteristics that may influence the occupational distribution of migrants interviewed. Bangkhen and Ratburana have a large number of factories; thus the proportion of migrants as production workers was higher than for other occupations. Phayatai is located in the core of the metropolis and has low-cost housing and second-class hotels, motels, and massage parlors; thus a small fraction of female migrants were found in these occupations. Bangkapi, which has been growing quite rapidly as a new suburb during the past decade, is mainly a residential area of the upper middle and the middle classes. Thus the pattern of occupations of migrants in this study is more or less a reflection of the characteristics of these areas.

Nonmigrants in this study are persons who were born in the sample areas and never moved out. Five hundred female nonmigrants in Bangkok metropolis were randomly selected among persons who lived next door to the sample migrants. As for nonmigrants at the origin, 300 women were randomly selected from the village of birth in Ayudhaya and Nakorn Pathom, for these two changwats had the largest number of out-migrants to the metropolis.

CHARACTERISTICS OF FEMALE MIGRANTS

AGE, MARITAL STATUS, AND FERTILITY PATTERNS

It is well known that migration is selective with respect to age. Migrants tend to be young adults. The female migrants in our survey were concentrated at ages 20–24 and 15–19; their median age was 22. As for marital status, a number of studies on migration have found that movement to the metropolitan areas occurs largely among the unmarried. (See, for example, Goldstein 1972 and the Thailand NSO, 1974.) This is true in the present study as well, for about 80 percent of the female migrants were single, only 18 percent were married, and the rest had divorced or separated from their spouses. The proportion of married migrants seems to increase with age, indicating that married women moved at a later age than the singles and tended to move with their families.

In Thailand, female migrants tend to marry at an age slightly higher than the average for rural women but lower than that for urban women. As for the female migrants in this study, their median age at first marriage was 20.7; at the time of interview, the average number of children was only two per woman. Almost one-fifth of the migrants had no children and only one in ten had five children or more. About 50 percent of these mothers said they had had enough children, while those who wanted more wanted only one more child.

ORIGINS AND TYPES OF MOBILITY

The largest proportion of female migrants came from the Central Region, followed by the Northeast, North, and South regions, respectively. Table 12.1 shows that the percentage distribution of migrants from various regions was similar to the distribution shown in the 1970 census (Thailand, NSO 1970:Bangkok–Thon Buri, table 9). Migrants from the Central Region came mostly from nearby changwats such as Ayudhaya, Lopburi, Ratchaburi, Angthong, and Suphanburi. As for the Northeast, the major-

Table 12.1 Percentage distribution of female migrants in Bangkok metropolis, by region of birth and region of last residence

Region	Birth	Last residence
Central	49.6	51.5
North	14.4	14.8
Northeast	26.6	25.0
South	9.4	8.7
Total	100.0	100.0
Total number	1,250	1,250

ity came from Nakhonratchasima, Ubonrajatani, and Khon Kaen; in the North they were from three major changwats: Chiangmai, Chiangrai, and Lampang. The South, which contributed the lowest number of migrants to the metropolis, had only two major contributing changwats: Nakhonsithammarat and Suratthani.

Some 60 percent of the migrants came from provincial urban areas while only 40 percent came from rural areas. It is interesting to note that the majority of female migrants moved alone to the metropolitan area, especially at young ages. Table 12.2 shows that 75 to 80 percent of the migrants at ages 15–19 and 20–24 moved alone. Only one in nine moved with the whole family and they were mostly in the age group 30–34. Approximately one in six moved with part of their family. About 90 percent had just made their first move; 6 percent had moved twice whereas only 1 percent had moved more than five times. The data seem to indicate that the migration of women is a recent phenomenon for most of them.

REASONS FOR MIGRATION

As mentioned earlier, migration in Thailand consisted predominantly of males before the 1970s. After the results of the 1970 census were released,

Table 12.2 Percentage distribution of female migrants in Bangkok metropolis, by age and type of mobility

| Age | Type of mobility | | | | |
	Total	Whole family	Part of family	Individual	Unknown
15–19	100.0 (381)	2.6	20.2	73.8	3.4
20–24	100.0 (621)	4.2	12.5	81.0	2.3
25–29	100.0 (107)	23.4	25.2	51.4	0.0
30–34	100.0 (70)	44.3	28.6	25.7	1.4
35–39	100.0 (32)	62.5	12.5	25.0	0.0
40–49	100.0 (28)	64.3	25.0	10.7	0.0
50+	100.0 (11)	54.5	18.2	27.3	0.0
All ages	100.0 (1,250)	10.9	17.2	69.7	2.2

however, an emerging trend of increasing female migration was detected. This new trend may be attributed to the growing modernization of Bangkok, the rising proportion of females enrolled in schools, the increasing participation of females in the nonagricultural labor force, and the weakening of traditional restrictions in rural areas (Mowat 1977). The trend toward the increasing importance of female migration is consistent with Bogue's observation (1969:765):

> Where migration may be accomplished cheaply and with security and especially where channels are well established and large numbers of former migrants at the place of destination are available to provide aid, the sex ratio of migrants tends to near 1 or to have a feminine balance. Where the movement is extraordinary . . . of a "pioneering," "invasion" or "new stream establishment" nature, . . . male migrants tend to outnumber females.

Bogue's generalization conforms rather well to the patterns of migration in Thailand. For the whole country, major migration streams were dominated by males except for migration to Bangkok metropolis, which was dominated by females. This pattern suggests that once the stream of migration to the metropolitan area had become well established, females came to outnumber males as in the 1965–70 period.

The increasing volume of female migrants has many causes. In general, female migrants in the metropolis are young and adaptable. For them, the city is where jobs are. In the rural areas, the combination of high fertility and a shrinking demand for labor has produced unemployment and underemployment. Thus the majority of women cite money as the principal reason for migration.

When female migrants were asked their main reason for migrating, almost one in two indicated economic motives such as coming to look for a job or to improve their standard of living (Table 12.3). Many migrants indicated poor conditions at previous places of residence; some came to look for work during the agricultural slack season. (These findings confirm other studies on migration to urban areas; see, for example, Meinkoth 1962; Thailand, NSO, 1974; Piampiti 1976.)

In addition to economic motives, social motivations must also be considered. Table 12.3 shows that about one in three migrants came for further study. This proportion corresponds roughly to the percentage of migrants who were students at the time of the survey. In the age groups 15–19 and 20–24 the percentages of migrants who came to continue studying were as high as 41 and 49, respectively. This finding may be traced to the uneven distribution of educational facilities in Thailand and the fact that urban children generally attain more years of schooling than rural children. The gap begins at the primary level and grows broader for girls than for boys.

Table 12.3 Percentage distribution of female migrants in Bangkok metropolis, by reasons for migration

Age	Total	Reasons for migration						
		Agri-cultural slack season	Poor con-dition at previous place	Looking for job	Better living condition	Continue studying	Followed husband, parents, or relatives	Others
15–19	100.0 (381)	3.7	3.7	39.6	1.6	40.9	8.7	1.8
20–24	100.0 (621)	1.4	3.7	37.5	1.6	48.8	5.8	1.1
25–29	100.0 (107)	0.9	7.5	50.5	2.8	6.5	27.1	4.7
30–34	100.0 (70)	4.3	8.6	38.6	5.7	2.8	37.1	2.8
35–39	100.0 (32)	0.0	12.5	37.5	3.1	0.0	46.9	0.0
40–49	100.0 (28)	7.1	14.3	21.4	10.7	0.0	35.7	10.7
50+	100.0 (11)	0.0	9.1	9.1	0.0	9.1	27.3	45.4
All ages	100.0 (1,250)	2.3	4.8	38.7	2.2	37.5	12.2	2.3

Hence educated rural youth join the stream of migration to Bangkok metropolis because of their desire for higher education.

Family reasons were also important. About 12 percent of the migrants moved because of marriage or followed their husbands or parents to the metropolitan area. Women who gave this reason for migration were mainly 25 years old or older, however. At ages 35 to 39, about 57 percent of the women cited family reasons for migration.

It should be noted that most female migrants had visited the metropolis before moving into the area during the 1974–75 period. Among 1,250 female migrants, 70 percent had come to Bangkok before; about one in three had never been in the metropolis but learned about the area from other sources. Friends and relatives played an important role, especially for the youngest age group, while mass media were a major source of information for migrants at age 20 and above. Nevertheless, in all age groups most of the migrants had visited the metropolis before their move.

About one in two migrants had received financial aid from parents, relatives, or friends. This proportion is rather high because many of the migrants are students. As the following results show, only a small fraction of migrants had to borrow in order to move to the metropolis:

Source of financing move	No.	%
Self	350	28.0
Parents, friends, relatives	852	68.2
Loan	7	0.6
Not specified	41	3.2

EMPLOYMENT AND EDUCATION

As stated earlier, most migrants are young adults. Almost 60 percent of female migrants were employed at the time of interview. Table 12.4 shows that the proportion of migrants not employed is composed mainly of students. Fewer than 1 percent of the migrants were unemployed and all were looking for work at the time of interview. As for work status, about 84 percent of the employed migrants were private employees; one in twenty migrants was self-employed or an unpaid family worker; only a small portion were employers.

Many migrants (about 50 percent) found work as soon as they moved into the metropolis. Their friends or relatives who had arrived earlier helped them find jobs; only 20 percent had to look for a job by themselves. As for those who could not obtain jobs when they arrived, the time they spent seeking a job ranged from three to six months. Migrants from the same origin tend to concentrate at the same area of destination. In Bang-

Table 12.4 Number and percentage distribution of female migrants in Bangkok metropolis, by employment and work status

Employment and work status	No.	%
Employed		
Total	722	57.8
Employer	6	0.5
Government employee	42	3.4
Private employee	607	48.6
Own-account worker	52	4.2
Unpaid family worker	15	1.2
Not employed		
Total	528	42.2
Students	461	36.9
Housewives	53	4.2
Retired	7	0.5
Unemployed	7	0.5
Total employed and not employed	1,250	100.0

khen district, for example, 15 percent of the female migrants came from the same origin (Changwat Ayudhaya) and were employed in the same factory at the time of interview. In short, migrants who had come earlier and who were succeeding in the metropolitan area doubtless persuaded friends or relatives to join them.

Table 12.5 shows that female migrants changed their occupations when they moved to the metropolitan area. All the migrants who were agricultural workers before migration had changed their occupation to other categories. A high proportion of them had become production workers and service workers (maids, waitresses, masseuses). Many migrants who were unemployed or family workers before their migration also shifted to these two occupational groups.[2] On the whole, the proportion of female migrants who were white-collar workers was rather low. This finding may be explained by their level of education. Regardless of age, almost 70 percent of the migrants had four years or less of formal education whereas only 5 percent had some vocational or university training. As a result, a high proportion of female migrants are employed as artisans, production workers, or service workers.

As for the student migrants, their level of education at the time of interview was much higher than that of employed migrants. All were in the age group 15–24. The largest number of student migrants were found at the highest level of education:

Table 12.5 Percentage distribution of employed female migrants in Bangkok metropolis, by current occupation, former occupation, or other work status

Current occupation	Former occupation							Other statuses		
	Total	Professional	Clerical	Sales	Farming	Crafts	Services	Unemployed or family workers	Students	Unknown
Total	100.0 (722)	100.0 (11)	100.0 (8)	100.0 (81)	100.0 (222)	100.0 (47)	100.0 (2)	100.0 (282)	100.0 (55)	100.0 (14)
Professional[a]	3.9	90.9	0.0	0.0	0.0	0.0	0.0	1.4	23.6	7.1
Clerical	9.7	9.1	75.0	0.0	7.2	10.6	0.0	6.0	34.6	42.9
Sales	7.8	0.0	0.0	21.0	8.6	0.0	0.0	6.7	1.8	0.0
Farming	0.0	0.0	0.0	0.0	0.0	0.0	0.0	0.0	0.0	0.0
Crafts[b]	53.7	0.0	0.0	48.2	59.0	66.0	50.0	58.6	29.1	35.7
Services[c]	24.5	0.0	25.0	29.6	24.3	23.4	50.0	27.3	10.9	14.3
Unknown	0.4	0.0	0.0	1.2	0.9	0.0	0.0	0.0	0.0	0.0

a. Includes administrative and government officials.

b. Includes production workers and laborers.

c. Includes maids, waitresses, and masseuses.

Level of education of student migrants	No.	%
5–7 years	3	0.7
8–10 years	22	4.8
11–12 years	114	24.7
Vocational, teacher training	108	23.4
University	214	46.4

It should be noted that about 70 percent of the student migrants came from provincial urban places and generally had a better education than migrants from rural areas. The educational institutions in Bangkok metropolis were major pull factors for these migrants, who knew that high-wage jobs could be obtained through higher education and training.

CHARACTERISTICS OF MIGRANTS AND NONMIGRANTS

Among 500 nonmigrants in Bangkok metropolis, 54.2 percent were employed at the time of the interview. Of the women who were not employed, 48.5, 34.9, 14.4, and 2.2 percent were students, housewives, retirees, and unemployed, respectively. Additional characteristics of migrants and nonmigrants are presented in Table 12.6 for comparison. On average, nonmigrants in areas of origin and destination were older than migrants. The median age for migrants was 22 as opposed to 34 and 24 for nonmigrants at origin and destination, respectively. The high median age of female nonmigrants at the origin may be due to the fact that most of them were wives of household heads. When standardized by age, the proportion of married women at the origin is highest: 77 percent. By contrast, 44 percent of female migrants in the metropolis were single and 51 percent were married. Among nonmigrants in the metropolis, 40 percent were single and 52 percent were married; 8 percent were widowed and divorced. A similar pattern of marital composition of Thailand's population was found by Goldstein (1972a:24) among males in 1960 and by Chamratrithirong (1976:136) among females in 1970. Goldstein noted that the "higher proportion of both single persons and of those widowed and divorced suggests that the city has particular attraction to individuals without immediate family ties, or at least that it is easier for such individuals to leave the rural areas for movement to the city" (1972a:23).

Regarding age at first marriage, our findings corroborate a study by Prachuabmoh et al. (1972), which shows that first marriage took place earlier on the average among women in the rural areas and latest among residents of Bangkok metropolis. The average ages at marriage were 20.6, 21.3, and 21.7 for women in the rural, provincial urban, and Bangkok-Thon Buri area respectively. Moreover, our study shows that the mean age

Table 12.6 Characteristics of female migrants in Bangkok metropolis and female nonmigrants at origin and destination

Characteristics	Migrants (%)	Nonmigrants Origin (%)	Nonmigrants Destination (%)
Age			
All ages	100.0	100.0	100.0
15–19	30.5	8.0	24.2
20–24	49.7	12.7	31.2
25–29	8.6	17.7	14.4
30–34	5.6	16.3	9.4
35–39	2.6	10.0	5.2
40–44	1.5	9.3	5.0
45–49	0.7	7.3	3.4
50–54	0.2	6.7	1.2
55–59	0.2	6.0	1.2
60+	0.4	6.0	4.8
Total no.	1,250	300	500
Median age	21.5	33.5	23.6
Marital status[a]			
Total	100.0	100.0	100.0
Single	43.9	18.0	39.6
Married	51.2	76.7	52.3
Widowed	1.0	3.3	5.8
Divorced or separated	3.9	2.0	2.3
Median age at first marriage	20.7	20.2	21.1
No. of living children[a]			
Total	100.0	100.0	100.0
0	22.2	5.7	15.3
1	23.2	17.5	22.9
2	17.8	20.7	16.7
3	17.4	13.0	15.2
4	5.2	12.6	12.9
5	9.0	8.1	8.3
6+	6.2	22.4	8.7
Total no.	240	246	222
Average no. of living children	1.9	3.8	2.7
Education of females not in school[a]			
Total	100.0	100.0	100.0
None	13.0	16.6	9.6
Primary 1–4 years	65.1	74.1	42.5
Primary 5–7 years	9.0	0.8	11.9
Secondary 3 years	8.3	4.9	19.2
Secondary 5 years	0.9	2.3	4.9
Vocational	2.4	1.3	6.8
University	1.3	0.0	5.1
Total no.	789	300	389

Table 12.6 *(continued)*

Characteristics	Migrants (%)	Nonmigrants Origin (%)	Destination (%)
Occupation[a]			
Total	100.0	100.0	100.0
Professional[b]	3.9	1.4	7.5
Clerical	11.7	0.0	18.0
Sales	13.8	15.2	32.6
Farming	0.0	54.2	0.0
Crafts	53.6	29.2	41.2
Services	17.0	0.0	0.7
Total no.	722	256	271

a. Standardized for age.

b. Includes administrative workers and government officials.

at first marriage of migrants falls between that of nonmigrants at origin and nonmigrants at destination. When the average number of living children is examined, again this pattern is found. Thus our findings seem to support Lee's hypothesis (1966:57) that the characteristics of migrants tend to be intermediate between the characteristics of the population at origin and the population at destination. When we look at other characteristics such as educational attainment and occupation, the data in Table 12.6 seem to support this hypothesis further. In terms of education attainment, 13 percent of the migrants had completed more than seventh grade while the percentages for nonmigrants at origin and destination were 9 and 36, respectively. The proportion of women having attained education beyond four years of primary school was highest among residents of Bangkok metropolis. Some 5 percent of nonmigrants in the metropolis had attained the university level versus 1 percent for migrants and none among nonmigrants at origin. As for occupational distributions, 4 percent of the migrants were in the professional category as opposed to between 2 and 8 percent for the nonmigrants. The highest proportion of women in the metropolis was found in the artisans and laborers category. Female migrants tended to be employed as service workers much more often than nonmigrants in the metropolis.

OTHER INFORMATION ON NONMIGRANTS

Apart from these characteristics of nonmigrants, other information was collected. Among 300 nonmigrants at the origin, 73 percent indicated that they had visited Bangkok metropolis. This proportion is quite high because of the short distances involved. The sample areas are only about 60 kilometers from the metropolis. Nearly half the nonmigrants had gone to Bangkok more than ten times. They usually stayed with friends or relatives in the metropolis for only a few days. Obviously, many of them went to visit their offspring or relatives. About one in nine went to see a doctor or go to the hospital. One in four went for business; the remainder went for recreation.

Thus these nonmigrants are quite well acquainted with the metropolis. Furthermore, 100 households out of 300 had a former member living in the metropolis at the time of interview. The number of out-migrants from the household was as high as five persons in two cases. In more than half the households, at least one person had left for Bangkok. Among 160 out-migrants, 79 percent were offspring of the respondents and the rest were relatives, parents or spouses. About equal numbers of males and females had moved to the metropolis; the sex ratio is 103 males per 100 females.

Nearly 16 percent of the out-migrants were under 20 years of age. Only eight persons or 5 percent were 45 years of age or older. On the whole, the average age of out-migrants was 25 with an age range of 10–50. The majority were recent migrants, for 38 percent had been living in the metropolis less than five years. Only 8 percent of the total out-migrants had been living in Bangkok metropolis for more than 25 years.

The distribution of occupations among out-migrants is quite similar to that mentioned earlier (Table 12.5) for migrants in the metropolis. Thirty-seven percent of out-migrants were employed as artisans or laborers and nearly 15 percent were government officials. One in 13 out-migrants from the households was studying in the metropolis at the time of interview.

Table 12.7 shows the percentage distribution of out-migrants to Bangkok metropolis by level of education. The proportion of migrants at the higher levels of education is quite high, possibly because of the inclusion of migrants who were studying at the time of interview. The majority of out-migrants had only four years of schooling, however.

Among these out-migrants, 87 percent had frequent contact with the family they had left; the rest had only occasional contact. The respondents also indicated that 35 percent of the out-migrants always send remittances home, 29 percent did so occasionally, but another 29 percent had never done so. The rest were students who still needed support from the family. The respondents stated that half the migrants would stay permanently in Bangkok metropolis; about 8 percent would stay temporarily; the respondents were uncertain how long the others would stay.

Among the 300 nonmigrants, only 2 percent thought of moving to Bangkok metropolis or other provinces. The rest had not desired to move elsewhere, for their present place of residence was their place of birth. This high proportion is not unexpected since the average age of nonmigrants in our survey is about 45 years. According to Morrison (1973:6): "The pro-

Table 12.7 **Percentage distribution of out-migrants from households in Bangkok metropolis, by education**

Level of education	%
None	3.1
Primary 1—4 years	48.1
Primary 5—7 years	6.9
Secondary 1—3 years	11.2
Secondary 4—5 years	8.2
Vocational and teacher training	5.6
University	2.5
Unknown	14.4
Total	100.0

Source: Survey of Female Migrants in Bangkok Metropolis, 1975.

pensity to migrate diminishes sharply with age. . . . Once beyond their 40th birthday, inertia sets in and, for better or worse, people pretty much pledge allegiance to where they are."

CONSEQUENCES OF MIGRATION

In this study, the effects of migration on individuals were gauged by asking migrants for their own evaluations. Some 60 percent of the 1,250 female migrants in Bangkok metropolis indicated that their living conditions had much improved while about one-third reported no change. The average income of all migrants was also higher than before migration. At the time of interview, the average monthly income of migrants employed as production workers, maids, and waitresses was 1,500 baht (20 baht = U.S. $1). As for migrants in other occupational groups such as professional workers and sales personnel, their average income was about 3,500 baht per month. And for the masseuses, their average income was also as high as 3,500 baht. Although the overall average earnings were rather low they can be considered high compared with former incomes in rural areas. About one in two migrants indicated that they sent remittances back home regularly.

Another effect of migration can be noted in the occupational mobility of migrants. Female migrants were drawn to the metropolitan area in response to a demand for service and production workers. During the past decade, female migrants who used to engage in agricultural work in rural areas came to fill the demand in certain sectors of the economy, especially in labor-intensive manufacturing, that required a high proportion of unskilled workers. Furthermore, female migrants concentrated in certain occupations, such as masseuses, bar hostesses, and prostitutes, that seem to create social problems in the metropolitan area. But for the migrants, the financial gain from these occupations was the important thing. Many migrants considered their migration experiences favorably.

Length of residence and the presence of friends or relatives in the city generally played a crucial role in the process of adjustment. The analysis is rather complex, though, as Morrison (1972:3) observes:

Generalizations about adjustment are difficult because: (1) the outward signs of adjustment vary from one subculture to another; (2) a migrant may be "adjusted" within the confines of his immediate group but not integrated into the broader community; (3) migrants' success in adjusting to a new environment is in part shaped by their motivations for moving.

In this study migrants were asked whether they had any problems adjusting to the urban environment. A quarter of the female migrants in our survey indicated that they had problems adjusting to the transportation system in Bangkok metropolis; another quarter said they disliked the urban environment. These two major problems—transportation and environment—caused nearly one in 20 migrants to decide to return home. The rest of the migrants cited only minor problems or none.

Regarding the impact of female migration on the area of destination, Bangkok metropolis, it should be noted that the population structure of the metropolitan area had been shifted by the high rate of female migration during the past decade. Between 1955 and 1960 male migrants outnumbered female migrants in the metropolis while between 1965 and 1970 this sex differential was reversed. Table 12.8 shows the sex ratio of the population in Bangkok metropolis in the years 1960 and 1970. In 1960, the ratio of males per 100 females at all ages was 104; in 1970 it was 98. Furthermore, because the majority of female migrants were young adults, the ratios of males per 100 females in the 10–39 age group was much lower in 1970. It should be noted, however, that the decline of the sex ratios may also be due to a greater undercount of females in the 1960 census than in the 1970 census.

At the area of origin, the impact of female migration cannot be directly detected for lack of appropriate data. Even so, the overall impact of out-migration of both males and females in some areas should be mentioned. In Ayudhaya, for example, a high rate of out-migration has been found in both the 1960 and 1970 censuses. The province experienced a substantial loss of population through migration during the decade, yet its annual rate of growth between 1960 and 1970 was about 0.5 percent due to the high rate of natural increase. Between 1955 and 1960 the rate of net migration

Table 12.8 Sex ratios of the population in Bangkok metropolis, by age: 1960 and 1970

Age	Sex ratio (males per 100 females)	
	1960	1970
All ages	103.9	97.7
0–9	104.5	104.3
10–19	102.8	97.9
20–29	109.4	95.0
30–39	106.4	97.8
40–49	107.2	100.0
50–59	101.0	93.9
60+	76.4	74.0

Source: Thailand, NSO (1960, 1970).

loss was 40 per 1,000 population; by 1970, this rate had increased to 73 per 1,000. In other words, Ayudhaya lost about 18,200 males and 14,000 females through migration between 1965 and 1970. Migration has changed the age distribution of population. The proportion of population in the economically active age group declined during the decade. The dependency ratio increased from 93 to 106. On the average, the population of the province was also younger, for the median age decreased from 20 years to about 17 years. Furthermore, as a result of the massive outward flow of women, the proportion of women in the childbearing years, ages 15 to 44, declined from 42 percent of all women in 1960 to 35 percent 1970. Partially because of these changes in age structure, the crude birth rate per thousand persons in Ayudhaya declined from 34 in 1968 to 26 in 1972. (Thailand, NSO, 1976b). It should be noted, however, that part of this decline was a consequence of the decline of the national birth rate during the same period. Finally, persistent migration away from Ayudhaya, especially among males, has led to an increasing proportion of elderly population and a more predominantly female population remaining in the province as shown by the declining sex ratio: from 95.3 to 93.9.

SUMMARY AND CONCLUSION

In the process of national development, the volume and rate of female migration in Thailand were found to have increased everywhere and to outnumber male migration in Bangkok metropolis, where the demand for service, clerical, and domestic workers was high. This new trend may be attributed to the modernization of the rural areas, the increasing proportion of females enrolled in schools, the growing participation of females in the labor force, and the weakening of traditional restrictions in rural areas. In this study, female migrants were found to be attracted to the metropolitan area for socioeconomic reasons. Opportunities for women in Bangkok metropolis substantially increased during the 1960s. The majority of female migrants were young adults and unmarried. They came for economic and social reasons but relied heavily on family or friends who had come earlier. Many changed their occupations and were satisfied with their current living conditions. Work opportunities, working conditions, and wages were found mostly satisfactory among female migrants. Their low level of education, however, limited their occupational choices in the metropolitan area. A number of female migrants were employed as masseuses, bar hostesses, and prostitutes. In this respect, a detailed study is needed to determine how migration affects the metropolitan area and the women's personal satisfaction.

The characteristics of migrants tend to fall between those of nonmigrants in the places of origin and destination—partly because they are already, to some degree, like the population at destination and unlike the population at origin with regard to age, marital status, age at first marriage, educational attainment, and occupation. The relatively poor situation of nonmigrants at origin may be in some degree a result of the massive outward movement of the young, the educated and the skilled, while the labor force left behind tends to be older, less educated, and less skilled. Thus, in the case of Ayudhaya, persistent out-migration has led to many changes in the population structure of the province.

These findings suggest that a national program of assisted female (and male) migration should be developed. This study shows that migration has enabled women to better themselves economically and socially. Migration has also acted as a mechanism for the adjustment of labor supply and demand. Yet the majority of female migrants rely heavily on their relatives and friends in deciding whether and where to go. In other words, they consider only a narrow range of alternatives regarding both destinations and job opportunities. Thus many female migrants in Bangkok metropolis end up with low-wage jobs or as bar girls and masseuses (although with higher incomes). The program would match an unemployed woman who cannot find work locally with a job elsewhere for which she is, or could be, qualified; it would enable her to relocate, if she so desires, with a minimum of disruption and risk. In this way, those who do move can be helped to migrate more effectively by choosing destinations based on economic judgments rather than hit-or-miss information from friends and relatives living elsewhere (Morrison 1973:19).

On the whole, this program should be consistent with national policy on population redistribution. Moreover, it should be developed in regional centers and their hinterlands so that assistance can be given to people *before* they move. Special attention and programs for women, especially the young and single, should be established with particular emphasis on occupational guidance and, if necessary, skill training for both female migrants and prospective migrants. The program's feasibility, however, would depend on further study including detailed analysis of the causes and consequences of female migration and the problems of adjustment.

NOTES

1. According to the registration procedure since 1947, a mover deregisters and then reregisters himself and those moving with him by filling out a form in duplicate and presenting it to the registration officer for certification. If the move is within a district, certification of the registration form completes the process; if the move is from one district to another, the registrant takes a copy of the form to the registration officer of the district to which he is moving; the process is complete when this form is certified (Sternstein 1976:9).

2. In the survey of migration in Bangkok metropolis conducted by the National Statistical Office in 1974 it was found that 60 percent of female migrants were employed as service workers while about 22 percent were production workers or laborers. In our survey, the proportion of production workers was higher than the service workers because of the choice of sample districts.

REFERENCES

Bogue, Donald J.
   1969   *Principles of Demography.* New York: Wiley.

Chamratrithirong, Aphichat
   1976   Fertility, nuptiality and migration in Thailand, 1970 census: the multiphasic response theory. Unpublished doctoral dissertation, Brown University.

Goldstein, Sidney
   1972a   *The Demography of Bangkok: A Case Study of Differentials Between Big City and Rural Population.* Research Report No. 7. Bangkok: Institute of Population Studies, Chulalongkorn University.
   1972b   *The Fertility of Thai Women.* Research Report No. 10. Bangkok: Institute of Population Studies, Chulalongkorn University.

Lee, Everett S.
   1966   A theory of migration. *Demography* 3(1):47–57.

Meinkoth, Marian R.
   1962   Migration in Thailand with particular reference to the northeast. *Economic and Business Bulletin* 14(4):3–45.

Morrison, Peter A.
1972   *The Impact and Significance of Rural-Urban Migration in the United States*. Santa
        Monica: Rand Corporation.
1973   *How Population Movements Shape National Growth*. Santa Monica: Rand Cor-
        poration.
1974   *Urban Growth and Decline in the United States: A Study of Migration's Effects in
        Two Cities*. Santa Monica: Rand Corporation.

Mowat, Susanne
1977   *Education and the Urban Migrant: A Comparative Analysis of Case Studies in
        Bangkok, Manila and Jakarta*. Bangkok: UNESCO Regional Office for Edu-
        cation in Asia.

Piampiti, Suwanlee
1976   Effects of migration on urban development in the southern region of Thai-
        land. Paper presented at the Seminar on Labor Supply, 21–25 June 1976.
        Manila.

Prachuabmoh, Visid, et al.
1972   *The Rural and Urban Population of Thailand: Comparative Profiles*. Research
        Report No. 8. Bangkok: Institute of Population Studies, Chulalongkorn
        University.

Sternstein, Larry
1976   *Migration to and from Khon Kaen Development Centre of Northeast Thailand Accord-
        ing to Population Registration Data for 1962 and 1972*. Occasional Paper No.
        59. Singapore: Institute of Southeast Asian Studies.

Textor, R. B.
1956   *From Peasant to Pedicab Driver*. Cultural Report Series, No. 9. New Haven:
        Yale University, Southeast Asia Studies.

Thailand, National Statistical Office (NSO)
1960   *Population Census and Housing*. Bangkok.
1970   *Population Census and Housing*. Bangkok.
1974   *The Survey of Migration in Bangkok Metropolis*. Bangkok.
1976a   *The 1970 Population and Housing Census: Economic Characteristics*. Subject Re-
        port No. 1. Bangkok.
1976b   *Statistical Reports of Changwat Ayudhaya*. Bangkok.

Chapter 13

The Migration of Rural Women to Taipei

Nora Chiang Huang

This chapter draws on data from a larger undertaking that includes an extensive survey of two village communities where out-migration has been notable in recent years. Female migrants to the Taipei metropolis from the two communities were studied in depth. The study examines the process of migration at the community, family, and individual levels and considers its causes and consequences for rural women in Taiwan.

Among Third World countries Taiwan is highly industrialized and urbanized. Traditional industry was transformed by first import and then by export substitution in the late 1950s and early 1960s. As a result, by 1976 the proportion of the labor force engaged in agriculture had decreased to 35 percent, while the proportion engaged in industry had increased to 21 percent (Galenson 1979). Over the same period the share of agricultural net domestic product declined from 36 to 13 percent, whereas that of industry increased from 13 to 30 percent (CEPD 1979a).

As the economy was undergoing these changes, the proportion of women in the labor force who were engaged in agriculture dropped sharply (64–39 percent between 1956 and 1976) and the proportion in manufacturing more than doubled (11–29 percent). By 1978 manufacturing accounted for 37 percent of the total national product and employed 779,000 women or 40.6 percent of the female labor force (DGBAS 1979).

The availability of female workers contributed to the development of light industries, led by textiles, electronics, and plastics. Involvement of the island economy in the international market has created a continuous demand for unskilled and relatively cheap labor.[1] Taiwan is considered by multinational corporations to be one of the major offshore manufacturing sites in Asia because of the quality of its female labor force and certain locational advantages.

The presence of manufacturing industries and services in the cities of Taiwan has resulted in a concentration of population in the urban areas of the western coastal plain. In the past, when the location of industries was unplanned, plants were located in or near the cities, which supplied them with facilities and services. As a result, the three nuclei of Taiwan's indus-trialization—Taipei, Taichung, and Kaohsiung—developed into metro-politan areas. The recent growth of those cities is due to the large number of migrants who moved to them from the countryside. Three-fifths of the population that is added to the Taipei metropolitan area each year, for instance, is of rural origin.

The proportion of women leaving villages for the cities has also in-creased in recent years. Comparison of male and female out-migration from rural households in western Taiwan in 1963, 1968, and 1975 reveals that the rate of female migration increased much faster than that of male migration. In 1975 one-third of out-migrants were females in a sample of 1,500 households in western Taiwan (Liao 1976), and among those who left their farms to work during 1973–75, 40 percent were women (CAFC 1977). Unfortunately, the number of those women who migrated to cities to work was not recorded. Research on factory workers in urban areas during the late 1970s (Huang 1977; Kung 1978; Diamond 1979) indicates that more than half the women workers were of rural origin. Rural women now constitute a substantial portion of the labor force in Taiwanese cities. Besides factory work, the opportunities offered by cities include commer-cial activities and services of various kinds, some of which require skills not taught in primary school, particularly those acquired in vocational training.

Rural women's participation in the labor force has grown not only because of the demand for their labor but also because of their rising edu-cation and aspirations. Given the opportunity for nine years of free educa-tion, women with a primary (six-year) school education are numerous in the rural villages. Some rural women have moved to cities for a better edu-cation or for vocational education. Compared with women of similar edu-cational status in urban areas, rural women are more likely to use their educational qualifications in the workplace.[2]

According to the 1973 agricultural census, among the 264,000 persons who left their farms between 1973 and 1975, some 46 percent moved to the Taipei metropolitan area for nonagricultural employment. Unlike big cities in most Third World countries, Taipei does not appear to have an unemployment problem.[3] Rather, its problem is one of underemploy-ment.[4] This issue will be discussed in the context of female migration to the major city of Taipei.

OBJECTIVES

In spite of the great interest shown in rural-to-urban migration, there has not been a study devoted to female migration in Taiwan. My interest in female migrants is based on the belief that men and women are subject to different migration situations (Chiang 1978). The approach used in previous migration studies was village-based (Huang 1971b; Liao 1970; Wu 1970; Kiang 1975), emphasizing economic motives for moving and neglecting the possibility that mobility might be stimulated by noneconomic motives. My research seeks not only to understand female migration but also to employ different approaches to illuminate the process of migration in general. The proposition that some mobility is generated by noneconomic motives will be tested.

My research covers both the sending communities and the major city to which migrants have moved. Both origins and destinations have been studied as "subsystems" driven by socioeconomic and geographic forces.[5] The female migrant who moves from one system to the other is the focus of this study. By studying both origin and destination and migrants from the rural community one can gain substantial information about the migration process.

The research is undertaken at the mesolevel and microlevel in order to understand the institutional roles, expectations, behavior patterns, beliefs, and values of a society. At the same time I wish to examine the decision-making processes of individual migrants and families. This approach requires one to look beyond economic motives for migration to discover attitudes regarding origins and destinations.

Several studies of factory women have been completed to date in the Taipei metropolitan area, and these have included a good proportion of rural women. By including women in a wider range of professions in the city and viewing them in terms of the city environment and the village communities from which they come, more insight is gained into the roles and problems of the female migrant. The findings of this research should provide a sound basis for raising issues relevant to women in the cities of the Third World. (For a good review of female migration in the Third World, see Youssef et al. 1979).

THE RESEARCH PROBLEM

The major questions guiding the research are:

1. What are the motivations for migration and to what extent are these goals achieved?
2. What are the push and pull factors in the rural and urban systems and how are these factors perceived by migrants?
3. In what ways does the rural background or the urban system pose problems of adaptation for migrants?
4. How do migrants support themselves as they seek jobs and housing? How do migrants adapt to their working and living environments?

5. How is social mobility achieved?

6. To what extent are connections maintained between female migrants and their home villages? Do migrant women contribute to the rural economy?

7. What determines whether a migrant continues to circulate or stays permanently in the city?

The two major stages in the migrant's experience—the decision-making process and adaptation to the city—form the focus of this study. My overriding hypothesis is that migration behavior and patterns are best understood in relation to the continuing ties between people at the origins and destinations.[6] The village woman who wishes to move on her own is still subject to parental approval based on trustworthy contacts in the city. Information on jobs and housing, for instance, is obtained from friends and relatives who are already in the city.

Hence my assumption is that the spatial and behavioral pattern of migration results from interactions between origins and destinations in the two stages of the migrant's experience. The decisions on where and how to move, as well as adaptation, are explained by the links of the family or potential migrants to friends or relatives in the city. These links may take the form of information flows, return visits, or remittances or exchange of goods.[7] Continuing ties between former migrants and the village alleviate anxiety for potential movers. Moreover, previous migrants create a channel for migration that amplifies the attractions of the city.[8]

Upon arrival in the city, the migrant depends on the informal network of friends and relatives for housing, introduction to jobs, and solace in her bewilderment. Two other strategies of adaptation are proposed here. First, the social and economic conditions of Taiwan create an urban system that is receptive to migrants. Certainly the urbanization prompted by industrial growth enables migrants to obtain jobs easily. Second, circulation between the city and the rural village eases the tensions of adjustment in the city environment.

THE RESEARCH DESIGN

Two rural communities consisting of 15 villages in two townships were selected for study on the basis of their high out-migration rates, underdevelopment compared to the rest of the island, a dearth of industrial development, and a high percentage of households engaged either in part-time or full-time work in agriculture.[9] The two rural communities in northern Taiwan send many migrants to Taipei in the north rather than to Taichung in central Taiwan or to Kaohsiung in the south. These two communities were selected from the 300 townships of 361 that experienced population declines in 1978 because of out-migration. There are differences between the two communities in terms of their physical environment, settlement pattern, economy, and spoken dialects. In the present research these differences are not related to out-migration patterns, but they do illustrate the range of villages from which out-migration is occurring.

Procedures for sampling households were based on the need for large numbers of representative rural households and the need to ensure a sufficient number of female migrants to Taipei. Different sampling methods were used in the communities according to their settlement patterns. The first community consists of three contiguous villages in a slopeland environment. (For a study of the demographic structure see Chiang 1979.) The villages consisted of 3,060 persons in 452 households in 1978. An attempt was made to interview every household because dispersed households tend to be heterogeneous. The second community is a rural township consisting of 12 villages with a total population of 22,747 persons in 4,044 households in 1978. Since nucleated villages tend to be homogeneous, a systematic cross-section of households was selected rather than a concentration of a few villages. In practice it was easier to handle the larger land area than in the first community because the houses are congregated on a plain. Approximately one out of seven households were selected from the household register. In all, 302 and 529 households, respectively, were interviewed via a structured questionnaire. Some 807 usable questionnaires were obtained from interviews carried out in December 1978 and February 1979 in the two communities.

A total of 338 female migrants to Taipei were identified in these interviews, including those who were married before moving to Taipei and those who married afterward. Addresses in Taipei were obtained for only half of these female migrants. In the second stage of fieldwork 98 female migrants were interviewed in dispersed locations throughout the Taipei metropolitan area (the city of Taipei and the county of Taipei). Since the number interviewed was far smaller than the number initially identified, raising the question of representation, significance tests of the differentials between the household characteristics of respondents and the others were carried out. No significant differences between the two groups were found.

A group of migrant women with different educational backgrounds and working experiences, at different stages of their life cycles and with different urban experiences, constitutes the sample. Included are single and married women between the ages of 15 and 40. A large majority (87.5 percent) of the married women were single when they first moved to the city. Only 10 percent were illiterate or had not completed elementary school. About one-third had completed elementary school, 30 percent had completed junior high school, 20 percent had completed senior high school, and 6 percent were currently in college.

Their present work in the city was diverse. A third of the respondents were working in factories. A few were in unskilled manual work such as construction, cleaning, and domestic service. A few worked in various urban services as waitresses, hairdressers, dressmakers, salesclerks, and bus conductors. A few were managing their own shops (such as a grocery store, a small garment factory, and a dressmaking shop), which were often operated with their husbands or relatives. One in 20 women were engaged in office work as clerks, typists, and accountants.

Working experience is related not only to education but also to stage in the life cycle. All the single women were either working, studying, or both. Among the 53 married women, only two had never worked; 28 worked only before marriage, 21 worked before and after marriage, and two started work only after marriage. One divorced woman worked before and after her divorce.

Although no attempt has been made to compare migrants with nonmigrants in the city, migrants in general are among the less well-to-do in Taipei. Forty percent of the migrants live in the suburbs of Taipei where the cost of living is lower.[10] Central city dwellings occupied by migrants are often dilapidated. Only 26 percent of the migrants owned their apartments; the remainder rented rooms or apartments (31.3 percent) or lived in housing provided by their employer (27 percent). Women who stay with friends and relatives (15.6 percent) are better accommodated. The women working in factories or shops usually live in the dormitories provided, taking bed space with six to eight other women in the same room. Salaries paid in various urban jobs are below the median income in the city, with 90 percent of the families of the married women earning less than NT$18,000 a month, the average income of the lower middle class in Taipei.

Three types of respondent are typical in the sample. The most common type is the single migrant who moved to the city to work after graduation from the village primary school. While working she may pick up skills or devote her evenings to formal schooling or to learning skills. The more fortunate women may come to the city for high school education and upon graduation remain to work. The second type is the married woman who continues to work after marriage because she needs to supplement her family income, because she is operating her own shop on the family grounds, or because she has a good education and a good job. The third type is the woman who quits her job after marriage if the husband's income is sufficient to support the family or she has young children.

MIGRATION DECISIONS

REASONS FOR LEAVING THE VILLAGE

Like all of the migration research on Taiwan, my village interviews show that the motivation for migration is usually economic. However, my interviews of women migrants indicate that the women have responded to different push factors in the villages, and to wider opportunities in the city.

The question "Why did you leave the village?" yielded a variety of answers. With the exception of a few women who said they had never considered the reasons for their move and a few who said they were not the decision-makers in their family's move to Taipei, most women gave *several* reasons for moving, reflecting push and pull forces operating in different degrees. Half the respondents gave reasons that are related to "the need to earn money." The decision whether to go to the city or not generally comes when a woman completes primary school or junior high school. (Education up to junior high school is provided by the government.) A woman's chance for further education is determined by her family elders and their economic situation. The only way to continue free education is to be admitted to a five-year teacher's training college after passing a college entrance examination. Eldest daughters are often obliged to sacrifice their chances for better education so that younger ones, especially males, can continue in school. There are, of course, women who do not want to continue after primary school, since the pressure for further education is not so strong for women as for men.

The second major reason for moving to Taipei is for education or to learn skills. Some villagers continue their schooling by attending senior high school in a town within commuting distance and then go on to college in the city. Because of the lower education standards in the villages, however, one often hears that students cannot pass the senior high school entrance exams and instead often attend vocational schools in the nearest town or in Taipei where there are more options. Women whose parents cannot support them through high school see this as an opportunity to continue their education by working, since opportunities for work are limited in the villages. The women who stay behind have to carry on domestic or farm work or find local jobs. The closest urban center contains shops of various kinds and government offices that employ people from nearby villages. In some villages women can commute to work in the nearest industrial towns. The migrant women, however, preferred to live and work in faraway Taipei. A small proportion (3 percent) of the women who went to Taipei said their major reason for leaving the village was "to experience city life"; 8 percent wanted to "leave the bitter life of the village" or "leave the control of the family." According to young village women, life was "bitter" because they had to join in the intensive farmwork.

Although women who move on their own are known as "autonomous" movers, the decision is rarely independent of parental supervision. Parental approval is often given on the condition that a woman must move with a friend or relative or have previous contacts in the city.[11] Often another family member who has already been to Taipei persuades the parents to agree to their daughter's request to leave for the city. A few women who gave as their reason "to help out some relatives in their businesses" were given approval easily by their elders. Attitudes toward male and female migration are similar in the village in most regards.[12]

IMAGES OF CITY LIFE

Most of the village women held certain images of city life, though these images often proved inaccurate. These perceptions of city life are based on hearsay, actual experiences, and impressions from the news media and especially from visiting former migrants. A commonly heard remark from village women is that "People in the city must be rich. My neighbors came back with beautiful dresses and makeup." Certainly the former villager driving back his own automobile would stir the envy of his neighbors.

Impressions of the city are also formed through the news media. In the evenings, families watch television soap operas of family life in Taipei. According to my village survey, 29 percent of villagers subscribe to newspapers from which they also learn about city life. Images of the city are also based on the actual experiences of villagers. Some 65 percent of the migrants had been to Taipei before they migrated, having visited relatives or participated in organized graduation trips at the end of their primary school education. A superficial knowledge of Taipei often was gained by visiting relatives who took them to see a glamorous part of town—something quite different from the village. These early visits provided them with the image of a Taipei "crowded with people and vehicles," "busy, prosperous, and colorful," and "convenient for shopping and traveling"—sharp contrasts to village life that are viewed with admiration.

Unfavorable stories of past migrants have also traveled back. Stories of past migrants who "met bad people," "failed in business," or "acquired extravagant styles of living" tend to tarnish the glamour of the city. A minority of the women interviewed had held negative feelings about Taipei before they moved: "City life is busy and full of tension." "It is a place where people are cold and indifferent." "It is a place of crime, disorder, and dark life."

REASONS FOR MOVING TO TAIPEI

Among the cities familiar to villagers, Taipei appears to be the best known —mainly through friends and relatives who have already moved there. A small percentage of migrants had lived in another small town or had commuted to work before coming to Taipei, but the 90 percent who moved to Taipei directly said they had not considered other cities before they moved. It surprised some that the question was even raised, because they had assumed that people in the villages move only to Taipei. As many as 21 percent of migrants replied that they could not think of a reason for going to Taipei, except that their friends were doing the same thing. Some 38 percent said they were following in the footsteps of former migrants whom they would join or rely on after arrival; 5 percent said they chose Taipei because their friends in the village were also going; the remaining 30 percent cited motives of work or study. These proportions suggest that among the reasons for going to Taipei are not only opportunities for work and education but also the pull of friends and relatives who have set up a "movement chain."

Since most of the migrants already had friends or relatives in the city before moving to Taipei, their decision to move and their adjustment are largely related to this extended social network from the village community. Now we will look at the adaptation of female migrants: their accommodations, job mobility, social life, and perceptions of their own experience.

ADAPTATION

Upon arrival in Taipei, the first place to settle is generally with friends or relatives or in one's own apartment. Women who moved with their families settled in their own residences. If the whole family moves together, it is often preceded by the husband who comes to arrange housing. Single women may stay in a dormitory (if they have a job before coming) or with relatives. It is common for a nuclear family to receive a relative from the countryside, who pays a small rent or helps with housework or the family business in exchange for accommodation. If a good relationship is maintained with the host family, the migrant stays on until she finds her own peer group of colleagues or classmates to stay with or takes a job in a distant location.

Work History

Village women are all employed within a short time after arrival in the city, reflecting the values placed on work and independence. Work is easily available in Taipei in various urban services and factories, often requiring only a primary school education. It is easier for a woman to find work than a man because companies place more restrictions on age for men and require the completion of military service.

A stroll through the city and a glance at the newspaper reveal advertisements for many jobs: salesgirls, waitresses, hairdressers, factory workers. As part of their recruitment program, factory personnel managers visit the schools, speak to students about employment at their factories, and invite them to visit factory grounds. There are also job recruitment centers in the city run by the government or private concerns.

None of the women I interviewed had resorted to government or private job placement centers, however. One of the reasons for the low response to government job placement services is the fact that the migrants often cannot fulfill the skill requirements. As a result, the city of Taipei faces a shortage of labor, especially in skilled work. Each year there are many more job vacancies than there are job-seekers. Three-quarters of the women I interviewed obtained work through a personal introduction; the rest did so by directly applying to factories or shops. Families in the village expressed the wish that their daughters "play safe" and depend on friends and relatives rather than other sources of help.

Because of the surfeit of job opportunities, most women found work within the first few weeks of their arrival. A majority of the women (64 percent) found work even before arriving in the city. When asked to give reasons for choosing their first job, most migrants cited "being introduced to the work by relatives" and "being able to work with friends." It is obvious that these migrants accepted whatever work was presented to them. A moderate proportion chose work requiring specific skills, such as hairdressing, dressmaking, accounting, and nursing. Very few had really compared alternatives and based their choices on salary, benefits, the nature of the work, the work environment, or the chance of learning new skills.

Table 13.1 compares the reasons for selecting the first job in the city and the reasons for choosing the present job. It is clear that friend-related reasons declined substantially in time. The numbers making choices on the basis of skills required and the terms of employment, and the numbers of those who now operate their own shops, all increased. The proportion of women not working also increased greatly, since many ceased work after marriage or after having children.

Table 13.1 Reasons for choosing first and present job in Taipei

Reason	First job (%)	Present job (%)
Recommended by friends and relatives	29.2	11.5
No choice	26.0	7.3
Can apply skills	10.4	17.7
Take care of own shop	6.3	13.6
Work with friends	5.2	3.1
Can study at same time	5.2	3.1
Acquiring skills	5.2	1.0
Terms of work	3.1	10.4
Not working	7.3	30.2
Unknown	2.1	2.1
All reasons	100.0	100.0

The most desirable jobs are in government service because these jobs offer stability, prestige, and fringe benefits. Working in an office is preferred to other situations. A job that involves "seeing people" is considered less prestigious. Domestic service jobs, despite the high pay, are the least preferred. When asked to give reasons for job changes, the migrant women in my sample frequently responded that it was easy to find work but hard to find a satisfying job.

Various conditions encourage workers to keep their job or leave it. The factory setting, with its regular hours of work, allows women to attend evening classes. Assembly-line work is dull and uncreative, however, and does not teach useful skills. The need to increase production under pressure often prompts people to leave. All the women who worked said they had to tolerate low salaries, long hours, poor working conditions, disagreeable managers and colleagues, and long commuter distances. Rather than adjust to these situations, they are able to quit and find other work in the city since jobs in Taipei are plentiful. Familiarity with job opportunities also increases with time. The lure of better pay or a better position elsewhere, as well as the opportunity to form a partnership or start one's own business, also accounts for the frequency of job changes. Jobs that provide skills are seen favorably by villagers and counterbalance undesirable qualities of the work. One woman said, "I need to stay in the shop until nine o'clock each day and until midnight at New Year's but I'm acquiring new skills in dressmaking. I can learn more patterns in the city than back in the village."

Personal relationships are highly valued at the place of work, so they are important in decisions to stay or go. One woman may stay on a job because she has good working companions; another may quit because her close friends have done so. Good company at the shop tends to break up boredom over routine work, and friendships provide solace for the homesick newcomer. The reasons given for satisfaction and dissatisfaction with present jobs are summarized in Table 13.2.

Long breaks in a migrant's work history are accounted for by similar reasons. It has become customary for villagers to quit work at New Year's. After they have collected their annual bonus, they return to the village and enjoy their holiday break. The high rates of turnover also reflect a low degree of commitment to work by women in general, since priority is given to family affairs and women are not usually depended upon as sole income earners. Although it is not the policy of companies to dismiss women after they are married, women often quit work after marriage or childbirth. One often hears this remark: "My husband thinks he can earn enough money for the family and there is no urgency for me to work. Now that I have children, I feel I should stay at home and take care of them."[13]

Turnover rather than initial recruitment is the major labor problem fac-

Table 13.2 Satisfaction and dissatisfaction with present job

Reason	Satisfied with work (%)	Dissatisfied with work (%)
Nature of work	17.7	14.6
Colleagues	10.4	2.1
Working hours	9.4	7.3
Operate own shop at home	9.4	0.0
Cannot work at home	0.0	1.0
Relationship with boss	4.2	1.0
Benefits	3.1	0.0
Short distance	3.1	0.0
Pay	1.0	6.3
Other reasons	0.0	12.5
No complaint	0.0	17.7
Not working (housewife or student)	33.3	34.4
Unknown	8.3	4.2
All reasons	100.0	100.0

Note: Columns do not sum to 100.0 percent because of rounding.

ing companies. Companies that hire workers through personal introductions fare slightly better. Foreign-owned companies have introduced salary increment systems to reward those who stay in their jobs, and they give bonuses to those who bring friends into the company.

The transition to a higher position is a difficult one for the rural migrant because exploitation is common in the lower ranks of occupation. The apprentice with a skilled job such as hairdressing or dressmaking can make the transition to regular employment only by changing to a new employer. One woman apprentice who worked in a hairdresser's shop said she had to work like a maid, sweeping the floor and washing hair, and very little of her work involved learning new skills. After acquiring some skills, she quit and became a regular employee at another shop.

There is also the blue-collar worker who planned to make the transition through evening school. Once she finished school, she expected to leap forward to office work even though she knows that her salary will not pay off her education. Rather, the aspiration for higher education justified her move to the metropolis and gave her a sense of achievement. It also gave her an alternative means of social mobility in the long run: marrying someone better than a blue-collar worker. White-collar workers are viewed as better off in terms of social mobility.

SOCIAL LIFE

Aside from friends and relatives already in the city, a woman tends to relate to her peer group at the workplace. It is customary for women to go out in groups after work for visiting, picnicking, shopping, or going to movies. Women tend to spend weekend time with friends they knew before coming to the city. Visiting the village constitutes a major pastime, and newcomers frequently return to relieve homesickness.

Attachment to people of rural origin in the same factory is stronger than to those from urban areas, but only a minority said they had stronger attachments to friends from the same village or township. Although there is no inclination to marry men from the village, it is said that men from villages are more "honest and reliable." Migrants are inclined to form friendships with people from the same dialect group, yet none joined a voluntary association formed by a religious or dialect group. School alumni groups formed in the village do not function in the city.

Apart from movement between village and city, there is little mobility within the city. Migrants report that they are only familiar with the neighborhoods around their place of work, home, or school, and shopping areas. Most migrants are unfamiliar with the greater part of the city, even after a long residence. They are financially limited to participation in various community services and entertainments.

Although 94 percent of the women said they had made new friends since they moved to Taipei, two-thirds of the unmarried women said they did not have boyfriends. (The majority of their colleagues at work are women.) Since students are sex-segregated in the schools during their early years, a young woman is often abashed to talk to men alone. One woman I met in the factory felt cautious about meeting young men in the factory because of what she read in the newspapers about sexual promiscuity there. Although there were parties organized by men on the weekends, she never joined them; in fact, she had never talked to any of the men in her factory. This attitude prevents many women from socializing with the opposite sex.

ADVANTAGES AND DISADVANTAGES OF CITY LIFE

The rural migrant often makes explicit comparisons between city and village. The city provides more comfort and convenience in its transportation, shopping, and public services such as schools and hospitals. The city has a higher standard of living and level of health than the village. Moreover, working in the city gives the migrant a regular income while farmwork does not compensate for the heavy demands of labor. Farmwork is considered harsher than city work. Many women object to exposure to the sun and getting rough hands from farmwork. Even though opportunities for commuting exist, the respondents prefer living in the city because commuting is so time-consuming. Women would still have to live under the auspices of their parents and devote energy to domestic tasks and farmwork.

The trade-offs for this convenience and freedom include overcrowded living conditions and air pollution in the streets. The lack of warm human relationships in the city is constantly brought up by villagers, as are a faster pace of life, pressures from work, and the high cost of living.

On the whole, migrants do not report serious problems of adapting. Dizziness on the buses, unfamiliarity with work or with people and other problems passed within a few months. Everyone felt homesick, though, even women who had lived in Taipei for many years.

REWARDS

Most of the women found their experience in the city rewarding. The most commonly stated reward is "the opportunity to relate to people and situations," a virtue emphasized in Chinese culture. "Being married" was the second most frequently cited reward; "skills and education" came in third; income-related reasons came last. Some also said that their personality had changed for the better—they had become more "flexible," "outgoing," "independent," "mature," "diligent," and "farsighted."

The salaries of the female migrants range from NT$3,000 to slightly more than NT$10,000. One-third to one-fifth of the total salary is earned by overtime work, used by employers as a work incentive. When business is good, women can earn up to NT$10,000 if they can endure the long hours of work. A large part of the income is spent on rent, food, and clothing; much of the rest is taken back home to parents. The villagers were realistic about making a living in the city; they admitted that the high rent and cost of food balance the relatively high pay. As a result, it is often the married men who move to the city to work and send back their earnings to the home village.

Do migrants receive more respect from other villagers? One woman voiced the feelings of many others: "Nowadays every family has someone living in the city. It's no big deal. Whether migrants receive any special respect depends on whether the individual is successful or not."

COMMITMENT TO THE VILLAGE

VISITS

Return visits by migrants make village life livelier. On public holidays one can see buses going south from Taipei packed with people from the villages, and visits are more frequent to villages close to Taipei. Migrants return for festivals, weddings, funerals, and to visit kin. They take long absences from work, for as long as two months, to relax from work, manage family affairs, take care of ailing family members, recover from illness, and help out with harvesting or postnatal care. Return visits account for the continued commitment of female migrants to the village, on the one hand, and reflect the ease of traveling between Taipei and the villages on the other. Visits help to cure homesickness, yet many migrants complained of boredom after a few days at home and said they were eager to return to the city.

Apart from contributing to the urban labor force, a majority of the migrant women have remitted part of their earnings home. As much as NT$6,000 was remitted, and most women sent between NT$1,000 and NT$3,000 every month. Bringing home money is an expression of filial piety, and even married women bring money home on their visits.

In most cases, cash is remitted regularly: monthly or bimonthly. Although few women thought their families would have suffered without them, their contributions to the village households are substantial. Besides supplementing living expenses at home, the second most common practice is to provide school tuition for younger family members. Other major uses are building or remodeling village homes and putting money into *huis* (savings associations). The main uses of the money are summarized in Table 13.3.

The migrants almost always send more to their villages than they receive in return. In a few cases, parents have loaned their children money to purchase an apartment in Taipei. Other types of help include looking after children and caring for married daughters who have returned for postnatal care. The mutual care system traverses both distance and administrative boundaries.

Table 13.3 Major uses of money taken or sent home by migrants

Use	No.	%
Supplement living expenses	20	20.8
School fees for brothers and sisters	17	17.7
Building house or remodeling	8	8.3
Savings	2	2.1
Indefinite	2	2.1
Use unknown	10	10.4
Does not send money home	37	38.5
All uses	96	100.0

Note: Percentages do not sum to 100.0 because of rounding.

Exchanges of goods take place mainly in the rural-to-urban direction. Gifts in the form of village products are brought by parents visiting their children in the city or are carried back to the city by children at the end of their village visits. Women on return visits to the village are more likely than men to bring back presents—often food—to the elderly. Durable goods are seldom brought back because they are readily available in rural areas. Most rural households are well-equipped with modern appliances.[14]

Migrants reported that their parents are quite familiar with their activities in the city—including knowledge of their work, their income, and their friends (but not their difficulties). As one women remarked: "My family does not know my frustrations about my work; I don't want to have them worry about me. When I have problems, I talk to friends or relatives in the city." The village always provides a backstop for the migrant, though. In 1973, during the economic slump, many migrants who were laid off returned to the village.

COMMITMENT TO URBAN LIVING

The degree of commitment to the village differs between males and females since women, unlike men, do not inherit land, do not hold religious positions, and move out of their villages permanently when they are married. Commitment exists in other ways, however. Women visit their villages more frequently than do men. Although a majority of migrants interviewed in Taipei regarded the village as their "first home",[15] most married women said they would reside in Taipei permanently. Single women were not sure. The common remark was, "I always consider the village my first home because I was born there. I am not sure if I will stay in Taipei forever, because I do not know whom I will marry and whether he will be staying permanently in Taipei."

The present movement pattern of single females between de facto urban and de jure rural residences reflects their dual commitment to the place of work and the home village. It forms a pattern of circular mobility based on the city.[16] For the rural female, circulation is the transition to becoming a permanent migrant in the city.

CONCLUSION

This study, based on individual female migrants who were followed up at their destination, shows that the motivations for migration include not just the need to earn money but also the desire for psychological and social satisfaction. The village, so removed from the hub of the nearby town, does not offer opportunities for young villagers who are better educated than their parents. Rather than material well-being for themselves and the village back home, many women felt that the wider experience of the city and marriage were their major achievements.

Friends and relatives already in the city have an important influence on the migrant's decision to move. They motivate the migrant to follow in their footsteps and provide reassurance for parents who permit their daughters to leave home. Moreover, by introducing prospective migrants to jobs, arranging accommodations, and offering comfort, friends and relatives take the place of institutions. Movement to Taipei is channeled by former migrants who reinforce the pull of the major city for potential migrants.

Before their arrival in the city most migrants are unskilled and ready to take whatever is offered them. Since their initial jobs frequently prove to be below their expectations, they continue through a series of job changes as their knowledge of job opportunities improves and they become less dependent on personal introductions.

Attachment to informal groups of colleagues and friends in the city eases the stresses associated with unfamiliar people and places. Returning to villages for visits and during breaks between job changes relieves homesickness and assures continued moral support from parents.

Even though job mobility is fluid, social mobility is limited. Few women make a long-term commitment to work. In fact, the transition from blue-collar work to marriage is often rapid. Those who merge a career with marriage are motivated by the wish to retain a prestigious white-collar job.

Although migrant women are not the principal providers, their remittances are important supplements to village households where farming is unprofitable. In spite of their long absences from the village, the women show their commitment by attending feasts, communicating by mail and telephone, and returning to care for ailing relatives or help with harvests. The migrant's base is clearly the city, though, and her returns to the village take on a circular pattern. Permanent residence in the city is established when a woman is married there.

The out-migration of rural females can be viewed as transferring unemployment and a surplus labor force from the village to the city. The willingness of rural women to be economically independent of their families, and their readiness to join the work force, indicates that they can make an important contribution to the city. They leave the village in search of better opportunities in the city, including paid indoor work and the chance to acquire education and new skills. The search for work that offers better pay and status while fitting their interests and skills continues and results in rapid job turnover. This turnover is not only undesirable from the viewpoint of private business; it also wastes human resources. To resolve this problem, the government must learn migrants' motivations, their methods of acquiring jobs, and their satisfactions and dissatisfactions with work, particularly their reasons for quitting, so that efficient recruitment systems can be devised. Job recruitment can be extended back to the villages in the form of vocational training in schools through 4-H clubs and farm associations. Improved recruitment would reduce both the social and private costs of labor turnover in the long run.

The salaries paid to migrant workers are not commensurate with the index of living costs in Taiwan. Women have extraordinarily long hours of work and some must tolerate variable work shifts as well. Unhealthy work environments and substandard accommodations are indirect ways of exploiting employees. In the face of labor shortages and rapid turnover, however, companies are beginning to improve salaries and benefits for employees.

The fact that women are receiving more education than before results in rising expectations and a desire for upward mobility. The Third World perception of women workers as unskilled, patient and tolerant, and easily available is now passé in Taiwan. Employment policies have to be modified to provide promotion opportunities to these aspiring migrants.

Although no insurmountable difficulties have been faced by rural females, their experiences in the city have in many ways failed to match their expectations. Their image of the city—rich, glamorous, and convenient—is created by the mass media, particularly television, and friends and relatives. This city of dreams turns out to be less than perfect in their actual experience, of course. Accurate information should be disseminated through the school system or television regarding both the advantages and disadvantages of urban life.

The methodology of this research—following up on rural women by obtaining their addresses at the village home—has been effective in compensating for the usual underreporting of out-migration. It should be noted, however, that this procedure often fails to identify women's special occupation groups. Village households may be reluctant to report addresses of daughters if they think they are not doing very well in Taipei.[17] Research on women migrants focusing on a wider variety of occupations would be of value. The spatial and behavioral patterns of rural men who have arrived at the Taipei metropolitan area should also be studied to provide a comparison with that of female migrants.

NOTES

1. Half (51.7 percent) of Taiwan's total production was manufactured for export in 1976.

2. According to Diamond (1973), middle-class women who are educated do not work—a symbol of their middle-class status.

3. In 1978 the number of job-seekers was 18,479 compared to 77,019 vacancies (BBAS 1979).

4. Liu has pointed out the problem of inadequate employment or labor underutilization. For males, inadequate utilization occurred with respect to income level, occupa-

tion, and education; for females, a mismatch of employment with income level predominated (Liu 1979).

5. The terms "urban control subsystem" and "rural control subsystem" have been used by Mabogunje (1970).

6. One reason why there is only a moderate amount of family movement is that villagers are obligated to keep land that has been inherited from their ancestors. Even when part of the family leaves, they maintain ties with the family of origin and expect to return in old age or to be buried.

7. "Rural-urban links" and "enduring ties" have been discussed in a number of Third World countries—for instance, in Nair (1978), Rempel and Lobdell (1978), and Adepoju (1974). However, it is a subject treated as a postmigration trait rather than a crucial factor influencing decisions to move.

8. As previous researchers have observed, "Friends and relatives in a metropolitan area of destination often provide information concerning perceived and/or potential job opportunities, and this helps determine why migrants choose one destination rather than another" (De Jong and Donelly 1973).

9. Over 50 percent of both communities have engaged in agriculture as their main occupation, according to CAFC (1977) and over 50 percent of the migrants moved to Taipei and Taipei County.

10. The suburbs of Taipei are growing faster than the city center because migrants from other townships usually take up residence in the suburbs. Besides, out-migration of urban residents from the center to the suburbs occurs as the residential areas in the center are turned over to commercial uses. See CEPD (1979b).

11. More than half the migrants had relatives in the city before moving; 75 percent were accompanied by friends and relatives when they moved to Taipei (not including those who came with their husbands).

12. Some parents expressed the wish that their children would stay to help on the farm; others thought the children should migrate to the city for wider experience besides earning money, to get a better education, and to learn skills. The expectation of women bringing an income is short-lived and overridden by the hope that she will marry into a good family.

13. It is commonly thought in Taiwan that a man "loses face" if he lets his wife work, because it shows that he is not capable of supporting the family. There was one case in my samples in which a husband resigned for the wife without her knowledge.

14. The percentage of households possessing appliances are: electric fan, 92 percent; rice cooker, 89 percent; radio, 54 percent; refrigerator, 66 percent; black and white TV, 63 percent; color TV, 25 percent.

15. None of the single women in my sample changed their address in the household registration record even though they had moved to Taipei a number of years before.

16. Circular rather than permanent mobility refers to "a great variety of movement, usually short-term, repetitive, or cyclic in nature, but all having in common the lack of any declared intention of a permanent or long-lasting change in residence" (Zelinsky 1971). Recent studies of circulation in the Third World are documented in Chapman (1982).

17. None of the families I interviewed reported female out-migrants in urban sex-related services, although interviewees in the city suggested that they have neighbors or classmates in such occupations, sometimes without the knowledge of their parents.

BIBLIOGRAPHY

Adepoju, A.
  1974   Rural-urban socio-economic links: the example of migrants in south-western Nigeria. In S. Amin (ed.), *Modern Migrations in West Africa*. London: Oxford University Press.

Bureau of Budget, Accounting, and Statistics, Taipei City Government (BBAS)
  1979   *The Statistical Abstract of Taipei City.*

Caldwell, J. C.
  1970   *African Rural-Urban Migration*. New York: Columbia University Press.

Chapman, Murray
  1982   Circulation. In John A. Ross (ed.), *International Encyclopaedia of Population*. New York: Free Press.

Chiang, Lan-Hung Nora
  1978   Male and female migration in Taiwan: an examination of characteristics and propensities to migrate. *Population Studies Journal* 2:60–81.
  1979   Population in a marginal environment—the case of Tsaochiao agricultural and pastoral community. *Science Report* 10 (December):29–41.

Committee on Agricultural and Fishing Census (CAFC)
  1977   *The Report of 1975 Agricultural Census of Taiwan-Fukien District of the Republic of China*. Vol. 11, bk. 1. Taipei.

Connell, John, et al.
  1976   *Migration from Rural Areas: The Evidence from Village Studies*. Delhi: Oxford University Press.

Council for Economic Planning and Development (CEPD)
  1979a   *The Comprehensive Development Planning of Taiwan*. Taipei. (In Chinese.)
  1979b   *A Research on the Development of the Taipei Metropolitan Area*. Taipei. (In Chinese.)

De Jong, Gordon F., and William L. Donelly
  1973   Public welfare and migration. *Social Science Quarterly* 54(2):329–44.

Diamond, Norma
  1973   The status of women in Taiwan: one step forward, two steps back. In Marilyn B. Young (ed.), *Women in China*. Michigan Papers in Chinese Studies, No. 15.
  1979   Women and industry in Taiwan. *Modern China* 5(3).

Directorate-General of Budget, Accounting, and Statistics (DGBAS)
  1979   *Monthly Bulletin of Labor Statistics, Republic of China*. December.

Galenson, Walter (ed.)
  1979   *Economic Growth and Structural Change in Taiwan: The Postwar Experience of Republic of China*. Ithaca: Cornell University Press.

Germani, Gino
  1965   Migration and acculturation. In P. Hauser (ed.), *Handbook for Social Research in Urban Areas*. Paris: UNESCO.

Hua, Yen
  1975   Female labor force of Taiwan. Paper presented at the Conference on Population and Economic Development in Taiwan, December 1975 to January 1976, Taipei.

Huang, F. S.
  1977   *Women Workers and the Industrialization in Post-War Taiwan.* Taipei: Cowboy Publishing Co.

Huang, T. C.
  1971a   Rural-urban migration in Taiwan. Unpublished doctoral dissertation, Cornell University.
  1971b   *A Study of Migration Intention Differential Among the Rural Youth in Taiwan.* Research Report, School of Agriculture, National Taiwan University.

Jelin, Elizabeth
  1977   Migration and labor force participation of Latin American women: the domestic servants in the cities. In *Women and National Development: The Complexities of Change.* Chicago: University of Chicago Press.

Johnson, G. E., and W. E. Whitelaw
  1974   Urban-rural income transfers in Kenya: an estimated-remittances function. In *Economic Development and Cultural Change* 22(3).

Kiang, Yu-lung
  1975   Determinants of migration from rural areas in developing countries—a contribution to the formulation of migration models, taking as example the rural region of Taipei and Taichung, Taiwan. Tung Hai Report 16:187–207.

Kung, Lydia
  1978   Factory women and the family in Taiwan. Unpublished doctoral dissertation, Yale University.

Liao, C. H.
  1976   *A Study of Rural Labor Force Migration in Taiwan.* Taipei: Department of Agricultural Extension, National Taiwan University.

Liu, C. Y.
  1976   *The Characteristics of Motivation of Return Migration of Labor Force in Taiwan.* Research Report No. 6501. Taipei: Department of Agricultural Extension, National Taiwan University.

Liu, Paul K. C.
  1979   Economic aspects of rapid urbanization in Taipei. *Academia Economic Papers* 7(1).

Mabogunje, A. L.
  1970   Systems approach to a theory of rural-urban migration. *Geographical Analysis* 11(1):1–18.

Mantra, Ida Bagoes
  1978   Population movement in wet rice communities: a case study of two dukuhs in Yogyakarta special region. Unpublished doctoral dissertation, Department of Geography, University of Hawaii.

Melville, Margarita B.
  1978   Mexican women adapt to migration. *International Migration Review* 12(2): 225–35.

Nair, S.
  1978   A study of population mobility from the rural areas of Fiji to the urban area of Suva. Unpublished M.A. thesis, Department of Geography, University of Hawaii.

Piampiti, Suwanlee
  n.d.   *Female Migrants in Bangkok Metropolis.* (Mimeographed.) Bangkok: School of Applied Statistics, National Institute of Development Administration.
  1979   Female migrants of selected service occupational groups in Bangkok metropolis. Unpublished manuscript.

Pryor, Robert J. (ed.)
  1975   *The Motivation of Migration.* Studies in Migration and Urbanization, No. 1. City Department of Demography, Australian National University.

Rempel, H., and R. A. Lobdell
  1978   The role of urban-to-rural remittances in rural development. *Journal of Development Studies* 14:324–41.

Ross, Marc H., and Thomas S. Weisner
  1977   The rural-urban migrant network in Kenya: some general implications. *American Ethnologist* 4:359–75.

Speare, A. et al.
  1975   A measurement of the accuracy of data in the Taiwan household register. *Academia Economic Papers* 3(2):35–74.

Sudarska, Niara
  1977   Women and migration in contemporary West Africa. *Signs* 3(1):178–89.

Whitford, Michael B.
  1978   Women, migration and social change: a Colombian case study. *International Migration Review* 12(2):236–57.

Wu, T. S.
  1970   A research on the out-migration and employment of rural youth in Taiwan. *Journal of Technology* 29:263–320.

Youssef, Nadia, et al.
  1979   *Women in Migration: A Third World Focus.* (Mimeographed.) Washington, D.C.: International Center for Research on Women.

Zelinsky, W.
  1971   The hypothesis of the mobility transition. *Geographical Review* 61(2):219–49.

Chapter 14

New Models and Traditional Networks: Migrant Women in Tehran

Janet Bauer

There is a tendency in studies of modernization and urbanization to presume a unilineal direction for the changes under investigation. It has been assumed, for example, that residence and increased participation in urban centers lead to the acquisition of modern attitudes and modern behavior. But urbanization and industrialization can have very different consequences for the two sexes—especially in societies where sex differences are an integral part of social organization.

Both Boserup (1970) and Boulding (1972) suggest that urban residence, for example, does not necessarily result in increased participation by women in modern urban life, since industrial urbanization undermines the traditional productive roles of women. Boulding assumes, however, that women's failure to participate in the urban infrastructure is due to "the extent to which the poverty trap catches the poor rural in-migrant and impedes the working of the urban-based communications network model of development" (1972:12). This model implies that increased access to information results in increased participation within the "industrializing infrastructure." Therefore, failure to participate is the result of residence in "isolated ghettos with distinct subcultures" where access to information networks is limited (1972:13). In suggesting solutions to low involvement, Boulding stresses improvement in the means of transmission and the quality of the message (1972:32–33).

It is the thesis of this essay that because access to sources and models of information are, in fact, unequally distributed on the basis of socioeconomic status and sex, access to information and the existence of infrastructure opportunities alone do not necessarily lead to increased participation in the modern sector or to a change in other behavior. I suggest, particularly in the case of Iran, that although women's access to information and models has increased, there are other obstacles preventing women from assuming the roles and behavior associated with urban living.

To understand what these obstacles are, how they limit women's participation, and how they can be eliminated, one must understand the idealized Islamic perceptions about men, women, and the family. Based on assumptions about the disruptive influence of women on the social order, a set of codes has been laid down for the regulation of women's behavior and the interaction between men and women, kin and nonkin. The responsibility for maintaining these codes is vested in the family, particularly the males. Appropriate female behavior and female virginity become symbolic, then, of the family's (that is, the males') fulfillment of this duty.

Over the last 15 to 20 years, families of migrants have streamed into Tehran, the capital of oil-rich Iran, in the hope of sharing in the developing market economy. The processes of industrialization and urban growth in which they become involved induce certain changes in the definition and use of space that directly threaten the traditional relationships between men and women. In Tehran, migrant males must deal with these challenges to the accepted sociocultural order (and to their control over women).

Because of the migrant males' interest in maintaining the accepted order, and despite the increase in models, information, and alternatives provided in Tehran, little change in women's participation, roles, or behavior can be expected to result from migration to the city. Controlled by its threatened males and aided by neighborhood networks, the family continues to define the context in which urban women must behave by controlling their perceptions of acceptable behavior. Consequently, there are disparities in the behavior and expectations of both men and women. While men's participation in the modern sector increases, their interest in maintaining the traditional codes for male/female separation is strengthened; while female participation and behavior are constrained to traditional responses, women's expectations become less traditional.

Boulding's model for ascertaining women's participation in the modern sector posits two contributing variables: traditional religious institutionalization of female roles and the industrializing infrastructures. This model is supported by statistical data on educational attainment, employment, and legal incentives. Such data do not explain why the emergence of women in the modern sector does not take place, however. Thus, I suggest, first, that more descriptive data are needed and, second, that additional variables must be evaluated. I begin by contrasting Boulding's two main variables —the traditional religious and cultural expectations found in the migrant places of origin and the challenges presented by the industrializing infrastructure encountered in Tehran. I then proceed to describe two intervening variables that are important in societies where sexual divisions are institutionalized: the role of men and the role of traditional social networks.

My data are based on one and one-half years of participant observation and interviews conducted among urban migrant and rural communities in

Iran. Four samples of rural and urban women were surveyed on a number of different variables using directed interviews. The urban samples are drawn from Tehran; the rural samples are taken from four different regions of Iran to represent statistically the sending communities of the migrant families who constituted the base sample for the entire project. Fieldwork was conducted prior to the culmination of the recent revolution in Iran. The implications of this revolutionary movement are discussed at the end of the chapter.

THE TRADITIONAL SOCIAL ORDER

The fact that female behavior is inextricably bound to male pride and family honor in traditional religio-cultural codes signifies that mechanisms for protecting female purity underlie basic social relationships. A man's honor depends on the reputation of his womenfolk. Consequently, social divisions have been elaborated in a series of regulations that separate men and women and encourage family ties over relations with nonkin. In contrast, the criteria defining segregation in the rural areas has been familiarity (stranger versus nonstranger). This distinction has allowed for a certain amount of interaction with a wide range of nonkin village males.

The importance of female chastity has certain repercussions for women: veiling and seclusion, early age at first marriage, little or no education, removal from positions of public authority, various prohibitions against contact with male strangers, and first-cousin marriage preferences. It demands virgin brides and obedient wives.[1]

It is difficult, however, to determine how these mechanisms were realized in preindustrial Iran. We cannot presume that contemporary village life represents the traditional past. Even the most remote villages have been affected by changes originating in the industrial urban centers. The traditional religious position now attributed to villages represents a historical shift in the locus of orthodoxism from preindustrial urban areas to the rural hinterlands (Rahman 1974:923). From a perusal of the literature and interviews with village women in Iran, it appears that conditions often worked against the strict implementation of what we assume the behavioral ideals to have been. For example, practical considerations often demanded exceptions to the ideal that women remain secluded or wear the *chador* (the long, flowing veil) wound tightly around their bodies. Such considerations also made allowances for conversation with nonkin males since everyone was familiar with everyone else in the village.

In contrast to urban society, traditional rural communities are characterized by the following traits: relative homogeneity, offering fewer role models and fewer decisions to be made; a limited mobility, offering practically no opportunity for venturing outside the village or village cluster; an

agricultural mode of production, demanding complementary contributions from both men and women; spatial and temporal arrangements that
keep the kin network undispersed, preventing women from excessive contact with male strangers; and the lack of a resource infrastructure—education, health, media, and religious facilities.

Because social contact is limited to a predictable set of circumstances
with a predictable set of family and friends, there is less necessity in the
rural village for complex behavioral prescriptions governing male/female
interactions (the constriction of female mobility, for example, and wearing
the veil in confining ways). The *chador*, always a symbol of social position,
was not even a part of standard dress in many rural communities until
about ten years ago. The rigors of agricultural work do not permit restrictive clothing for women.

A rural woman's life is a predetermined path from birth to early marriage, motherhood, and widowhood. The major transitions are controlled
by the men in her household: father, brothers, husband, and finally sons.
The nature of agricultural society, however, demands cooperation between
the sexes and a less hierarchical assignment of role status than is found in
industrial urban societies; both men and women must assume heavy burdens in agricultural production. Women also had important roles in the
negotiation of family affairs—the arrangement of marriage, for example,
especially when it involved negotiation with familiar village people.

Because the rural family had, until recently, remained relatively undispersed and because few material resources were at hand, family relationships took on great significance. The image of the big, happy, and har-
monious extended family is greatly exaggerated, however, for frequent
face-to-face contact between family members inevitably leads to disagreements. Given the range in inheritance patterns, moreover, close family
members may or may not reside in close proximity—even in the village—
and "neighboring" is still an important village activity.

In summary, then, a woman is expected to be chaste before marriage,
compliant in her family's choice of spouse for her, fertile, and obedient to
her husband. It is clear that there have always been those who did not
adhere perfectly to this ideal, but the public nature of the village and the
lack of culturally sanctioned alternatives left little room for deviation.

THE URBAN CHALLENGE TO TRADITION

From this traditional and rural background male migrants and their families have flowed into various parts of Tehran. The first arrivals were able to
settle in regional or *ta'efe* quarters.[2] As the shortage of both urban space
and economic resources began to prohibit this pattern of settlement, migrants out of necessity settled more randomly in neighborhoods across the

south of the city. Therefore, neighbors reflect the heterogeneity of urban life in the variety of regional, linguistic, and cultural traditions they represent, although they share a common working-class status. Migrants, despite their separation by distance, do maintain contact with family in other neighborhoods of Tehran and in the villages through holiday visits, weddings, and funerals. Moreover, rural relatives also make trips to the city for business and for pleasure.

The neighborhood chosen for this study—suppose we call it "X"—is typical of the numerous migrant neighborhoods in Tehran, not only in its heterogeneity but also in the economic motivation that brought migrants to the city, the nuclear organization of the households, the average length of residence in Tehran, and the families' socioeconomic status. The neighborhood's 25,000 inhabitants are packed into one square kilometer on the southern edge of the city. Most of these families speak Azeri Turki, having come from the areas north and west of Tehran. Most male heads of household have arrived within the last 8 to 15 years. They migrated both as a result of the growing industrial sector and as part of the displacement of agricultural labor following land reform.[3] Some of the families came directly from the village; others moved to X from different sections of Tehran. X is the most recent of the migrant settlements; it was incorporated into the city in the late 1970's.

The population of X can be categorized as migrant according to the Statistical Center's definition, which classifies anyone who is not living in the place of his or her birth at the time of enumeration as a migrant. By this definition approximately 80 percent of the men and women between the ages of 35 and 65 living in Tehran are migrants (PBO 1976).[4] X, however, displays the attributes usually associated with migrant ghettos in the rural origin of its population and their lower socioeconomic standing. When the men came in search of work, their wives, daughters, and mothers followed. The majority of adult women are illiterate and have little knowledge of the Persian language. For the most part they do not work outside the home.

In contrast to the traditional environment described earlier, the urban environment of Tehran is characterized by greater heterogeneity and mobility, which provide new models and experiences and fill social spaces with increasing numbers of strangers. Changes in the means of production, moreover, widen the separation between domestic and nondomestic space, depriving women of their traditional productive role and constricting them to the shrinking domestic sphere. Rearrangements in the use of time and space separate kin groups by greater distances; rearrangements of work limit the time for events, such as weddings and funerals, that ritualize family solidarity. Thus the social space between kin and nonkin, men and women, is diminished. Furthermore, there is an expansion of the resource infrastructure to include a wide variety of services—health, education, and media—and information offering men and women the opportunity for new roles and behavior.

These features of the urban environment make it difficult to maintain the acceptable boundaries between men and women. Since people's networks are increasingly filled with strangers, there is a redefinition of space and a redistribution of behavior. These changes have limited women's participation in nonsex-segregated public activities and have led to the use of formalized behavior to control contact between males and females.

In the urban setting there is a greater number of social situations that can be called public. Public spaces are characterized by interaction between members of the opposite sex who are both unrelated and unfamiliar—that is, they are strangers. Formal behavior is required in these public spaces to emphasize the separation between men and women. This behavior involves both an intensification and an accommodation of traditional behavior. For example, a "public" label is assigned to most spaces outside the household because of the frequency with which women encounter men who are complete strangers. Therefore, in almost every sphere, including walks to the neighborhood shops, traditional formal behavior—wearing the veil tightly wrapped around the body with only the eyes showing, for example, and abstaining from conversation with males, is occasioned more and more often, even in interactions with familiar but unrelated males.

By demanding more formal behavior and controlling access to public spaces, men restrict women's behavior in the public domain and confine women's roles as much as possible to domestic activity. This restriction occurs despite optimistic predictions that the new industrial infrastructure will create new opportunities, models, and information with which "women can take on attributes of modernism in a social setting [Muslim society] that has traditionally produced highly constrained and confined women" (Fox 1973:520).

NEW ROLES AND BEHAVIOR

The primacy of Tehran in providing an urban support system is indicated by the number of educational institutions, health facilities, media sources, and bureaucratic establishments that offer the possibility of employment. For example, 20 percent of all radio transmitters, 26 out of 30 newspapers, 53 out of 57 magazines, and 23 out of 31 weeklies are found in Tehran (PBO 1973–74, 1976).

These establishments provide the models and information about behavior that figure in social learning theory (Bandura 1977). Modeling is defined as the process by which an individual can observe (and learn) other people's actions, words, and social experiences. This information can then be used to shape the individual's own actions. This is one reason why the media have such powerful social consequences. Television, radio, printed matter, and movies; institutionalized educational experiences (mostly nonformal); contact with higher-status women from beyond the neighborhood —these are the sources that have the greatest effect on the lives of adult women in the migrant neighborhoods.

Most studies of modernization attribute the most influential role in the formation of modern attitudes and behavior (especially among the illiterate) to the mass media (Thompson 1974; Fox 1973). In the migrant neighborhoods of Tehran, television, radio, and popular magazines are major sources of information for women about products, life-styles, and male/female relationships. In the rural areas, radio is the primary source of information because of demands made by agricultural chores, lack of good television reception, and widespread illiteracy. Freed from the burdens of agriculture and restricted from other activities, urban migrant women spend about five hours a day watching television or browsing through popular magazines. Popular television programs include both Iranian and foreign films and foreign serials like "Get Christy Love," "The Bionic Woman," and "Charlie's Angels"—programs in which the main characters are aggressive professional women who make their own way in the world of men. Projecting women into nontraditional situations and into nontraditional contact with men, they increase women's experience and affect their expectations.

Radio talk programs present none of the visual images of television, but they do provide a forum for discussion of marriage, divorce, and mothering within the urban context. These programs are an effective means of transmission in a basically illiterate female society. The most widely read magazine in migrant households, *Javanan,* runs stories of illicit and ill-fated love, suicide, murder, and rape—complemented by illustrations that reach the literate and illiterate alike.

The cinema is all but off limits to women, except when Hindi "slice-of-life" films are shown. Admittedly, most films shown in the southern part of Tehran are the worst examples of the westernized sex flick and would be objectionable to most western women too.

Formal and nonformal educational institutions transmit factual information and provide successful role models in the form of male and female instructors, many from outside the immediate neighborhood. The direct educational facilities available to wives and mothers in X consist of literacy classes and the miscellaneous services offered by the Women's Organization's family welfare centers. Here women may avail themselves of instruction (in literacy, dressmaking, typing, and dollmaking), child-care services, or advice on legal matters, birth control, and health problems. Through its teachers, lawyers, and staff, the Women's Organization has an explicit policy of discouraging the veil and projecting an image of the modern, progressive woman. Through their children, women also have access to information that is disseminated by formal educational institutions (elementary schools, secondary schools, and universities). Of course, this information can be a source of intergenerational conflict when children insist that they are more knowledgeable on certain matters than their parents.

In fulfilling their increasing responsibilities for representing the family in contact with local institutions and agencies, women encounter women from beyond the local community whose educational attainment and roles outside the home contrast sharply with their own. These contacts include the teachers in their children's schools, doctors and nurses in clinics, and women working with agencies in the surrounding community. Neighbors represent a variety of backgrounds, but their experiences, behavior, and expectations are likely to be similar to a woman's own. The direct and indirect sources of information about roles, behavior, and life-styles project women who are unveiled, sexually active, and transgress the social norms demanded by the migrant neighborhood. Women in X have a great deal of knowledge (though sometimes inaccurate) about what women in the middle- and upper-class and foreign neighborhoods eat and wear, how their families live, and what they think on numerous subjects. The women in X like much of what they see in these other women.

Women's Adaptation and Participation

Most migrant women's urban participation can be classified into three geosocial spaces: the household, the neighborhood, and the wider community of kin and nonkin. The redefinition of public and private space has sharpened the distinction between public spaces (defined by the presence of more strangers, less sex segregation, and more formal behavior) and private spaces (more familiar individuals, more sex segregation, and less formal behavior). Private space is almost completely limited to the domestic scene.[5] Thus, in the move to the city, women find themselves even more confined to the private, domestic sphere, where less formal behavior is demanded. They are discouraged and prevented from participating in the public sphere. Very few women in the low-income, migrant neighborhood of X work outside the home.

Thus it is the adaptation of women as wives, mothers, and daughters that we will investigate. Certain changes in roles and behavior do occur, but these are, for the most part, accommodations that reinforce the boundary between men and women and compensate for the dispersion of the kin network.[6] In effect then, these changes result in the intensification of traditional behavior.

WOMEN IN THE HOUSEHOLD

Although in general women's participation in subsistence economic production is eliminated in the city, wives do have an increasing share in managing the household. Because of her husband's absence during the work day and because of the growing nuclear nature of the urban family (where mothers-in-law are either absent from the immediate household or have no control over domestic affairs), wives have been given the major responsibility for daily purchases and minor encounters with various public agencies (the school, the health clinic, the gas company). Mothers-in-law who do reside with their sons' families no longer have a monopoly over knowledge and skills that were once associated with age. Younger women now have more familiarity with the handling of daily urban life.

These circumstances dictate that some of the decision-making power in the household be shared with women. Most wives report receiving a weekly or daily allowance for household operations. Men, however, retain control of major decisions—large purchases, trips, domestic negotiations. Men also control women's use of nondomestic spaces by granting or withholding permission for their various activities—becoming employed, going to school, visiting friends, attending weddings. Most wives have permission to leave the house for the purpose of carrying out these domestic tasks, which are usually performed within a 15-minute radius of the home.

When a woman does venture into the public world she comes into contact with complete strangers. As a result, more formal behavior is demanded. Even within close range of the compound, the *chador* should be worn in a formal manner covering all but a small portion of the face. (When worn informally, it leaves the arms free.) A woman does not talk or smile on the street, even when she casually passes family or friends in public.

Exceptions to the limits on movement are applied according to age and marital status. An adolescent girl is restricted from unchaperoned movement except to attend school, when she is accompanied by friends, brothers, and sisters, and for short errands if there are no younger brothers or sisters to do them. The adolescent girl is usually refused permission to visit school friends residing just a few streets away. Young wives, especially those who have only recently arrived in the city, are likewise restricted in their movements. Widows, divorcees, and women past menopause have the greatest freedom of mobility. Not only do they have less "sexuality" but fewer males are directly responsible for their behavior.

Although permission is necessary for most movements, women insist there is a mutual understanding between husband and wife concerning the destinations that are always acceptable—a neighbor's house, a nearby relative's, a shopping trip to the bazaar just an hour away. The fact that women acknowledge the implicit bounds placed on their mobility by their husbands, fathers, and brothers, despite the male's absence from the household, attests to the increasing role of neighbors in reinforcing socially accepted behavior.

WOMEN IN THE NEIGHBORHOOD

In contrast to Wirth's pronouncement that the urban neighborhood plays an insignificant part in the lives of its residents (1938:20–21), urban women declare that the effects of the migrant neighborhood are profound. Their sons, they say, learn bad habits from neighborhood youth and their own affairs are monitored by neighbors who, although unrelated, are intensely curious about one another's lives.

The urban migrant neighborhood falls between two types: the neighborhood where public and private space is sharply divided (residents are from the middle and upper occupational levels) and the neighborhood where there is little distinction between public and private (the rural village). There is a certain amount of informal behavior on the streets of X. Many women wash their clothes at the public water hydrants, for example, and gossip in their doorways. The audience in these neighborhoods is not as anonymous as one might expect in urban areas. What the neighbors see and think matters a great deal; the neighborhood exercises the social control that the family, through loss of face-to-face contact, cannot.

Housewives are often separated by long distances from the family and friends on whom they have always relied. A visit means travel over some distance and close encounters with strange men in buses or taxis. Thus a woman spends a good part of her day interacting with neighbors. Because urban women have more free time and fewer household activities than their rural counterparts, they spend a greater part of each day gossiping. While their daughters form friendships at school, older women can only enter into loose alliances with neighbors determined by length of acquaintance and proximity of households.

In day-to-day emergencies, as well as in major life-cycle events, women considered their obligations to their neighbors to be of equal importance to those of their extended families (*famil dur*) and in some cases equal to those of members of their very close families (*famil nazdik*).[7] When asked who assisted them most when the initial move to the city was made, most women answered that it was a neighbor. Friendly relations with neighbors offset the strain that can develop in extended family relations over money, marriage alliances, and reciprocity in visiting. While preferring to have members of their nuclear family nearby, women often feel that it is better to have strangers living next door because of the disagreements that inevitably arise in daily interaction. In these cases one cannot fight with family but can do so with neighbors.[8]

Yet the closest nonkin relations that develop are with those same neighbors—especially the ones with whom the family has long been acquainted. In interaction with these neighbors, prohibitions against contact between men and women may be relaxed because of familiarity. This relaxation is signified in the way one wears the *chador* in the presence of those males. In general, however, women of all ages and marital statuses wear the veil more confiningly in the city than in the village.

There are two occasions when neighborhood women have the opportunity to exchange social information: one is the informal visiting that occurs between morning chores and during the late afternoon when women stand in their doorways waiting for dusk; the other is the neighborhood *roseh,* a religious meeting that ritualizes these informal associations.

Through informal gossip networks women become acquainted with the intimate details of one another's lives. On various matters—failure to wear the veil, inappropriate dress, conversation with the opposite sex, the presence of male strangers in the household, employment in nonsegregated establishments, unaccompanied travel—the informal neighborhood network dispenses disapproval or—as in the case of early marriage, hasty remarriage, and immediate and continuous fertility of new brides—registers approval.

The other opportunity for social exchange is the local *roseh,* a religious meeting where the story of the martyrdom of the Prophet's grandsons is read and ritualized crying takes place as a display of faith. These occasions, as much social as religious, are used to redistribute surplus wealth and accumulate status. A woman organizes a *roseh* after making a vow concerning the recovery of a loved one or the favorable outcome of some event. It is, perhaps, indicative of women's powerlessness in public that the incidence of both *rosehs* and *sofrehs* (similar occasions involving the preparation of elaborate foods) increases with the move to the city. It is also an indication that women have more time to divert to nonhousehold activities but few places to direct it. Consequently almost every day there is a *roseh* somewhere in X. Before, during, and after the *roseh* program women have the chance to talk to (and about) one another.[9]

WOMEN IN THE COMMUNITY

The most noticeable thing about a woman's relationships outside the neighborhood circle is that her male relatives—husband, father, brothers—mediate this world for her. Although the extended family carries weight in some decisions, this influence is diminishing. The arrival of a suitor, for example, can still necessitate the calling together of close relatives in order to evaluate the young man and his family. Increasingly, however, it is the men of the household, rather than the larger family network, who exercise singular authority in regulating women's behavior.

Women's mobility outside the neighborhood is restricted because of the threat of interaction with strange males. Women are discouraged from continuing their education or seeking employment in the public domain. Although women travel out of their local neighborhoods to visit shrines, to drop in on relatives in other migrant neighborhoods, and to fulfill obligations to relatives in the village, they rarely make these trips alone but rather in the company of men of the household or other females.

A formalized system of reciprocal visiting *(deed* or *baz deed)* has evolved to maintain relationships with relatives in other parts of the city. Weekends and holidays are spent visiting with members of the extended family. Most families also have daily family visitors from their own neighborhood or other parts of Tehran. The crucial family events—births, deaths, weddings —further renew family ties throughout the city and into the countryside.

Family relations are often marred by disagreement—who receives wedding invitations and what type, whether there should be male/female segregation at a particular event, whether a wedding should be held in a home or a *boshgah* (something like a club), whether loans have been repaid.[10] Just as family relations in the village are not free from discord, physical abuse, and attack, so too the urban family is beset by these tensions. The discord is to some extent relieved by the associations formed with neighbors and the physical distance separating family members. In a study on the maintenance of primary groups, Litwak and Szelenyi (1969) found that neighbors were sought in short-term emergencies while family was relied upon in long-term crises.

Men and women interviewed throughout the migrant neighborhoods of Tehran expressed a preference for borrowing money from close friends rather than extended family. Still, more long-term loans are made to family members than to friends. Men and women profess to confide in close friends while in reality they discuss weighty matters with parents or brothers and sisters. The extended family continues to be an important resource in the migrant areas, as studies by Litwak and Szelenyi (1969) and Firth and Forgue (1969) indicate for other urban areas.

At the same time, a number of changes occur in the frequency of family interaction. The urban migrant family becomes more private, for example; that is, more family interaction is confined to the immediate nuclear family, which increasingly becomes defined as an entity separate from the rest of the community (Laslett 1973). Urban family relationships become more emotional and voluntary (Kerckhoff 1972), and the nuclear family finds it beneficial to maintain relations of mutual support with both the husband's and the wife's family.[11]

THE ROLE OF MEN AND TRADITIONAL NETWORKS

In socialization theories, particularly social learning theory (Bandura 1977), individuals take into account the social repercussions of an action in making decisions about behavior. Reinforcement of women's behavior in X is provided by the traditional neighbor and family networks and particularly by their male relatives. After discussing these two forces—networks and men—I wish to examine the religious rationalization that accompanies the circumscription of women's behavior and determine why women themselves support these limitations.

Male relatives govern the participation of urban migrant females in nondomestic activities by controlling their access to public spaces and their interactions with male strangers. Men grant permission to leave the house for various reasons: to travel, to go to school, to find employment. Certain behavior, reserved for encounters with strangers in rural society, is assigned to the increasing number of public situations in the city. Walking on the streets, traveling on public transportation, working, going to school—these activities, if they are permitted at all, necessitate intensifying behavior such as the wearing of the formal black veil, covering one's mouth when talking to men, suppressing of smiles or laughs, sitting in the formal position (upright with legs crossed), and declining to discuss certain topics.

COURTSHIP AND MARRIAGE

Family and neighborhood networks collaborate with male relatives in reinforcing certain behavior. This collaboration is evidenced in the cycle of courtship and marriage. Although education for females has been gaining approval, early marriage (ages 15 to 18) is still very much favored. Girls who do not marry before age 20 can be the subject of gossip within the family and throughout the neighborhood. After a girl has reached puberty, her movements in the migrant neighborhood become more restricted. Her behavior is cause for scrutiny by neighbors and relatives who know she is on the marriage market.

When a suitor appears at her house (perhaps he has noticed her on the street or a friend or relation has suggested the girl as a possible mate) the girl's family convenes to consider the match. The men then carry out their research, which often takes them to towns or villages outside of Tehran. The power of neighbors over the fate of other women is also exemplified in this aspect of urban marriage. The mechanisms of research have been devised because increasing numbers of males are seeking unrelated women in marriage. Males in both the girl's and the young man's families visit homes and stores in the neighborhood and places of work (if the prospective spouse is employed) seeking information and recommendations for the prospective *namzad* (fiancé). Pictures and visits are then exchanged.

Traditionally, village marriages were negotiated informally by the women of the two families in the *hamum* (bath) or in the doorways. With the advent of marriage to strangers, more formal negotiations were necessitated and are now undertaken by men. The *mehrieh* (the bride's portion of the marriage payment, which is supposed to provide security for her in the event of divorce) and the *shir baha* (literally, milk money—given to the bride's mother for having raised her from infancy but generally used to purchase the *jahaz,* the dowry of appliances and utensils for setting up the new house) are also subject to the approval of the family, particularly the bride's father or an older male relative. Furthermore, contractual signatures are required when the goods or money are exchanged. A girl may be asked if she approves or disapproves of the young man, but even if she disapproves a father can force her—especially when he is anxious to marry her to a child of his brother or sister. In over half the cases I investigated, first-cousin marriage occurred (either cross-cousin or parallel). Cousins are often preferred by girls themselves because they at least have some foreknowledge of the male relatives, their behavior and appearance. Unrelated suitors in the urban areas are usually strangers to the family.

After the contract is agreed upon, a girl's movements are even more closely circumscribed. Now the groom's family is observing her behavior. At every step of the marriage path there is the possibility for disagreement between families over some aspect of the arrangements or protocol.

The *shirini xordan* (literally, the eating of sweets) marks the giving of formal consent for the marriage by the two families. Although the agreement may be dissolved at any point up to the *akd kanun* (the official wedding ceremony), it cannot be done without compensation—mainly monetary. During the period preceding the marriage, the urban couple may be allowed to go to parks or the homes of relatives alone. If this is the case a *sigeh* is read by the mullah (the Muslim holy man). This proclamation binds the couple morally and legally to one another and justifies their being seen together in public. The girl's family, however, will not be relieved from anxiety until the night of the *arusi* (the wedding celebration) when proof of their daughter's virginity—upon which the honor of the family rests—is brought to the girl's mother.

THE PSYCHOLOGY OF ENCAPSULATION

Sociologists confirm that women have a need for the supportive networks of family, friends, and neighbors in the process of geographic mobility (McAllister et al. 1973). Women in the migrant neighborhoods of Tehran are certainly surrounded by such networks. On the one hand, these networks support the woman's entry into the urban environment; on the other, they encapsulate women. Salzman (1978) uses the image of encapsulation to describe the situation of Middle Eastern tribes surrounded by dominant national governments. In each case there were individuals in the tribe who served as mediators with the outside world. In a similar manner, migrant males in Tehran mediate the relationships of their female relatives at each level of contact with the outside world.

Women are denied the right to participate in public activities and to hold positions of authority on the basis of established religious and cultural conceptions that construe women to be emotional and irrational beings. In interviews with the significant males of women's networks, the men voiced a lack of confidence in women's ability to think, handle money, and deal with nondomestic problems. At the same time, even young educated men often expressed a preference for women with a limited education over high school graduates as marriage partners. These men enjoyed access to all parts of the city, places of work, theaters, parks and other places of leisure, and educational facilities. They were better educated, better traveled, and displayed a greater degree of bilingualism than women. They also had more experience dealing with a variety of situations. The advantages that men enjoy in the urbanization process are inextricably linked with the notion that women are less capable than men.

Awareness of their lack of experience not only enables women to evaluate their own limitations realistically but also leads them to believe there is something deficient in their own natures. When asked what occupations they envisaged for their children, most women replied that they were unqualified to hold expectations of this kind. When pressed they pointed to their lack of exposure and unfamiliarity with the range of possible careers. When asked if they would like to work outside the home, they said they did not have the skills.

While the admission of personal shortcomings is commendable, the attribution of these limitations to innate inferiority is inhibiting. Women were characterized by both men and women as inferior in thinking capacity. They were, at the same time, held responsible for flaws in *men's* behavior. Even women said that *matalak* (the discourteous things men say to women on the streets) is the fault of the women's conduct, dress, and mannerisms. Women (especially rural women) viewed a man's beating his wife as sinful only if she were innocent.

The extent to which women support the prevailing image of the Irrational Woman prevents them from asserting their case for greater participation in the world at large. Youssef (1978:76) calls it seclusion—"women's volitional response to resist forces of social modernity"—as opposed to exclusion—the limitations imposed on women by men and the social system. That is, in maintaining the restrictions on women's behavior and in registering disapproval for certain behavior, men are aided by women

themselves, who have been conditioned by years of constraint and exposure to Islamic prescriptions of the appropriate female alternative: the
chaste mother figure.

Many women accept the image of women as less capable than men
when they see that their only form of security lies in measuring up to the
cultural standards of female behavior and recognize that improvement of
their status lies in furthering the status of their men and the family unit.[12]
As a result, women conspire against themselves by demanding the same
behavior from each other.

The dominant images have powerful support from religious tradition in
Iran, drawn from Koranic passages and precedents from the Prophet's
life. Sura IV on women—especially verse 34: "Men are in charge of
women, because Allah hath made the one of them to excel the other"—is
used to legitimize male dominance (Pickthall 1953). Islamic conceptions of
nature attribute contrasting characters to men and women. Men are rational; women, irrational. Women's impulses must be controlled in the interests of social order and to prevent men from being distracted in their
orderly quest for knowledge of God and the universe. It is for these reasons
that regulations governing the behavior of women have been instituted
(both to minimize and to formalize male/female interaction).

These ideas are expressed in the apologetic writings of certain religious
thinkers. Fischer outlines the writings of various Iranian holy men who
assert the innate inferiority of women by arguing that a woman's testi-
mony is worth only half that of a man, that her brain is biologically smaller
and less capable than a man's, that it is in society's best interest if women
do not take positions of public authority (Fischer 1978:193–97).

Religious treatises written for popular consumption argue for the assignment of roles that complement the "natural abilities" of men and
women: Men should assume roles of leadership in the home and in public;
women should bear children and organize the household. In another Islamic book, *Hejab,* written for young girls and distributed in Koran
classes, the authors rationalize that women who wear the *chador* are "freer"
than women in western society who, because of their "nakedness," are left
to the mercy of men, powerless to protect themselves from men's carnal
desires. That belief exemplifies what Mernissi (1975) calls the implicit and
explicit nature of the women's position: While implicitly the sexual power
of women can destroy men, explicitly women are submissive.

These images of women are disseminated among the illiterate female
population through religious stories told by grandparents and parents in
the home and through the *roseh* and Koran classes. At the *roseh* women's
perceptions are again guided by a male—the mullah—interpreting the
precepts of Islam. Before or after the reading of the stories of Hasan and
Hossein, the mullah discusses the teachings of the Koran and other bodies

of religious knowledge. The religious model that women are encouraged to heed is simple: the obedient, strong, and chaste daughters, wives, and mothers.

The Koran, a document of legal reform in its day, does grant rights to women in certain areas such as inheritance (although it is not an *equal* right). Males, however, firmly control the implementation of these rights. The secular legal reforms of the past decade have followed the spirit of the Koranic law as traditionally implemented in Iran. Certain inequalities were institutionalized; others were changed. Women were also granted greater means of achieving their rights in marriage, divorce, and inheritance. (See Mernissi 1976 for a similar state of affairs in Morocco.) Still these secular measures have not gained the approval of the religious community and are not executed where women lack the awareness to pursue their rights. Reforms emancipating women from traditional constraints were opposed by the mullahs as early as 1918, and their opposition has continued to the present day (Bagley 1971:48).

With respect to the hope often voiced in research that the creation of legal reforms can provide the impetus for breaking down traditional prejudices against women's education, employment, and the postponement of marriage, for example, Youssef (1978:76) points out that Muslim society "contains few explicitly official legal injunctions discriminating against women in public life." It is prevailing cultural ideals, she says, that "render many options in different life sectors totally unacceptable for women."

Thus attempts to emancipate women by establishment of a minimum age for marriage, the right of women to initiate petitions for divorce, compulsory education, and equal inheritance have neither removed all the sex-based inequities from the law nor ensured that women will be permitted to marry later, continue their education, or accept portions of inheritances. The latest Iranian Family Protection Law raised the legal minimum age at marriage for women to 18. This measure does not prevent families from marrying their daughters below the minimum age by performing a *sigeh* (in effect, a temporary marriage) ceremony until the girl reaches 18. A woman's fear of losing her children may cause her not to file for divorce, even though the latest divorce laws leave the decision of custody to the courts in more situations than in the past. Often women who initiate the divorce thereby forfeit their *mehrieh* and are deprived of an important means of support.

ATTITUDES VS. BEHAVIOR

Although they are restricted from full participation in the public domain, women are exposed to new sources of information, role models, and alternatives in the urban setting. As a result, women's evaluation of certain behaviors may differ from how they actually behave under the influence of various constraints.

Women were asked to evaluate nine kinds of behavior according to whether the behavior was positive or negative, whether they were permitted to engage in it, and whose approval (husband, neighbors, or religious authorities) they would have to secure if they wanted to change it. Few women rated behavior as negative on religious grounds, especially when given specific situations, although abortion was consistently rejected on moral grounds. Television viewing, on the other hand, although objectionable for religious reasons, was admitted to be a regular activity in homes where television reception was possible.

A large number of women said they approved of education for their daughters, individual choice of a marriage partner, and a later age for marriage (usually 18 to 20). While professing these attitudes, women are in most cases prevented from realizing them because their behavior is limited by social networks—especially the males in these networks.

Most of the women interviewed indicated that if they lived in a different neighborhood, they would be more likely to engage in a specific kind of behavior, although permission of the principal male relative remained of primary importance. The implication here is that a husband's insistence upon certain behavior might be affected by the social environment. Many women expressed the desire to live in neighborhoods farther north where neighbors were perceived to be less inquisitive.

Greer Fox, in a study on the modernization of Turkish women (1973: 521), delineates four types of women: "two types whose behavior and attitudes match in terms of modernism or traditionalism and two whose behavior is inconsistent with their attitudes." The majority of women interviewed in the migrant neighborhood of X would be considered Type III —the "constrained moderns" whose attitudes are more modern than their behavior.

CONCLUSIONS AND IMPLICATIONS

The religious and cultural images that govern Iranian society, the need to minimize male/female contact and control women's access to public spaces, and the delegation of that responsibility to men, the family, and neighbors—all have contributed to keeping urban poor women from participating fully in life outside the migrant neighborhoods. Despite the increase in information about new roles and behavior, which is often presumed to lead directly to the formation of modern attitudes, there is still a great disparity in the ideas and behavior of both men and women—not only because women are physically restricted in their movements but also because they know what the social consequences of their actions will be.

While the male migrant's participation in urban life expands, the woman's access becomes ever more limited. On the one hand, men become more determined to preserve traditional values (which demand the separation of men and women). On the other, women are learning new patterns for interaction, even though they cannot realize them under the present circumstances of encapsulation.

Women's interaction is more or less limited to the household and the neighborhood, yet it is precisely these traditional networks that are least likely to reinforce the new roles and behavior. Mernissi (1976) says that Muslim women must look beyond the family network if they are to change their roles. She describes the Muslim family in Morocco as a ghetto for women. Muslim women should not so much "attempt to modernize the family structure," she says, "as to seek access to nonfamily networks" (p. 37). Although sexual discrimination may be officially illegal, it is difficult for women to gain access to public spheres without the social support of family and neighbors.

Time-budget studies support the proposition that the family and household are the last strongholds in maintaining traditional relationships, roles, and expectations. Even in the socialist countries of Eastern Europe, where large numbers of women work outside the home, women continue to carry the burden of responsibility for household chores. In the process of industrialization women do double duty—they take on jobs away from home and still do most of the work inside the home (Szalai 1975).

Conceptions of proper conduct held by women in the migrant areas are beginning to change. Wives are given more responsibility on behalf of their families. Young girls attend high school and perform well. They are learning new behavior and are beginning to realize that they are just as capable as men. The subsequent restrictions on their behavior and the double burden of work they must endure can create tension between male and female family members.

This tension becomes evident when the nuclear and extended family attempt to impose decisions on women—when a wife wants to establish a dressmaking business over the objections of her husband, when a widow in financial difficulty must cross an obstinate brother's protests and take a job, when a woman does not want to remarry despite the insistence of parents, uncles, and neighbors.

Mernissi (1978) contends that the authority of the Moroccan patriarch is being undermined by economic insecurity and the expansion of government services. Tension is caused because men can no longer perform their roles as economic providers, while the state becomes, in Mernissi's words, the "factual father." Although providing for one's family does become more difficult and may contribute to the male's insistence on his women keeping the "traditional female place," the authority of male family members in Iran is still supported by the tenets of Islam. In any case, the family patriarch was never the absolute source of family authority. Under the traditional landlord/peasant agricultural system, landlords too exerted influence, even in personal decisions of their village families.

It is the reorganization of the household, with its emphasis on the nuclear family and the geographic distances separating the extended family, as well as the disparity between access to information and control over its use, that challenges the traditional ordering of family authority.[13] Not only are the relationships between male and female family members affected but also those between women—especially the relationship between mother-in-law and daughter-in-law. Mothers-in-law cannot expect to enjoy control over the behavior of daughters-in-law who have more experience in dealing with the urban environment. Once women were married to men twice their age. During their early years of marriage they were supposed to be submissive to their husband and his mother. At least they could look forward to dominating their future daughters-in-law and perhaps having a greater voice in family affairs when their husband reached the age of senility. Now women are marrying men closer to their own ages and as daughters-in-law are no longer so pliable. They no longer wait on their husband's mother nor refuse to show affection toward their children in the presence of their husband's father. On interview questions, young rural and urban girls said they no longer heeded the proverbial admonition to keep their husband's shoes lined up by the door and to obey his parents. Relations between sisters-in-law also become strained as they vie for their brothers' resources.[14]

Accompanying this tension within the family, which focuses on the roles and behavior of women, is a change in the ties between family members. This change is noticeable in the husband/wife relationship. There are fewer incidences of wife beating (prevalent in rural areas), wives begin to assume the role of companion to their husbands, and women are given (out of necessity) greater responsibility in administering the urban household. In Kerckhoff's terms, family relationships become emotional and voluntary; the conjugal relationship is emphasized at the expense of the consanguinal tie (Kerckhoff 1972). In the migrant neighborhoods of Tehran this is a nascent shift. Yet it is significant that while tensions are being created in some aspects of family relationships (especially authority roles), discord is partially offset by ongoing change in the underlying nature of family association.

THE PROSPECTS

These observations on the adaptation of women to life in south Tehran have been drawn together from a period of inquiry preceding the resolution of the revolutionary movement in Iran. At the time of this research,

families in south Tehran were in a peripheral position vis-à-vis their relationship to the industrial sector of the economy (most heads of household
were unskilled construction workers, drivers, or unskilled office workers)
and their involvement in middle-class urban life. Their position was also
peripheral to the revolution and did not play a central role in the initial
protests and rallies.

In prerevolutionary Iran, options and behavior were differentiated not
only on the basis of gender but also on the grounds of geosocial class.
While all societies are organized to some extent according to cultural inter-
pretations of gender, distinctions in roles on this basis appear to increase
with urbanization. This fact was evident in contrasting the activities of
women in the different urban classes and rural Iran. Among the upper
classes of Tehran, the ways of the west were evident. Women went to
school, moved about without veils, drove cars, held jobs in various sectors
of the nondomestic economy, and wore the latest clothes. The middle- and
lower-income urban women, in contrast, adopted seclusive behavior. The
poorest women (usually divorced and widowed), both in Tehran and the
villages, could not afford to indulge in this restrictive (but status-denoting)
behavior. Out of necessity, the rural women moved about the village and
fields in agricultural activities while the urban women sought work as
cooks and domestics (often suffering a consequent loss of status). Regardless of their personal hopes and convictions, women were circumscribed by
their economic situation and the behavior enforced within their social
class.

Throughout the revolution, it was upper- and middle-class women and
students—of more secure means, longer urban residence, and more education and exposure—who circulated information and marched in the pro-
test demonstrations. While they were generally more autonomous than
their sisters in south Tehran, many of the middle-class women and students wore the veil or adopted some kind of covering *(hejab)* out of sympa-
thy with the Islamic spirit that consolidated the revolution. While it is not
evident that their participation was motivated by expectations of furthering sexual equality, a number of "covered" *(bahejab)* women have demanded a clarification of the rights of women in Islam—rights ensured to them
by the Koran but, they say, denied to them during the years of indirect
colonial domination and industrial development.

To many in the non-Islamic world, the sight of veiled feminists may be
an anomaly. The veil itself may be a vehicle for the eventual emancipation
of women, however. While women in X would not necessarily agree that
the veil symbolizes one's capabilities or "goodness," they did maintain that
it has everything to do with one's social reputation. Thus if the veiled
women—particularly the largely illiterate female population of south Tehran, provincial towns, and the villages—can be given socially acceptable
but active public roles, they will have the opportunity to engage in activi-

ties from which they can gain confidence and create new images of women in Iran.

Clearly the achievement of sexual segregation as a religious and cultural ideal (or a channel for ordering society) retains a good deal of importance among the middle- and lower-class religious community who invested heavily in the outcome of the revolution. Prior to the revolution, many of them espoused an explanation of the differentiation among women in Iran that gave preeminence and status to the veiled women who attended to their religious duties but were educated, forward thinking, and committed to equal but separate gender roles. Today the Islamic state appears to be not only maintaining separation of activities and roles but also constricting the alternatives that some Iranian women enjoyed in employment and education. In Iran as in other societies experiencing radical change, it has become evident that a revolutionary context itself does not ensure a positive direction for women's control over their lives.

NOTES

1. For complete discussions concerning the status, life cycle, and roles of women in Iran, as well as the basic religious and cultural rationale behind the idea of male/female separation in Muslim society, see Fischer (1978), Vieille (1978), Youssef (1978), Mernissi (1975), Papanek (1973), and Gulick and Gulick (1978).

2. *Ta'efe* is an extended-family identification (often no longer meaningful); Lambton (1961:221) defines *ta'efe* in this sense as clan.

3. For various political reasons, the northwest Azeri Turki-speaking region of Iran was partially excluded from the early growth of state industry (Fisher 1963:16).

4. The most recent migrants to the city are hidden from standard surveys that interview heads of household. Aside from seasonal workers, they are single people (almost exclusively male) who are cycled into Tehran as workers, students, and army recruits —often while they are still of high school age. They live with family or friends until they marry, sometimes returning to the village to acquire a bride. The young couple can then expect to be renters, perhaps in the home of a relative for the first few years of married life. Thus by the time a man sets up his own household, he has already been a resident in Tehran for several years.

5. Laslett does not argue that the family is becoming more nucleated; she maintains that the nuclear family has been a traditional phenomenon and focuses instead on the increasing privacy of the family. That is, a greater amount of family interaction occurs within the domestic establishment and away from public scrutiny and social control (Laslett 1973).

6. Certain accommodations have been made to allow for male/female interaction in public spaces—in buses, taxis, certain places in pilgrimage—besides situations when the man and woman are well acquainted with one another.

7. Proximity is an important consideration in assessing family relationships. Women sometimes admitted they felt less at ease with brothers and sisters who lived far away than with the friends and neighbors they see every day.

8. The Gulicks record similar remarks made by women in their sample of migrant and nonmigrant women in Isfahan, Iran (Gulick and Gulick 1978).

9. Although few women in X attend Koran classes, girls and women in the areas surrounding X do attend classes in various parts of Tehran. The classes themselves form a network linking women all over the city. Some groups hold classes in more than one area of the city; in other cases, the same teacher gives instruction to more than one group of women.

10. Family events in south Tehran are usually segregated by sex. A wedding held in a public place like a *boshgah* can be segregated in two ways: by the absence of women altogether or by their wearing of a formal black veil and refraining from activities such as dancing (which is then performed by men).

11. Vatuk (1972) details changes in traditionally patrilineal urban Indian families toward the exploitation of both matrilineal and patrilineal family ties.

12. Remy (1975:370) reports similar findings in Nigeria, where women depend on husbands, kin, and ethnic associations for security. "Maintaining 'correct behavior' insures the continuation of this security while at the same time making it necessary," she says. In other words, women themselves reinforce the limitations that are placed on their behavior.

13. Mernissi (1978) speaks of the "atomization" of the family into small nuclear-type units, as do many others who associate the increase in nuclear organization of the household with urbanization and industrialization. However, a number of researchers have urged caution about assuming that the traditional household organization was the extended family (Laslett 1973). Today in Iran the incidence of nuclear family types is, in fact, greater in the rural areas (PBO 1973–74).

14. A sister depends on her brother for support, especially if she is divorced or widowed. Many divorcees set up house with their brothers' families. This bond is symbolized and renewed on occasions such as the Persian New Year, when brothers are expected to give their sisters presents.

BIBLIOGRAPHY

Bagley, F. R.
    1972   The Iranian Family Protection Law of 1967. In C. E. Bosworth (ed.), *Iran and Islam*. Edinburgh: University of Edinburgh Press.
Bandura, A.
    1977   *Social Learning Theory*. Englewood Cliffs, N.J.: Prentice-Hall.
Boserup, Ester
    1970   *Women's Role in Economic Development*. New York: St. Martin's Press.
Boulding, E.
    1972   Women as role models in industrializing societies: a macro-system model of socialization for civic competence. In M. B. Sussman and B. E. Cogswell (eds.), *Cross National Family Research*. Leiden: E. J. Brill.
Denich, B.
    1976   Urbanization and women's roles in Yugoslavia. *Anthropological Quarterly* 49(1):11–19.

Fischer, M.
1978   On changing the concept and position of Persian women. In L. Beck and
        N. Keddie (eds.), *Women in the Muslim World*. Cambridge, Mass.: Harvard
        University Press.

Fisher, W. B.
1963   Physical geography. In W. B. Fisher (ed.), *Cambridge History of Iran*, Vol. I.
        Cambridge: Cambridge University Press.

Firth, R., J. Hubert, and A. Forgue
1969   *Families and Their Relatives*. London: Routledge & Kegan Paul.

Fox, G. L.
1973   Some determinants of modernization among women in Ankara, Turkey.
        Journal of Marriage and the Family 35(3):520–29.

Gulick, J., and M. E. Gulick
1978   The domestic social environment of women and girls in Isfahan, Iran. In
        L. Beck and N. Keddie (eds.), *Women in the Muslim World*. Cambridge,
        Mass.: Harvard University Press.

Kerckhoff, A.
1972   The structure of the conjugal relationship in industrial societies. In M. B.
        Sussman and B. E. Cogswell (eds.), *Cross National Family Research*. Leiden:
        E. J. Brill.

Lambton, A. K. S.
1961   *Persian Vocabulary*. 2nd ed. Cambridge: Cambridge University Press.

Laslett, B.
1973   The family as a public and private institution: an historical perspective.
        Journal of Marriage and the Family 35(3):480–94.

Litwak and Szelenyi
1969   Primary group structures and their functions: kin, neighbors and friends.
        American Sociological Review 34(1):465–81.

McAllister, P., et al.
1973   The adaptation of women to residential mobility. *Journal of Marriage and the
        Family* 35(2):197–204.

Mernissi, F.
1975   *Beyond the Veil: Male-Female Relationships in a Modern Moslem Society*. Cam-
        bridge, Mass.: Schenkman.
1976   The Moslem world: women excluded from development. In I. Tinker and
        M. B. Bramsen (eds.), *Women and World Development*. Washington, D.C.:
        Overseas Development Council.
1978   The patriarch in the Moroccan family: myth or reality. In J. Allman (ed.),
        Women's Status and Fertility in the Muslim World. New York: Praeger.

Papanek, H.
1973   Purdah: separate worlds and symbolic shelter. *Comparative Studies in Society
        and History* 15:289–323.

Pickthall, N. M.
1953   *The Meaning of the Glorious Koran*. New York: Mentor Books.

Plan and Budget Organization (PBO)
1966   *Statistical Yearbook of Iran.* Tehran: Statistical Center of Iran.
1973–74 *Statistical Yearbook of Iran.* Tehran: Statistical Center of Iran.
1976   *National Census of Population and Housing.* Tehran: Statistical Center of Iran.

Rahman, Fazlur
1974   Islam. *Encyclopedia Britannica.* Vol. 9.

Remy, Dorothy
1975   Underdevelopment and the experience of women: a Nigerian case study. In R. Reiter (ed.), *Toward an Anthropology of Women.* New York: Monthly Review Press.

Salzman, P.
1978   The study of "complex society" in the Middle East: a review essay. *International Journal of Middle Eastern Studies* 9:539–57.

Swan, E.
1977   Highlights of the 1966 census of Iran. In D. A. Momeni (ed.), *The Population of Iran.* Honolulu: East-West Center Population Institute/Pahlavi University.

Szalai, A.
1975   *The Situation of Women in the Light of Contemporary Time-Budget Research.* U.N. E/ConF/66/Bp/6. New York: United Nations.

Thompson, R.
1974   Rural-urban differences in individual modernization in Buganda. *Urban Anthropology* 3(64):78.

Vatuk, S.
1972   *Kinship and Urbanization.* Berkeley: University of California Press.

Vieille, P.
1978   Iranian women in family alliance and sexual politics. In L. Beck and N. Keddie (eds.), *Women in the Muslim World.* Cambridge, Mass.: Harvard University Press.

White, E.
1978   Legal reform as an indicator of women's status. In L. Beck and N. Keddie (eds.), *Women in the Muslim World.* Cambridge, Mass.: Harvard University Press.

Wirth, L.
1938   Urbanism as a way of life. *American Journal of Sociology* 44:1–24.

Youssef, Nadia
1978   The status and fertility patterns of Muslim women. In L. Beck and N. Keddie (eds.), *Women in the Muslim World.* Cambridge, Mass.: Harvard University Press.

ECONOMIC ACTIVITY AND ADJUSTMENT OF FEMALE MIGRANTS: ANALYTIC MODELS

Chapter 15

Migrant Women at Work in Asia

Nasra M. Shah
Peter C. Smith

This chapter attempts to answer four questions: How do female labor-force participation rates vary among the five countries under study? Are participation rates for female migrants to Asian cities systematically different from those of urban natives? What are some of the constraints and facilitators associated with differentials in female participation rates, especially differences between migrants and others? How do the occupational structures of migrant and nonmigrant women vary within and among the five countries?

It is important to study these questions for several reasons. Participation in the labor force is one of the traditionally significant motives for male migration to the cities in Asia and is becoming increasingly significant for females. A migrant woman's entry into the urban labor market has important implications for her adjustment. The type of economic activity that she enters into is crucial not only for her initial adjustment to the city but also for her future social mobility within the urban environment. Several researchers have studied the preponderance of female migrants in domestic service in diverse countries (Jelin 1977; Sudarkasa 1977; Ibarra 1980; Youssef et al. 1979). They have generally agreed that domestic service is a dead end; few migrant women seem to have an opportunity to move into better-paying or higher-status jobs. Admittedly, however, direct longitudinal evidence on this point is lacking. The subject of female migration has attracted attention only in the last few years, and labor-force participation among migrant women has not been researched extensively so far.

A group of researchers at the International Labour Office (ILO) has studied the labor-force participation of migrant women. Standing (1978b), examining the likelihood of migrant women's entering the urban labor force, concludes that their participation rates are likely to be higher than those of nonmigrants. For one thing, migrants have lower wage aspirations than nonmigrants because they come from areas where incomes are low and the range of jobs is limited; migrants therefore have a greater probability of employment in wage labor. Migrants are more likely to accept menial or degrading jobs because anonymity is possible in their case. If male migrants obtain only low-income jobs, their wives are more likely to become secondary workers, and this would make the activity rate of migrant women higher than that of nonmigrants (Standing 1978b:chap. 8). Mazumdar (1979) adds to these arguments the notion that migrants, because they are largely young and single, have lower living costs and thus are able to accept lower wages. Empirical evidence from several Latin American studies supports the positive relationship between migrant status and labor-force participation, particularly in the case of women. (See, for example, several case studies in Standing and Sheehan 1978.)

The relationship between female migration and employment in Asian countries has not been studied extensively. Moreover, the few studies that have been done offer mixed results. A study in Sri Lanka showed an insignificant relationship between the two variables (Standing and Sheehan 1976). In Bombay, India, length of residence in the city was found to be negatively associated with the female labor-force participation rate but positively associated with the male rate (Zachariah 1968). Chaudhury (1979) found in a study of migrants to Dacca, Bangladesh, that 62 percent of the migrant women were working compared with 45 percent of the nonmigrant women. Results from Thailand show that more of the migrant women to Bangkok metropolis were in the labor force than were nonmigrant women (see Chapter 8 of this volume).

Whether a migrant woman enters the labor force depends on various factors. It should be emphasized that the concept of labor-force participation is difficult to measure and that the economic activities of women are seriously underreported in census data in some countries. Underreporting may be due to a misperception of the labor-force question by respondents; it may also be due to respondents' genuine belief that certain economic activities of females do not qualify as labor-force activities. Furthermore, respondents (male as well as female) may deliberately underreport female economic activity. Despite these weaknesses of measurement, a comparison of participation rates for various countries does provide a rough indication of economic activity. Hence a discussion of the forces that constrain and promote these rates remains useful.[1]

Thadani and Todaro, in developing a theory of female migration in Chapter 3 of this volume, include the pattern of employment opportunities as a significant cause of female migration. Migration from rural to urban areas is regarded as a function of the rural/urban (formal-sector) wage differential and the probability of obtaining formal urban employment, taking into account the direct and indirect effects of sex discrimination. Thadani and Todaro suggest that migration will result in a greater positive

Figure 15.1 Framework for analyzing influences on female labor-force participation

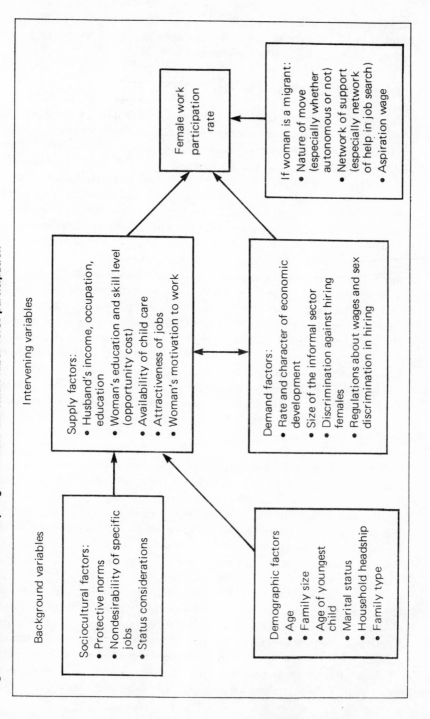

differential for women than men in cases where women have little autonomy and power in rural areas but are able to control their own income
from the informal sector in urban areas.

AN ANALYTIC FRAMEWORK

Figure 15.1 presents a conceptual framework within which the labor-force
participation behavior of women in general, and that of migrant women in
particular, may be explored. Many of the factors discussed by Standing
(1978a, 1978b) are considered important here. Moreover, we emphasize
the normative structures that define female work in either positive or negative terms. The factors affecting female labor-force participation can be
divided into two broad categories: background variables and intervening
variables. The background variables are further subdivided into sociocultural factors and demographic factors. Individual and societal conceptions
about the propriety of female work have a strong influence on a woman's
desire for work and her eventual participation in the labor force. Some
societies are highly protective of female chastity and honor; only jobs that
ensure minimal contact between the sexes are permissible. Examples of
such normative structures from India and Pakistan can be found in Singh
(1978), Korson (1970), and Papanek (1971). Furthermore, status is important in deciding whether a wife or daughter should be allowed to enter the
labor force. Jobs that enhance the family's status may be encouraged
whereas those that reduce the family's status may be forbidden or con-
cealed (and thus underreported). These general normative structures may
vary according to a family's level of destitution—for example, *any* job
might be defined as culturally permissible if the woman is the sole bread-
winner of the family.

Demographic variables such as the wife's age must be considered because of the cultural limits on permissible work for very old or very young
persons. Family size has often been found to have a positive effect on work
participation, and the age of the youngest child may act as a positive or
negative influence depending on the alternatives for child care and whether the job is outside the home. As for marital status, widowed and divorced
women are theoretically likely to have a greater need to enter the labor
market than other women in most societies.

Two sets of intervening variables are important in the labor-force participation of women: supply factors (including individual motivation to
work) and demand factors. The supply factors and the level of individual
motivation are influenced by the background variables. The demand for
certain jobs may change if the regulations about wage rates change. Even
though the model presented in Figure 15.1 deals with females only, the relative supply and demand for the labor of males and females is likely to

influence female labor-force participation. Standing (1978a) found in Jamaica that female migrants were willing to work much longer hours than nonmigrants and had lower aspirations for wages: The lower the aspiration, the greater the probability of a migrant woman's employment. Furthermore, in some countries the informal sector has a fairly high absorptive capacity and migrants can participate in the labor force as marginal workers although they may be seriously underutilized (see Chapter 8).

Personal motivation to work is important both in entering the labor force and in keeping a job. Individual motivation may be meaningless, however, if a woman has no other option except working to earn her livelihood. Many low-income women in developing countries belong in this category, particularly if they are widowed or divorced and the head of their household. In the case of more affluent women who have the (theoretical) option not to participate in the labor force, work commitment is probably a significant factor in participation.

How does this general framework apply specifically to migrant women? Migrant women might differ from nonmigrant women in several respects. Migrants might bring with them different attitudes regarding the permissibility of work in general and specific types of jobs that would affect the female migrants' participation. The migrants' family structure might be very different from that of nonmigrants—especially in countries where the predominant pattern of female migration is autonomous rather than based on the family. In these countries, where women move autonomously (and perhaps even alone) in order to find jobs, it is reasonable to expect that work participation is higher among migrants than among nonmigrants. In these cases a network of support appears to play a considerable role in the decision to move. It has been shown that in some countries certain groups of autonomous movers have a well-integrated network—prostitutes in Bangkok (Piampiti 1980), for example, and domestic servants in Manila (Ibarra 1980). Another factor that could facilitate labor-force entry for migrant women is their greater willingness to take up unskilled and low-paying jobs (such as domestic service) as in the Jamaican case discussed above. Similar findings have been reported for migrants to several Latin American cities (Jelin 1977) and to Jakarta, Indonesia (Suharso et al. 1975).

The foregoing framework does not list all the variables that enter into a woman's decision whether to enter the urban labor market, but the structure does allow us to compare the data for five Asian countries. Since empirical data are available for only a few of the variables, we do not test the framework but rather use it as a guide for the comparative analysis of limited data. We hope to test parts of the model presented in Figure 15.1 more rigorously as more data become available.

THE DATA

The five countries compared in this study are Indonesia, Malaysia, the Republic of Korea, Thailand, and Pakistan. Our analysis is based on the following data:

1. Indonesia: 1976 Intercensal Survey, Phase 2 (SUPAS II)
2. Malaysia: 2 percent sample of the 1970 census
3. Korea: 1 percent sample of the 1970 census
4. Thailand: 2 percent sample of the 1970 census
5. Pakistan: 1973 Housing, Economic, and Demographic (HED) Survey (a sample survey of about 250,000 households designed to supplement the 1972 census)

We analyze female work participation both in terms of activity rates—calculated as percentages economically active among females in a specified age group and other population categories—and in terms of occupational distributions. We also analyze unemployment rates for various groups. Except for Korea, where persons 14 years old and more are included in the labor force, information about work participation pertains to persons aged ten and over. The reference period to which the labor force pertains is the survey week for all countries. We chose the reference week in preference to another measure such as work participation over the previous year because all the countries had comparable data on the former measure.

All the countries provide occupational data based on the guidelines provided by the International Standard Classification of Occupations (ISCO) and therefore generally comparable. We regrouped the nine broad categories into five groups to provide a summary comparison between migrant and nonmigrant females. A detailed comparison using a 38-category classification has been developed (see Smith and Crockett 1980) for Thailand. Even though all the countries in this study follow the general pattern of coding provided by ISCO, there may be subjective differences in the coding of specific occupations. Moreover, the nature of the same occupation might vary considerably from country to country. Such differences should not affect the broad groupings, however.

We divided migrants into two groups: recent migrants and long-term migrants. Recent migrants are defined as those who moved to urban areas in the recent past, that period being defined variously as from five to eight years before the survey. (Residence eight years prior to the survey was used in the case of Pakistan.) In the case of Korea, Indonesia, and Pakistan, long-term migrants are defined as persons whose residence five (eight in the case of Pakistan) years prior to the survey was different from their birthplace. In the case of Malaysia and Thailand, long-term migrants are defined as those who moved 5 to 20 years prior to the survey because data on duration of residence are available for these two countries.

We selected four independent (or control) variables for the purpose of examining the forces that constrain or promote the labor-force participation of migrant and nonmigrant women. The four variables are age, marital status, education, and whether the respondent was a head of household. We have used wife's education as a proxy for the family's socioeconomic status. Age and marital status represent the respondent's demographic status and have been shown to be important variables in the work history of migrant women (Standing and Sheehan 1978). Headship status is used to measure a woman's need to enter the labor market. In some societies, women are reported as heads of households only if they are destitute and clearly do not have adult male supporters. Work participation is generally considered to be permissible for such women, even in societies where female work is in general not acceptable.

The analysis is based on cross-tabulation of data on the variables specified above. We compare the activity rates and unemployment rates of migrants and nonmigrants after controlling for the sociodemographic variables. The analysis is largely descriptive and designed to provide a broad picture of female work participation within the urban areas of each country.

THE RESULTS

The overall percentage of women who are economically active varies dramatically among the five countries—from a low of 4 percent in Pakistan to a high of 40 percent in Thailand (Table 15.1). Data from other national surveys in Pakistan have shown that female participation is actually similar to the level in Indonesia and Korea: about 20 percent (Shah and Shah 1980). The data for Pakistan must therefore be interpreted with caution. Male activity rates are quite similar for the five countries when we compare males aged 25 and above. As expected, 90 to 95 percent of all males aged 25 to 44 are in the labor force. Age-specific activity rates for females differ notably among countries. The pattern in Pakistan shows little variation by age; Korean women have exceptionally high rates among the very young (10–24), whereas Indonesian women have much higher rates among those over 25; the activity rates for Malaysian women are higher among those under age 45; and the Thai pattern for females is similar to that of Thai males, with 53 percent of the Thai women aged 25–44 in the labor force.

When we compare overall participation rates of recent migrants and nonmigrants, the former generally have higher participation rates in all countries (Table 15.2). In Indonesia and Korea, rural-to-urban migrants

Table 15.1 Urban labor-force participation for males (M) and females (F), by age and marital status: Indonesia, Korea, Malaysia, Pakistan, Thailand

Age group and marital status	Indonesia		Korea[a]		Malaysia		Pakistan		Thailand	
	M	F	M	F	M	F	M	F	M	F
All ages	58.8	23.6	72.8	21.9	63.1	26.1	61.3	4.2	64.2	39.9
10–24	**28.7**	**17.5**	**42.0**	**31.8**	**42.7**	**26.5**	**41.9**	**2.9**	**40.0**	**33.6**
Single	22.9	18.1	40.7	37.0	40.6	28.2	37.8	2.7	37.4	34.2
Married	90.6	12.6	93.1	6.5	85.2	16.1	77.9	3.2	92.4	29.7
Widowed	86.1	38.7	0.0	50.0	57.1	42.9	35.3	11.8	80.0[b]	66.4
Divorced	66.7	45.4	50.0	52.4	50.0	50.0	30.2	11.1	63.2	47.9
25–44	**93.3**	**29.7**	**94.9**	**16.9**	**94.3**	**29.1**	**89.7**	**5.1**	**91.8**	**52.7**
Single	71.6	55.7	83.5	50.5	90.0	67.0	80.2	21.6	85.2	77.5
Married	97.4	22.4	97.1	12.0	95.8	21.6	92.6	3.7	95.5	44.6
Widowed	91.7	63.7	80.4	57.2	86.7	45.2	74.2	17.9	90.8	74.8
Divorced	85.1	60.6	88.4	59.2	86.4	52.6	56.3	18.4	81.2	71.9
45+	**76.5**	**29.0**	**74.3**	**14.7**	**70.5**	**17.0**	**73.4**	**5.5**	**73.4**	**31.8**
Single	66.1	37.7	50.0	0.0	64.9	42.3[b]	56.8	22.7	69.7	46.9
Married	79.4	25.5	77.1	14.6	73.1	16.3	78.4	4.0	77.7	33.8
Widowed	47.3	30.6	33.8	14.0	45.4	15.5	51.2	7.1	43.1	24.2
Divorced	61.1	48.3	65.4	46.0	58.3	33.3[b]	56.4	23.5	67.6	45.9

a. Data for Korea in this and subsequent tables pertain to persons 14 years old and above.

b. Fewer than 30 unweighted cases.

Sources: Sample tapes from 1970 censuses. See text for details.

Table 15.2 Female labor-force participation, by marital status for nonmigrants, long-term migrants, and recent migrants: Indonesia, Korea, Malaysia, Pakistan, Thailand

Country and marital status	Number (unweighted)	All women	Nonmigrants	Long-term migrants	Recent migrants Rural-urban	Recent migrants Urban-urban
Indonesia	45,628	**23.6**	**22.2**	**25.2**	**36.0**	**22.7**
Single	18,134	20.5	16.8	28.1	45.1	26.8
Married	20,973	20.7	22.2	20.0	16.2	13.9
Widowed	4,929	38.0	38.5	36.7	56.6	35.6
Divorced	1,592	53.7	52.4	53.5	66.8	57.3
Korea	32,902	**21.9**	**21.1**	**19.0**	**29.7**	**21.1**
Single	10,620	37.8	24.4	35.0	60.8	41.1
Married	17,908	11.9	14.7	12.6	9.7	10.5
Widowed	3,985	21.2	26.4	20.2	19.7	20.2
Divorced	389	56.3	57.1	49.2	69.5	56.8
Malaysia	15,367	**26.1**	**25.0**	**25.4**	**27.9**	**32.0**
Single	7,732	31.7	28.5	35.2	40.2	45.4
Married	6,552	19.6	19.5	20.5	16.5	19.8
Widowed	969	22.3	22.7	21.0	15.2[a]	26.6[a]
Divorced	114	44.7	41.9	52.6[a]	50.0[a]	47.6[a]
Pakistan	233,197	**4.2**	**3.4**	**5.2**	**4.4**	**5.6**
Single	85,979	3.8	2.9	9.8	5.2	6.1
Married	128,809	3.7	3.5	3.8	3.3	4.6
Widowed	17,348	8.9	7.8	9.5	9.8	9.7
Divorced	1,061	19.2	12.9	19.6	26.4	31.0
Thailand	177,413	**39.9**	**38.7**	**41.1**	**38.3**	**48.1**
Single	79,636	40.3	36.1	47.8	43.2	61.2
Married	78,904	39.5	41.8	39.2	33.5	30.2
Widowed	13,434	31.4	33.2	29.7	27.4	35.1
Divorced	5,439	59.6	58.9	60.5	58.5	62.8

a. Fewer than 30 unweighted cases.

have higher participation rates whereas urban-to-urban migrants and nonmigrants have similar rates. In Malaysia and Thailand, in contrast, it is the urban-to-urban migrants who have distinctly higher participation rates.[2] The participation rates of long-term migrants are in general not very different from those of nonmigrants.

Controlling for marital status, we find the differences between the nonmigrant and recent migrant women to be generally greatest among the single. In Indonesia, for example, more than two and one-half times the proportion of rural-to-urban, recent migrant, single women are in the labor force compared with nonmigrants (45 and 17 percent, respectively). In Malaysia and Thailand, more than one and one-half times the proportion of urban-to-urban single migrants are in the labor force as among nonmigrants. Divorced migrant women have consistently higher participation rates than divorced nonmigrant women, but the differences are much smaller than among single women. Furthermore, divorced women in all the countries have much higher participation rates than do women of other marital statuses. Divorce seems to create greater economic need among all women, particularly among migrant women, thus leading to higher participation rates. Among widowed women, the differences between migrants and nonmigrants are generally small except in Indonesia, where 57 percent of the rural-to-urban widowed women are in the labor force compared with 38 percent of the nonmigrant widows.

The pattern for married migrant women is usually the opposite of that for single and divorced women; that is, a similar or smaller proportion of the married migrant women are in the labor force than among married nonmigrants. The differentials for three of the five countries (Korea, Malaysia, and Pakistan) are negligible, but in Indonesia and Thailand notably smaller proportions of married migrant women are in the labor force. The lower participation rates of migrant married women are perhaps related to their lower economic need for entering the labor force. Their participation is probably discouraged too by the lack of child-care facilities at their place of origin. Since married women constitute a significant proportion of the sample in all the countries (from 43 percent in Thailand to 55 percent in Pakistan), their lower participation rates are an important component of the participation rates for all migrants.

It may be concluded from the data shown in Table 15. 2 that marital status is a significant variable that should be controlled in an analysis of the labor-force participation of migrant women. Single, divorced, recent migrant women seem much more likely than married women to enter the labor force in urban areas. The former category probably includes large numbers of autonomous female migrants who migrated in order to find employment. These women are likely to be in greater need of employment than married women and therefore less particular about the number of hours, wages, and overall social status of work they take up.

When we analyze participation rates after controlling for age and marital status, a clear pattern for all countries emerges: significantly higher rates among young (under 25), single, recent migrants compared with nonmigrants (Table 15.3). The proportion of women working is one and one-half to two times higher among recent migrants than among nonmi-

Table 15.3 Female labor-force participation, by age and marital status for nonmigrants, long-term migrants, and recent migrants: Indonesia, Korea, Malaysia, Pakistan, Thailand

Country and marital status	Total			Nonmigrants			Long-term migrants			Recent migrants		
	<25	25–44	45+	<25	25–44	45+	<25	25–44	45+	<25	25–44	45+
Indonesia	17	30	29	15	32	31	21	27	27	26	31	26
Single	18	55	38	15	51	31	24	27	50	32	71	9[a]
Married	13	22	25	13	24	29	13	21	22	11	18	21[a]
Widowed	39	64	31	31[a]	64	32	37[a]	63	29	64[a]	61	30
Divorced	45	61	48	39	61	53	49[a]	58	47	71	70	27[a]
Korea	32	17	15	22	21	17	30	16	15	40	16	12
Single	37	50	0[c]	24	42	0[b]	33	53	0[b]	50	53	0[c]
Married	6	12	15	8	16	15	7	12	15	6	11	12
Widowed	50[a]	57	14	0[b]	59	19	50[a]	58	14	50[a]	56	12
Divorced	52[a]	59	46	33[a]	59	67[a]	60[a]	47	53	60[a]	66	34
Malaysia	27	29	17	25	29	16	27	28	18	33	31	16
Single	28	67	42	25	64	32	29	70	60[a]	41	76	54[a]
Married	16	22	16	18	21	15	17[a]	22	18	12	23	16[a]
Widowed	43[a]	45	16	60[a]	42	16	0[b]	47[a]	16	0[b]	53[a]	13[a]
Divorced	50[a]	53	33	40[a]	46[a]	36[a]	50[a]	57[a]	50[a]	67[a]	78[a]	11[a]
Pakistan	3	5	6	3	5	5	5	5	6	4	6	9
Single	3	22	23	2	18	13	5	25	26	4	27	28
Married	3	4	4	3	4	4	5	4	4	3	5	5
Widowed	12	18	7	6	15	6	17	21	8	20	17	8
Divorced	11	18	24	8	12	19	12	20	21	15	32	38

Table 15.3 *(continued)*

Country and marital status	Total			Nonmigrants			Long-term migrants			Recent migrants		
	< 25	25–44	45+	< 25	25–44	45+	< 25	25–44	45+	< 25	25–44	45+
Thailand	33	53	32	31	55	34	36	51	31	42	48	26
Single	34	77	47	30	76	48	38	81	45	48	80	42
Married	30	45	34	33	47	36	29	44	33	24	38	28
Widowed	66	25	24	61[a]	75	25	63[a]	75	24	76[a]	72	19
Divorced	48	72	46	45	70	48	52	75	45	53	72	40

a. Fewer than 30 unweighted cases.

b. No cases in the cell.

c. The cell has some cases but no employed women.

grants. In Indonesia, for example, 32 percent of that group was in the labor force compared with 15 percent of their nonmigrant counterparts; the comparable figures for Korea are 50 percent and 24 percent. The participation rates of similarly defined long-term migrants seem to be intermediate between those of nonmigrants and recent migrants. The pattern of higher participation persists among single recent migrants aged 25 to 44, although the differences are much smaller. Among older single women (age 45 and above) in Malaysia and Pakistan, recent migrants have higher participation rates than nonmigrants, but this pattern is reversed in Indonesia and Thailand. Thus employment seems to have a significant influence on the migration of young, single, recent migrants in all the countries although the participation rates in Pakistan are much lower than in other countries. These findings are consistent with the trend toward increased female migration of young, single women to take up employment in the cities of Southeast Asia.

In all the countries, married recent migrants at all ages have lower participation rates than nonmigrants (Table 15.3). Differences by age are small for widowed women. One other subgroup for which participation rates are consistently higher among recent migrants than among nonmigrants is divorced women under age 45. Older (45 and above) divorced recent migrants are less likely to be in the labor force than older divorced nonmigrants in all countries except Pakistan. It is possible that older divorced women move in order to live with relatives rather than to take up employment; this speculation deserves exploration especially in light of findings from other studies (Youssef et al. 1979; United Nations 1980). These subgroups are generally very small, however, so the present findings must be interpreted with caution.

EMPLOYMENT BY EDUCATION AND MARITAL STATUS

Work participation varies within each country by level of education. Moreover, the work pattern too varies with education from country to country (Table 15.4). In Indonesia, for example, activity rates are significantly higher among the illiterate than among the educated; but in Malaysia it is the educated who are employed in larger proportions—36 percent of those with primary or higher education compared with 21 percent of the illiterate. These variations persist when migration status is controlled. Despite this overall variation, the subgroup of single illiterate women presents a highly consistent picture across countries. That is, single, illiterate, recent migrants have significantly higher participation rates than their nonmigrant counterparts. In Indonesia, 58 percent of these migrants are economically active compared with 30 percent of nonmigrants; comparable figures for Korea are 71 and 39 percent. Thus single illiterate women seem to represent a group whose need for employment is particularly great

Table 15.4 Female labor-force participation, by education and marital status for nonmigrants, long-term migrants, and recent migrants: Indonesia, Korea, Malaysia, Pakistan, Thailand

Country and marital status	Total			Nonmigrants			Long-term migrants			Recent migrants		
	Illiterate	Primary or less	More than primary	Illiterate	Primary or less	More than primary	Illiterate	Primary or less	More than primary	Illiterate	Primary or less	More than primary
Indonesia[a]	**32**	**20**	**22**	**33**	**19**	**20**	**30**	**22**	**25**	**42**	**27**	**22**
Single	35	19	20	30	16	17	37	30	25	58	37	26
Married	26	17	22	30	18	23	23	16	23	18	10	18
Widowed	36	41	45	36	44	48	35	38	43	46	43	29[c]
Divorced	60	51	48	55	51	50	63	46	48	72	61	35[c]
Korea[a]	**18**	**26**	**19**	**22**	**27**	**17**	**17**	**21**	**17**	**18**	**30**	**22**
Single	60	57	28	39	40	18	56	53	27	71	68	38
Married	18	12	10	22	15	12	18	13	9	15	10	9
Widowed	14	33	36	19	39	42	13	31	35	12	32	35
Divorced	60	60	49	85[c]	56[c]	43[c]	52[c]	52	42[c]	57[c]	66	55
Malaysia[a]	**21**	**23**	**36**	**21**	**22**	**32**	**21**	**20**	**39**	**19**	**30**	**44**
Single	40	29	33	36	26	30	52	30	37	52	41	45
Married	17	14	43	17	15	43	19	14	43	12	12	41
Widowed	19	26	46	20	25[c]	50[c]	19	25[c]	33[c]	18[c]	33[c]	57[c]
Divorced	40	47	58[c]	45[c]	37[c]	50[c]	44[c]	57[c]	67[c]	20[c]	75[c]	67[c]

Pakistan[a]	**4**	**3**	**9**	**3**	**2**	**7**	**4**	**4**	**12**	**4**	**5**	**8**
Single	3	2	8	3	1	7	7	3	17	5	5	8
Married	3	4	8	3	4	9	3	3	9	3	6	7
Widowed	8	13	20	7	13c	18	9	12	20	7	20c	18
Divorced	17	33	18	12	4c	32c	22	28c	16	25c	62c	21c
Thailand[b]	**34**	**40**	**43**	**35**	**38**	**41**	**33**	**42**	**50**	**34**	**46**	**37**
Single	51	41	35	49	35	34	53	50	43	63	60	31
Married	35	37	58	35	40	61	35	37	59	30	28	47
Widowed	23	52	60	24	53	60	24	50	55	17	53	81
Divorced	50	63	70	53	60	70	47	68	67	49	63	72

a. For Indonesia, Korea, and Malaysia educational levels are: no grades, grades 1–6, and grade 7 and above.

b. For Pakistan and Thailand educational levels are: illiterate, ≤ grade 7, and grade 8 and above.

c. Fewer than 30 unweighted cases.

and migration helps in meeting that need. For women in other marital statuses the differences in activity rates are neither as consistent nor as significant as among the single.

In all countries, married recent migrants at all educational levels have lower participation rates than similar nonmigrants. It seems that married migrants have a lesser need for work than single women. Married women probably move with their husbands who are likely to be the principal breadwinners. Another explanation for the lower activity rates of married recent migrants is the possibility that their economic activity may be reported less often than the activity of single, widowed, and divorced women. Underreporting is likely to be particularly severe when it is the husband who responds to the labor force questions. It is not clear, however, whether married migrants are any more likely to underreport such activity than married nonmigrants. The lower participation rates of married migrant women, even among the illiterate, seem to contradict the hypothesis about higher participation among migrant women whose husbands are in low-paying jobs.

The pattern for widowed and divorced women varies by country. In Indonesia, larger proportions of the illiterate divorced and widowed who are recent migrants are in the labor force than among nonmigrants. In Korea, recent migrant divorcees of all educational levels have consistently lower participation rates than their nonmigrant counterparts. Educated, divorced, recent migrant women in Malaysia have notably higher participation rates than nonmigrants, but their numbers are too small in our data to warrant further comment. In Thailand, the only subgroup having a higher participation rate among recent migrants than nonmigrants is widowed women with more than a primary school education.

Thus participation rates vary considerably from country to country when educational level is controlled together with marital status. The only consistent patterns are the higher participation of illiterate, single, recent migrants and the lower participation of recent married migrants—both compared with nonmigrants. Participation rates of educated and uneducated widowed and divorced women vary from country to country. These patterns are probably the result of cultural constraints on work by certain subgroups and the forces of demand and supply that apparently differ for women of diverse marital and educational status.

HOUSEHOLD HEADSHIP

In recent years considerable attention has been given to the prevalence of female-headed households as an aspect of women's role and status. Buvinic et al. (1978) found that about 18 percent of the households they studied in 74 countries contained "potential" female household heads; the figure for Asia was 15 percent.[3] They estimated the proportion of potential female household heads to be 23 percent for Indonesia, 21 percent for Korea, and 17 percent for Thailand. When we calculated the percentages of females aged ten and over who were reported to be household heads, we found the proportions to be much smaller. Some 7 percent of all women in Indonesia and Korea, 9 percent in Thailand, 10 percent in Malaysia, and 2 percent in Pakistan were reported as household heads. Among widowed and divorced women, however, one-third to one-half were reported as household heads. The figures of Buvinic and colleagues and our own are not strictly comparable because they have different denominators, but they do provide a basis for comparison of actual versus potential female headship. The literature on the subject suggests that women who are heads of household are likely to be more migratory than other females. Female heads are also much more likely to enter the labor force than others. For the five countries in this study, seven times as many heads as nonheads are in the labor force in Pakistan and 1.2 to 2.7 times as many in the other four countries. In all countries, single household heads have particularly high participation rates compared with single nonheads.

When we compare recent migrant heads of household with nonmigrant heads, the differences are not very great (Table 15.5). The significant difference is that obtaining between heads and nonheads, regardless of migration status. In all countries except Korea, recent migrant heads are somewhat more likely to be in the labor force than nonmigrant heads. When marital status is controlled in addition to headship, the numbers are generally too small to allow meaningful conclusions. Headship apparently involves a pressing demand for employment; large numbers of migrant as well as nonmigrant women who head households enter the labor force. Furthermore, the female head herself is likely to be the respondent in the survey gathering labor-force information. Because she is likely to give more accurate information about her economic activity than a male household head would give, we can expect that the labor-force participation of female heads is more accurately reported than that of female nonheads.

UNEMPLOYMENT RATES

If migrants have a greater need for jobs, lower wage aspiration, and fewer reservations about the type of work they do and the number of hours they are required to work, then they should have lower unemployment rates. Table 15.6 shows that migrants have consistently lower unemployment rates than the nonmigrants in the four countries surveyed. (Pakistan was not included in Table 15.6 because of data problems.) This finding holds true at all educational levels. Larger proportions of the educated women, however, among both migrants and nonmigrants, reported themselves to be unemployed. This finding points again to the importance of a person's need for a job, which is likely to be greater among the illiterate and poor

Table 15.5 Female labor-force participation, by headship and marital status for nonmigrants, long-term migrants, and recent migrants: Indonesia, Korea, Malaysia, Pakistan, Thailand

Country and marital status	Total[a]		Nonmigrants		Long-term migrants		Recent migrants		% H/% NH
	H	NH	H	NH	H	NH	H	NH	
Indonesia	56.9	21.3	56.3	20.0	58.0	22.2	53.0	27.0	2.7
Single	62.8	20.1	55.5	16.6	79.8	27.2	42.2[b]	34.2	3.1
Married	46.3	20.5	40.4[b]	22.1	52.1	19.7	40.6[b]	14.5	2.3
Widowed	54.7	24.6	54.5	24.4	55.0	22.0	54.2[b]	41.3	2.2
Divorced	67.3	47.0	67.8	45.1	66.5	44.5	69.0[b]	61.0	1.4
Korea	44.1	20.2	52.2	19.3	41.8	16.8	43.1	23.4	2.2
Single	65.5	37.3	71.4[b]	24.1	58.1	34.7	66.2	50.3	1.8
Married	38.2	11.0	51.2	13.6	37.2	11.9	34.8	9.3	3.5
Widowed	41.8	9.9	49.2	12.2	41.0	8.4	38.8	10.7	4.2
Divorced	56.1	56.5	69.2[b]	48.6	55.7	41.4	52.7	67.6	1.0
Malaysia	30.7	25.5	28.1	24.7	30.7	24.6	40.6	29.7	1.2
Single	73.6	30.9	73.0	28.0	68.6	34.0	77.0	42.0	2.4
Married	23.5	19.1	21.0	19.2	26.5	19.6	27.1	17.8	1.2
Widowed	27.2	15.6	26.9	15.1	27.6	11.6	28.0[b]	21.0[b]	1.7
Divorced	47.6	41.2	44.9	36.0[b]	44.4[b]	60.0[b]	80.0[b]	37.5[b]	1.2

Pakistan	26.7	3.8	21.5	3.2	27.8	4.5	58.0	4.6	7.0
Single	71.0	3.6	53.9	2.9	78.0	9.0	24.7	4.7	20.3
Married	22.0	3.6	18.9	3.4	24.4	3.6	74.5b	4.0	6.1
Widowed	23.6	5.9	20.1	5.4	25.9	5.9	77.7b	8.4	4.0
Divorced	45.9	17.6	53.4b	10.9	41.2b	18.2	50.0b	28.0	2.6
Thailand	56.8	38.2	56.8	37.2	55.0	39.0	66.2	40.8	1.5
Single	78.3	39.0	76.0	35.2	82.1	45.6	78.2	50.1	2.0
Married	55.2	38.7	58.1	41.1	53.0	38.5	51.6	31.4	1.4
Widowed	45.2	15.9	45.5	17.6	45.0	12.2	45.2	22.0	2.8
Divorced	69.0	51.2	69.8	50.7	68.5	50.6	67.8	53.9	1.4

a. H—head; NH—nonhead.

b. Fewer than 30 unweighted cases.

Table 15.6 Percentage unemployed among females ten years old and over, by education and migration status: Indonesia, Korea, Malaysia, Thailand

Country and education	Total	Nonmigrants	Long-term migrants	Recent migrants
Indonesia	8	10	6	5
No grades	5	6	4	2[a]
Up to primary	8	11	5	3[a]
Above primary	11	14	9	10
Korea	5	7	5	4
No grades	1	1[a]	1[a]	1[a]
Up to primary	3	5	3	3
Above primary	8	10	9	7
Malaysia	14	16	9	10
No grades	5	6[a]	3[a]	3[a]
Up to primary	11	14	5[a]	7[a]
Above primary	20	24	17	15
Thailand	4	5	2	4
No grades	2	2	1	3
Up to primary	4	5	2	3
Above primary	6	7	4	7

Note: Unemployment is defined as participation in the labor force but not being employed during the week prior to survey.

a. Fewer than 30 unweighted cases.

than among the educated. It also reflects the general oversupply of educated labor that pervades Asia. When unemployment rates are examined in relation to headship status, women who were household heads had very low unemployment rates compared with nonheads. This was true for women at all educational levels and in all countries (data not shown). Thus, as stated earlier, headship seems to intensify the need for a job and results in high participation rates and low unemployment rates.

Occupational Structures and Migrant Status

One objective of this study is to compare the occupational structures of migrants and nonmigrants. Table 15.7 summarizes the occupational structures for four of the five countries. (Pakistan was again excluded because of data problems.) Migrant women are again divided into long-term and recent and the two groups are compared with nonmigrant women.

One of the most striking differences between recent migrant and nonmigrant females in all countries is the heavy concentration of recent migrants

Table 15.7 Summary of occupational structure of nonmigrant, long-term migrant, and recent migrant females: Indonesia, Korea, Malaysia, Thailand

Country and migration status	Unweighted no.	Total %	Major occupations (%)					
			Professional, administrative, clerical[a]	Sales	Farming	Production, transport, mining[b]	Service	Domestic[c]
Indonesia								
Nonmigrants	8,711	100.0	15.5	35.6	13.3	17.4	18.3	(11.6)
Long-term migrants	3,337	100.0	16.5	40.9	6.1	12.5	22.1	(15.2)
Recent migrants	858	100.0	18.6	18.9	3.3[d]	10.0	50.0	(45.0)
Korea								
Nonmigrants	5,658	100.0	15.4	24.5	11.2	27.0	21.9	(9.7)
Long-term migrants	2,340	100.0	11.1	30.8	12.1	26.1	19.8	(8.2)
Recent migrants	3,564	100.0	13.8	18.0	3.0	25.6	39.6	(26.4)
Malaysia								
Nonmigrants	3,781	100.0	25.5	8.0	10.3	37.1	19.1	(11.4)
Long-term migrants	771	100.0	27.7	9.3	12.2	30.9	19.8	(11.8)
Recent migrants	803	100.0	28.2	4.5	2.1	31.6	33.5	(23.3)
Thailand								
Nonmigrants	39,752	100.0	19.4	33.1	7.1	23.6	16.8	(4.7)
Long-term migrants	17,607	100.0	19.4	34.3	2.7	21.5	22.2	(7.5)
Recent migrants	11,600	100.0	18.0	19.1	4.1	20.4	38.3	(24.6)

a. Includes the following broad groups: professional, technical, and related; administrative, executive, and managerial; and clerical and related.
b. Includes miners, quarryworkers, well drillers, and related occupations; transport equipment operators; and all production-related workers.
c. Cooks and maids in domestic service only.
d. Fewer than 30 unweighted cases.

in the service workers category. In Indonesia the proportion of persons in service work was more than two and a half times greater among recent migrants than among nonmigrants—50 percent versus 18 percent. In the other three countries, the proportion was almost doubled. Some 40 percent of all recent migrants in Korea, 34 percent in Malaysia, and 38 percent in Thailand were employed as service workers. The majority of service workers in each country consisted of cooks and private maids—in other words, domestic servants. As noted earlier, domestic services constitute an important sector that absorbs many migrants, especially in Latin America and Asia. The data analyzed in this study clearly support this generalization.

It should also be noted that only the recent migrants are concentrated in the service sector. The percentage of long-term migrants in this sector is not very different from that of nonmigrants. In Thailand and Indonesia rather more of the long-term migrants than nonmigrants were in service occupations, but the differences are relatively small. Perhaps this finding implies that as migrants become settled in their new environments they are able to move out of service occupations into other work such as sales. It is difficult to specify this process in the absence of adequate longitudinal data, however, and the collection of such data is an important research priority. What does seem clear is that in all countries the occupational structures of the long-term migrants are much more similar to those of the nonmigrants than to those of recent migrants. Nonmigrants and long-term migrants were concentrated in either sales occupations or handicrafts, although the amount of concentration varied from country to country.

Besides domestic service, production and related work also absorbed substantial numbers of both migrant and nonmigrant women. Almost one-third of the Malaysian, one-fourth of the Korean, and one-fifth of the Thai recent migrants were engaged in these activities. When the professional, administrative, and clerical workers are grouped together there are only small differences between migrants and nonmigrants within each country. More of the nonmigrants and long-term migrants were in sales occupations than were recent migrants. Similarly, fewer of the recent migrants than nonmigrants were in agricultural occupations. Recent migrant males, unlike the females, were not concentrated in the service sector. In fact, the occupational structures of recent migrant and nonmigrant males were quite similar to each other in most countries (data not shown).

SUMMARY AND CONCLUSION

We have analyzed census data from five Asian countries to study the patterns of labor-force participation of migrant and nonmigrant females. Migrants were divided into two groups, long-term and recent, on the basis of their length of residence. The analysis was restricted to urban areas only. We found that recent migrant women were more likely to be in the labor force than were nonmigrant women, whereas the participation rates of long-term migrants were quite similar to those of nonmigrants.

Certain patterns of labor-force participation resulted when we controlled the four factors hypothesized as constraining or promoting participation (age, marital status, education, and household headship). When age and marital status were controlled, young, single, recent migrants had a consistently higher labor-force participation rate than their nonmigrant counterparts. Married recent migrants, in contrast, had consistently lower participation rates than nonmigrants in all age and educational categories. Relatively young (under 45) divorced recent migrants had higher participation rates whereas the rates of widowed recent migrants were not very different from those of their nonmigrant counterparts.

Women who were household heads had consistently higher participation rates than nonheads among both migrants and nonmigrants. Among women who were heads, there were differences by country between migrants and nonmigrants. In Indonesia and Korea, fewer of the recent migrant heads were employed; in the other countries considerably more of the recent migrant heads were in the labor force than were nonmigrant heads. The percentage of recent migrants who were heads was generally quite small, however.

Thus the groups that had higher participation rates among recent migrants seem typically to be those who had the greatest economic need for employment—young single women and divorced women, particularly those who were heads of household. Single and divorced women were more likely to be autonomous migrants than married women, and they were more likely to move to urban areas in search of employment. We speculate that more of the recent migrant married women can afford to remain out of the labor force because they have husbands to support them. Furthermore, it is likely that single and divorced (unattached) recent migrants are less particular about the types of jobs they are willing to take up. It is probably for such reasons that the unemployment rate of migrants was consistently lower than that of nonmigrants. Moreover, the high concentration of recent migrant employed women in service occupations, such as cooks and private maids, suggests that migrant women are more willing to work in these low-paying jobs than are nonmigrants.

Half of all recent migrant females in Indonesia and more than one-third in Korea, Malaysia, and Thailand were employed as service workers, compared with much smaller proportions among nonmigrants and long-term migrants. Our findings about recent migrants are consistent with those from earlier studies in Latin America that found a high concentration of recent female migrants in domestic service. If the current occupational structure of long-term migrants is any guide, it is likely that many of the recent migrants will be able to move out of domestic service into other occupations such as sales and handicrafts. This process can be analyzed adequately, however, only with longitudinal studies or reliable occupational histories of female migrants in cities.

It might be reasonable to conclude from the available information that recent female migrants fill very specific vacancies in the urban occupational structure—vacancies that are usually low-paid, demand long hours of work, and are in most cases beyond the protection of labor unions or government regulation. It may be the very existence of such vacancies that encourages female migration. The extent to which migrant female workers actually gain from their migration and entry into such occupations is beyond the scope of this study but remains an important question.

NOTES

1. The problem of measurement may be particularly serious in countries where social norms do not support female labor-force participation. Furthermore, male respondents, who are usually the suppliers of information for censuses, may underreport participation rates more often than female respondents. For an example of such a bias from Pakistan, see Shah and Shah (1980). For a comparative analysis of sex biases in reporting economic activity, see De Souza (1980).

2. Researchers analyzing Malaysian data usually disaggregate the country into its Chinese, Malay, and Indian ethnic groups. Although we recognize significant differences among these ethnic groups, we have not analyzed them separately—primarily because of the small number of cases we would have to work with and also because we want to compare Malaysia as a whole with other countries. The participation rates (percentages) for Chinese, Malays, and other women are as follows:

Group	Nonmigrants	Long-term migrants	Recent migrants
Chinese	28	30	40
Malays	19	20	24
Others	17	18	21

3. They defined "potential" female heads as all adult widowed, divorced, or separated women and single mothers as a proportion of the total "potential" male heads, who were defined as all adult males ever married (Buvinic et al. 1978:37–38).

REFERENCES

Buvinic, Mayra, Nadia Youssef, and Barbara Von Elm
    1978   Women headed households: the ignored factor in development planning. (Mimeographed.) Washington, D.C.: International Center for Research on Women, Agency for International Development.

Chaudhury, Rafiq-ul-Huda
1979 Marriage, urban women and the labour force: the Bangladesh case. *Signs* 5(1):154–63.

De Souza, Stan
1980 The data base for studies on women: sex biases in national data systems. In Alfred de Souza (ed.), *Women in Contemporary India and South Asia*. New Delhi: Indian Social Institute.

Ibarra, Teresita
1980 Domestic helpers in metropolitan Manila as migrants: an exploratory study. Paper presented at the 11th Summer Seminar in Population, East-West Population Institute, Honolulu.

Jelin, Elizabeth
1977 Migration and labor force participation of Latin American women: the domestic servants in the cities. In Wellesley Editorial Committee (ed.), *Women and National Development*. Chicago: University of Chicago Press.

Korson, J. Henry
1970 Career constraints among women graduate students in a developing society. *Journal of Comparative Family Studies* 1(1):82–100.

Mazumdar, Dipak
1979 *Paradigms in the Study of Urban Labor Markets in LDCs: A Reassessment in the Light of an Empirical Survey in Bombay City.* World Bank Staff Working Paper No. 366. Washington, D.C.

Papanek, Hanna
1971 Purdah in Pakistan: seclusion and modern occupations for women. *Journal of Marriage and the Family* 33(3):517–30.

Piampiti, Suwanlee
1980 Female migrants of selected service occupational groups in Bangkok Metropolis. Paper presented at the 11th Summer Seminar in Population, East-West Population Institute, Honolulu.

Shah, Nasra M., and Makhdoom A. Shah
1980 Trends and structure of female labour force participation in rural and urban Pakistan. In Alfred de Souza (ed.), *Women in Contemporary India and South Asia*. New Delhi: Indian Social Institute.

Singh, Andrea Menefee
1978 Rural-urban migration of women among the urban poor in India: causes and consequences. *Social Action* 28(4):326–56.

Smith, Peter C., and Virginia Crockett
1980 Some demographic dimensions of occupations: research implications from an urban Thailand case study. Paper presented at the Meeting on Intermediate Cities in Asia, East-West Population Institute, Honolulu.

Standing, Guy
1978a Aspiration wages, migration and urban unemployment. *Journal of Development Studies* 14(2):232–48.
1978b *Labour Force Participation and Development.* Geneva: International Labour Office.

Standing, Guy, and Glen Sheehan
  1976   *Labour Force Participation in Sri Lanka.* (Mimeographed.) Geneva: International Labour Office.
  1978   *Labour Force Participation in Low Income Countries.* Geneva: International Labour Office.

Sudarkasa, Niara
  1977   Women and migration in contemporary West Africa. In Wellesley Editorial Committee (ed.), *Women and National Development.* Chicago: University of Chicago Press.

Suharso et al.
  1975   *Migration and Education in Jakarta.* Leknas-Lipi: National Institute of Economic and Social Research, Indonesian Institute of Sciences.

United Nations
  1980   *Patterns of Urban and Rural Population Growth.* Population Studies, No. 68. New York.

Youssef, Nadia, Mayra Buvinic, and Ayse Kudat
  1979   *Women in Migration: A Third World Focus.* (Mimeographed.) Washington, D.C.: International Center for Research on Women.

Zachariah, K. C.
  1968   *Migrants in Greater Bombay.* Research Monograph No. 5. Bombay: Demographic Training and Research Centre.

Chapter 16

Female Asian Immigrants in Honolulu: Adaptation and Success

Robert W. Gardner
Paul A. Wright

In the 60 years preceding the Great Depression, immigration from Asia was the major source of Hawaii's population growth. Between 1930 and 1965, this flow was reduced to a trickle because the demand for plantation labor dropped and legal restrictions tightly controlled the number of Asian immigrants entering the United States. Since 1965, as a result of changes in the immigration law, Asian immigration has once again become a significant component of population growth in Hawaii. Of the recent immigrants, nearly three-fifths have been females, thus reversing the pattern of earlier days when a large proportion of the immigrants were males, mostly destined for agricultural work on the plantations.

At least nine-tenths of the foreign-born Asians in the state of Hawaii are Chinese, Filipino, Japanese, or Korean.[1] This study focuses on the female immigrants of these four groups living in the City and County of Honolulu,[2] where more than four-fifths of the foreign-born Asians in Hawaii, as well as four-fifths of the total state population, live. With the use of data from a 1975 sample survey, the following central questions are addressed:

1. How do female Asian immigrants fare economically and socially compared with U.S.-born females having similar characteristics?
2. How do female Asian immigrants fare economically and socially compared with male Asian immigrants having similar characteristics?
3. Are there differences among female Asian immigrants of the different ethnic groups and between the recent (1965–75) female arrivals and earlier female immigrants?

The analysis is in two parts. First, we examine several variables that give a general description of Honolulu's population, especially the immigrants. Included here are variables that can be hypothesized to be the major determinants of immigrant success and adaptation. Second, we examine several measures of success and adaptation, both singly and in combination, controlling for the effects of the other variables when possible. This analysis will allow us to say what factors seem to be most important in determining the success and adaptation of female Asian immigrants in Honolulu.

The literature on adaptation of migrants, which is voluminous and well known, will not be reviewed here.[3] For the purposes of this study, adaptation is defined as the "success" (in the form of labor-force participation, employment, occupation, and income) enjoyed by immigrants compared with that of the native-born population when one controls for objective factors assumed to contribute to success (education and occupational training, for example). In this study we are somewhat constrained by the nature of the data, which come from a survey not specifically designed to study migrant adaptation. The data provide no subjective impressions of adaptation, happiness, or success of the migrants themselves, for example, nor do they allow comparisons with the prior situations of the migrants or with those individuals left behind. (See Goldlust and Richmond, 1974, for a discussion of objective and subjective dimensions of migrant adaptation.)

Nevertheless, we are able to draw a fairly clear picture of the objective aspects of migrant adaptation in Honolulu for two reasons. First, the survey did collect data on several crucial variables, especially income, which is our basic measure of success; second, we can compare various migrant and nonmigrant groups to determine their relative standings for these variables. Thus, insofar as "adaptation" implies a coming together of certain migrant and local-born characteristics, we can use our data to examine the three questions posed earlier.

The data were obtained from a 5 percent sample survey of all households on Oahu conducted by a local survey firm in April 1975 for the U.S. Office of Equal Opportunity (SMS 1976). This survey questionnaire was similar to the 1970 U.S. census questionnaire, but, unlike the census, it included a question on the length of residence in Hawaii. We are thus able to distinguish recent from earlier arrivals, an impossible task with census data.

THE FOREIGN-BORN POPULATION OF HAWAII

Before we examine the basic descriptive data of the population of Honolulu in 1975, it is important to discuss one distinctive feature of Hawaii demography—the large military population. In 1975, almost one-fifth of the estimated 704,500 Oahu residents were associated with the military (serving in the armed forces or dependents of such persons). Because few persons in the military community come to Hawaii voluntarily and almost all depart at the end of one or two tours of duty, only individuals unrelated to the military are considered in the following discussion. Military-related individuals constituted about 7 percent of all foreign-born Asians on Oahu in 1975, including 9 percent of foreign-born Asian females.

The estimated nonmilitary (hereafter called "civilian") population of Oahu in 1975 was approximately 556,000 (Table 16.1). Almost half of this total and nearly 80 percent of the foreign-born were "Asian" (i.e. Chinese, Filipino, Japanese, and Korean). Recent (1965–75) Asian immigrants comprised 55 percent of all Asian immigrants, and females made up 55 percent of those recent arrivals.

The Japanese are by far the most numerous of the Asian groups, but among all foreign-born Asian females nearly half are Filipino and among the recent immigrant Asian females almost 60 percent are Filipino. These figures reflect the historical patterns of migration to Hawaii (Nordyke 1977). The Japanese arrived in large numbers but much earlier than the Filipinos, who have been coming in large numbers since the change in the U.S. immigration law in 1965.

Whereas the typical recent Asian immigrant is a young adult, the average long-term Asian immigrant, not surprisingly, is near or past retirement age. But whereas the median age of the long-term male immigrant is 65 years, the corresponding median among the long-term females is only 53 years (data not shown). By contrast, the median age of the recent female Asian immigrants is 29, somewhat higher than the male figure of 26 years. These age differentials reflect past patterns in which males migrated first and later sent for spouses. More recently, many of the females have married servicemen abroad and come to Hawaii with their spouses when military service, often lasting many years after the initial marriage, is completed.

RESIDENTIAL CONCENTRATION

Residential clustering of a group's members can be interpreted as a sign that the group has not assimilated into society at large or as evidence of discrimination by society. Although Hawaii enjoys a largely deserved reputation of having nonsegregated neighborhoods, Asian immigrants, especially the most recent, are clustered in only a few neighborhoods.

Among the recent immigrants the Filipinos are the most residentially concentrated and the Japanese the least. Some 65 percent of recent Filipino immigrants but only 37 percent of their Japanese counterparts aged 18 and over live in census tracts in which recent Filipino and Japanese immigrants, respectively, constitute more than three times their share of the Oahu population.[4] Furthermore, as evidenced by the residential concentration of immigrants living in Hawaii for more than ten years, the rate of dispersal is much more rapid among Japanese than among Filipinos.

Table 16.1 Civilian population (in thousands) by ethnicity, sex, place of birth, and years in Hawaii: Oahu, 1975

Ethnicity	Total population					% of ethnic group				Sex ratio[a]			
	Total	Foreign-born by years in Hawaii			U.S.-born	Foreign-born by years in Hawaii			U.S.-born	Foreign-born by years in Hawaii			U.S.-born
		Total	0–10	11+		Total	0–10	11+		Total	0–10	11+	
Total	565.7	77.5	45.5	30.9	480.2	13.7	8.0	5.5	84.9	89	79	110	105
Male	283.9	37.3	20.6	16.2	242.1								
Female	281.7	40.2	24.9	14.8	238.1								
Total Asian	275.8	61.0	33.7	26.3	212.8	22.1	12.2	9.5	77.2	93	81	114	101
Male	137.6	29.6	15.1	14.0	107.0								
Female	138.2	31.4	18.7	12.3	105.9								
Chinese	37.8	7.3	4.4	2.7	30.0	19.4	11.6	7.1	80.2	78	75	83	103
Male	18.7	3.2	1.9	1.2	15.4								
Female	19.1	4.1	2.5	1.5	14.9								
Filipino	63.9	33.8	21.0	12.6	28.9	52.9	32.9	19.7	45.2	126	90	222	101
Male	34.1	18.7	9.9	8.7	14.5								
Female	29.9	15.0	11.1	3.9	14.4								
Japanese	164.8	15.7	5.0	10.1	148.6	9.4	3.0	6.1	90.2	61	62	61	100
Male	80.4	5.9	1.9	3.8	74.3								
Female	84.3	9.7	3.1	6.3	74.3								
Korean	9.3	4.2	3.3	0.9	5.1	45.2	35.5	9.7	54.8	63	67	52	122
Male	4.4	1.6	1.3	0.3	2.8								
Female	4.9	2.6	2.0	0.6	2.3								

Note: Not all totals equal the sum of parts because some questions (such as years in Hawaii) were not always answered, some respondents were born in U.S. possessions, and fractions were rounded.

a. Sex ratio = M/F X 100.

(Fifty percent of Filipinos and less than 7 percent of Japanese living in Hawaii for more than ten years reside in census tracts in which they account for more than three times their respective shares of the Oahu population.) In fact, whereas areas containing the highest concentrations of immigrant Filipino adults are the same as or immediately adjacent to those of high concentrations of U.S.-born Filipinos, the areas of high concentrations of given immigrant Oriental groups are generally distant from those of their U.S.-born counterparts.

Among the recent Oriental immigrants, males are residentially more concentrated than females. Among Japanese adults, who represent an extreme case, 50 percent of males but only 31 percent of females live in census tracts in which the recent Japanese immigrant adults comprise more than three times their overall proportion on Oahu. This phenomenon is at least in part the result of the higher percentage of Oriental females who are married to U.S.-born spouses. In contrast, the recent Filipino male and female immigrants show the same degree of residential concentration, notwithstanding the great numbers of females among them. Many of the Filipino females are married to Filipino males who migrated earlier.

Although we cannot give a more detailed discussion of residential concentration here, it is worthwhile to note that public housing areas contain high concentrations of Filipino, Chinese, and Korean, but not of Japanese, recent immigrants. These concentrations reflect poverty rather than voluntary choices.

Concentrations of native-born Chinese and Koreans in upper-middle- to upper-class areas and concentrations of native-born Japanese in middle- to upper-middle-class areas (predominately single-family housing), provide dramatic evidence of the material success enjoyed by many offspring of Oriental immigrants. However, the concentration of U.S.-born Filipino adults in lower- to lower-middle-class areas reflects both a much slower rate of upward mobility among the Filipinos and the fact that their Filipino immigrant forbears arrived more recently than did those of the Chinese and Japanese.

EDUCATIONAL ATTAINMENT

There is an American myth that anyone can rise to the top of the social and economic scale, but in reality a good education is generally essential if "success" is to be attained. In Table 16.2 we look at the educational attainment of the various groups. It should be kept in mind that this table does not tell us where the education was received; a person could have studied only abroad, in the United States, or in some combination of the two sites. Because most immigrants come to Honolulu as adults, however, it is probable that most of them received their formal education in their home countries.

Table 16.2 Percentage distribution of the civilian population 25 years old and over, by schooling, place of birth, years in Hawaii, and sex: Oahu, 1975

| Years of schooling | Foreign-born Asians by years in Hawaii | | | | | | U.S.-born Asians | | All persons | |
| | Total | | 0–10 | | 11+ | | | | | |
	M	F	M	F	M	F	M	F	M	F
Under 8	45	36	24	30	59	43	6	8	11	11
8–11	14	14	11	11	16	17	17	17	16	16
12	16	25	18	26	15	25	39	42	33	39
13–15	11	12	17	14	6	10	18	17	18	18
16+	15	14	30	20	5	6	21	17	22	17
Total	101	101	100	101	101	101	101	101	100	101

Note: Percentages may not sum to 100 because of rounding.

Foreign-born Asian females tend to have a much lower educational attainment than U.S.-born Asian females. They are characterized by a much higher percentage of grade-school dropouts and a lower percentage of college graduates. The recent female arrivals on the whole are much better educated than their predecessors, however, and a higher percentage of them than of the U.S.-born Asian females hold college degrees. Nonetheless, almost 30 percent of the recent female arrivals but only 8 percent of the U.S.-born Asian females did not complete eight years of formal education.

Compared with their male counterparts, foreign-born Asian females tend to have lower proportions at both extremes of educational attainment. Among the long-term immigrants, the females tend to be better educated. They were generally much younger than the husbands who sent for them and were thus beneficiaries of improving educational systems in their home countries. In contrast, among the recent immigrants, males tend to be considerably better educated than their female counterparts. A common case is the college-educated professional who is granted an immigrant visa and brings his less well educated wife with him.

Among the long-term female immigrants, all ethnic groups are characterized by low educational levels. Among the recent arrivals, the Japanese females are unique in that few are either highly or poorly educated. More than 60 percent have completed exactly 12 years of schooling, fewer than 10 percent have a college degree, and fewer than 5 percent are grade-school dropouts. The recent Filipino immigrants display the opposite pattern: Only about 12 percent have completed exactly 12 years, 20 percent did not complete grade school, and 22 percent completed four or more years of college.

In summary, female Asian immigrants are less well educated than U.S.-born Asian females, largely because of the poor education of the early arrivals. Compared with their male counterparts, fewer of them have college degrees. They are also less likely to be grade-school dropouts. Recent arrivals on average are much better educated than the early migrants.

MARRIAGE PATTERNS

Marriage patterns of interest here include the age at marriage—because it is related to a person's educational and occupational attainment and fertility—and intermarriage, which can be viewed as an indicator of assimilation or adaptation. One striking feature of the U.S.-born Oriental population in Hawaii is the late average age at first marriage. Late marriage is conducive to economic success because it reduces the number of potential children, facilitates the gaining of higher education and work experience, and increases the potential economic resources that can be brought into a marriage. For U.S.-born Oriental females, this late marriage represents at least partly an adjustment to local conditions, as indicated by the finding that marriages generally take place two to four years earlier in the countries of origin.

Asian immigrants are characterized by singulate mean ages at marriage (SMAMs) that are similar to those existing in the countries of origin; Filipino SMAMs, for example, are about two years lower than Oriental levels.[5] If delayed marriage among females promotes their economic success, the immigrant Oriental females have an advantage over their Filipino counterparts in this respect. Whereas the SMAM of U.S.-born Oriental females (27.2 years) is 2.6 years higher than that of the female Oriental immigrants, the corresponding difference is only a year among Filipino females. This finding suggests a slower move toward "economic maximization" among native-born Filipinos.

In patterns of out-marriage, the three Oriental groups again display characteristics quite distinct from those of the Filipinos. Among Oriental females residing in Hawaii ten years or less, fewer than half have foreign-born spouses (almost invariably of the same ethnicity), more than a quarter have Hawaii-born husbands and two-ninths have mainland-born (almost invariably Caucasian) spouses. In contrast, seven-eighths of the Oriental males living in Hawaii ten years or less have foreign-born spouses and only a twentieth have mainland spouses. Among the Filipinos, almost all immigrants of both sexes have foreign-born (Filipino) spouses.

Among Oriental immigrants living in Hawaii ten or more years, three-fifths of the males and five-eighths of the females have Hawaii-born spouses. (Most of the widowed in this group were undoubtedly married to foreign-born spouses, for almost all Japanese and Korean women arriving in Hawaii prior to 1924 migrated with husbands or were "picture brides" —brides chosen through a system of supplying photographs of potential wives to men already in Hawaii). In contrast, 68 percent of the long-term Filipino immigrants and 86 percent of their female counterparts have foreign-born spouses. A high proportion of Filipino immigrant males took Hawaii-born spouses because of the shortage of immigrant Filipino women that existed prior to World War II.

Many of the marriages of female Oriental immigrants to mainland-born husbands undoubtedly took place when the spouses were serving abroad in the military. In the sense that mainland-born individuals who moved to Hawaii are "outsiders" in the local culture, marriages to mainland-born spouses do not suggest a significant assimilation into the local society, although they do undoubtedly facilitate the learning of American values.

In summary, then, if the patterns of out-marriage are accurate indicators of assimilation, the Filipino immigrants are assimilating far less rapidly than their Oriental counterparts, regardless of sex or time lived in Hawaii. Even the U.S.-born Orientals seem more "local" than their U.S.-born Filipino counterparts in that a much higher proportion have Hawaii-born mates. Among the Oriental immigrants, the females appear to assimilate more than the males. The reverse, however, appears to be true for the Filipino immigrants.

MEASURES OF SUCCESS AND ADAPTATION

In this section we consider three measures of success, all economic: employment status (working or not), occupation (concentrating on three key occupational categories), and median income (the most easily quantified measure of success in the modern world, if not the best from all points of view). We first view these variables separately for Asians as a whole and then discuss them for each ethnic group. We next investigate the factors that seem related to differences in occupation and income among the immigrant and U.S.-born male and female Asians.

EMPLOYMENT STATUS

Since 1960, increasing proportions of American women have entered the labor force. Because of high living costs in Hawaii, the female labor participation rate is the highest in the United States. Partly because of the rapid increase in the number of females in the state's labor force, the unemployment rate in Hawaii since 1970 has usually exceeded the national average.

We consider the labor-force participation and unemployment rates only of people between ages 18 and 64, because those below the age of 18 are in school and most above the age of 64 are retired. We also treat age groups

18–24 and 25–64 separately, as many in the former group are attending college or are handicapped by inexperience in gaining and holding employment, and most women above age 25 are married and many have children.

Among young adults (ages 18 to 24), Asian immigrants of both sexes show labor-force participation rates (the proportion of a group that is working or seeking work) quite similar to the rates of the total population (data not shown). Recent arrivals, especially females, show lower rates, whereas the rates of long-term female Asian immigrants are the highest of any group. This finding may reflect a progressive weakening of cultural norms against women entering the labor force, a change brought on at least in part by financial necessity.

Young adult Asian immigrants do not seem to be particularly disadvantaged, compared with U.S.-born Asians, in proportions unemployed and unemployment rates. In fact, immigrant rates of unemployment are lower than the level for the total population between the ages of 18 and 24. That many of the U.S.-born in this age group are seeking employment for the first time reduces their advantage over the immigrants.

Long-term young adult Asian immigrants have especially low unemployment rates, perhaps because of their favorable attitudes toward accepting any employment, combined with a knowledge of "local ways" learned from growing up in Hawaii. Among the young immigrants, both recent and long-term, the females are characterized by proportions unemployed and unemployment rates similar to those of males. In general, however, we find few marked differentials among young members of the Honolulu labor force.

In the age group 25–64, we find that compared with the younger group, participation rates are higher for males and lower for females no matter what their migration status (Table 16.3). This finding reflects a pattern of males entering the labor force after school and training and females leaving the labor force for marriage and children. Nevertheless, impressively high proportions of females of all categories are in the labor force.

Female adult Asian immigrants show a participation rate close to that of the total population but somewhat lower than that for U.S.-born Asian females. As is true for the younger adults, the long-term adult immigrants have higher participation rates than the more recent arrivals. For females, however, the difference is small.

Regarding unemployment in the 25–64 age group, we find that whereas foreign-born males have slightly lower rates than the general population, female immigrants have higher rates. In fact, no matter what the status of the group, female unemployment rates are higher than male rates.

Two groups stand out as having exceptionally low unemployment rates. U.S.-born Asians have rates well below those of the total population; but

Table 16.3 Percentage of labor-force participation and unemployment of the civilian population 25–64 years old, by place of birth, years in Hawaii, and sex: Oahu, 1975

Labor-force status	Foreign-born Asians by years in Hawaii						U.S.-born Asians		All persons	
	Total		0–10		11+					
	M	F	M	F	M	F	M	F	M	F
In labor force	89.1	61.2	94.8	60.9	85.4	61.7	91.8	68.7	89.6	60.8
Employed	86.1	53.7	89.7	50.6	85.4	59.1	90.6	65.8	86.1	55.1
Unemployed	3.0	7.5	5.1	10.3	0.0	2.6	1.2	2.9	3.5	5.7
Not in labor force	10.0	38.8	5.2	39.1	14.6	38.3	8.2	31.3	10.4	39.2
Unemployment rate[a]	3.4	12.3	5.4	16.9	0.0	4.2	1.3	4.2	3.9	9.4

a. Unemployment rate = (unemployed/labor force) × 100.

long-term Asian immigrants, especially the males, show almost no unemployment. Whatever the obstacles between the immigrant and employment, they seem to operate mostly in the first years of a migrant's residence. These obstacles may include a general lack of local contacts for employment purposes, poor English skills, and professional licenses received abroad that are invalid in Hawaii. There do appear to be, for both sexes, values held by Asian immigrants that enable them to hold employment well, once the initial disadvantages associated with their immigrant status are surmounted. Similar values held by U.S.-born Asians may account for their low unemployment rates.

It is of interest to examine the employed population to see how many hours are being worked per week. In the past, most women in the U.S. labor force were part-time workers. This is certainly not true today, however, at least in Hawaii. If a full work week is defined as being at least 35 hours, 83 percent of the immigrants and 86 percent of the U.S.-born among Asian adult females were working a full week in 1975. Approximately 95 percent of all employed Asian males in all migration categories were working full time. In practice, then, employment in Hawaii means full-time work.

Data on the number of hours worked lend no support to the stereotype of the superindustrious immigrant working 60 hours a week at two jobs. Few females, regardless of migration status, work more than 40 hours a week; among the Asian males, the proportions working more than 40 hours a week are 12 and 17 percent among the short-term and long-term migrants, respectively, but 20 percent among the U.S.-born. In fact, it is the migrants from the mainland who are most likely to work more than 40 hours a week (Gardner and Wright 1980).

So far we have treated the Asians as a single group. There are many differences by ethnicity, however, especially between the Filipinos and the three groups comprising the Orientals. Those differences are especially great among the U.S.-born. Among the immigrant females there are interesting differences that do not follow the Oriental/Filipino dichotomy. For example, half of the recent Japanese but approximately two-thirds of the other recent adult female immigrants are in the labor force. In Japan, women generally do not hold gainful employment after marriage and it is possible that the cultural norms do not change immediately after the move to Hawaii. They seem to change later, however, because long-term Japanese female immigrants have participation rates that are not significantly lower than those of other ethnicities.

Unemployment among recent immigrant Japanese women between the ages of 25 and 64 (6 percent) is much lower than among the other Asian women. Among the long-term female immigrants, nearly two-thirds in all groups are in the labor force; in no group does unemployment exceed 3.3 percent. For males, unemployment is virtually nonexistent among all groups of long-term Asian immigrants.

In summary, female Asian immigrants have labor-force participation rates lower than those of their male counterparts and lower than those of local-born Asian females as well. Within the Asian female migrant groups, there are important differences in labor-force participation; recent Japanese immigrants have especially low rates. Young female immigrants have levels of unemployment similar to those of local-born Asians, but older female Asian migrants have rates higher than those of the Hawaii-born. These patterns conceal great differences by duration of residence, however; unemployment rates are low among long-term female Asian immigrants. Nevertheless, female unemployment rates are higher than male rates for all categories.

OCCUPATIONAL DISTRIBUTION

In comparing the occupational distribution of the immigrants and the U.S.-born, we consider only employed persons between ages 25 and 64. Many of those under the age of 25 are continuing their education; in most cases the students work part time and at jobs that may bear little resemblance to future employment. Attention is given here to three broad occupational categories: professional, technical, managerial; clerical and sales; and service. The first category generally requires a college education; clerical jobs generally require at least a high school diploma; service jobs are characterized by minimal educational requirements and low salaries. Major occupations not considered here are mainly blue-collar jobs, which are generally intermediate between the clerical and service jobs in prestige and remuneration.

Table 16.4 portrays an occupational distribution among Asian immigrants of both sexes that is strikingly service-oriented. (The participation of Asian immigrants in the service sector is vital to the tourist industry, the most important industry in the state.) Compared with the U.S.-born Asians, low proportions of male and female Asian immigrants are engaged in professional and clerical occupations and high proportions work in the service sector.

Compared with male Asian immigrants, female Asian immigrants have low percentages in professional jobs and high percentages in service occupations. Longer residence in Honolulu seems to have little effect on the occupational distribution of Asian female immigrants; the proportions in professional jobs are nearly identical among recent and long-term residents, but figures do rise somewhat with longevity for clerical and service jobs. It should be kept in mind that occupational prestige is highly correlated with educational attainment and the recent immigrants tend to be much better educated than their predecessors. Whether in fact considerable upward mobility is apparent when education is controlled is the subject of a later section.

The three U.S.-born Oriental female groups in the 25–64 age group are characterized by a similar occupational structure: nearly a third in professional occupations, more than two-fifths in clerical and sales jobs, and a seventh in the service trades (data not shown). By contrast, fewer than a quarter of the U.S.-born Filipino women are in professional occupations and nearly a fifth are in service jobs. Among the men there are similar differences, although the Japanese are somewhat less likely to be engaged in professional occupations than either the Chinese or the Koreans. Only a tenth of the Filipinos but a third of the Japanese and half of the Koreans and Chinese are in professional occupations. The proportion employed in service occupations ranges from under a quarter among Filipinos to more than a third among Japanese.

Among the long-term female immigrants, about a fifth of the employed Japanese females are professionals and about three-tenths are in service occupations; at the opposite end, the proportions of Filipinos in professional and service occupations are less than a tenth and nearly half, respectively.

Almost 60 percent of long-term immigrant Japanese males are in professional employment and only a twelfth are in service occupations; by contrast, less than a tenth of Filipinos are in professional employment and nearly three-eighths of Chinese are in service occupations.

To summarize, female Asian immigrants show a poor occupational distribution compared with local-born Asian females and male Asian immi-

Table 16.4 Percentage distribution of employed members of the civilian labor force 25—64 years old in selected occupations, by place of birth, years in Hawaii, and sex: Oahu, 1975

Occupation	Foreign-born Asians by years in Hawaii						U.S.-born Asians		All persons	
	Total		0—10		11+					
	M	F	M	F	M	F	M	F	M	F
Professional, technical, managerial	19.7	14.7	21.0	14.9	18.0	14.6	38.9	30.0	37.9	31.8
Clerical, sales	7.2	27.1	7.9	25.4	6.2	29.9	15.1	43.6	11.9	38.6
Service	23.0	33.6	24.2	31.7	21.5	36.8	6.8	15.4	10.0	18.8
Other (blue-collar or unclassified)	50.1	24.6	46.9	28.0	54.3	18.7	39.2	11.0	40.2	10.8
Total	100.0	100.0	100.0	100.0	100.0	100.0	100.0	100.0	100.0	100.0

grants. Duration of residence seems to have only a small effect on the occupational distribution. Among the Asians, Filipinos are definitely at the lower end of the occupational ladder.

Before we examine the third measure of success, income, we should pause to consider the relationship between education and occupation. Occupational status is usually highly correlated with educational level. Given the high proportion of poorly educated among the immigrants, it is reasonable to expect their general occupational levels to be lower than those of the native-born. Thus if we find that occupational levels of the immigrants and U.S.-born are similar when the level of education is controlled, the immigrants can be said to have adjusted very well in gaining employment commensurate with their educational qualifications. Data pertaining to this topic are found in Table 16.5.

First we consider those who never completed primary school. Notable for all groups is the heavy concentration of females in the low-paying service occupations, where considerable proportions of immigrant males are also found. There appears to be no substantial upward mobility of either males or females with increasing length of residence (although females do move more into service jobs), but the foreign-born Asians do not ¬ppear to be greatly disadvantaged in occupational competition with the poorly educated native-born Asians.

In looking at the Asian high school graduates who progress no further, we find that considerably lower proportions of the foreign-born than of the U.S.-born are employed in professional and clerical occupations, whereas more of the foreign-born Asian females are employed in service occupations. In this educational category the foreign-born Asian males are characterized by a much lower occupational status than the U.S.-born Asian males, but what is perhaps most surprising is that a higher proportion (40 percent) of the recent male arrivals with a high school education are working at service jobs than is true for either the female high school graduates (34 percent) or the poorly educated immigrant males (29 percent). Perhaps the explanation is that in Asia the well educated are expected to shun "dirty" work such as construction. Therefore, many of the immigrant high school graduates who cannot find clerical employment may opt for "clean" service jobs in preference to more remunerative jobs requiring hard physical labor. Compared with their female counterparts, a higher proportion of male Asian immigrants who are high school graduates are in professional occupations and much smaller proportions are in clerical and sales occupations. Length of residence in Hawaii does result in some upward occupational movement out of service and into clerical employment for male, but not female, high school graduates. Nevertheless, the longer-term immigrant males have a smaller proportion in professional jobs than the more recent arrivals.

Table 16.5 Percentage distribution of the employed Asian members of the civilian labor force 25–64 years old, by schooling and occupation, place of birth, years in Hawaii, and sex: Oahu, 1975

Years of schooling and occupation	Foreign-born Asians by years in Hawaii				U.S.-born Asians	
	0–10		11+			
	M	F	M	F	M	F
Less than 8 years						
Professional, technical, managerial	1.4	2.9	3.4	0.0	4.0	8.0
Clerical, sales	3.5	5.8	1.3	6.1	4.5	5.4
Service	28.6	48.5	24.5	63.3	24.8	64.6
Other (blue-collar and unclassified)	66.5	42.8	70.8	30.6	66.7	22.0
Total	100.0	100.0	100.0	100.0	100.0	100.0
12 years						
Professional, technical, managerial	15.7	12.1	11.8	9.0	25.7	19.2
Clerical, sales	2.0	35.1	8.4	42.6	19.2	54.9
Service	40.5	33.8	21.1	31.9	6.4	14.2
Other (blue-collar and unclassified)	41.8	19.0	58.7	16.5	48.7	11.7
Total	100.0	100.0	100.0	100.0	100.0	100.0
16+ years						
Professional, technical, managerial	49.9	34.9	87.5	53.2	80.3	73.9
Clerical, sales	12.7	36.9	9.5	21.6	12.2	19.5
Service	10.2	14.8	0.0	9.4	3.5	3.0
Other (blue-collar and unclassified)	27.2	13.4	3.0	15.8	4.0	3.6
Total	100.0	100.0	100.0	100.0	100.0	100.0

A look at the Asian women who hold at least a B.A. degree reveals that whereas three-quarters of the U.S.-born have professional jobs, far fewer of the recent and long-term immigrants have such occupations. About half of the highly educated recent male arrivals are in professional employment; this finding suggests they are much more successful in securing high-status employment than the well-educated females arriving with them. Nevertheless, they are at a severe disadvantage in competition with the well-educated U.S.-born males and with earlier male arrivals. The earlier arrivals (mostly Japanese) are doing as well or better occupationally than the native Asian males. Thus, although marked improvement for both sexes is evident over time, the males but not the females are eventually able to achieve parity with their U.S.-born counterparts.

We thus find that in general, for a given level of educational achievement, immigrants have less prestigious jobs than the native-born. Males fare better than females and there is some indication of improvement with length of residence, especially among college graduates.

INCOME

In view of the finding that many of the Asian immigrants are poorly educated and hold menial jobs, one can anticipate that their annual incomes are lower, on the average, than those of the native-born. In considering incomes we include only employed persons between the ages of 25 and 64. The rationale is that incomes earned by those under age 25 tend to be low (and also tend to be poor predictors of later income), that those unemployed can be expected to have low incomes or none at all, and that most people aged 65 and over are employed part time if at all.

Table 16.6 portrays median income by migration status and ethnicity. Turning our attention first to the U.S.-born, we find that the median income of Asian males is virtually identical to that of all males in the general population, but the median income of Asian females is above that of females in the general population (data not shown). Considering the widespread discrimination against Asians that existed prior to World War II,[6] the upward advance of the descendants of the immigrants is indeed impressive.

Not unexpectedly, however, the overall economic picture is much less bright in the case of the Asian immigrants, who lag considerably behind the native-born Asians. Median incomes of recent immigrant Asian males and females are 30 and 33 percent, respectively, below those of the U.S.-born Asian males and females. Among Asian immigrants living in Hawaii more than ten years, the income differences narrow to 17 and 24 percent, respectively. Thus the income differential declines at a much slower rate for females than for males.

More striking is the income gap between males and females, regardless of migration status. Overall the median yearly income of all Asian females is only 53 percent of that of all Asian males. That this figure ranges only from 48 percent among the long-term immigrants to 53 percent among the recent immigrants and 55 percent among the native-born is evidence of institutional forces that greatly discriminate against females of all places of birth in the job market, at least with respect to income. Before addressing this issue further, we discuss the income characteristics of the different Asian ethnic groups.

Table 16.6 Median income of employed civilian Asians 25—64 years old, by hours worked, education, occupation and occupation combined: Oahu, 1975

Control	Median income ($ in thousands)						Females' income as percentage of males'			Income of foreign-born as percentage of U.S.-born income			
	Foreign-born Asians by years in Hawaii				U.S.-born Asians		Foreign-born		U.S.-born	0–10		11+	
	0–10		11+				0–10	11+					
	M	F	M	F	M	F				M	F	M	F
Total	8.9	4.7	11.3	5.4	13.6	7.5	53	48	55	70	67	83	76
Hours worked a week (40)	9.3	5.1	11.2	6.3	13.4	7.8	55	56	59	67	63	84	78
Education													
16+ years	11.7	5.5	16.8	8.6	16.8	11.3	47	51	67	70	48	100	76
12 years	7.9	4.9	13.1	5.9	13.3	7.0	62	45	52	59	70	99	85
0–7 years	7.1	4.1	9.3	4.7	9.7	4.3	58	51	45	74	95	96	110
Occupation													
Professional[a]	10.3	5.4	14.1	9.2	16.5	10.5	52	66	64	63	51	85	86
Clerical, sales	9.5	5.8	10.8	6.3	11.3	7.4	60	58	66	84	78	95	85
Service	6.8	4.2	8.1	4.7	10.2	5.2	62	58	51	67	82	79	90
Occupation and education													
Professional,[a] 16+	11.8	5.7	20.7	9.8	18.2	12.3	48	47	68	65	46	114	79
Clerical, sales, 12	b	7.0	b	7.1	12.9	7.4	b	b	57	b	94	b	97
Service, 0–7	6.2	3.8	6.9	4.3	8.2	4.6	62	62	56	75	83	85	94

a. "Professional" refers to professional/technical/managerial.
b. Too few in the sample population for a reliable estimate.

Among the various local-born ethnic groups, the Orientals and Caucasians are the most well-to-do in Hawaii. By contrast, the Filipinos (and Hawaiians) are characterized by a generally low socioeconomic status.[7] One reason for the relative affluence of all three U.S.-born Oriental groups is the high proportion of females in the labor force. Another reason is the low unemployment rate of Orientals of both sexes.

The recent Korean, Chinese, and Filipino female immigrants fare poorly, but Japanese women are characterized by incomes above those of U.S.-born Filipino females. Their much higher average income appears somewhat surprising in view of the high proportion of Japanese who work only part time and their low participation in professional occupations. The explanation may be that knowledge of Japanese language and culture is a valuable asset in the tourist industry (a fifth of the tourists are Japanese) and the many businesses that have overseas contacts with Japanese firms. Knowledge of the other languages and cultures confers no such advantage in the local job market.

Koreans have the lowest median income of recent male immigrants and Chinese the highest. It is difficult to explain the low median income of Japanese men, as they have the knowledge of Japanese language and culture that seems to benefit Japanese women, and a higher proportion of them (more than a third) than of any other group work more than 40 hours a week.

As in the case of the recent immigrants, for long-term immigrant females incomes are highest among the Japanese. Notably, only long-term Filipino immigrants characteristically have higher incomes than their counterparts among the recent arrivals. The median income of the long-term Japanese immigrants is well above that of their native-born counterparts, and that of the Chinese is comparable to the median for all native-born males. The median Filipino income, however, is nearly a quarter below the median for all U.S.-born Asian males.

These specific comparisons should not be allowed to obscure two basic findings. First, as a whole the immigrants are characterized by a much less enviable occupational distribution and lower incomes than the U.S.-born Asians (although their incomes rise with time). And second, incomes of women regardless of their ethnic or migration status are generally between 50 and 55 percent of those of men of comparable ethnicity and migration status.

How can we explain these patterns? There are several factors that might account for the income differentials between Asian immigrants and native-born residents and between female and male immigrants. Suppose we examine the differences in proportions working full time and educational and occupational levels.

Male/female differentials are reduced but slightly when only persons working 40 hours a week (the norm in Hawaii) are considered. Thus the notion that a substantial part of the male/female differential is due to the presence of many part-time female workers can be safely rejected. Nor can the differences between the native-born and foreign-born be ascribed to differences in the number of hours worked.

Because educational levels of the immigrants are generally well below those of the U.S.-born, it is reasonable to expect that income differentials to some extent reflect differences in educational levels. In fact, though, Table 16.6 shows that poorly educated immigrant females are not at a competitive disadvantage compared with the native-born. The reason appears to be that generally only the most menial jobs are available for poorly educated females, irrespective of migration status. That this pattern does not apply to males probably results from the existence of many well-paying jobs (especially in the construction industry) that are available to poorly educated males, and these jobs tend to go to local-born persons.

Among the recent Asian immigrant females there is a competitive disadvantage, and it increases with increasing education. Although the income differentials for immigrant females decline with increasing residence, they do not disappear. In contrast, income differentials between male Asian immigrants and U.S.-born Asian males do tend to disappear with time and increased education.

We have shown that the well-educated immigrants are often underemployed, especially at first, in jobs for which in theory their level of education should qualify them. This is one explanation for the generally low income of the immigrants. Nonetheless, Table 16.6 shows the stubborn persistence of income differentials by immigrant status and sex, no matter what broad occupational category is considered. Differentials between foreign-born and U.S.-born do tend to decline with increasing residence in Hawaii.

Male/female differentials are not reduced when occupation is controlled for. What is most striking is the persistence of these differentials, irrespective of occupation and immigration status. Although the male/female differential for immigrant Asians employed in professional occupations does appear to decline with increasing duration of residence, this is not true in the clerical and service occupations. The sex differential in income is least among long-term Asians holding professional employment. Note that male/female differentials among U.S.-born Asians are similar to those of the immigrants.

Among recent immigrant Asian females the competitive disadvantage vis-à-vis the U.S.-born Asian females is greatest in the professional ranks and least in the service category. A marked improvement in relative income among the long-term female immigrants is apparent in all three broad occupational categories. Except in service occupations the differentials in favor of the native-born are greater for females than for males. Thus well-educated immigrant Asian women are doubly disadvantaged— both in gaining employment commensurate with their educational levels and in remuneration for those fortunate enough to obtain white-collar jobs.

When education and occupation are both controlled, differences among the immigrants by years of residence, between immigrants and the native-born, and between males and females still remain. In a comparison of the Asian males and females, the relative differences are greatest for both the short-term and the long-term immigrants with at least four years of college education and in professional occupations, whereas the differences are least among the native-born Asian professionals.

Differences between the recent immigrants and the U.S.-born are greatest among the college-educated Asians, especially females, in the professional categories. Although improvement with time is evident, earnings of well-educated professional females in Hawaii 11 years or more remain 20 percent below those of the native-born females. The median income of the well-educated professionals among the recent Asian male immigrants is more than a third below that of the U.S.-born Asians, but the long-term immigrants in this category (mostly Japanese) are strikingly successful.

In summary, then, no matter what controls are used within the limits set by the data, the median incomes of immigrants are far below those of the native-born, although the differences usually diminish with increasing duration of residence in Hawaii. Incomes of the females are far below those of males in comparable migration categories—usually in the neighborhood of 40 to 50 percent lower, irrespective of the controls one chooses. This finding is evidence of systematic discrimination against women that affects the native-born and immigrant alike. The relative disadvantage of being female is greatest among the well-educated female immigrants, both in gaining professional employment and in remuneration in the professional occupations.

SUMMARY AND CONCLUSION

In this study we have examined the economic adaptation and assimilation of female Asian immigrants in Hawaii compared with male immigrants and the native-born female Asians. Data for the study are from a 5 percent sample survey of all households on the island of Oahu conducted in 1975.

Patterns of residential distribution of native-born Asians suggest that the Orientals have experienced much more upward mobility than the Filipinos. Among the recent immigrants, the female Orientals are more residentially dispersed than the males; among the Filipinos there is no difference. The immigrant Filipinos are more residentially concentrated than the Orientals; furthermore, the latter disperse at a more rapid rate. Both economic necessity and cultural forces account for the residential patterns of the immigrant Asians.

Educational levels of the early immigrant females are low relative to those of the native population, but they are somewhat higher than those of the early immigrant males. Although the educational levels of the recent female immigrants are much higher than those of the early immigrants, they are somewhat lower than those of recent immigrant males and U.S.-born Asian females.

Asian female immigrants are, on the average, two years younger than U.S.-born Asian females at the time of marriage. Of those who out-marry, most who marry mainland-born husbands are recent arrivals. Oriental women are most likely and Filipino men least likely to be married to a U.S.-born spouse.

Labor-force participation of the immigrant females is high by national standards, although it is somewhat lower than that of the U.S.-born Asian females in Hawaii. This participation rate rises with increasing duration of residence in Hawaii. Unemployment is a serious problem among recent immigrants, both male and female. In contrast, unemployment is low among the long-term immigrant females and almost nonexistent among their male counterparts. This finding suggests cultural values that enable success in obtaining and holding employment, once initial barriers are overcome. Most of the immigrant females in the labor force are employed full time.

Most immigrant females hold menial jobs; relatively few are in professional occupations. This finding also holds true for the immigrant males; but the immigrant females are worse off—and, in addition, upward mobility with increasing duration of residence is more evident for males than females. In relation to educational levels, the occupational structure of the immigrant females is highly disadvantageous compared with that of U.S.-born Asian females and moderately so compared with that of male immigrants. This occupational disadvantage is most apparent among the college-educated immigrant females. Whereas immigrant males eventually achieve rough occupational parity with U.S.-born males having comparable education, the same is not true of the immigrant females.

Incomes of the immigrant females are very low initially but improve substantially with increasing duration of residence. Nevertheless, even among immigrant women in Hawaii more than ten years, the median income remains more than 25 percent below that of the U.S.-born Asian women. More striking is the sex differential: The median incomes of females of all migration groups average 40 to 50 percent less than those of the males in comparable groups. This differential is substantial for all groups but is greatest among the long-term immigrants. Differentials by sex and immigrant status remain almost unchanged when education, occupation, and hours worked are controlled. Income differentials are greatest in the professional category, again showing that relative disabilities are greatest for the well-educated professional females.

Superficially, many of these findings conform to a theme that is not only a part of American mythology but also a staple of sociological studies: "Immigrant starts out at the bottom but eventually makes good." They show initial residential concentrations in a few less-desired areas, low initial rates of intermarriage, high rates of unemployment, and low occupational levels and incomes in relation to skills and aspirations. All these characteristics become less marked with increasing duration of residence. That the native-born Orientals are doing very well by local standards (although this is not true of the local Filipinos) completes the typical American saga. The outcast arrivals have "made it." They have become "American."

What differs in this study is the focus on females, which reveals the economic price paid by women who immigrate. This price is paid by all female immigrants, but the sex differential in income and occupational prestige is greatest among the long-term migrants, especially those with a college education. Supporting the facade of the "fun-filled" Honolulu tourist experience are many foreign-born Asian women working at service occupations well below their capabilities and training and at minimal wages.

This differential is especially ironic because if out-marriage and residential dispersion are good indexes of assimilation, the immigrant Asian females have changed their cultural norms more rapidly than the males. Furthermore, among the long-term immigrants the females tend to be better educated; yet it is in this group that the male/female differential in income is greatest.

In short, the Asian female immigrants suffer the double disadvantage of being immigrants and being women. As a group, their talents are underutilized and the pay for the work they do is far below that of male immigrants. It follows that if their economic position is to be substantially improved, concerted efforts must be made to improve opportunities for immigrants in general and to remove institutional barriers that hinder true equality between the sexes.

NOTES

1. Because of certain similarities discussed later in this essay, Chinese, Japanese, and Koreans are sometimes grouped together as "Oriental"—sharing a common cultural heritage different from that of the Filipinos. For a discussion of the "Oriental ingroup" and reasons why Filipinos are not considered members, see Samuels (1970).

2. Honolulu City and County is effectively coextensive with the island of Oahu. All

parts of the island are within commuting distance of Honolulu City, which contains about half the population. Less than 2 percent of the labor force is in agriculture and two-thirds of this number is in plantation agriculture, which in Hawaii is organized much like an industrial enterprise. For a description of the "urban" aspects of plantation agriculture in Hawaii, see Lind (1955).

3. There are many good works dealing with adaptation of migrants, among them: Brody (1970), Findley (1977), Goldlust and Richmond (1974), Gordon (1964), Graves and Graves (1974), Richardson (1967), and Richmond and Verma (1978).

4. We consider only adults in measuring residential concentration because children have no choice in residential location and the location of U.S.-born children, especially Filipinos, depends on the location of foreign-born parents.

5. The SMAM, as developed by Hajnal (1953), is based on an assumption of "marital stability"—unchanging age patterns of marriage in the past several generations. If this assumption is not met, the SMAM is not necessarily an accurate estimate of current marriage patterns. Nevertheless, it is often used because it is a concise way of summarizing point-in-time marital-status distribution by age groups.

6. For a discussion of the various tactics used by the Caucasian elite to keep the Asians in Hawaii from rising economically and politically, see Fuchs (1961).

7. Surveys of the civilian populations of Oahu, Maui, and Hawaii in 1975, conducted by the U.S. Office of Economic Opportunity (OEO), revealed the median *family* income to be $16,486. Among families headed by Hawaii-born Chinese, Japanese, and Koreans, the medians were $20,732, $19,722, and $19,561, respectively. The median income of families headed by mainland-born non-Portuguese Caucasians living in Hawaii 11 years or longer was $20,752. By contrast, the median for families headed by Hawaii-born Filipinos was only $14,053.

REFERENCES

Brody, Eugene B. (ed.)
   1970   *Behavior in New Environments: Adaptation of Migrant Populations.* Beverly Hills: Sage Publications.

Findley, Sally
   1977   *Planning for Internal Migration: A Review of Issues and Policies in Developing Countries.* Washington, D.C.: U.S. Bureau of the Census.

Fuchs, Lawrence
   1961   *Hawaii Pono: A Social History.* New York: Harcourt Brace Jovanovich.

Gardner, Robert W., and Paul A. Wright
   1980   Kamaainas and malihinis. Unpublished manuscript. East-West Population Institute, Honolulu.

Goldlust, John, and Anthony Richmond
   1974   A multivariate model of immigrant adaptation. *International Migration Review* 8(2):193–226.

Gordon, Milton
   1964   *Assimilation in American Life.* New York: Oxford University Press.

Graves, Nancy B., and Theodore D. Graves
    1974   Adaptive strategies in urban migration. *Annual Review of Anthropology* 3: 117-51.

Hajnal, John
    1953   Age at marriage and proportions marrying. *Population Studies* 7(1):111-36.

Lind, Andrew W.
    1955   *Hawaii's People.* Honolulu: University of Hawaii Press.

Nordyke, Eleanor
    1977   *The Peopling of Hawaii.* Honolulu: University Press of Hawaii.

Richardson, Allen
    1967   A theory and a method for the psychological study of assimilation. *International Migration Review* 2(1):3-29.

Richmond, Anthony, and Ravi P. Verma
    1978   The economic adaptation of immigrants: a new theoretical perspective. *International Migration Review* 12(1):3-38.

Samuels, Frederick
    1970   *The Japanese and Haoles of Honolulu: Durable Group Interaction.* New Haven: College and University Press.

Survey and Marketing Services, Inc. (SMS)
    1976   *OEO 1975 Census Update Survey: Oahu.* Honolulu.

Chapter 17

Philippine Urbanism and the Status of Women

Rodolfo A. Bulatao

The adjustments in social structures and in individual life-styles that urban living demands may be welcomed or feared—welcomed for the comforts and diversions the city can supply, feared for the erosion of social networks and the toppling of traditional verities. This essay suggests that, in appropriate measure, both reactions may be right for Filipino women— Philippine urbanism may be seen as a qualified good (or a qualified bad) when one considers its effects on women's status, depending on which aspects of status are emphasized.

The elements involved are obviously complex. Urbanism means not just a new economic setting but also renewed contact with western culture— contact that in the past apparently had little effect but may, in the modern context, be more potent. The complex of factors associated with urban life may well be a major cause of change, but any change is likely to be evolutionary: "Filipinos have known how to adapt their traditional patterns to the exigencies of urban life" (Carroll 1970:16). Moreover, they know how to transform western culture to their own purposes. There is also in the urban setting the uncertain effect of colonial attitudes, possibly more prevalent among the educated, regarding the proper role of women: the Maria Clara complex (after the heroine in Rizal's novel—coy, retiring, subservient), also called *feminismo*. Castillo (1976:250) defines the complex thus: "The Filipino woman wants to get married; to have children (childlessness or even a one-child marriage is not preferred); to be subordinate yet equal; to be seductive without being seduced; to be a companion to her husband and a mother to her children." Urbanism could reinforce such images or destroy them.

The significant difference that the urban context makes is evident in Castillo's (1976:245) conclusions regarding women in the Philippines:

> In examining the ten different aspects of the Filipino woman's life, it is not the inequality between males and females but rather the disparities between rural and urban and between women in Metro Manila and the rest of the country

which come out as the most significant disparities. The urban and especially the Metro Manila female shows advantages and characteristics quite distinct from other Filipino women.

In education, income, and the amenities of life, the urban and particularly the Manila woman is assumed to be well ahead of her rural counterpart. If the status of women is defined in terms of material comforts, the results of the urban/rural contrast are easy to predict. The status of women may also be compared, however, to that of men. In this case, one is concerned with sexual inequality in all social classes. From this perspective, the effect of urbanism is less easy to predict.

One might see the modernizing influences in urban life as loosening traditional restraints on women (see Patai 1967). Or one might argue that the urban setting confirms western images of the independent woman and frees men from their own dependence on a wife's labor. One might see expanded educational opportunities for women in the city; but one might also see greater segregation of the sexes in higher education and see women entering less demanding fields (Tinker 1976). One might maintain that the city opens up economic opportunities for women; but one might also focus on the tendency to assign women to less responsible, less remunerative, and less secure jobs (Boserup 1970). It is not evident a priori that urbanism must promote or eliminate sexual inequality. It is even possible that, like Spanish and American colonialism, its net effect is minor and largely superficial.

The analysis of survey data presented here is designed to assess the impact of urbanism on women's status—defined broadly to cover occupation, family, social participation, stereotypes and attitudes, and personal satisfaction. Rural/urban comparisons will be made cross-sectionally using data from a single survey; this strategy limits what can be said about the dynamics of the situation, but it also avoids the fallacy of focusing on a certain group of advantaged or disadvantaged women. After comparing urban and rural women, we will compare migrants and nonmigrants.

THE DATA

The data on the status of women come from a nationwide survey on women conducted between December 1975 and March 1976 by the Social Research Laboratory, University of the Philippines.[1] This survey covered 1,598 women, both married and single, between the ages of 18 and 59. It also covered 399 of their husbands, but these data will not be considered here.

The female sample was stratified into four areas: the primate city, other large cities, small cities, and rural areas. To represent rural areas, one province in each of ten regions was chosen, and barrios (excluding *pobla-ciónes* or town centers) were chosen within these provinces. For the primate city, the city of Manila itself and seven immediately surrounding cities or municipalities were covered. The population of this area, which may be called Greater Manila to distinguish it from the broad area officially labeled Metro Manila, was about 3.2 million in 1970. Considered large cities for the purposes of the survey were the next four cities in size: Cebu, Iloilo, Bacolod, and Davao. Cebu City, the largest of the four, with about 350,000 people, had only 11 percent of the population of Greater Manila. Davao City, the smallest, had 180,000 people, 6 percent of the Greater Manila population. The small cities ranged in size from 10,000 to 50,000 and included these nine in order of decreasing size: Cotaboto, Jolo, Zamboanga, Legaspi, Dumaguete, Ozamis, Digos, Tuguegarao, and Puerto Princesa. These cities ranked between twenty-seventh and sixty-fifth in size among Philippine cities as of 1970.

Some characteristics of respondents, by type of area, are provided in Table 17.1. Manila respondents were slightly younger and more likely to be single; rural respondents were more likely to be married and to have more children. As could be expected, a level of living score based on household items was highest for Manila and lowest for rural areas. Less expected was the pattern for education: Rural respondents were at the bottom of the educational ladder, but Manila respondents were not at the top; women from the small cities proved to have more education.

All respondents were interviewed using a questionnaire that took one to two hours of interview time. The questionnaire covered a variety of topics, including household characteristics, community participation, childrearing and socialization, gender-related attitudes, and personal satisfaction. The questionnaire was designed in English and Tagalog, translated into local dialects, and then back-translated to check for accuracy. (For a detailed description of the methodology see SRL 1977.) In the next section I consider responses to the survey relating to occupational characteristics, family relations, community participation, stereotypes and attitudes, and satisfaction and relative social position.

RURAL/URBAN CONTRASTS

Occupational characteristics of women in each type of urban and rural area are presented in Table 17.2. About 43 percent of women in the sample were earning money (higher than official rates because women under 18 were not studied). Most of the remaining data in the table pertain only to working women, except time spent working (obtained for all women) and age started working (obtained for any women who had ever worked).

The patterns in Table 17.2 were unexpected. In most aspects, small-city

Table 17.1 Sociodemographic characteristics of sample rural and urban women: Philippines, 1976

Characteristic	Barrio	Small city	Large city	Primate city	Com- bined
Age (%)					
18–24	20	23	23	23	22
25–34	32	33	33	35	33
35–44	28	27	24	30	27
45+	19	17	19	12	18
Marital status (%)					
Single	12	19	19	23	16
Married	84	75	77	73	80
Separated	4	6	4	4	5
Mean no. of children	4.0	3.2	3.1	3.0	3.6
Mean desired no. of children	5.3	4.9	5.4	4.2	5.1
Education (%)					
Did not finish grade school	42	13	25	8	28
Completed grade school	30	16	18	28	25
Did not finish high school	11	15	23	20	14
Completed high school	17	56	34	44	33
Mean level of living score	2.3	4.1	3.6	4.9	3.2
Number of respondents	799	480	160	159	1,598

women were better off occupationally than barrio women and also better off than women in larger cities. More small-city women worked, more worked outside their neighborhood, more worked as professionals. Small-city women spent more time working, had higher occupational prestige, and earned more money: Almost half of them earned 300 pesos or more a month. Like women in other areas, most of them emphasized the monetary rewards of working; but when other rewards were asked about, small-city women were more likely than others to mention self-development or professional development. Finally, they saw the greatest chances for advancement and were the most satisfied with their jobs. (As with the other contrasts to follow, most of these differences persisted when education was controlled.)

The occupational situation of Manila women, surprisingly, was not as good. Only as many Manila women were working as in rural areas, and the proportion in professional jobs was no greater. Job satisfaction and chances for job advancement were also relatively low. Working women in

Table 17.2 Occupational characteristics of sample rural and urban women: Philippines, 1976

Characteristic	Barrio	Small city	Large city	Primate city	Combined
% earning money	35	59	41	35	43
Place of work					
At home	38	40	39	49	40
In barrio or neighborhood	41	27	34	24	33
Outside barrio or neighborhood	20	33	27	27	27
Occupational group					
Professional	14	26	17	11	19
Clerical	1	14	7	9	7
Sales	25	23	13	26	23
Skilled	13	13	25	22	15
Unskilled	5	3	6	6	4
Service	11	20	24	22	17
Farm	31	2	8	4	15
Mean occupational prestige score	30	42	34	35	36
Monthly income in pesos					
0–99	48	17	43	21	33
100–299	30	34	32	37	32
300+	22	49	25	42	35
Mean time spent working (minutes)	157	248	214	148	188
Mean age started working	24	26	25	26	25
Main reason for working					
To earn money, to meet basic needs	52	48	50	40	49
To supplement husband's income, to help parents, to send children to school, to add to savings	41	46	44	49	44
Satisfaction in work, for the experience, training	5	5	6	11	5
Other	2	1	0	0	1
Advantages to working besides money					
To meet basic needs	15	7	4	13	11
To supplement husband's income, to help parents, to send children to school, to add to savings	17	12	25	28	16
Self-development, for the experience, professional development	5	28	8	3	15
Work is enjoyable	34	29	39	31	32
To meet people, to help others	10	16	10	8	12
To keep physically fit	14	7	8	15	11
Other	4	1	6	3	3

Table 17.2 *(continued)*

Characteristic	Barrio	Small city	Large city	Primate city	Combined
% with good chances of advancement in job	27	45	22	24	33
Mean job satisfaction					
From direct questions	3.57	3.77	3.63	3.64	3.66
From ratings of job aspects	14.59	15.39	14.16	14.72	14.88
% who would like a different type of work	53	49	53	43	50

Manila did, however, have higher incomes, though they still earned less than small-city women.

Are these occupational differences accompanied by differences within the family? Table 17.3 presents data on household task allocation, decision-making, household problems, and marital satisfaction. In general, small-city women again came out best. For six specified household tasks, wives usually had the main responsibility. In the small cities, however, this was less often so than in other areas. The tasks were assumed not by husbands—small-city husbands also performed fewer household tasks—but most often by servants. It is notable that Manila women fared worse than women in any other type of area, whether urban or rural, and were the most often burdened with these tasks.

Family decision-making patterns did not vary in comparable fashion, however. Wives seldom made decisions by themselves in any region. As has been generally found for the Philippines, most wives managed the family finances, but this number was lowest for the small cities. A related set of questions asked whether wives needed their husbands' permission for certain activities. (Respondents were not asked about husbands' activities that required the wife's permission, though, of which there probably are some). Small-city wives required their husbands' permission less often than rural or large-city wives, but more often than Manila wives.

On questions regarding family problems and marital satisfaction, the advantage of small-city wives was again evident. They reported the fewest problems and the greatest satisfaction. More than other urban women, they emphasized a husband's love and understanding more than his merely being responsible for supporting the family.

It might be expected that occupational advantages would translate into greater community participation. From the limited set of measures available (Table 17.4), this did not appear to be so. It was rural women, more than any urban women, who more often belonged to organizations and

Table 17.3 Family characteristics of sample rural and urban women: Philippines, 1976

Characteristic	Barrio	Small city	Large city	Primate city	Com- bined
% of wives who handle each task					
Doing the cooking	85	77	89	93	84
Washing the dishes	64	50	65	83	62
Cleaning the house	77	55	77	84	71
Washing the clothes	83	65	80	91	78
Looking after the children	80	72	82	95	79
Disciplining the children	51	57	61	92	58
Mean no. of tasks wife is responsible for	4.30	3.67	4.44	5.34	4.23
Mean no. of tasks husband is responsible for	3.89	3.45	3.81	4.00	3.77
Mean time wife spends in housework	393	318	367	402	370
% of wives making family decisions					
On major purchases	18	15	15	15	16
On family business	15	14	18	14	15
Holding the money	95	86	89	91	91
Winning disagreements with spouse	22	24	22	17	22
% of wives requiring permission to					
Buy clothes for self	67	59	81	34	63
Go out with friends	93	91	95	85	92
Lend money to relatives	93	90	92	89	91
Mean no. of household problems	2.38	1.97	2.29	2.34	2.25
% for whom spouse's being away from home is a problem	47	37	44	37	43
% who often discuss personal problems with spouse	62	66	78	71	65
% who say husband treats them very well	38	57	24	46	43
Why husband's treatment is good					
Husband loves, understands, pays attention to, respects wife	40	40	33	35	39
Husband has no vices, does not deceive, admits faults	5	4	4	5	5
Husband does not hurt wife, beat wife, quarrel	13	11	9	11	12
Husband is good, responsible, supports family, treats wife well	31	34	40	39	33
Other	6	5	6	5	6

Table 17.3 *(continued)*

Characteristic	Barrio	Small city	Large city	Primate city	Com- bined
% who consider their marriage happier than average	53	72	52	58	59
Who has more advantages?					
Married women	60	49	51	49	55
Same	9	11	11	12	10
Single women	31	40	38	39	35

Table 17.4 Community activities of sample rural and urban women: Philippines, 1976

Characteristic	Barrio	Small city	Large city	Primate city	Com- bined
% belonging to some organization	42	39	32	37	39
% participating in neighborhood activities	58	39	47	23	48
Neighborhood activities for women					
Cleanliness, beautification	34	22	20	77	31
Social welfare activities	13	16	18	3	14
Other civic projects	17	20	13	11	17
Celebration, religious activities	28	29	46	6	29
Other	9	13	3	3	9
Mean time spent in community activities	12.95	7.78	8.49	8.77	10.55

participated in neighborhood campaigns and socials and who spent time in community activities. The neighborhood activity more common for rural women than for urban women was beautification—in connection, one assumes, with one of the ubiquitous civic campaigns of Imelda Marcos. The implication is that rural women may simply be easier to mobilize; by this measure, community participation does not count for much.

Apart from their positions in institutional networks, the status of women depends on how they are viewed and how they view themselves. Table 17.5 reports relevant findings. Some measures require explanation. Using self-ratings on eight adjectives, a masculinity score was developed through discriminant analysis between female and male respondents (SRL 1977). This masculinity score assumed positive loadings for the adjectives "aggressive," "ambitious," and "independent" and negative loadings for the adjectives "religious" and "delicate." Parallel to the masculinity score was a gender stereotype differentiation score based on whether the respondent assigned each of these five adjectives to the "proper" sex. This differentiation score is reported in the first row of Table 17.5. The mean was lower for rural than for urban women, suggesting that urbanism may crystallize perceived differences between the sexes. Among urban respondents, the score was marginally higher for Manila women. A separate question asked whether the respondent considered men or women to have a stronger sex drive. As with the stereotype differentiation score, Manila women were the most extreme in choosing men.

Table 17.5 Stereotypes and attitudes of sample rural and urban women: Philippines, 1976

Characteristic	Barrio	Small city	Large city	Primate city	Combined
Stereotypes					
Gender differentiation	2.54	2.73	2.72	2.78	2.64
Stronger sex drive					
Women	5	7	8	4	6
Equal	35	29	36	30	33
Men	60	63	57	67	61
Self-ratings					
Masculinity	10.13	10.20	9.84	10.29	10.14
Efficacy	10.72	12.05	11.48	11.38	11.26
Most important life goal					
Comfortable life	21	15	19	37	21
Sense of accomplishment	2	4	3	9	3
Family security	20	29	15	29	23
Self-respect	3	7	5	13	5
Social recognition	3	0	1	1	2
Salvation	51	44	59	13	46
Adjusted mean ratings of life goals					
Sense of accomplishment	-0.14	-0.07	-0.13	0.02	-0.10
Self-respect	0.02	0.16	-0.01	0.05	0.06
Mean attitudes scores					
Disapproval of women working	17.66	16.04	16.98	17.12	17.05
Belief in traditional division of labor	11.22	10.17	10.87	10.67	10.81
Belief in women's fulfillment through homemaking	8.06	7.51	7.69	8.18	7.87

Self-ratings contrasted somewhat with these stereotypes. On the masculinity score, the Manila women were the highest, although they perceived the greatest contrasts between men and women. (The differences, though slight, were significant in a one-way analysis of variance.) Small-city women came next on the masculinity score. On a separate attitude scale for personal efficacy, small-city women scored highest, perceiving themselves as most in control of their own lives. Life goals among women in each region varied. Salvation was the dominant goal among rural, small-city, and large-city women; a comfortable life was dominant for Manila women. For small-city women, as for Manila women, family security was a secondary goal. Respondents answered ten Likert-scale items on women's roles. Factor analysis led to the identification of three dimensions among these items: "disapproval of women working," "belief in division of labor by sex," and "belief in women's fulfillment through homemaking." Scores reflecting each dimension showed small-city women to be lowest on each dimension or most in favor of sexual equality. Rural women were highest on the first two dimensions; Manila women were highest on the third.

How respondents summed up these different occupational, familial, community, and attitudinal characteristics might be determined from their views of their own welfare and status. Respondents were asked how happy they were in general and where they would place themselves on a ten-rung ladder of satisfaction with their life (Table 17.6). On both measures, small-city women were clearly more satisfied. The other three groups did not differ on the first measure, but on the second measure the Manila women ranked themselves lower than the other two groups. A more impersonal question was put to the respondents: "Would you say that men are generally treated better in this society or are women generally treated better?" Again the small-city women were most positive: More of them than of the other groups said women were treated better. What were the reasons for this attitude? Small-city women emphasized social advantages: women being respected, protected, tolerated. But Manila women—who saw fewer advantages for women—focused mainly on familial matters: being closer to the children, being able to care for the family. Respondents were asked, finally, whether women's position in society needed improvement. The majority thought so, except in Manila, where only 42 percent agreed.

The comparisons suggest that Manila women are indeed different from other women—in placing less emphasis on salvation, in being able to earn higher incomes, in being more burdened with housework, in being somewhat freer from their husbands' authority, in being less concerned with improving their position—but not necessarily better off. In fact, it was small-city women who came off better in the majority of comparisons. Recalling that small-city women reported the highest educational levels,

Table 17.6 Satisfaction and relative position of sample rural and urban women: Philippines, 1976

Characteristic	Barrio	Small city	Large city	Primate city	Com-bined
% very happy	16	21	16	16	17
Mean present ladder rating	4.62	5.42	4.64	4.10	4.81
Mean past ladder rating	4.27	5.16	4.11	3.90	4.49
Mean future ladder rating	5.94	7.61	6.01	5.58	6.40
Which sex is treated better					
Women	10	19	14	8	13
Equal	51	55	63	55	53
Men	39	26	23	37	33
Ways women are treated better					
Occupational: need not work, lighter work	8	6	5	13	7
Familial: care for family, closer to children	18	8	5	37	13
Social: respected, protected, tolerated	51	66	58	37	58
Personal: attractive, loving, patient, companions for men	17	10	21	13	14
Other	6	10	11	0	8
Advantages of being a woman					
Occupational	6	6	12	2	6
Familial	66	48	60	71	60
Social	7	21	4	9	11
Personal	17	18	19	11	17
Other	4	7	4	7	5
% saying position of women needs improvement	64	72	72	42	65

we may ask whether education is the reason for their advantages. To investigate this question, the variables in previous tables were analyzed with a breakdown of the sample into three roughly equal education groups: those who did not finish grade school, those who completed grade school, and those who completed high school (data not shown).

Controlling education did not eliminate the advantages that small-city women had over other women, except for occupational prestige. In each education group, small-city women were the most likely to be employed. Their occupational prestige was not necessarily the highest in each education group, however, though no other group was clearly higher in prestige. This finding was connected with the distribution of professionals: Almost all professionals had completed high school, but, of those who had completed high school, rural and small-city women were more likely to be professionals than large-city or Manila women. Incomes, as before, were higher for employed small-city women except at the highest educational level, where Manila women did slightly better. Job satisfaction, however, was clearly highest for small-city women at each educational level.

Controlling education did not change the relationship between area and the sharing of household tasks: Small-city women still did less than others; Manila women did more. Nor did it affect the amount of time spent in housework, which followed the same pattern. Regarding decision-making, the education control made little difference; in no area were women consistently more likely to make family decisions. The education control also confirmed the previous relationship between area and women's asking permission for their activities from their husbands: This finding was less expected, in each education group, among Manila women. In each education group, too, small-city women reported fewer family problems, said their husbands treated them very well more often, and rated themselves as more satisfied with their marriage.

Within each education group, as overall, rural women were the most active in organizations and in the neighborhood (primarily in beautification and cleanliness campaigns) and spent the most time in community activities. Within each education group, also, rural women had relatively low stereotype differentiation scores. Manila women were more likely than other women to assign a stronger sex drive to men, except in the highest education category. Regardless of education, Manila women were the least enamored of salvation as a life goal and the most committed to seeking a comfortable life. Small-city women, in contrast, had the strongest sense of efficacy at each education level and were the least likely to believe that women should not work, that there should be a division of labor by sex, or that women's fulfillment comes through homemaking. On the measures of personal happiness, small-city women were not consistently highest, but on ladder ratings they were highest in each education group. And in each education group, too, small-city women were more likely to feel that the society treated women better than men.

Since small-city women were more often employed, it is reasonable to ask whether employment was responsible for their various advantages. Analyses by employment status were carried out to address this issue. As with education, controlling employment did not eliminate the advantages of small-city women. In fact, it left the relative positions of women from each type of area roughly the same on most variables.

THE STATUS OF URBAN MIGRANTS

The degree to which female migrants share in the higher or lower status of women in the community is an important topic in its own right, but it also has implications for the understanding of status differentials between communities. Although we can make some comparisons between migrants and nonmigrants, because of data limitations they will not be fully satisfactory.

Urban migrants, for purposes of this analysis, were those currently living in an urban area who reported at least one other previous residence and who mentioned at least one rural area (either *población* or barrio) among their previous residences. This definition is based on ever having migrated from a rural to an urban area—rather than, as is more common in the literature, having migrated within a specific time period. By this definition, the number of urban migrants was close to two and a half times the number of urban nonmigrants in each type of urban area.

As Table 17.7 shows, the migrants by this definition were different from the nonmigrants on a number of demographic characteristics. In each type of urban area, they were older, more often married, and had more children. They also had less education and a lower level of living score, especially in Manila. These differences may be responsible for some of the other contrasts to be described next (Table 17.8).

On occupational characteristics, the migrant/nonmigrant comparisons had different results in small cities and in larger cities. In comparison to nonmigrants, migrants were generally better off in small cities—more often employed, higher in occupational prestige, receiving better incomes, perceiving better chances of advancement. Migrants were generally worse off in larger cities and in Manila, however. On job satisfaction, migrants were lower in each type of area. On a number of family characteristics, small-city migrants were better off than nonmigrants, but migrants in larger cities were less well off. Small-city migrants were responsible for fewer household tasks, spent less time on housework, and considered themselves better treated by their husbands. In large cities and in Manila, the differences between migrants and nonmigrants on these variables were reversed. On other family measures, the contrasts were less clear.

Regarding community participation, the one clear contrast was between migrants and nonmigrants in Manila: The former were less likely to participate in organizational or neighborhood activities. Regarding attitudes, migrants in each type of urban area were slightly less in favor of sexual equality. And where personal satisfaction was concerned, migrants were slightly less satisfied with their lives.

Given the broad definition of migrants and the demographic distinctiveness of the group so identified, the precise meaning of these contrasts can-

Table 17.7 Sociodemographic characteristics of urban migrants and nonmigrants, by city size: Philippines, 1976

Characteristic	Barrio	Small city		Large city		Primate city		Combined
		Migrant	Non-migrant	Migrant	Non-migrant	Migrant	Non-migrant	
Age (%)								
18–24	20	20	32	19	34	19	35	22
25–34	32	33	33	33	34	38	25	33
35–44	29	29	20	29	17	30	27	28
45+	20	18	15	18	15	13	13	18
Marital status (%)								
Single	11	16	26	16	24	18	35	15
Married	84	80	66	78	76	78	63	80
Separated	4	4	8	6	0	5	3	4
Mean no. of living children	4.0	3.5	2.6	3.4	2.6	3.3	2.4	3.6
Mean desired no. of children	5.4	4.8	4.7	5.6	4.9	4.3	4.0	5.1
Education (%)								
Did not finish grade school	42	13	11	25	13	9	5	28
Completed grade school	31	17	15	18	17	32	13	25
Did not finish high school	11	17	14	20	30	22	16	15
Completed high school	17	54	60	37	40	37	65	33
Mean level-of-living score	2.3	4.1	4.2	3.6	4.4	4.7	5.7	3.2
Number of respondents	788	303	128	99	41	112	40	1,511

Table 17.8 Selected characteristics of urban migrants and nonmigrants, by city size: Philippines, 1976

Characteristic	Barrio	Small city		Large city		Primate city		
		Migrant	Non-migrant	Migrant	Non-migrant	Migrant	Non-migrant	Combined
% earning money	35	64	48	38	49	34	37	42
% professional	14	23	28	14	25	8	13	18
Mean occupational prestige	30	41	39	32	39	33	38	35
Monthly income in pesos								
0–99	49	15	29	39	42	25	10	34
100–299	29	34	33	34	32	41	30	32
300+	22	51	38	26	26	34	60	34
Mean job satisfaction, from ratings of job aspects	14.59	15.31	15.74	13.78	15.16	15.16	14.31	14.91
Mean no. of tasks wife is responsible for	4.30	3.63	3.94	4.61	3.84	5.44	4.96	4.24
% requiring permission to buy clothes	66	60	59	82	81	36	24	63
% who say husband treats them very well	37	59	50	23	26	44	52	42
% who consider their marriage happier than average	53	68	76	60	52	55	72	58
% participating in neighborhood activities	58	39	35	49	34	21	25	48

Table 17.8 *(continued)*

Characteristic	Barrio	Small city		Large city		Primate city		
		Migrant	Non-migrant	Migrant	Non-migrant	Migrant	Non-migrant	Combined
% who say men have stronger sex drives	60	61	63	53	63	68	60	61
Mean ratings of gender stereotype differentiation	2.54	2.69	2.85	2.71	2.68	2.70	3.03	2.64
Self-ratings								
Masculinity	10.13	10.28	9.98	9.81	9.85	10.16	10.67	10.13
Femininity	10.71	12.09	11.92	11.67	12.07	11.46	11.33	11.26
Most important life goal								
Comfortable life	21	13	14	20	15	34	43	20
Family security	20	27	28	11	24	36	11	3
Salvation	52	48	45	63	51	9	19	47
% very happy	16	20	23	15	19	13	27	17
Mean present ladder rating	4.63	5.34	5.63	4.69	4.97	4.05	4.28	4.82
Which sex is treated better?								
Women	10	21	19	17	7	8	10	13
Equal	50	53	55	62	65	55	55	53
Men	39	26	26	21	27	37	35	34

not be determined. It is notable, however, that small cities again are unusual, often showing contrasts that are the reverse of those in larger cities.

CONCLUSION

Urbanism appears to have a salubrious effect on women in small cities. In large cities, its effect is clearly less favorable. These effects are statistically significant and may eventually lead to socially significant changes. Nevertheless, many pre-Hispanic descriptions of the status of women remain valid even in urban areas (Infante 1975). Beyond this conclusion, this study must leave more questions than answers. Why indeed are small-city women more favored? From these data, no answer can be given. One might speculate about differences in economic structure, such as the absence of a large proletarianized labor force. Or one might speculate about the virtues of small communities—the rural networks and traditions that are easier to maintain and the freedom from the pressures of the metropolis. Or one might cite migrant selectivity and the possibility that the less advantaged end up in large cities at the bottom of the ladder. Only further research can determine whether these explanations are valid.

One final issue deserves mention. Small Philippine cities may share many characteristics, but they are certainly not all alike. This study has ignored distinctions among communities based on region, ethnicity, and economic base. Yet these characteristics are certainly important. The frontier character and the economic potential of a region determine the relative size of the female component in the migration stream (Flieger et al. 1976), and very likely they affect the status of female residents. What urbanism means for women's status will be fully understood only when such variations among cities can be taken into account.

NOTES

This chapter, which was prepared for the Working Group Meeting on Women in the Cities, has not been updated.

1. Support for the survey was provided by the Philippine Social Science Council; fieldwork was conducted by the council's research network.

REFERENCES

Boserup, Ester
    1970   *Woman's Role in Economic Development*. London: Allen & Unwin.

Castillo, Gelia T.
1976   *The Filipino Woman as Manpower: The Image and the Empirical Reality.* College, Laguna: University of the Philippines at Los Banos.

Flieger, Wilhelm, Brigida Koppin, and Carmencita Lim
1976   *Geographical Patterns of Internal Migration in the Philippines: 1960-1970.* Manila: National Census and Statistics Office.

Infante, Teresita R.
1975   *The Woman in Early Philippines and Among the Cultural Minorities.* Manila: Unitas.

Patai, Raphael
1967   *Women in the Modern World.* New York: Free Press.

Social Research Laboratory (SRL)
1977   *Stereotype, Status, and Satisfactions: The Filipina among Filipinos.* Quezon City: Department of Sociology, University of the Philippines.

Tinker, Irene
1976   The adverse impact of development on women. In Irene Tinker and Michele Bo Bramsen (eds.), *Women and World Development.* Washington, D.C.: Overseas Development Council.

Chapter 18

Adaptation of Polynesian Female Migrants in New Zealand

Nancy B. Graves

Although New Zealand has drawn most of its wealth from rural exports, its population has been primarily urban since the colonial period. As in Australia, cities began as entry points and developed as administrative and trade centers (Thorns 1977). Since New Zealand never had a large rural population to be attracted to the city, urban growth has come mainly from overseas migrants. These historical circumstances have led to a situation where a predominantly European and largely English-speaking majority depends heavily today in its major cities on the "unskilled" labor of persons from various Polynesian cultures who are first- or second-generation migrants.

THE CONTEXT OF POLYNESIAN FEMALE MIGRATION

In this report I concentrate on the adaptation of Polynesian migrants to the two largest cities of New Zealand: Auckland with a population of approximately 650,000 and Wellington, the capital, with a population of about 300,000. Since most research has not focused on male/female differences in migrant adaptation and frequently does not analyze data by sex, this report must extrapolate to community studies from material gathered by those few studies that do differentiate the responses of female migrants.

THE INTERNAL MIGRATION OF MAORIS

Until World War II, Maoris were mainly subsistence farmers living in close proximity to other members of their own tribes and descent groups, gathering on the common meeting ground for these groups, the *marae*, but largely withdrawn from Pakeha (European) society. Less than 20 percent had migrated to one of New Zealand's 24 "urban areas" by the end of the war; but by the 1971 census, only 25 years later, a majority of Maoris were living in these same urban areas. The Maori population as a whole has grown by more than 400 percent in the past 50 years, however, so that even those remaining behind have almost doubled in number. Thus urbanization has largely come about through land pressure resulting from this increased population and the diminution of Maori holdings.[1] Secondarily, resettlement in towns and cities has been encouraged by the Maori Affairs Department in the belief that this approach would assimilate the Maori people into New Zealand life.

At first the migrant stream consisted mainly of young single persons, often financed by various government preemployment and apprenticeship schemes that brought Maoris from the country, housed them in hostels, and attempted to give them vocational skills, find them jobs, and orient them gradually to city life. These programs continue, but many young people today prefer to escape from the supervision of authorities, whether the government or their own elders, by migrating on their own and living with peers (Gillespie 1973). Moreover, in recent years more Maoris are migrating in family units (Rowland 1969). Overall the migrant stream has been fairly equally balanced as to sex. In Auckland, where 40 percent settle, the sex ratio is 971; the urban population remains young, however, as two-thirds of Maoris in the city are under 25 years of age (Walsh 1971).

IMMIGRANTS FROM OVERSEAS: THE PACIFIC ISLANDERS

Pacific Islanders have been coming to New Zealand in small numbers since the turn of the century, but significant migration only began following World War II. Today most Pacific Islanders come to New Zealand through a process of "chain migration" sponsored and financed by kinsmen already living in New Zealand. These sponsors, naturally, are very sensitive to economic conditions in the urban areas where they live and tend to discourage migrants who might become a burden on them when jobs are scarce. Thus the migration flow for all groups is far more sensitive to fluctuations in the New Zealand economy than to changes in government regulations.

The in-migration of Pacific Islanders took a startling jump during the 1970s, perhaps compensating for the fewer migrants during the recession of 1968–69. Although migration rates have slowed in the last few years, this dramatic growth over the last 30 years has resulted in a sizable group of Pacific Island residents in New Zealand. Only about one in 40 of the total population are Pacific Islanders, but in Auckland their proportion is double this figure.

Male and female migration rates have not differed greatly overall. Women tend to follow behind male migrants, so women joining families continue to migrate in the years when migration is low, evening out the sex ratio. Young single women appear to migrate at about the same rate as young single men (Graves and Graves 1976), and in some island groups (Cook Islands, the Tokelaus) they were the first to go, hired as domestics with fares paid by their employers.

Motives for Female Migration

The Rural Opportunity Structure. Pacific Islands adult migrants interviewed in New Zealand repeatedly stress the importance of economic motives for migration. It is also clear that, as a large community of migrants was established in New Zealand cities, these communities themselves constituted a pull to the city (Curson 1970; NZDL 1979; Pitt and Macpherson 1974). It is therefore difficult to speak only of the rural end of the migration continuum. The fact that there are few wage labor jobs for women on most islands does provide an incentive for young women to migrate. Still, many might have preferred to remain at home were it not for the needs of the larger kin network, both in the islands and in New Zealand. Shankman (1976) noted that young women were chosen by their *'aiga,* or extended family, to migrate in order to earn money for important family projects. They were preferred for support over young men, who are perceived as more likely to spend their earnings on entertainment and drinking. Young women are generally sent to live with elder relatives who will supervise their conduct. The extent to which these women's desires to migrate or stay home coincide with their family's wishes needs further research.

In the Cook Islands too it has long been a practice to send young women to New Zealand to the homes of relatives, but mainly to help care for children while the mothers work. Today they are sent by parents even more often than by extended kin—a reflection of a nuclearization process that is discussed later.

Another consideration for women is the fact that until very recently, despite bilateral descent and choice of residence after marriage, females had few opportunities for prestige or leadership in the islands. In Samoa, women are seen as representing "the back of the house" (the kitchen area); in fact, this sentiment was expressed by a prominent Samoan male leader in Auckland recently during a speech to a Pacific Islands women's group. Although women can achieve a *matai* (chief) title in Samoa, few have done so (Pitt and Macpherson 1974; Shankman 1976). Since *matais* direct all productive labor in agriculture, distribute its earnings, and are the only persons who can vote or run for office, most women in Samoa must gain power by influencing men. In Tokelau, Huntsman and Hooper (1973:5) conclude, "A man's life is outside, active and public, and a woman's inside, sedentary and private." Migration can be seen as the path to an alternative status system for women, as they can gain status in the migrant community as well as earn money that influences decision-making, not only in their own nuclear household but among more distant kin.

Proportionately more Cook Islands women than Samoan women hold titles, but these women do not hold political power and prestige equivalent to the Samoan *matai* titles. The major route for women to prestige in the

Cook Islands is in civil service posts, nursing, or teaching. The number of these jobs is limited. Since those who gain them have more than average education and are more modernized than others, they are also most likely to be attracted to opportunities in New Zealand. Among the first migrants from the island I studied were teachers originally sent for short teacher-training courses in New Zealand. After this brief exposure to New Zealand life, many returned to New Zealand and induced others to follow. Thus there is a brain drain that overrides motives of occupational prestige in the islands themselves.

Finally one must consider the lack of educational and vocational training opportunities in the islands. In 1977 the Cook Islands government compiled a labor-force training plan through 1982 with many new positions specifically tailored for women; most of the training for these jobs had to be received overseas in either New Zealand or Fiji. Once they are trained, it is often hard to induce the recipients to remain at lower salaries in the islands. Education for their children is one of the most frequently expressed reasons for the migration of Samoan and Cook Islands families (NZDL 1979; Pitt and Macpherson 1974).

The Urban Opportunity Structure. Most island migrants come to New Zealand with eight to nine years of schooling (the equivalent of seventh or eighth grade in the United States). Their English language skill is variable, but most find that "island English" is quite different from that spoken around the factories where they are able to obtain jobs (Graves and Graves 1977a; Haman 1978; NZDL 1979). The concentration of Pacific Islanders and Maoris in the lower-paid, "unskilled labor" jobs has not changed since World War II (Lee 1975; Macpherson 1977). Islanders with higher qualifications usually are downwardly mobile occupationally in New Zealand because they cannot afford to retrain to meet New Zealand requirements for their professions. Only since 1976 has a government-financed retraining program made it possible for teachers (and later, nurses) to become qualified to practice their profession in New Zealand, and only 12 to 17 women a year have been through the program. Many are unwilling to give up the paying jobs they have established in the meanwhile, however, and say that migration and employment in New Zealand confer status enough to satisfy them.

It would seem, then, that the children of migrants would have a better chance of moving into higher occupations. Studies have shown, however, that island-raised children brought to New Zealand for higher schooling do better than those raised under the New Zealand system despite their parents' belief in its superiority (Clay 1974). Island children raised in New Zealand and New Zealand Maori children have similarly low rates of educational attainment. (Hohepa, 1977, estimated that between 78 and 80 percent never obtain their School Certificate, the minimal high school degree.) Since School Certificate and University Entrance passes increasingly are required for entry to trade apprenticeships and white-collar jobs, Polynesian young people continue to swell the ranks of the unskilled.

In short, due to pressing financial needs and low educational qualifications, most Polynesian women migrants find blue-collar jobs like their men, and proportionately more Polynesian women are working than among majority group women. Slightly more Maori women than Pacific Islanders have clerical jobs, and even in factory samples (Haman 1978; Graves and Graves 1977a) it is found that Maori women have more education than island women.

Research is needed on the relative status of women who go to work versus those who stay home and mind children among Polynesian and Pakeha groups. Island and Maori women incur no particular stigma for being working mothers, as is the case in the majority group, and it is more often grandmothers or eldest children who care for the young ones while mothers work.

Polynesian women, regardless of age or occupation, realize for the first time in the city what it means to hold minority group status. In their home areas there are few Europeans, and these are regarded as outsiders; the loss of control over their own affairs may come as a shock and an affront to dignity. Apart from their low status vis-à-vis Pakehas, Polynesian women encounter many different tribes and factions from their own ethnic group as well as people from other Polynesian cultures. The question of the relative status and privilege of these groups within the Pakeha world creates practical problems on the street as well as in the workplace (Graves and Graves 1973, 1977a).

ADAPTATION IN THE CITY

A Theoretical Framework

It is helpful to look not just at the specific *tactics* that migrants use for coping with typical life problems, such as housing, jobs, financing, and social security needs, which have been studied worldwide (Graves and Graves 1974a), but the underlying *adaptive strategies* that guide their choices among alternative tactics. Three general strategies are being employed with varying frequency by all ethnic groups in Auckland, both Polynesian and non-Polynesian. (Graves and Graves 1977a:8):

> In coping with the world around them, individuals have a variety of alternative resources which they can call upon: their own, those of the "nuclear" family which they have founded . . . , those of their "extended" family . . . , those of their friends and neighbors, and those of the wider society, as provided through more impersonal agencies and institutions. We will refer to persons' choices

among these alternative resources, and the associated behavior which these choices entail, as their adaptive strategy. In the *kin-reliance* strategy individuals typically call on resources of the wider circle of relatives beyond the nuclear family; in *peer reliance* they turn to persons of roughly their own generation and social standing, whereas in *self-reliance* they depend on their own resources, those of their nuclear household, or the impersonal institutions of the wider society.

The migrants' choice of strategy depends on a number of factors: the extent of their own resources and their access to those of others; their cultural tradition and personal experience; and finally the fact that each strategy requires a heavy investment of the migrant's time and energy—both to keep networks current and to reciprocate for aid given. Consequently, although most people draw upon resources from all these sources at different times and for different purposes, they can usually be characterized by the predominant source to which they turn: kin, peers, or self. I refer to this source as the migrants' preferred adaptive strategy.[2]

APPLICATION TO RESEARCH

There are two kinds of research to which this framework may be applied. First, my colleagues and I have done research that explicitly applies this paradigm. We have published reports from a study of 157 factory workers —72 men and 85 women—in Auckland (Graves and Graves 1977a, 1977b, 1980; Graves 1978) and are currently engaged in a project involving approximately 750 randomly sampled respondents identifying themselves ethnically as Maori, Samoan, Cook Islander, or Pakeha living in various areas of Auckland (Graves et al. 1979c). In addition, Renée Haman, while a research fellow with the South Pacific Research Institute, contributed two studies of female factory workers using many of the same measures and concepts (Haman 1977, 1978), although she did not measure adaptive strategy directly.

The second kind of evidence comes from studies of Pacific Islanders or Maoris that do not examine adaptive strategies but discuss many of the same issues of migrant adjustment. Missing in most of these studies are male and female comparative data, even though females have usually been included in the samples. Moreover, very few provide data for comparing Polynesian groups with Pakehas. The material, therefore, has been used mainly to support or extend the research findings from Graves and Haman.

The adaptive strategies concept is outlined in Table 18.1. Note that behavioral items are used—that is, items the respondent can report on with a fair degree of accuracy. We also used many nonverbal aids such as counters to facilitate memory. Respondents are given a total score in each of the three adaptive strategies and then are classified according to their

Table 18.1 Measurement of adaptive strategies: 1976—77

Indicator[a]	Kin-reliant	Peer-reliant	Self-reliant
Household composition	Living with parents or kin of parents' generation or as member of a three-generation extended family	Living with friends or relatives of own generation (brothers, sisters, cousins)	Living alone or with conjugal family members only (spouse and children)
Use of money	Regularly helps support a relative	Goes to pub at least once a week[b]	Savings account for own or conjugal family needs
Spare-time activities	Visiting relatives mentioned during last 2 weeks	50% or more with friends	More than 50% alone or with conjugal family members
Social networks	Saw 5 or more relatives or exclusively relatives during last 2 weeks	Saw 6 or more friends during last 2 weeks	Saw fewer than 6 friends and fewer than 5 relatives, but not exclusively relatives during last 2 weeks
How obtained present job	Relatives	Friends	Self
Work mates	One or more relatives work in same factory	Sees one or more work mates socially outside of work	Does not see any work mates socially outside of work

Note: One point is given for each of the six factors present for each of the three scales.

a. In subsequent research questions regarding the exchange of goods and services with relatives and friends have been added as a seventh factor and systems of emotional support as an eighth.

b. In subsequent research, where we wanted to explore the relationship between preferred adaptive strategy and drinking behavior, we substituted loans of money to friends for this item.

predominant strategy choice. Correlational analyses in this study allow for a quantitative continuum of strategy choices.

In our 1977 study of workers in two factories we found consistent differences between ethnic groups in major adaptive strategy (Table 18.2) Generally Europeans of both sexes prefer a self-reliant adaptation. New Zealand-born or educated Polynesians (including those of either Pacific Islands or Maori cultural heritage) more often choose peer reliance, while Pacific Islands immigrants tend to prefer kin reliance. Thus, while adaptive strategy is not synonymous with cultural background and persons

Table 18.2 Sex and ethnic differences in preferred adaptive strategy

Ethnic group	Kin-reliant (%)	Peer-reliant (%)	Self-reliant (%)
Europeans			
Men (N = 16)	0	38	**62**
Women (N = 14)	14	7	**79**
N.Z.-educated Maoris and islanders			
Men (N = 26)	35	**46**	19
Women (N = 28)	28	**36**	36
Pacific Island immigrants			
Men (N = 27)	**41**	22	37
Women (N = 43)	**56**	2	42

from each ethnic group fall in each adaptive category, there is sufficient association to permit extrapolation to other studies. It must be remembered, however, that self-reliance as a choice for an immigrant Pacific Islander formerly closely tied to kin is quite a different thing than for a New Zealand Pakeha who has grown up in a western nuclear family stressing individual independence. These subtleties will be discussed throughout this essay.

Male/Female Comparisons of Adaptive Strategy. Although it is clear from Table 18.2 that women in general were similar in adaptive strategy to men of the same ethnic group, there were differences. First, more women in every ethnic group adopted self-reliant strategies. Second, fewer women than men in every ethnic group took a peer-reliant strategy. There are a number of interrelated explanations for these facts. In general, persons choosing self-reliance, regardless of sex, tended to be about nine years older than the average of those choosing other adaptive strategies, were married, and were living in nuclear family households. The fact that more women than men chose this strategy, however, although as many men in the sample were married, indicates that women may be more influenced by their marriage role than are men or that they are using this adaptive strategy for reasons connected with being married rather than by choice.[3] This preference for self-reliance is related to the fact that our sample was composed strictly of working women. In addition to holding down their factory jobs, these women were expected to handle domestic chores and child care. The fact that fewer men in the self-reliant category had working wives than did men in the other categories may indicate that they expected these chores to be done by the women. This expectation appears to continue even when the wife works, leaving her little time for the development of kin-support or peer-support networks. Although 65 percent of the kin-reliant men were married, only 44 percent of the kin-reliant women managed to combine nuclear and extended-family obligations. And, as we will see, self-reliant women got in very little visiting or other social activity. Thus the working wife, isolated in her home catching up on chores on the weekend, depends increasingly on her husband for support of all types. Women frequently rely on their spouses for obtaining employment; men never do. For the working wife, self-reliance does not mean independence as it may for the single woman leaving either a nuclear or extended family to be on her own. Rather it can mean that while she runs her household and contributes to family income, she is also isolated and overworked.

Another factor mitigating against a peer-reliant adaptation for women is insufficient opportunity for casual meeting. In the rural environment, Polynesian women meet while washing clothes at the stream, at the village hall, or in family festivals and working bees. In the city, where men in factory jobs congregate in the pubs after work, few women feel comfortable doing so. Pub attendance is more permissible for Maori women than for those from other groups, and this is a common way to reintegrate with family and friends when visiting one's home town. An observational study of public bar behavior in Auckland (Graves et al. 1979b) found that over half of Maori drinking groups included women; few Pacific Islands women were seen; Pakeha women mainly attended exclusive lounge bars where dress regulations are strict. Young single women in our factory study not only chose peer reliance more often but had higher rates of pub attendance than other women in the sample. They seemed to pay for their recreation, however, by earning a bad reputation among their work mates (Graves and Graves 1977a).

Alternative socializing settings for women of this socioeconomic level are the parent-run preschools (play centers), various sports and social clubs, and church groups. Among working women attendance at all these settings was low, due mainly to family and kin obligations. For many women, the short breaks at work are their only opportunity to socialize with friends.

Ethnic Variations in Adaptive Strategy. Another way of meeting needs for socializing and providing mutual support is by having more relatives in the home. Both the Graves study and the Haman study (1978) showed that Pacific Islands women, especially those who were kin reliant in other ways, were more likely than European and Maori women to live with relatives or, when married, to have relatives living with them and their husband. This tendency resulted in a fairly low ratio of children to adults despite having more children in the home for Pacific Islanders compared to most native New Zealanders, either Polynesian or Pakeha. Maori women, like Pacific Islanders, had children of all ages, and without relatives to help out they were saddled with an excessive child-care burden. Friends, evidently, do not help much with this crucial problem. The nuclear family is now the norm for New Zealand-raised Polynesians as well as Europeans, but there are few economical child-care facilities to substitute for the functions formerly filled by extended-family members. As legislation against immigrants not of working age grows more restrictive, many Pacific Islands women are being deprived of the opportunity to use a kin-reliant strategy. They, too, will then be forced into a reduced family situation with its attendant problems of isolation and lack of support.

ADAPTIVE STRATEGY AND MIGRANT ADJUSTMENT

All migrants to the city face problems of housing, financial assistance, employment, establishing an urban social network, and relating to the urban host society. In this section we consider how a migrant's adaptive strategy can affect her decision-making.

ASSISTANCE TO COME TO NEW ZEALAND

In our study almost all female migrants were assisted financially to come to New Zealand, or else they came as part of a family group. This finding was less true for men. For both sexes, kin-reliant migrants were more likely to have had their fare paid by relatives than were the self-reliant.

For the New Zealand Labour Department study (NZDL 1979:35–36) we have breakdowns by island group but not by sex. Of their total sample of 250 males and 103 females, 69 percent were assisted by relatives other than parents, and a further 16.5 per cent were helped by parents. Some were assisted by friends (2.5 percent), indicating peer reliance, and the rest by impersonal sources (employer, 3.4 percent; home government, 5.5 percent). "Other," which presumably consists of using one's own resources, accounted for only 2.2 percent—adding up to a total of 11 percent for self-reliant strategies.

The Labour Department study notes that Samoans were most likely to have fares paid by the extended family (two-thirds of this ethnic group), while Tokelauans and Tongans received half their fares from this source. Cook Islanders and Niueans tended to be more dependent on parents for their fares, often receiving a trip to New Zealand as a reward for completion of school studies. The Tokelau Islanders were the only group to receive government assistance.

Haman's study (1978) gives statistics on women by island group. Haman found that 38 percent of Cook Islands women had assistance from kin for airfares, housing, or jobs (all combined in her data) compared to 69 percent of Samoan women migrants. She did not differentiate between parental aid and help from extended kin. An interesting question posed by this study is whether these women gave such assistance, in turn, to other relatives. While 40 percent of Samoan women gave all three types of assistance and 53 percent gave four or more types of assistance to relatives, only 37 percent of Cook Islanders gave this much aid, while 38 percent gave only one type of aid and 25 percent gave none at all to subsequent migrants. Haman relates this finding to the differing immigration requirements for the two groups.

OBTAINING HOUSING

Our factory study found that all Pacific Islands immigrants (male and female) except one lived with kin upon arrival in New Zealand. The Labour Department study does not have data on this question, but Haman studied this matter in detail, concerning herself with the type of kin chosen. She found that Samoan women migrants chose lineal kin more often than Cook Islands women, who tended to choose collateral kin of their own generation. (Fifty percent chose cousins or siblings.) This finding accords with the Graves's (1977a) finding that Cook Islanders (16 percent) more often chose peer reliance than Samoans (10 percent). Thus living with collateral kin may be a way station in moving to a peer-reliant strategy.

Haman (1978) also found that 12 percent of Cook Islands women came as heads of their own domestic units, compared to only 6 percent of Samoan women in her sample. Moreover, 25 percent of the Cook Islands women stayed at a school or place of employment upon arrival, whereas no Samoan women did so. Samoan women relied heavily on parents' siblings for housing (38 percent).

The initial coping tactic of choosing family, friends, or one's own nuclear unit to live with upon arrival may or may not be maintained after the immigrant has been in the city a while. A common shift is from kin reliance to peer reliance as a person gets to know a wider circle of friends. For women, however, this shift seldom takes place after marriage because of the lack of opportunities discussed earlier. Keeping a kin-reliance strategy is not easy in an individualistic society where, for instance, the bureaucracy does not recognize the extended family as an entity for the purpose of buying houses and obtaining loans. Pacific Islanders dedicated to this strategy get around these problems by pooling their money in a family credit union, buying houses for extended-family members until all are accommodated, and financing these houses from family funds more often than using stringent government loans. New houses are preferred because of low down payments.

OBTAINING A JOB

We noted in discussing Table 18.1 the tendency for Polynesians to rely on kin or friends as opposed to impersonal sources of information discovered by individual effort. This finding is particularly true for women. All three major studies cited in this review agree, however, that relatives are resources for the first job much more often than for subsequent jobs (Graves and Graves 1977a, 1977b; Haman 1978; NZDL 1979). Table 18.3 shows this shift, which holds for all ethnic groups: Relatives are used *more* by Pacific Islanders and Maoris at all stages of job-seeking, but all groups tend to rely on friends or self more for later jobs. Similarly, the Pacific Islanders in the New Zealand Labour Department study turned mainly to relatives for their first job, (57 percent) while only 16 percent had found their present job (at time of interview) from that source (NZDL) 1979:59–60). Some of this shift took place because of growing peer reliance; 12 percent used friends to find their first job, 16 percent for their present job. But a much more significant proportion were simply learning their way around the society and used a self-reliant strategy to find their current job. Self-reliant sources included self-search, newspapers, and help from organizations such as the home government, the Labour Department, and churches. This strategy accounted for only 30 percent of the sample on the first job but 66 percent on the present job.

Haman's all-female sample shows the same pattern: Use of friends increases slightly, but the major change is to an increased self-reliance in subsequent job searches. Haman suggests that ethnic differences in the use of relations to find first jobs may be traced to two causes: Not only do many Pacific Islanders need job guarantees before coming to New Zealand but also Polynesian and European attitudes about the employment of women may differ.

A related issue concerns reasons cited for the choice of subsequent jobs. In our study we found male/female differences on only one factor, consid-

Table 18.3 Alternative strategies for obtaining employment

	Relative		Friend		Self	
Ethnic group	First job	Present job	First job	Present job	First job	Present job
Europeans (N = 30)	43% → 20%		4% → 18%		53% → 62%	
N.Z.-educated Maoris and islanders (N = 53)	47% → 36%		11% → 23%		42% → 41%	
Pacific Island immigrants (N = 74)	66% → 35%		7% → 14%		27% → 51%	

ering the sample as a whole. Men differed significantly from women (chi square = 6.88, $p < :01$) in more often choosing a job for reasons of self-growth, which includes opportunities for achievement not explicitly linked to more pay or comments about the intrinsic value of the work (Graves and Graves 1977a:18). When the data are broken down by ethnic group and sex (see Table 18.4), however, we see that this sex difference is accounted for by differences between Pakeha men and women; Polynesians, both male and female, rarely mention self-growth. A small proportion of Pakeha women (10 percent) also gave self-growth reasons for leaving their *previous* job, compared to 7.5 percent of all Polynesian women. But 44 percent of Pakeha men left their jobs for self-growth reasons, compared to 22 percent of New Zealand-educated Polynesian and no Pacific Islands men. Hence this characteristic appears mainly to be linked to western individualism, imparted by schools perhaps primarily to men but particularly to men from modern western cultures.

Most Polynesian men and women emphasize instead social relations as the major reason for choosing one job over another; secondary in their hierarchy of values is the rate of pay. While social relations receive major emphasis from European women as well, the percentage who mentioned this factor is still low compared to Polynesians. Pacific Islands women are also concerned that the job be close to home, probably because they are unlikely to own a car. Polynesian women are also more mindful than Europeans of the need for a high rate of pay. This concern is probably due more to their bigger family expenses than to contrasting salaries earned by

Table 18.4 Reasons for choosing their present job

Reason	Pacific Island immigrants		N.Z.-educated Polynesians		Pakehas/ Europeans	
	Women (%)	Men (%)	Women (%)	Men (%)	Women (%)	Men (%)
Self-growth	0	0	4	4	0	31
Social ties	67	63	68	73	36	31
Distance	40	20	29	38	21	44
Pay	26	17	21	4	14	12
Type of work	7	17	4	12	21	0
Working conditions	0	3	4	4	0	0
Hours	7	0	11	38	21	6
Number of respondents	43	27	28	26	14	16

Note: N = 154 New Zealand factory workers. Percentages sum to more than 100 in each column because subjects were permitted to mention more than one reason. Missing data prevented classification of three additional subjects interviewed in this study.

spouses, since European men did not earn more than Polynesian men in the factories surveyed. Haman (1978:79) points out that since pay is used by Pacific Islands women to validate status in their kin groups through ability to contribute to the needs of family members, it has a meaning for social relations that does not apply as much to Pakehas.

ESTABLISHING SOCIAL NETWORKS

Once the migrant was on the job, social relations were a powerful predictor of satisfaction or dissatisfaction. Some 93 percent of the women (and 83 percent of the men) mentioned relations with coworkers as key reasons for liking or disliking their job; 90 percent of Polynesians mentioned this reason, compared with 74 percent of Pakehas. Men had fewer complaints about fellow workers than did women, and Polynesians complained less than Pakehas.

We have seen that many Polynesian women migrants choose a job, particularly their first one, because relatives or close friends work there as well. We were interested in whether relatives would continue to be preferred work mates for female migrants as they remained longer in the city. Therefore we asked our respondents to tell us the number of close friends they had on the job and whether these were also relatives and then to use 12 chips to constitute their ideal work group, indicating both the ethnic group and relationship of work mates.

Peer-reliant women reported having more friends on the job (a mean of 4.4) than either kin-reliant or self-reliant women (3.6 and 3.2 respectively). As might be expected, kin-reliant women had the most friends on the job who were also relatives. Were these friendship networks by choice or happenstance? When asked to choose their ideal work group, kin-reliant women chose 14 percent of the group to be relatives, compared to 11 percent for peer-reliant women and 10 percent for self-reliant women. All women chose about the same proportion of work mates to be unrelated members of their own ethnic group (27–28 percent). Self-reliant women, however, were often concerned that the ideal work group have an even distribution of *all* ethnic groups—30 percent of them chose an equal number from each ethnicity represented compared to 15 percent of the kin-reliant women and only 8 percent of the peer-reliant women. Men showed this result even more strongly, with 44 percent of the self-reliant choosing an even ethnic distribution. For Europeans, this measure was undoubtedly influenced by New Zealand's strong ethic of equality among races. For Polynesians choosing self-reliance, it may reflect an effort to leave behind ties and integrate with the Pakeha majority. Some Pacific Islanders explained that they wished to perfect their English and learn Pakeha ways; having such a work group, they said, would help them.

Their adaptive strategy strongly affected their perception of whether they worked alone or in a group. The group-oriented kin-reliant and peer-reliant women tended to perceive themselves as "working in a group" even when objective analysis would indicate they were doing individual tasks on separate machines (67 percent of these strategy types compared to 42 percent for self-reliant women). Furthermore, self-reliant women were more likely to see themselves as "working alone " even when they were placed in a work group where coordinated efforts were necessary. This finding was true for men as well (Graves and Graves 1977a).

Haman's results (1978:182–85) support the Graves's findings. Pakehas, who generally choose a self-reliant strategy, were most likely to prefer a job "on my own" (75 percent), compared to only 19 percent of Maoris and 42 percent of Pacific Islanders, who generally prefer group-oriented strategies. Moreover, 81 percent of Maoris (the most strongly peer-reliant group) indicated a preference for working with friends, compared to 54 percent of Pacific Islanders and only 25 percent of Pakehas. In her sample, no Pakehas or New Zealand-educated Polynesians preferred to work with relatives. Some 58 percent of Maoris reported kin employed in the factory where they worked, however, as did 66 percent of Pacific Islanders; only 16 percent of Pakehas had relatives working there (Haman 1978:185).

All groups reported they had the most contact and the closest friendships with members of their own ethnic group. The value of these monocultural groups for immigrants in terms of social support and work motivation is dealt with by Haman in an earlier paper (1977). Pakehas and New Zealand-educated Polynesians said they would prefer an ethnically mixed work group, however, either because it was more interesting or because they considered a monocultural work group bad in some respect. Again, Pacific Islanders said that perfecting language skills was their major reason for preferring a mixed group.

For kin-reliant persons, social life centers on the wide network of extended-family members. By definition, they see more relatives from outside their own household each week and are more likely to consider visits to relatives one of their major spare-time activities. These women initiate more social contacts than women in the other two strategy groups. In general, women are more active in seeing relatives than are men in all strategy groups.

As noted, the public bar serves as an informal club and contact center for peer-reliant persons. Some 83 percent of peer-reliant men and 67 percent of these women attended a pub at least once a week, compared to only 20 percent of kin-reliant women and 15 percent of peer-reliant women. Self-reliant persons tended to base their social life on their own home and nuclear family. They were far more likely to be isolated socially, to have few friends, and to see them less frequently. Self-reliant women had initiated the fewest social contacts in the past two weeks (28 percent of their total contacts compared to 40 percent for kin reliant and 33 percent for peer reliant). Despite their ethic of equality, their social behavior does not show much cross-ethnic contact.

Women in all strategy groups are more confined to the home than men, having a smaller proportion of out-visits to total visits per week. Nevertheless, women in all three categories have done more visiting than have the men, suggesting that keeping up social ties is more important for them. The only exception to this finding is in the greater visiting of nonrelatives by peer-reliant men. (No doubt this visiting could include group gatherings at the pub.) Overall, women have a social network averaging 13 persons whereas men average 9.6.

We also inquired about the extent to which social ties on the job were pursued outside work. Peer-reliant women saw more of their work mates outside the job than did any other group; self-reliant women did so the least. Kin-reliant women saw an intermediate number during off-work hours, but most of these work mates were relatives.

Again there were male/female differences. Self-reliant men were more isolated on the job than were self-reliant women, while men and women in the other two strategy groups were more alike. This finding indicates that perhaps Pakeha men's greater emphasis on the self-growth goal of achievement may cut down on time for affiliation. Women were also more likely than men to report relatives as close friends, regardless of their adaptive strategy. Women have higher mean scores on the kin-reliance index, and their higher rate of visiting relatives and greater numbers of relatives at work in all groups may indicate that women are more willing than men to depend on relatives. This finding is even more true for Polynesian than for Pakeha women.

Haman (1978) found the same ordering of ethnic groups for social relations when away from work as she found on the job. Polynesians visited work mates when off the job more than Pakehas, and Pacific Islanders did so more than Maoris. Maori women also had a higher dependency ratio, which could keep them busy at home during weekends and evenings. Some 63 percent of women with high dependency scores had no contact with work mates off the job, compared to 42 percent of the women with low dependency ratios.

In Haman's sample, 75 percent of the Pakeha women spent time off the job in solitary activities, compared to only 32 percent Maoris and 54 percent of the Pacific Islanders. The islanders focused mainly on family activities whereas Maoris split their time between family and friends, which is in keeping with their peer-reliant strategy. Only 8 percent of Haman's Pakeha sample spent time with friends.

With respect to visiting, all the women in Haman's sample spent the majority of their time with their own ethnic group. Maoris saw the most persons from other ethnic groups, which corroborates our evidence concerning peer-reliant persons. Pacific Islanders had the highest rates of visiting in general, but they saw mainly relatives. While 87 percent of the Pacific Islanders lived near kin, and 68 percent of the Maoris, only 50 percent of the Pakehas did so. Although Maoris had more kin in the city than the other groups, they did not visit them as often as did Pacific Islanders. Similar results were found for these groups in the Graves and Graves study.

Other corroborative evidence comes from studies done in public bars and public schools. Graves et al. (1979a) found that Pakehas most often drink alone or in pairs in bars, whereas Pacific Islanders and Maoris drink in groups of four to six persons. Also N. Graves (1975) found in a survey of all preschools and a sample of primary schools in the Auckland metropolitan area that Pakeha teachers, parents, and children preferred solitary activities or those involving no more than two people, while Polynesians preferred to work and play in groups of three or more.

In summary, then, most Polynesian women have chosen group-oriented strategies of adaptation that require keeping up social networks both at work and at leisure. Those who have chosen, or are required by circumstance, to adopt a self-reliant strategy focused on the nuclear family have fewer mutual obligations to kin and friends, but they pay for this independence by having a higher dependency ratio and less social support both at work and at home. A peer-reliant strategy does not seem to help married women with major problems of domestic chores and child care.

Formal and Informal Organizations

The general adaptive strategy chosen by a female migrant greatly affects whether or not she will associate with organizations and what type of organization she will choose. Kin-reliant women spent much of their time in informal kin meetings to decide on family business, raise funds for helping relatives in the city or in the islands, and prepare for family events such as weddings, funerals, or title ceremonies.

Samoan women, for example, are active along with their men in running family credit organizations called *kalapu* (Pitt and Macpherson 1974; Macpherson 1975). Kin-reliant women are also more active than women pursuing other strategies in church groups and activities. For example, Graves and Graves (1977a) found that while 44 percent of the kin-reliant women reported they needed lots of money for their church activities, only 28 percent of the self-reliant and 8 percent of the peer-reliant women conceded this. Similarly, 58 percent of Pacific Islands women (compared to only 7 percent of Maoris and New Zealand-educated islander women and no Pakehas) said they needed large sums of money for their church.

For Pacific Islanders, the church is a way to unite different kin groups within the ethnic community, and many social welfare programs are initiated by the Pacific Islanders Presbyterian Church and other churches. In a list of 149 voluntary associations geared to the needs of migrants produced by the Pacific Islanders Educational Resources Center (PIERC), 25 percent were church-related; of these, 35 percent were Samoan. Hamilton (1974), in her study of the political integration of Samoan migrants, found that most regarded community affairs as church-related activities. Samoans also have the custom, not uniformly followed by other Polynesian groups, of contributing fine mats, food, and large sums of money in the name of relatives who are members of a new church just opening. This is done regardless of whether the contributors are themselves members of the church; in turn, those in whose name the donations were made are obliged not only to contribute their own gifts to the church but to repay relatives for their generosity. These customs, along with the many financial obligations to relatives in the islands, place a heavy burden on Samoan women in particular and help to account for their emphasis on the importance of pay in choosing a job.

Peer-reliant persons do not, in general, care much for formal organizations, with the exception of sports clubs. They prefer informal gatherings where financial aid takes the form of ad hoc associations and lotteries; social support and job opportunities are garnered through conversation with mates. Moreover, the young peer-reliant woman finds that most of the formal women's organizations are run by married women and first-generation migrants, while she herself is likely to have been raised or educated in New Zealand. Peer-reliant men have formed a number of peer groups labeled in Auckland as gangs; these groups are occasionally involved in territorial conflicts centering on neighborhood pubs (Graves et al. 1979b). Women sometimes associate with male gang members, but they do not themselves form gangs. Feminist groups are becoming more popular among some Maori women, especially those with more education. By and large, however, young peer-reliant women end up in largely male-dominated settings due to a lack of youth organizations. Since most peer-reliant persons have broken with church as well as kin authority, young people's groups organized by churches are unpopular. More research needs to be done on the sports and social clubs, which appear to be a middle path between pub and church.

Migrants choosing a self-reliant strategy tend either to use the formal organizations and agencies on their own through official channels or to join interest-based organizations with a modern structure and format. PIERC lists 67 government or city agencies that minister to the social needs of Pacific Islanders. Most of these agencies serve the majority group as well and were not specifically set up to handle Polynesian problems. Nevertheless, efforts have been made to hire Polynesians in the police (where a special interracial J-[juvenile-]team handles youth problems and educates the public on cultural differences), the Maori Affairs Department (which includes Island Affairs), and the Vocational Training Council. The Consumer's Reseach Bureau hired Polynesian officers to educate Polynesians on the dangers of hire purchase, false advertising, unwholesome modern food, and the need for budgeting in an urban environment, as well as for handling specific complaints. The Race Relations Conciliator's Office mediates cases of alleged discrimination in housing, jobs, and other areas of public life. And Auckland Hospital has trained a number of Polynesian medical social workers and community workers to go directly to homes and consult on a variety of health or adjustment problems.

PIERC itself was established by the government to meet the needs of this population. It does so mainly by educating interested Pakehas who may come in daily contact with Pacific Islanders as employers, teachers, or members of the general public. Apart from providing the directory of services, PIERC has classes in island languages and cultures, provides consultation services for schools and businesses, and is developing a series of pamphlets and age-graded books on Polynesian cultures and their viewpoints. It also provides home tutoring in English as a second language. But due to one problem or another in implementing the program, most Polynesian women continue to learn English from relatives or friends.

Citizen's Advice Bureaus operate in many neighborhoods where there is a high proportion of migrants, referring persons for legal advice and providing information on dealing with government agencies. These bureaus have few bilingual officers, however, so migrant women with language problems usually cannot use them. A Samoan women's organization has offered to operate a bureau in a heavily Polynesian district, but the government has thus far declined to support an organization for only one island group.

A number of women's voluntary associations with ethnic origins have arisen to address welfare and "uplift" issues. The most venerable of these groups is the Maori Women's Welfare League, founded in 1951, which receives funds from the government and lobbies for the interests of Maori families and youth. A recent counterpart for Pacific Islands women is PACIFICA, which now has government support. These organizations attempt to unite Polynesian women on common social problems, hold regular meetings and conventions where they remit proposals to government bodies, raise funds, and provide some scholarship support. These formal organizations mainly attract women who are upwardly mobile or middle class, however, most of whom follow a self-reliant strategy. Kin-reliant women, especially if they have jobs, are usually too busy. And these associations hold little attraction for non-English speakers, since meetings are conducted in English. Traditional Pacific Islands women may find the

European style of conducting meetings uncomfortable as well. PACIFICA is attempting to broaden the base of its membership by holding neighborhood meetings in homes, a policy that may lead to the development of a new social support system for some women. Meetings of these smaller groups tend to focus on everyday problems—dealing with children's teachers, how to get legal advice, and so forth—which may prove to be of greater help to migrants than conspicuous national conventions.

Other formal organizations are composed of specific ethnic or island-of-origin groups: the Council of Samoan Women, the Samoan Action Organization, and associations for people from each of the various Cook Islands (even certain villages within them), the Tokelaus, Tonga, and Fiji. Many Cook Islanders prefer such organizations to church-related or government-sponsored groups, as they combine hometown social conviviality with welfare assistance.

Pacific Islanders have not been very active in forming political organizations or taking part in the political issues of society at large. Furthermore, Hamilton (1974) found that Samoan women had even less interest in political matters, possessed less political information, were less interested in voting, and felt less obligation to New Zealand as their adopted nation than did Samoan men. Young Pacific Islanders and the more educated of the older generation are beginning to change this pattern, but it is likely that they will need to use the ethnic organizations if they wish to involve the average migrant.

RELATIONS WITH THE HOST SOCIETY

How does a Pacific Islands female migrant relate to members and institutions of the host society? Her relations are patterned by her immigrant status (temporary or permanent resident), by whether she is employed and in what industry, and by whether or not she lives closely with others of her own ethnic group. Maoris vary too by whether they are first- or second-generation urban residents and by the extent of their kin ties within the city and in the home area. Finally, all Polynesians are inevitably affected by the European style of major societal institutions with which they are in daily contact, as well as the attitudes, behavior, and norms of Pakeha society.

Linguistic and cultural contrasts abound. The significance of these differences for intergroup contact began to make an impression on government and the general public only in the mid-1970s. Government policy until recently has been forthrightly assimilationist, but now there is increasing talk of pluralism and multiculturalism. Still, in 1976 the prime minister told a national convention of Pacific Islands women that their request for a radio station broadcasting in various Polynesian languages was not only unnecessary (since Polynesian music could be played on present stations) but harmful, since it might retard the learning of English.[4]

Until recently there were separate schools for Maoris in rural areas. There is still a separate Maori electoral roll by which Maori representatives can be voted for by persons with one-half or more Maori blood. Like American Indians, Maoris in general prefer to retain whatever governmental representation and programs they have gained over the years, but at the same time they feel a growing resistance to what Hohepa (1978) has called the "one-people" myth of New Zealand society. The last five years have seen the beginning of more pluralistic programs in education: units on Maori and Pacific Islands cultures (which, however, function largely as cultural enclaves in the midst of a basically unchanged western individualistic classroom).

Considerable research has been conducted over the years on the attitudes of the Pakeha majority toward Polynesians, mainly Maoris (Ausubel 1960; Archer and Archer 1970; Thomas 1970; Trlin 1971; Vaughan 1962). Many of these studies show paternalistic attitudes toward Polynesians, and most are social distance studies that conclude that Pakehas generally prefer to associate with people who are physically and culturally similar to themselves (see T. Graves 1976:1). In our own research, we chose a more open-minded approach to the description of other ethnic groups (Graves and Graves 1974b; T. Graves 1976). We found that white New Zealanders placed themselves intermediate along a cultural continuum that grouped British-based cultures at one end and Polynesian cultures at the other. Although they perceived themselves as more like Polynesians than any other English-based group, Pakehas still saw themselves as significantly different in personality from both Maoris and Pacific Islanders. It should be noted, however, that on the evaluative dimension, Pakehas present more favorable stereotypes of Polynesians than they do of themselves or their British cultural cousins, with the exception of Canadians.

In its study of Pacific Islands workers, the New Zealand Labour Department asked respondents directly what things about New Zealand life and society seemed difficult to them. The most significant topic was the threat of crime and violence; islanders noted that fights were more common than on their home island. Others objected to the influence of alcohol, the absence of respect for others (particularly older people), the use of foul language, and the limited role of the church.

Adjustment to the host society seemed to entail different problems at different stages of adaptation. At first, language difficulties occupied much attention, along with adjustment to the faster pace of life and unaccustomed modes of transportation, the colder weather, the more routinized work patterns, and the expense and difficulties of obtaining favorite island foods. Many mentioned the noise and generally hectic atmosphere of the city compared to their quiet and orderly village. They also mentioned the personal style of New Zealanders, which was seen as cold and "not wanting to mix with us."

During the second stage of adjustment migrants are still concerned with their language skills, but now they find housing, problems at work, and discrimination and nonhelpfulness of Pakehas taking precedence. As more migrants move away from the relatives who initially gave them accommodation on arrival—and Cook Islanders do this sooner than Samoans (Haman 1978:61)—they must become more aware of their landlords, neighbors, work mates. In a study of Auckland landlords, Spoonley (in Macpherson 1977:110) noted that Pacific Islanders were perceived by 67 percent of his sample as lowering the value of surrounding properties. With few exceptions, attitudes toward them as tenants were very negative. Observations indicated that offices offering rentals required more personal information and guarantees of good intentions from Polynesians than from Pakeha clients (Graves and Graves 1973).

A series of observational studies was done to assess the behavior displayed by members of the host society toward Polynesians contacted in public places (Graves and Graves 1973). We found four major types of interethnic contact, each of which carried its own norms of appropriate behavior: transitory, asymmetric, egalitarian, and reverse asymmetric.

Transitory situations—as on the street, on public transportation, in shops or waiting rooms—call for avoidance behavior and attempts by Pakehas to maintain privacy. Polynesians frequently violated these norms by speaking louder than approved, singing, or sitting too near by Pakeha standards. Other Polynesians, however, were acutely aware of Pakeha standards and reacted by withdrawing and becoming mute and shy. Some felt under covert surveillance to such an extent that they would leave waiting rooms at doctor's offices and wait outside until called. In either case, Polynesians frequently feel unwelcome, since friendly smiles, gestures, or conversation are not among the norms prescribed for this kind of situation in Pakeha society. Since transitory situations are very rare in island life and small rural Maori towns, Polynesians tend to characterize the city as cold and unfriendly.

In the second sort of situation, roles of participants are *asymmetric* and the Polynesian is subordinate. This situation does, of course, occur in Polynesian hierarchical societies, but the behavior appropriate to a subordinate role in island culture may not suit the norms of Pakeha culture. An example of this situation involved a Tongan woman who brought a basket of food to an immigration official from whom she was seeking an extension of visa. This was a perfectly appropriate gesture of commoners seeking audience with an official in Tonga, but in Auckland it shocked the official, who saw it as an invitation to corruption. Pakehas in these situations generally act in one of three ways: by "playing the book," sometimes overplaying the dominant role according to the strict rules of their office; by adopting a paternalistic way of being helpful to the Polynesians; or by being helpful to the Polynesian, even if it means bending the rules somewhat. We found more instances of the first two responses than the third, but the response depends also on the advantage to the Pakeha. Employers, for example, many of whom value their Polynesian workers highly, hired personnel officers (and increasingly these are Polynesian and female) to help employees with all types of personal problems.

Polynesians generally adopt one of four responses to the behavior of the dominant Pakeha in these situations. They may be extremely shy and rely on acculturated relatives or friends to intercede for them; this response is more typical of females than males. They may resent their subordinate status and show extreme discomfort and nervous reactions; these responses are commonly found among Maoris and second-generation Pacific Islanders. They may try to evade the demands of the other person through subterfuge or feigned misunderstanding, even "stupidity." Or, finally, they may take advantage of the paternalism and subtly manipulate the Pakeha. If an egalitarian person in a legitimate position of authority is trying to help, however, Polynesians are usually approving and cooperative. In our sample of factory workers, 55 percent of Pacific Islanders and 52 percent of New Zealand-educated Polynesians desired an egalitarian attitude on the part of their supervisor at work, compared to only 30 percent of Pakehas. Moreover, 80 percent of Pacific Islanders and 67 percent of Maoris wanted supervisors to help with personal problems, and 68 percent of both groups preferred a supervisor who would work alongside employees on occasion when needed. Men and women felt the same about this matter, except that even more women (71 percent) than men (58 percent) preferred a supervisor who would join in the work (Graves and Graves 1977a:47–48). This finding reflects the fact that traditionally Polynesian leaders are generally elected by consensus, and usually they must maintain that consensus through considerate behavior toward subordinates or lose their position (Macpherson 1975).

The other two types of situation—the *egalitarian,* where roles are equal, and the *reverse asymmetric,* where Polynesians are dominant and Pakehas are subordinate—are rare but very instructive. Pakeha reactions when they are of equal status to Polynesians, as in work situations where they have the same jobs and eat in the same cafeteria, fall generally into four patterns. First, they may reject the situation as unnatural and refuse to eat with Polynesians, or otherwise avoid interaction, associating with their "own kind." Second, they may become passive, cease to initiate the interaction as Pakehas generally do when they are clearly dominant, and allow Polynesians to initiate eye contact and conversation while they themselves participate minimally. This behavior has been observed among bar patrons, for example, who drink with Polynesians but never meet their glance or begin a conversation. Third, they may attempt to subvert the situation into one where they are dominant, calling attention to the differences rather than similarities between themselves and Polynesians. Finally, Pakehas may try to respond in an egalitarian fashion as they would with a Pakeha friend, often making comments to emphasize that although there are differences, they consider the other person to be an equal. Only where Pakehas have frequent contact with Polynesians and work and live near them do these relations assume a natural character without self-conscious remarks.

Situations in which the Polynesian is dominant are rare. They occur, for example, at cross-racial weddings where the hosts are Polynesian, and at meetings of Polynesian organizations to which Pakehas are invited. Since often the Pakehas present are culturally aware, the interactions go smoothly and they try to enter into the spirit of the occasion even if they are not always certain of the norms. Of particular note, however, is the fact that Polynesian hosts go out of their way to welcome strangers to their way of life. Now it is the Pakeha who seems shy and ill at ease.

These observations suggest a sort of "Peter principle" of interracial relations operating in New Zealand society. Because the situations in which Polynesians are placed in subordinate roles are much more common that those in which they are equal or superordinate to Pakehas and can therefore display their competence, most Pakehas form impressions of Polynesians as inadequate or childlike. Opportunities to interact in egalitarian settings or on Polynesian home ground are increasing, however—as in Polynesian-run preschools with mixed clientele, mixed work groups, and the increasing likelihood of encountering Polynesian women as supervisors, officers, and service personnel. The work of PIERC and a series of pamphlets by the Vocational Training Council on understanding the different island groups and Maoris (as well as one for Polynesians on "Understanding Pakehas"), along with the work of the Race Relations Conciliator, are also helping to bridge the cultural gap.

As the economic scene worsens and resentment of urban Maoris and second-generation Pacific Islanders mounts, however, the climate of racial interaction may deteriorate in New Zealand. To date there has been more unintentional misunderstanding than serious racial hatred in the majority of cases, but if nothing is done to change the severe imbalance in socioeconomic status—which is creating what Macpherson (1977) has called a new "eth-class"—New Zealand could lose its reputation as an egalitarian society.

CONCLUSION

Historical circumstances have created in New Zealand a situation analogous to that in the United States. In both countries a white, British-based culture dominates the economic, political, and social life. Similarly, policymakers have tended until recently to adhere to the old melting-pot theory of assimilating ethnic minorities to a typical "New Zealand" way of life, which was that of British immigrants as it evolved over several generations. Labor shortages led to dependence on a racially and culturally distinct minority for laborers in secondary industry and other blue-collar employment. And because Pakeha institutions were either unaware or unwilling to adjust to a multicultural population, the unequal socioeconomic status of this rapidly growing Polynesian minority has been reinforced through the educational system.

Attempts to remedy the situation and help these urban migrants adjust to city conditions—and these efforts have been considerable—have largely taken the form of expanding existing agencies or creating new organizations to cater to Polynesian needs. This is a typical approach in modern western societies. There is little recognition that it does not fit the adaptive strategies of most Polynesian migrants, who are group-oriented and prefer informal, face-to-face organizations and modes of operation. A more effective way of helping these people is through their ethnic organizations, clubs, and informal networks.

Moreover, Pakeha institutions themselves could benefit by an injection of Polynesian group orientation. In the modern world, more and more industries are undertaking "human relations" training and social service jobs are increasingly replacing those that call for "object relations." Most Polynesians have well-developed social skills from years of coordinating group efforts in family and community. Schools may find that group-oriented learning is more fun than competitive, individualistic learning modes; indeed, this style increases academic performance, as research in the United States has recently shown. Not only would Polynesian students learn more readily, but Pakeha students would benefit as well.

Another point is worth emphasizing here. Despite the sharp contrast between Polynesian cultures and the Pakeha way of life, not all Polynesian groups and individuals are alike in their style of adaptation. A strong case is made by the studies cited here for intragroup variability in adaptive strategy. Flexibility should be built into public policies so that these variations can be recognized and dealt with in differing ways.

Finally, female Polynesian migrants have a number of distinctive problems that must be considered in planning programs. Marital status affects women's adaptation far more than men's. Women carry the major burden of responsibility for domestic chores and childrearing even when they are employed. New Zealand policy-makers tend to downplay the concerns of female workers in general, and the urgent social problem of inadequate child-care facilities has not received sufficient attention (PMC 1976). Authorities deplore "overcrowding" of Pacific Islanders' homes with additional relatives, but they have not acknowledged the real function these relatives perform in reducing the dependency ratio of these households. Nor has there been recognition of the positive functions of peer-oriented gatherings such as at public bars, although there is much outcry about Polynesian drinking and violence. Migrants themselves have taken these issues seriously, though, and Polynesian bar managers are changing the atmosphere of pubs by innovative, group-oriented methods to conform to the traditional social gathering common in rural settings (Graves et al. 1979b). The new pub still does not meet the needs of many Pacific Islands women, however, who need informal gathering places but do not drink.

In short, the Polynesian group-oriented example could be used to enrich Pakeha society and institutions, which are, according to many critics, detrimentally individualistic and alienated. While Polynesian women are already contributing significantly in the workplace, their talents could be used to even greater advantage if the benefits accrued from their group-oriented style of life were fully utilized, instead of requiring them to become like Pakehas in order to operate in a white world. Polynesian women have already shown they can assimilate what modern western culture has to offer. A great many of their problems now stem from the inflexibility of Pakeha institutions themselves, which are failing to assimilate Polynesian values and virtues into the mainstream of a truly multicultural New Zealand society.

NOTES

The research by Graves and Graves cited in this report was made possible through grants from the Royal Society of New Zealand (James Cook Fellowship), the National Institute of Mental Health (Grant No. 2 RO1 MH30139-03), the National Institute of Alcohol Abuse and Alcoholism (Grant No. 1-RO1-AA-03231-03), and the New Zealand Department of Labour, Community Service Programme.

1. Initial migration was from farms to small rural towns, and this pattern still continues (Metge 1964; McCreary 1968). But rural jobs are too scarce to absorb the growing Maori labor pool, a trend foreseen by Belshaw after the census of 1936 (Belshaw 1940:192–98).

2. It should be noted that strategy types depend on the national or regional setting. Reliance on patrons or pressure groups could be more important in some settings than in others, for example.

3. Our current study adds a measure of strategy *preference* to control for persons, par-

ticularly women, who desire a strategy other than their present one but are constrained by circumstances.

4. Privately run radio stations were not allowed for some time in New Zealand, and support from the government broadcasting system was sought for a Polynesian station. As a compromise, Radio Pacific was established. It broadcasts in Maori and different Pacific Island languages on certain evenings but broadcasts most programs in English.

REFERENCES

Archer, Dane, and Mary Archer
    1970   Race, identity, and Maori people. *Journal of the Polynesian Society* 79:201–18.

Ausubel, David P.
    1960   *The Fern and the Tiki.* Sydney: Angus and Robertson.

Belshaw, Horace
    1940   Economic circumstances. In I. L .G. Sutherland (ed.), *The Maori Situation.* Wellington: H. H. Tombs.

Clay, Marie M.
    1974   Polynesian language skills of Maori and Samoan school entrants. In D. H. Bray and C. G. N. Hill (eds.), *Polynesian and Pakeha in New Zealand Education.* Vol. 2: *Ethnic Difference and the School.* Auckland: Heinemann.

Curson, P. H.
    1970   The Cook Islanders. In K. W. Thomson and A. D. Trlin (eds.), *Immigrants in New Zealand.* Palmerston North: Massey University, Caxton Press.

Gillespie, H. M
    1973   An investigation into the adaptive strategies employed by rural Maori youth for coping with urban life. Unpublished M.A. thesis, University of Auckland.

Graves, Nancy B.
    1975   *Inclusive versus Exclusive Interaction Styles in Polynesian and European Classrooms: In Search of an Alternative to the Cultural Deficit Model of Learning.* Auckland: South Pacific Research Institute.

Graves, Nancy B., and Theodore D. Graves
    1973   *Culture Shock in Auckland: Pakeha Responses to Polynesian Immigrants.* Research Report No. 2. Auckland: South Pacific Research Institute.
    1974a   Adaptive strategies in urban migration. In Bernard Siegel (ed.), *Annual Review of Anthropology.* Vol. 3. Stanford: Annual Reviews.
    1977a   *Understanding New Zealand's Multi-Cultural Workforce.* Report to the Polynesian Advisory Committee of the Vocational Training Council of New Zealand. Wellington: Vocational Training Council.
    1977b   Preferred adaptive strategies: an approach to understanding New Zealand's multi-cultural workforce. *New Zealand Journal of Industrial Relations* 2:81–90.

Graves, Theodore D.
   1976   *Would You Want Your Daughter to Marry One?* Research Report No. 11. Auck-
           land: South Pacific Research Institute.
   1978   Polynesians in New Zealand industry. In Cluny Macpherson, Bradd Shore,
           and Robert Franco (eds.), *New Neighbors . . . Islanders in Adaptation.* Santa
           Cruz: Center for South Pacific Studies.

Graves, Theodore D., and Nancy B. Graves
   1974b   *As Others See Us: New Zealander's Images of Themselves and of Immigrant Groups.*
           Research Report No. 4. Auckland: South Pacific Research Institute.
   1976   Demographic changes in the Cook Islands: perception and reality: or,
           where have all the mapu gone? *Journal of the Polynesian Society* 85(4):447–61.
   1980   Kinship ties and the preferred adaptive strategies of urban migrants. In
           S. Beckerman and L. Cordell (eds.), *The Versatility of Kinship.* New York:
           Academic Press.

Graves, Theodore D., et al.
   1979a   *Patterns of Public Drinking in a Multi-Ethnic Society: A Systematic Observational
           Study.* Research Report No. 20. Auckland: South Pacific Research Insti-
           tute.
   1979b   *Drinking and Violence in a Multi-Cultural Society.* Research Report No. 21.
           Auckland: South Pacific Research Institute.
   1979c   *The Role of Alcohol in Migrant Polynesian Adaptation.* NIH Research Project
           No. 1 RO1 AA 03231-03. Bethesda, MD: National Institute of Health.

Haman, Renée
   1977   *Situational Factors in Inter-Group Relations: Pacific Island Women in a New Zealand
           Factory.* Research Report No. 14. Auckland: South Pacific Research Insti-
           tute.
   1978   Polynesian women in industry: participation, motivations, and orientation
           in a multi-cultural factory situation. Unpublished M.A. thesis, Depart-
           ment of Sociology, University of Auckland.

Hamilton, Linda
   1974   The political integration of the Samoan immigrants in New Zealand. Un-
           published M.A. thesis, University of Canterbury, Christchurch, New Zea-
           land.

Hohepa, Patrick W.
   1978   Maori and Pakeha: the one-people myth. In Michael King (ed.), *Tihe
           Mauri Ora: Aspects of Maoritanga.* Wellington: Methuen.

Huntsman, Judith, and Antony Hooper
   1973   Gender in Tokelau. In Goodale and Silverman (eds.), *Gender in the Pacific.*
           Buffalo: Association of Social Anthropology in Oceania.

Lee, Margaret
   1975   *Nga Kaimaki: Polynesians in Industry.* Wellington: Vocational Training Coun-
           cil of New Zealand.

Macpherson, Cluny
   1975   *Migrant Polynesians and the New Zealand Factory—A Case for the Application of*

Human Relations Theory. (Mimeographed.) Auckland: University of Auckland, Department of Sociology.

1977   Polynesians in New Zealand: an emerging eth-class? In David Pitt. (ed.), *Social Class in New Zealand.* Auckland: Longman Paul.

McCreary, John R.
1968   Population growth and urbanisation. In E. Schwimmer (ed.), *The Maori People in the Nineteen-Sixties.* Auckland: Blackwood and Janet Paul.

Metge, Joan
1964   *A New Maori Migration: Rural and Urban Relations in Northern New Zealand.* London: Athlone Press.

New Zealand Department of Labour, Research and Planning Division (NZDL)
1979   *The Work Experience of Pacific Island Migrants in the Greater Wellington Area.* Wellington.

Pitt, David, and Cluny Macpherson
1974   *Emerging Pluralism. The Samoan Community in New Zealand.* Auckland: Longman Paul.

Prime Minister's Conference (PMC)
1976   *Report on Women in Social and Economic Development Conference.* Wellington: Committee on Women.

Rowland, D. T.
1969   The Maori population of the Auckland urban area: a study of their distribution, mobility, and selected demographic and social characteristics. Unpublished M.A. thesis, Geography Department, Auckland University.

Shankman, Paul
1976   *Migration and Underdevelopment: The Case of Western Samoa.* Boulder, Colo.: Westview Press.

Thomas, David R.
1970   Ethnic prejudice in Australia and New Zealand students. *Australian Psychologist* 5:154–56.

Thorns, David C.
1977   Urbanisation, sub-urbanisation, and social class in New Zealand. In David Pitt (ed.), *Social Class in New Zealand.* Auckland: Longman Paul.

Trlin, A. D.
1971   Social distance and assimilation orientation: a survey of attitudes towards immigrants in New Zealand. *Pacific Viewpoint* 12:141–62.

Vaughan, Graham M.
1962   The social distance attitudes of New Zealand students towards Maoris and fifteen other national groups. *Journal of Social Psychology* 57:85–92.

Walsh, A. C.
1971   *More and More Maoris.* Auckland: Whitcombe and Tombs.

CONCLUSION

Chapter 19

Women in Asian Cities: Policies, Public Services, and Research

Siew-Ean Khoo
Judith Bruce
James T. Fawcett
Peter C. Smith

The migration of women—especially to large cities—is both a reflection of ongoing social change and an indication of changes to come. Particularly striking are the implications of increasing numbers of young single women moving to cities. The proportion of women in urbanward migration streams is increasing, and women migrants to major urban areas outnumber men in many Asian countries. Such changes are occurring in countries where women's traditional roles have heretofore been sharply constrained, such as Korea and Malaysia, as well as in more open social systems, such as Thailand and the Philippines. There are also important differences within countries—as between the north and south of India—and there are countries where very little change is evident—Pakistan is a notable example.

In addressing the migration of women in Asia and their urban adaptation, the preceding chapters have related this spatial mobility to prevailing cultural norms as well as to changing social and economic conditions. The theoretical and empirical perspectives offered by these chapters are important contributions to our understanding of the role of women in the migration process in Asia. Among the countries represented in this volume, the diversity of patterns in female migration is apparent, reflecting the variety of cultural, developmental, and urbanization patterns in the region. Yet similarities also exist in the profiles of migrant women, their participation in the urban labor market, and the impact of their migration, suggesting common issues that deserve the attention of policy-makers and scholars. In this concluding chapter, we summarize the main policy, planning, and research issues related to female migration and women in the cities.

DEVELOPMENT PLANNING AND FEMALE MIGRATION

Two aspects of development appear to have a profound effect on the migration of women to cities in Asia. One is the increasing level of female education. The other is the strategy of industrialization adopted in several East and Southeast Asian countries.

The increase in educational opportunities for women has affected the pattern of female migration in several ways. The profiles of female rural-to-urban migrants delineated in this volume indicate that migrant women, just as men, tend to be more educated than those remaining in the rural areas. Exposure to formal schooling has a modernizing effect on young people in rural areas, prompting them to seek urban wage employment. This effect of schooling appears to be greatest among women. In the Philippines, for example, the educational selectivity of female migrants is much stronger than that of male migrants; moreover, the proportion of women with some high school education among female migrants is more than twice that among nonmigrant rural women.

An urban bias in the quality and availability of educational facilities contributes powerfully to the educational selectivity of migrants. A significant proportion of young female migrants in the Republic of Korea, the Philippines, and Thailand now migrate to the cities to continue their education. In the urban economy, a reasonably high level of education is required for even clerical positions. Although rural-to-urban female migrants are generally more educated than nonmigrant women in the rural areas, they are usually less well educated than female urban residents and male migrants. A large proportion have only a primary school education, which is insufficient to qualify them for middle-level positions in services, sales, or manufacturing. Many migrant women work in low-status jobs because their options for other employment in the city are limited.

The low educational level of female migrants compared to migrant men reflects the fact that education is considered less important for women in many societies. This is particularly true of traditional rural families. Consequently, when the family's resources are limited it is the females who are more likely to be withdrawn from school. Often they are sent to work in the cities to help support the education of male siblings. In some countries, such as Pakistan and India, only a small elite group of women has any exposure to education. The rest, when faced with the necessity to earn income, must use informally acquired skills such as cooking, sewing, child care, handicrafts, and small-scale marketing.

The industrialization strategy adopted by some countries has created employment opportunities for women in the export-oriented manufacturing sector—another reason why families decide to send daughters to the city. In an effort to utilize their young and literate labor force, these countries have chosen to attract foreign investment in light labor-intensive industries such as the production of microelectronics components and textiles. Factories of this kind tend to cluster around large cities such as Seoul, Taipei, Kuala Lumpur, and Penang, and their preference for female labor has provided a strong incentive for young rural women with a little education to move to the city. In Korea, production workers have become the largest occupational group among urban migrant women; and if present trends in Malaysia continue, production workers will soon replace service workers as the largest occupational group among female urban migrants.

The expansion of industrial employment opportunities for migrant women has occurred mostly in the rapidly developing countries in East and Southeast Asia. In these and other countries, however, many female migrants—especially those who are young and single and have recently arrived in the city—continue to be employed as domestics and other service workers. These occupations are marked by low status, low wages, and hard working conditions. In some countries, prostitution is a common form of employment for single women migrants. Other female migrants are self-employed in the informal sector. These are often older women who work as hawkers and vendors in the marketplace. Their working hours may be long and their incomes small and uncertain. The flexible working hours may be beneficial to women who are mothers and household heads, however, and even a small income may make a critical difference when the earnings of several household members are pooled.

The woman's financial contribution to her family's resources and the link she can provide in the city for new arrivals from the village enhance her status within the family. For many young Asian women, earnings from jobs in the city bring new and greater personal freedom from parental control in their consumption and marriage patterns. It is for reasons such as these that young female migrants, despite their limited options for employment in the cities, continue to move there to work in low-status jobs in the informal service and manufacturing sectors.

Are the changing patterns of female migration desirable? Are they consistent with national development objectives or social norms? Such questions have become prominent public issues in some countries. In many societies, male migration is more compatible with traditional culture, while there is concern about the migration of young single women to cities and its impact on family structure and social values. This has been the case in Malaysia, where public concern has led to formation of a task force to look into the welfare of young female migrants in the cities. Often elders are concerned that the women migrants will adopt modern ideas and attitudes that can threaten their authority; others fear that the migrants will marry urban residents and not return to their villages to look after elders. The exposure of young women to modern ideas in the city can also lead to lower fertility, however, owing to a smaller desired family size and a more favorable attitude toward family planning—which happen to be the objectives of many national population and development plans.

One aspect of female migration that should be of interest in countries concerned with the rapid growth of their primate cities is the dominance of women in migration streams, particularly to large metropolitan areas. The development strategies that have created urban jobs, particularly in the manufacturing sector, have not been consistent with the aims of population policy (even though they may have prevented a labor surplus in rural areas among the cohort of educated youth in the postwar period).

Important policy issues arise in connection with sending areas as well. Rural-to-urban migrants tend to be in the 15–29 age group, and women migrants are usually younger than men. The out-migration of these young people in the highly productive ages may cause serious imbalances in certain rural areas. The demographic and socioeconomic consequences of this imbalance can be considerable. With more children and old people depending on each remaining person of working age, the dependency ratio is increased. Older men and women and children may have to compensate for the loss of farm and household labor by assuming additional work in the fields and at home. Unless migration is motivated by push factors such as lack of agricultural land and underemployment in the rural sector, a labor shortage can occur and crop cultivation may be disrupted. Such effects have been documented in Thailand and Indonesia.

In settings where migrants are predominantly of one sex, an imbalance in the sex ratio in the peak migration ages will also occur. This imbalance can alter marriage patterns and, where agricultural tasks are sex-specific, cause changes in labor practices. If women are more likely to migrate because their contribution to agricultural fieldwork is less important, their out-migration could have a negligible impact on agriculture and farming. However, this will depend on whether their labor has become redundant due to technological change or replacement by other workers, or they contribute less agricultural labor because their remuneration is poor. The effect of rural-to-urban migration on agriculture is also mitigated if it occurs mainly during the agricultural slack seasons and is mainly in the form of circulation or temporary migration.

Another important effect of migration on rural sending areas is the value of remittances received by family members remaining behind and their use of the remittances. Research on Taiwan, for example, has demonstrated two important uses of remittances sent by urban women migrants to their families in the villages: supplementing the family's living expenses and financing the education of siblings. More information is needed on the proportion of female migrants who remit to their families in the rural areas, the size of the remittances, and how this income is used for consumption or investment.

We have highlighted some of the main connections between development planning and female migration. Many of these connections have been hidden because there was little research on female migration in Asia and emerging trends were slow to be recognized. Moreover, it appears that sectoral development policies usually are pursued without sufficient consideration of their effects on population distribution—either in the aggregate or separately for men and women. Examples are the concentration of higher education facilities in capital cities and the encouragement of new industries whose need for female workers cannot be met in the immediate vicinity of the factory. Most development policies do have migration-related effects, and these will only be understood when there are more comprehensive studies and better analysis of population distribution. In the final section of this chapter we identify the research priorities.

URBAN PROGRAMS AND SERVICES

Regardless of future trends and how they may be affected in the long run by policy, there are many practical needs of women now living in cities and those sure to migrate to urban areas in the years immediately ahead. On the whole, not much attention has been given to women in planning urban services—mainly because planners have assumed that most women are dependent wives and that, if they do work, their incomes are not essential. In view of the changes occurring in many Asian countries, both these assumptions must be challenged. Moreover, a strong case can be made that planning is usually more effective when the population is examined in a disaggregated manner. One useful form of disaggregation is the examination of differentials by sex.

Further, more efficient and responsive services can be designed if low-income urban and migrant women are regarded not as a single client group but as several groups identified by age, marital status, economic activity, and family responsibilities. Those particularly in need of urban services can be placed in four categories: working women who are salaried employees, working women who are self-employed, working mothers, and women heads of household. We will discuss each type in turn.

Female salaried employees are most often domestic servants or factory workers. Many female migrants in Korea, Malaysia, the Philippines, Taiwan, and Thailand are in this category. These young women face long working hours, low pay, and vulnerable tenure. The environment in textile, garment, and electronics factories is stressful. Often female workers live in factory-provided dormitories, as many do in Korea, or they rent shared quarters that may have more conveniences than their rural homes but are also overcrowded, as is usually the case in Malaysia. Being on their own, they may also embark on a freer life-style and more open relationships with men, which may expose them to the risk of unwanted and culturally shameful pregnancies.

These salaried women workers need diversified training programs to expand their employment prospects. They also need health care, especially family planning services. Both may create more options for young single women in urban areas who may be locked into domestic service, prostitution, or unrewarding factory work. They also need inexpensive and adequate housing with access to clean water and modern sanitation facilities.

Women who are self-employed, often married and working in their homes, fit their jobs in between other household tasks. There are many self-employed women among migrants to the cities in India and Thailand. The work they do usually makes use of their manual skills and local materials to produce goods for sale. Some of these workers may be well integrated into community handicraft enterprises; others are extensions of a manufacturing operation on a "putting-out" basis, where they obtain basic materials from the factory and return the finished product. Still others produce goods on their own for direct sale in the marketplace or through informal outlets. Others are engaged as hawkers or vendors retailing goods produced by others. In any case, their situation contrasts sharply with salaried factory workers or domestics with respect to the services that would enhance their living standards.

The essential needs of self-employed women, whether working principally in their homes or on the streets, as producers or sellers, are access to low-cost materials, ready cash and credit on reasonable terms, and access to markets. The issue of market access is especially important. These women must be able to get to markets quickly and cheaply to ensure long trading hours and reasonable profit margins.

Working mothers represent an overlapping category—that is, they may be salaried or self-employed. Working mothers balance responsibilities for child care, cooking, and household maintenance or food production with whatever work they carry on for cash. Women who must work outside the home without child-care services may have to leave children uncared for or under the loose supervision of neighbors. Women who work at home have less of a problem, but still they must trade off work time against time devoted to child care. In some cases, older children may be held back from school to care for younger siblings.

Day-care or *crèche* programs at reasonable cost are the primary need of working mothers. Such programs must be located near their homes or workplaces to be of value to low-income women, since long detours and transportation costs would cut into work time and household incomes, thus discouraging women from using the service. The *crèche* programs located near construction sites for the convenience of women coolies in some Indian cities are a good example of planning according to the needs of working mothers.

A number of women migrants in cities are also heads of household, and these women are likely to have particularly urgent economic and social needs. They may be the poorest among low-income groups in urban areas; often they are the sole providers for their families. The divorced and widowed migrants in Indian cities belong to this group. Some of these women moved to the city because they were unable to support their families alone in the village; others became household heads through unfortunate circumstances after migration.

More information on low-income urban women, including better measures of family structure and labor-force participation, is needed to assess the prevalence of female-headed households and the extent of their economic needs. It seems certain, however, that women heads of household should have high priority for access to programs offering income-generating opportunities in the home. They also have special needs with respect to support services such as transportation, training, credit, and child care. In some countries, the right to housing in the woman's name may be an issue of critical importance to women who are heads of household.

We can suggest two general issues that should be considered when evaluating what urban and migrant women need from public and private services: support for women's multiple roles and support for income and employment. Suppose we examine these issues in greater detail.

A woman's multiple roles as mother, housekeeper, and income earner have important implications for urban planning. If new housing is planned, for example, it would be useful to know how women use space as they move between childrearing, household maintenance, and income-producing activity in the home or the community. From such information would come specific plans for new housing schemes—for example, work space might be provided every 10 or 20 housing units to encourage women to work together in a collective area but still be near their children. Urban planning can also reduce the distance and time needed for women to use critical services such as health, child care, and job training programs. More numerous community-based services are often preferable to larger, more sophisticated, but less acccessible facilities.

Access to credit may be crucial for self-employed women. Legal and social changes may be needed to allow women as individuals to obtain loans. Credit programs can encourage entrepreneurship and financial independence among migrant women. Similarly, efforts by planners to shorten the distance between home and workplace and to reduce the expense of traveling will encourage the participation of women in the labor force. Such arrangements will also benefit male workers, of course, and if they are married they will find it easier to help with household maintenance and child care. In many societies, however, men are still reluctant to take on these responsibilities.

The participation of client groups—the general public—in planning and decision-making is important in the design of responsive urban services. If women participate in planning and decision-making about relevant community facilities, such as schools, shops, and child-care centers, they will be more likely to use them and take on management responsibilities. Thus client-oriented planning can lead to more cost-effective facilities and can reduce the maintenance burden after facilities are in place.

RESEARCH ISSUES

The preceding discussion of development planning and urban policy has indicated numerous issues on which we need more information. But other aspects of female migration and urban adaptation also merit further research for both scientific and practical reasons. We conclude by discussing some of the main research needs.

The rising trend in female urbanward migration and related patterns of sex selectivity in migration streams pose interesting research questions about the relationship of these patterns to cultural forces, the pace of urbanization, and strategies of development. Sometimes the patterns may have historical causes relating to the redress of sexual imbalances in past migration streams. In other instances, the predominance of female migrants is in fact destabilizing and tends to reduce sex ratios that are already too low.

Several topics might be investigated in order to understand changing sex ratios in migration streams: rural inheritance patterns and family structures and their effects on the relative mobility of the sexes; imported sex-role ideologies as they affect differential recruitment into modern occupations; images of the city and urban men and women in the mass media; the labor force's structure in each society and its relation to the global economy; ideologies of education and the nature and distribution of educational institutions; and class and ethnic divisions that may have relevance in a variety of indirect ways. For most of these topics, as well as for other aspects of government intervention, public policies and programs can provide incentives for migration that are greater for one sex than for the other. Such incentives are usually unintended, but it would not be difficult to design public policies that explicitly address the issue of sex ratios in migration streams. The main instruments would presumably be education and employment policies, including information programs directed to appropriate audiences.

The consequences of sexual imbalance in migration streams are also important. Courtship and marriage patterns in both rural and urban areas are often directly affected, and beyond this the consequences vary widely. There are consequences for family structure and authority, both in the rural and urban settings. There are consequences for childbearing and childrearing. There may be political consequences in emergent social or moral issues that various interest groups may exploit. There may be economic consequences tied to the employment of migrants and the remittances they send to relatives remaining behind. Of particular importance is the impact of migration streams on class structure and inequality: the degree to which the stream creates or feeds a distinct urban class and the degree to which it reduces or exacerbates rural/urban inequalities. Female migration may have different consequences in this regard than male migration.

Causes and consequences are intertwined, of course, and this becomes apparent when a microlevel perspective is adopted—that is, when the focus is on the individual migrant. Traditional norms, values, and attitudes tend to affect female migration much more than male migration, particularly in imposing restrictions on female mobility. In a specific setting, research may be designed to determine whether migration leads to an undesirable amount of independence in women or the degree to which migration is thought to offer women a more satisfactory life and improve their status. The relation between marital status and migration should also be investigated further. Of particular interest is the question of how norms, values, and attitudes on marriage and childrearing are related to female migration and whether they affect the form of migration (commuting, circulation, or permanent settlement). Such influences should be explored in the areas of origin as well as destination.

Social and family networks can be important influences on the migration decision and the migrant's adjustment to life in the place of destination. Research should take into account the diversity, size, and degree of support of social networks affecting female migration compared to male migration and the extent to which women use these networks to gain information before migration and to cope with the urban environment afterward.

Migrants in the cities usually maintain links with relatives or friends in the rural areas. Besides the family and kin obligations that are implied, such links may be a form of insurance for the migrants should they need to return to the village. Other research questions on male/female differences are relevant to the understanding of female migrants' adaptation in the city: economic and social links, the frequency with which these links are used and reaffirmed, the reasons for their maintenance, and how they affect the migrant's adjustment to new surroundings. The use of remittances as a link is a particularly important research and policy issue that should be examined in relation to its impact on the rural sending areas.

Several empirical studies in this volume present profiles of female migrants that include their work patterns and socioeconomic status at the urban destination. There is often no information on how this status compares with their status before migration, however. What happens to migrants after they move to cities? Does geographical mobility also mean social mobility in most cases? In what ways are migrants better off and worse off after migration? Few studies have addressed these issues in the context of differential impacts on male and female migrants. Current interest in the life-cycle approach for demographic analysis should stimulate interest in the premigration status of migrants and changes in their economic, demographic, and social behavior after a change of residence.

Overall three research areas deserve high priority:

1. The changing demographic picture: what is happening to the sex and age distribution and other characteristics of different types of migration streams (rural to large city, rural to intermediate city, urban to urban, urban to rural, and so forth)
2. The need for public services and facilities for two groups in particular: single female migrants from rural areas and female heads of household in large cities
3. The impact on rural sending communities—especially regarding farming practices and productivity—of different rates and patterns of female out-migration

The multiple causes of sex-selective migration patterns also need investigation, of course, especially the causes related to diverse development strategies. Tracing causes is a long-term goal, however, whereas the topics listed above can be expected to have a much more immediate impact on policy. They deal with the basic facts of female migration, which are urgently in need of better documentation, and with the key consequences for poor migrants and poor rural communities. Research of this kind will highlight the immense social changes that are under way and will, we believe, lay the foundation for more effective and equitable public programs related to the many facets of female migration and urban adaptation.

4403   52